Mining Capitalism

Mining Capitalism

*The Relationship between Corporations
and Their Critics*

Stuart Kirsch

UNIVERSITY OF CALIFORNIA PRESS

University of California Press, one of the most
distinguished university presses in the United States,
enriches lives around the world by advancing scholarship
in the humanities, social sciences, and natural sciences.
Its activities are supported by the UC Press Foundation
and by philanthropic contributions from individuals and
institutions. For more information, visit www.ucpress.edu.

University of California Press
Oakland, California

Library of Congress Cataloging-in-Publication Data

Kirsch, Stuart.
    Mining capitalism : the relationship between
corporations and their critics / Stuart Kirsch.
        pages   cm
    Includes bibliographical references and index.
    ISBN 978-0-520-28170-7 (cloth : alk. paper) —
    ISBN 978-0-520-28171-4 (pbk. : alk. paper) —
    ISBN 978-0-520-95759-6 (e-book)
        1. Mineral industries—Environmental aspects—
Papua New Guinea.   2. Mineral industries—Political
aspects—Papua New Guinea.   Copper mines and
mining—Papua New Guinea—Ok Tedi Region.
4. Gold mines and mining—Papua New Guinea—
Ok Tedi Region.   5. Ok Tedi Mining.   I. Title.
    HD9506.P262K57   2014
    338.209953—dc23
                                            2013040294

Manufactured in the United States of America

23 22 21 20 19 18 17 16 15 14
10 9 8 7 6 5 4 3 2 1

To Rex Dagi and Alex Maun, *ne angotmi bot-korokman*, in recognition of their sacrifices and achievements.

Contents

Illustrations

Acknowledgments

The movement of this project across scholarly and activist communities has increased the number of people and organizations to which I am indebted. A fellowship in Urgent Anthropology from the Royal Anthropological Institute and Goldsmiths College, University of London, provided me with the opportunity to conduct timely research and frame this project in anthropological terms. The University of Michigan generously supported my research through the Center for International Business Education; the College of Literature, Science, and the Arts; the Department of Anthropology; the Office of the Vice President for Research; and the Rackham Graduate School. The Program in Agrarian Studies at Yale University provided a stimulating environment in which to think through, discuss, and begin writing about these issues. An ESRC-SSRC fellowship supported my participation in a collaborative research project at Manchester University on Territory, Conflicts, and Development in the Andes, which provided me with a valuable comparative perspective on resource politics. A fellowship from the American Council of Learned Societies and a Michigan Humanities Award enabled me to complete the manuscript.

This work has benefitted significantly from discussion with colleagues and graduate students at the University of Michigan and elsewhere, especially Anthony Bebbington, Denise Humphreys Bebbington, Mark Busse, Tony Crook, Michael Dove, Steven Feld, Kim and Mike Fortun, Bob Foster, Katherine Fultz, Lawrence Hammar, the late Olivia Harris,

Federico Helfgott, Matt Hull, David Hyndman, Bruce Knauft, Fabiana Li, Jimmy McWilliams, Lynn Morgan, Steve Nugent, Dinah Rajak, Elisha Renne, Doug Rogers, Jessica Smith Rolston, Suzana Sawyer, Jim Scott, K. Sivaramakrishnan, Marilyn Strathern, Jim Trostle, Jimmy Weiner, Marina Welker, Michael Wood, and Anna Zalik. My collaboration with Peter Benson on the anthropology of the corporation has been especially rewarding. Many of the arguments presented in this book have been honed through debates with my regular sparring partners on mining issues in Melanesia, Glenn Banks, John Burton, and Colin Filer, although neither they nor anyone else is responsible for the views expressed here.

During the campaign against the Ok Tedi mine, I came to rely on Brian Brunton, Simon Divecha, Geoff Evans, Igor O'Neill, Helen Rosenbaum, Lee Tan, and later Techa Beaumont and Matilda Koma for information and insight. At Slater & Gordon, Nick Styant-Browne, John Gordon, Peter Gordon, Ikenna Nowokolo, and later Ben Hardwick provided an invaluable backstage view of the legal proceedings without imposing any restrictions on my work. Lewis Gordon, David Hunter, Lawrence Kalinoe, Jacob Kopas, and David Szablowski fielded legal queries. David Nelson has generously shared his knowledge about the environmental impacts of mining for many years. I have also benefited from long-running exchanges with Peter Adler, Robert Bryce, Joji Cariño, Luis Manuel Claps, Bong Corpuz, Catherine Coumans, Al Gedicks, the late Robert Goodland, Jamie Kneen, Fergus MacKay, Roger Moody, Gavin Mudd, Geoff Nettleton, Vicky Tauli-Corpuz, Ximena Warnaars, Viviane Weitzner, Andy Whitmore, and David Wissink. Kathy Creely, Jennifer Nason Davis, and Vikki John helped me track down important references. Sandhya Murali and Steve Hurvitz assembled a wealth of financial data. Bonnie Campbell, Katherine Fultz, Ken MacDonald, and Nina Glick Schiller generously allowed me to make reference to their unpublished work. Discussions with the members of the Mines and Communities network have influenced this work more than I can acknowledge. I am also indebted to the Association of Indigenous Village Leaders in Suriname, the Forest People's Programme, Indigenous Peoples Links, the Middlesex University School of Law, the Mineral Policy Institute, the North-South Institute, the Office of the United Nations High Commissioner for Human Rights, and the Tebtebba Foundation for including me in their research projects and workshops.

Some of the examples from chapters 2 and 3 initially appeared in "Indigenous Movements and the Risks of Counterglobalization," published in *American Ethnologist* in 2007. Some of the material in chapter 5 was originally published in a short essay called "Sustainable Mining," which appeared in a special issue on corporate oxymorons in *Dialectical Anthropology* in 2010 and in the chapter "Mining Industry Responses to Criticism" in Edward F. Fischer, ed., *Cash on the Table: Markets, Values, Moral Economies* (SAR Press 2013).

This work has also benefitted from discussion at the University of Auckland, Bowdoin College, Columbia University, the University of Heidelberg, the Maurer School of Law at Indiana University, the University of Michigan, the University of Munich, the Universidad del Rosario, the School for Advanced Research, the University of Wisconsin Law School, and Yale University. I am particularly grateful to Heinz Klug for encouraging me to write in a more hopeful vein. Matt Hull and his seminar on corporations; Kedron Thomas, Peter Benson, and their reading group at the University of Washington in St. Louis; and the students in my seminars on engaged and environmental anthropology provided insightful comments on the manuscript. Jeri Sawall applied her keen editorial eye to the first draft. Zeynep Gürsel, Dominique Nabokov, and Randal Stegmeyer provided valuable advice and assistance regarding the images for the book; Ben Pease produced the three elegant maps. I also wish to thank my colleagues at the University of California Press: Reed Malcolm, who supported the project from the outset and guided it through the review process, and Wendy Dherin, Jennifer Eastman, Stacy Eisenstark, and Rose Vekony, who oversaw its transformation into a book. The comments from the three anonymous reviewers were exceptionally helpful in guiding the final revisions.

Were it not for the courage of the local activists who sought to bring ecological reason to the Ok Tedi and Fly Rivers, this book would have a very different story to tell. The book is dedicated to Rex Dagi and Alex Maun, whose heroic exploits figure prominently here, although I would be remiss if I failed to express my admiration and gratitude to Dair Gabara, Gabia Gagarimabu, Robin Moken, Moses Oti, Barnabus Uwako, the members of ENECO, and the many other people who have fought so hard to protect their rivers and forests; it has been a great privilege to work with them and write about their extraordinary and inspiring efforts.

Finally, for never losing faith in this project or the larger struggle for justice, I offer my enduring gratitude to Janet Richards.

Introduction

The corporation is one of the most powerful institutions of our time. Corporations organize much of the world's labor and capital, shape the material form of the modern world, and are a prime mover of globalization. But corporations are also responsible for a wide range of harmful effects, including the use of technologies with deleterious consequences for human health and the production of environmental hazards that threaten the planet. The situation is exacerbated by neoliberal economic policies that view the market as the most efficient means of solving these problems and assert that effective management of these issues by the corporation can substitute for regulation.[1] These policies have led the state to transfer many of its regulatory responsibilities to corporations and markets. Yet the failure of market-based policies and corporations to address these concerns—or, in many cases, to even acknowledge their existence—reproduces the status quo. This allows corporations to continue externalizing the costs of production onto society and the environment, despite making widely publicized claims about the social benefits of their activities, their commitment to abide by existing laws and regulations, their willingness to cooperate with the state, and their responsibility as corporate citizens. The risks associated with production are normalized and naturalized as the inevitable consequence of modernity rather than contingent relations between states, corporations, and the environment that can be reorganized and improved.

However, the risks posed by corporations to people and the environment are increasingly contested by social movements and nongovernmental organizations, or NGOs. Critics of the corporation document existing problems, challenge harmful practices, inform the public, enroll supporters, seek to influence electoral politics, harness the power of the law, and even resort to violence. They address problems ranging from regional issues like mountaintop removal by coal miners in Appalachia to global environmental concerns like the contribution of carbon-based fuels to greenhouse gases and climate change. They target specific companies for past events, such as Dow Chemical for the Bhopal gas tragedy (Fortun 2001), or entire industries for the risks they pose to future generations, such as uranium mining and nuclear power (Hecht 1998, 2012). They invoke the discourses of responsibility, sustainability, and transparency in their critique of corporate practices. The remarkable proliferation of NGOs since the 1980s includes organizations that express diverse political ideologies. For example, organizations focused on environmental issues range from radical groups like Earth First to more moderate and populist NGOs like Greenpeace, as well as to NGOs that routinely partner with corporations to achieve their objectives, such as Conservation International and the Nature Conservancy. Some opposition movements organize on the basis of ethnicity or identity, such as Penan protests against logging in Sarawak (Brosius 1999), while in other cases, unexpected alliances have formed between groups that were previously antagonistic, such as the coalition of Native Americans and sport fishers that collaborated in blocking the development of a proposed zinc and copper sulfide mine in northern Wisconsin (Gedicks and Grossman 2005; Grossman 2005).

Many of these campaigns operate through "transnational action networks" that make international resources available to new categories of actors (Keck and Sikkink 1998). The resulting forms of mobilization have been described as enacting a "politics of scale" (Escobar 2001a, 166). They are also known as counterglobalization movements because of their innovative use of the architecture of globalization in challenging transnational corporations. Although the participants in these campaigns may be relatively few and far between, their cumulative influence can be significant. By harnessing new communication technologies ranging from the Internet and cell phones to satellite imaging, they are able to track and report on corporate activity in approximately real time, wherever it occurs. New social media extend their outreach. They stage protests and ask questions at annual shareholder meetings. They also exert pressure on the international financial institutions and multilateral organizations that facilitate the global flow of capital, turning these institutions into de facto regulatory bodies. These networks replicate the geographic distribution of capital by putting pressure on the corporation wherever it operates.

Corporations have thus been forced to adapt to pressure from their critics. They regularly employ a variety of "corporate social technologies" intended to manage their relationships with the public (Rogers 2012). They seek to assuage concerns by promoting uncertainty and doubt. They manage the politics of time by manipulating scientific research, concealing or delaying recognition of significant problems. They co-opt the discourse of their critics by promoting themselves as responsible, sustainable, and transparent. They also seek to enhance their reputations by forging strategic partnerships with NGOs, fostering division among their critics. These strategies help corporations withstand critique and weather crises. Their ability to neutralize criticism often leaves the public resigned to the harms they produce.

This book examines the relationship between corporations and their critics. I argue that the underlying dilemmas associated with capitalist modes of production can never be completely resolved; they can only be renegotiated in new forms. Given the efficacy of corporate social technologies in co-opting and adapting the strategies and discourses of their critics, social movements and NGOs must continually develop new approaches to these problems. Consequently, the dialectical relationship between corporations and their critics has become a permanent structural feature of neoliberal capitalism. Ethnographic attention to these interactions can help to answer the following questions: Why do efforts to reform corporate practices often fall short of their goals? How do corporations counteract the discourse and strategies of their critics? Which political strategies are more effective in curtailing the human and environmental costs of production? These questions have both analytical significance in terms of understanding one of the fundamental dynamics of contemporary capitalism and political implications for countering the politics of resignation, in which the perpetuation of the status quo appears inevitable (Benson and Kirsch 2010a).

I seek to answer these questions by examining the dialectical relationship between the mining industry and its indigenous and NGO critics. Mining moves more earth than any other human endeavor. Mining companies routinely externalize a significant proportion of the costs of production onto society and the environment. For example, mining companies rarely pay the full costs of the water they use, including the opportunity costs for other users, such as farmers. They regularly fail to assess their responsibilities in time frames commensurate with the longevity of their environmental impacts. Thus, in the United States alone, more than 156 abandoned hard rock mining sites have been targeted for federal cleanup, an intervention that will cost the U.S. government an estimated $15 billion, more than ten times the annual Superfund budget for all environmental disasters (Office of the Inspector General 2004, i). Requiring payment for the externalized costs of production would not only erode the profitability of the mining industry, but it would also mean that many mining projects are no longer economically viable.

The mining industry is defended on both economic grounds, in terms of the creation of wealth and employment, and on technological grounds, in terms of the widespread need for and use of metals. Mining is also presented as a mode of development that can help alleviate poverty, even though dependence on natural-resource extraction is inversely correlated with economic growth in a relationship economists call the "resource curse" (Auty 1993; Sachs and Warner 1995; Ross 1999). Since the late 1990s, however, the industry has promoted the view that mining contributes to sustainable development through the creation of economic opportunities that extend beyond the life of the project, although the definition of *sustainability* employed in these claims completely elides the concept's original reference to the environment.

Previous anthropological research on the mining industry addressed questions about labor, capitalism, and modernity (Ferguson 1999; June Nash 1973; Powdermaker 1962; Taussig 1980). Ethnographers of Latin America introduced readers to Tío, the devil spirit to whom Bolivian miners made offerings of coca and alcohol in return for his help in finding a rich vein of ore (June Nash 1973; Taussig 1980, 143). Michael Taussig (1980, xi) describes the devil as a "stunningly apt symbol of alienation" that condenses "political and economic history." With its reflective eyes and gaping mouth, the devil of the tin mine became an iconic image for a generation of ethnographers seeking to combine symbolic anthropology with the study of political economy, especially scholars studying resistance to capitalism. The resulting struggles over lands and livelihoods rocked Latin America during the 1960s and 1970s, including the CIA-supported coup d'état in Chile in 1973, after the country nationalized ownership of its copper mines, including substantial holdings by the U.S. companies Kennecott and Anaconda (Finn

1998). The new Chilean economy became an incubator for the experiments in economic policy that gave rise to neoliberalism (Harvey 2005).

The subsequent spread of neoliberal economic policies facilitated the investment of mining capital around the world, unearthing new ore bodies to supply the expanding global economy. In the wake of the collapse of a socialist alternative to capitalism in 1989, the World Bank came to view its investment in natural-resource extraction as "the 'spear point' of open trade policies and neo-liberal economic reform" that would encourage recalcitrant states to lift restrictions on foreign investment (Danielson 2006, 17). Pressure from the World Bank led to reform of the mining codes in dozens of countries (Moody 1996, 46), dismantling regulatory regimes that provided at least nominal protection of labor, the environment, and the persons and peoples displaced and dispossessed by mining projects. These developments led to the expansion of investments in mineral exploration in Latin America by a factor of six, by four in the Pacific, and by two in Africa (Reed 2002, 205).

New technologies of mining have also transformed labor politics since the publication of the classic anthropological works on mining in the 1970s. The underground tin mines of Bolivia employed a large, unskilled labor force that worked under hazardous conditions. Labor was easily replaced if workers went on strike or were injured or killed in mining accidents. In contrast, the new open-cut mines are capital intensive. They employ relatively few workers, and their ability to organize has been weakened by new regimes of temporary and subcontracted labor (Smith and Helfgott 2010). Although labor conflict in the mining industry has not disappeared, its political significance has been greatly diminished (Szablowski 2007, 41–42; Helfgott 2013).[2] As James Ferguson (1999) notes with regard to Zambia's copper industry, the promise of modernity continues to elude mine workers on the margins of the global economy.

The new generation of open-cut mines also produces fifty times the waste rock of underground mining (Ripley et al. 1978, 36). These projects turn mountains into craters in a matter of years. Many of these mines are gigantic, completely out of proportion to human scale, which contributes to the hubris of mining engineers who assume they can master the forces of nature. Although these mines leave behind vast holes in the earth up to several kilometers in diameter, it is usually the handling of tailings, waste rock, and overburden that results in lasting environmental problems. The impacts of these projects increase exponentially when these materials are discharged directly into rivers or the sea.

Many of these new mines are located in places where indigenous peoples retain control over lands and territories not previously seen to have economic value. Communities dependent on natural resources for subsistence are especially vulnerable to the environmental impacts of mining. Their values may also be incompatible with industrialized modes of resource extraction. Writing about the response of the people living in Bougainville, Papua New Guinea, to the environmental impact of the Panguna copper and gold mine, which was the catalyst for a land-owner rebellion that led to a decade-long civil war, Jill Nash (1993, 17–18) observes that "the destruction of the landscape has enormous power—it is a cataclysmic event—in a subsistence society like Bougain-ville. . . . The land is not only for material benefit, which compensation payments reduce it to; it encodes their history and identity and is a major source of security." In extreme cases, the environmental impacts from large-scale mining projects can be so pervasive that people come to question their fundamental assumptions about the natural world (Kirsch 2006).

As a result, mining projects have become the target of unprecedented conflict on almost every continent. Protests against mining address a range of interrelated concerns, including claims to political autonomy and the rights to lands and territories, environmental impacts, the poli-tics of livelihood, and cultural survival. The participants in these strug-gles circulate petitions, stage demonstrations, and set up roadblocks. They collaborate with international NGOs and church groups. They file legal cases in domestic courts concerning pollution and compensation, and they engage lawyers to bring suit against transnational mining com-panies in the countries in which the companies are incorporated. They have also instigated rebellions and civil wars. Referenda against mining are debated and passed in cities and *pueblos* across Latin America, demonstrating that the proposed projects lack a "social license to oper-ate," and leading outraged state officials to criticize voters for taking democracy into their own hands. In contrast, politicians who question why their predecessors signed agreements that effectively gave away their nation's patrimony, allowing mining companies to reap windfall profits, are accused of "resource nationalism" by the mining industry when they seek to rectify the imbalance.

Conflicts between mining companies and communities are generally classified as examples of "new social movements," because they focus less on the concerns of labor and class and more on other aspects of identity and rights, including civil rights, environmentalism, and indigenous rights (Melucci 1980; Touraine 1985). Although the "newness" of these movements has been challenged (Calhoun 1993; Tucker 1991), there are clear differences between these forms of mobilization and the political activism of the late 1960s and early 1970s, when June Nash conducted her fieldwork among Bolivian tin miners. The earlier movements responded to "accumulation by exploitation" through union membership, labor action, and the nationalization of resources, while the new movements oppose the practice of "accumulation by dispossession" through which resources and rights are appropriated and privatized (Harvey 2003).

The escalation of mining conflicts coincided with the emergence of environmentalism as an international political movement during the 1980s and 1990s. Many of the new social movements are engaged in what Joan Martinez-Alier (2003) calls the "environmentalism of the poor," which recognizes that marginal communities are especially vulnerable to environmental degradation and therefore more likely to engage in political action to protect their access to resources. This view challenges the post-materialist hypothesis that identifies environmentalism as a value that arises only after individuals have already fulfilled their basic needs (Inglehart 1977, 1990). It also differs from environmentalism focused on the protection of "wilderness" in the form of national parks and conservation areas that separate people from nature (Cronon 1996).

Another important focus of mining conflicts has been the distribution of economic benefits (Filer 1997a; Arellano-Yanguas 2012). People living in rural areas often expect mining companies to provide them with access to higher standards of living, better education and health care, and new economic opportunities. Yet mining companies rarely fulfill such expectations and often fail to keep the promises they do make. Communities affected by mining often find themselves caught betwixt and between old and new lives when environmental damage compromises subsistence production and the limited economic benefits they receive do not allow them to achieve their aspirations for modernity (Kirsch 2006).

Many of the actors in the new social movements against mining identify as indigenous. As Arturo Escobar (2001b, 184) suggests, indigeneity is one of the ways in which "peoples' sense of belonging and attachment to place continue to be important sources of cultural production and mobilized to various ends." Rather than an autonomous social formation, indigeneity is a relationship between peoples with histories of conflict and differential access to power (de la Cadena and Starn 2007). Despite acquiring legitimacy through their relationships to place, the politics of indigeneity operates in part by connecting the participants to politics beyond the state, providing new resources to solve conflicts stalemated at local or national levels (Niezen 2003). The international legal status of indigenous peoples has developed through a series of multilateral conferences and agreements (Anaya 2004; Barsh 1994), although the definition of indigeneity remains unsettled in many national contexts (T. M. Li 2000). Some states do not recognize the existence of indigenous peoples within their boundaries. In other countries, people disagree among themselves about whether they wish to be identified as indigenous.

Indigenous politics has long been shaped by interactions with extractive industry (Gedicks 1993, 2001; Sawyer and Gomez 2012). This remains true today, as mining interests continue to influence the politics of recognition. For example, the prime minister of Peru recently declared that the Quechua and Aymara peoples of the Andes were not considered indigenous for the purpose of laws about consultation in relation to natural-resource extraction (Reuters 2013). Mining also influences relationships between indigenous peoples and NGOs. In conflicts over mining, indigenous peoples have found strong allies in environmental and human rights groups, but conservation organizations are increasingly likely to partner with the mining industry rather than indigenous communities (Chapin 2004). It may not be an exaggeration to claim, as I have heard from parties on both sides of these conflicts, that mining companies and indigenous peoples regard each other as their greatest threat.

Sustained critical attention from NGOs and increasingly effective strategies of resistance by indigenous peoples during the 1990s took the mining industry by surprise. The remote location of most mining projects has long afforded them relative freedom from oversight or interference, allowing the industry to maintain a low profile. This can be contrasted with branding in the petroleum industry, in which consumers engage directly with corporations at the pump.[3] The comparative obscurity of the mining industry is compounded by the fact that most metals are sold to other companies rather than consumers. The resulting anonymity of metals—it is impossible, for example, to trace the source of the copper wire in my computer or the gold in my wedding ring—means that the mining industry is largely immune to consumer politics.[4] Thus, until recently, the mining industry lacked the kind of public relations machinery commonly employed by industries with longer histories of engagement with their critics. But with the global rise of indigenous, environmental, and NGO politics, the mining industry faced unprecedented challenges to its legitimacy and the threat of external regulation, forcing it to develop new strategies for engaging with its critics.

MINING CAPITALISM

My interest in these questions stems from more than two decades of ethnographic research and participation in the indigenous political movement that challenged the environmental impact of the Ok Tedi copper and gold mine in Papua New Guinea (Kirsch 2002, 2006). Since the mid-1980s, the mine has discharged more than two billion metric tons of tailings, waste rock, and overburden into the Ok Tedi and Fly Rivers, causing massive environmental degradation downstream. In the first half of this book, I examine how an alliance of indigenous peoples, environmental activists, and lawyers mounted an international campaign that sought to stop the Ok Tedi mine from polluting the local river system. In chapter 1, "Colliding Ecologies," I examine the reaction of the people living downstream from the mine to its social and environmental consequences. Pollution from the mine has caused extensive deforestation, making it impossible for the people living on the Ok Tedi and Fly Rivers to feed their families using traditional subsistence practices. Although the state continues to follow the development paradigm that encourages less-developed countries to improve their economic standing through natural-resource extraction, the environmental devastation downstream from the Ok Tedi mine illustrates the microeconomic version of the resource curse, in which mining immiserates these communities instead of benefiting them economically.

Chapter 2, "The Politics of Space," addresses the ways that a group of charismatic leaders from the Ok Tedi and Fly Rivers collaborated with international NGOs in their campaign against the Ok Tedi mine. They faced a steep learning curve. Their initial protests and petitions were largely ignored by the mining company and the government. It was only by taking their campaign global that they were able to challenge Broken Hill Proprietary Ltd. (BHP), the majority shareholder and managing partner of the mine. They followed the movement of copper ore from Papua New Guinea to smelters in Europe and Asia. They attended the 1992 "Earth Summit" in Rio de Janeiro and met with environmental NGOs in New York and Washington, DC. They presented their case at the International Water Tribunal in Amsterdam and discussed German investments in the Ok Tedi mine with members of the Parliament in Bonn. They testified at public hearings held to assess BHP's bid to acquire a billion dollar diamond concession in Canada's Northwest Territories, and information they provided about the environmental problems caused by the Ok Tedi mine helped to deter BHP's copper prospect in the Caribbean. Through their encounters with other peoples facing similar threats, they first began to see themselves as indigenous. This identity has proven to be a productive way to frame the issues in their campaign and forge political alliances, even though the state of Papua New Guinea denies that its citizens are indigenous. For a time, they also became heroes of Australia's green community and celebrities on the environmental NGO circuit. The chapter discusses both the strengths and compromises of these alliances, which in this case operated less like the horizontal mode of democratic power-sharing associated with network politics than a form of distributed action in which the participants were not always aware of each other's activities. Although the international support they received helped to legitimize their claims, they were unable to stop the mining company from polluting their river and destroying their forests.

The impasse prompted the leaders of the campaign to file a lawsuit against BHP in Melbourne, where the company is based. Their legal action is the subject of chapter 3. The 1994 litigation represented thirty thousand people living downstream from the mine against one of Australia's largest corporations. The case was notable in that it sought to hold a transnational corporation accountable in its home country for its operations overseas, establishing an important precedent subsequently taken up in other legal claims against the mining industry. The case was settled out of court in 1996 for an estimated $500 million in compensation and commitments to stop discharging tailings, the finely ground material that remains after the valuable ore is extracted, into local rivers. The plaintiffs were forced to return to court in 2000, however, after BHP failed to implement the tailings containment stipulated by the earlier agreement. The second lawsuit was settled in 2004, after public pressure forced BHP to transfer its 52 percent share in the Ok Tedi mine to a development trust, which may eventually cost the company three billion dollars in lost revenue. The title of chapter 3, "Down by Law," refers to both the success of their first lawsuit, which initially appeared to be a victory over BHP, and the outcome of the second case, which ultimately failed to protect the environment. The shortcoming of their campaign suggests an important limitation of the politics of space: the many years that it took to mobilize their campaign and put pressure on the mining company, during which pollution from the mine continued unabated. The chapter also weighs the pros and cons of international tort claims, which can provide legitimacy to opposition movements, establish important legal precedents, and advance the cause of indigenous peoples against the mining industry, but may also fall short on grounds that have little to do with the merits of the case or the rights that have been violated. The top-down management of the litigation process that replaced the horizontal networks of the original campaign also restricted participation and reduced political commitment to the legal proceedings, weakening them in the process.

This book draws on long-term ethnographic research with the Yonggom people living on the Ok Tedi River. In my previous work, I considered whether culture continues to matter in the context of such overwhelming power disparities, showing how questions of meaning were at the heart of their political struggles (Kirsch 2006). In contrast to the a priori commitments of engaged anthropologists whose choice of fieldwork projects is driven by their political interests (e.g., Juris 2008; Speed 2008), I viewed my participation in the campaign against the mine as a "logical extension of the commitment to reciprocity that underlies the practice of anthropology" (Kirsch 2002, 178). By the time George Marcus (1995) was astutely commenting on the emergence of multi-sited ethnography, I was already moving between radically different fieldsites, discussing the problems caused by mining and potential interventions with villagers, state officials, employees at the mine site and executives at the corporate headquarters in Melbourne, lawyers in Australia, and NGOs on several continents. Marcus (1995, 113), however, did not anticipate that the "constantly mobile, recalibrating practice of positioning . . . as well as alienations from . . . those with whom [one] interacts" may stabilize over time. Although my research methods and questions varied according to the context, my relationships with the people affected by pollution became the constant in these interactions and the basis on which I gained access to the participants on both sides of a highly charged political contest (Kirsch 2002).

My participation in the Ok Tedi case also resulted in invitations to a pivotal series of international meetings about the relationship between indigenous peoples and extractive industry. I attended these workshops and conferences not only to present the results of my research or because they represented novel sites for the collection of ethnographic data, but also for the opportunity to contribute to these debates as a political actor (Ramos 1999). This presented new challenges and learning opportunities, as well as risks, including potential repercussions for violating the academic norms that separate scholarship from political engagement. However, the stakes in these conflicts for the people living along the Ok Tedi and Fly Rivers, and for other people facing similar problems, far outweighed any risks to my career.

In an exceptionally thoughtful essay on these matters, Gaynor Macdonald (2002) suggests that the positions anthropologists advocate as political actors and expert witnesses in legal proceedings may be incompatible with the partial, open-ended character of postmodern ethnography. But in writing this book, I have found it impossible to adopt a neutral position, a response that is informed by decades of engaged research on mining conflicts. A degree of skepticism and perhaps even cynicism is required to analyze the mining industry's relationship to its critics—and between corporations and their critics more generally—including how these interactions shape global capitalism. I leave to the reader to weigh the strengths of this orientation against the potential blind spots that result from having worked with the people living downstream from the Ok Tedi mine, one of the worst mining disasters in recent decades in terms of its social and environmental costs.

The first half of the book analyzes the forms of protest and legal action undertaken by critics of the mining industry, with a focus on the Ok Tedi case as both an ethnographic context for understanding these dynamics and in terms of the case's historical significance for subsequent relationships between mining companies and their critics. The second half of the book entails a shift from writing about resistance to what Laura Nader (1972) calls "studying up" by focusing on the mining industry, which is the subject of chapters 4 and 5. Contemporary ethnographic research on the corporation ordinarily entails participant-observation in a variety of contexts, from the boardrooms where important decisions are made to the public protests, shareholder actions, and courtrooms where corporations face resistance, as well as in the fields, factories, markets, and homes in which production and consumption take place. However, conducting ethnographic research within the corporation poses a risk of co-optation, because the tendency of ethnographers to empathize with the subjects of their research may influence their findings or temper their critical perspectives. Thus, these two chapters suggest alternative models for studying corporations by examining how they produce and manipulate science in order to influence their critics and avoid regulation, the subject of chapter 4, and how they respond to their critics through various corporate social technologies, the focus of chapter 5. This discussion takes the dialectical relationship between corporations and their critics as its object of study rather than conducting ethnographic research within the corporation.

Chapter 4, "Corporate Science," begins by asking how the engineers and scientists working at the Ok Tedi mine could have missed the slow-moving environmental disaster that it set into motion downstream. It then considers how different industries use science in managing their relationships to the public, both industries in which profits are predicated on harm, such as the tobacco and mining industries, and the pharmaceutical industry, which is dedicated to improving human health and therefore held to higher ethical standards. The chapter finds unexpected similarities across these industries in their manipulation of scientific research and findings, arguing that these shared strategies are intrinsic to contemporary capitalism rather than restricted to specific corporations or industries.

In chapter 5, "Industry Strikes Back," I examine the strategies and tactics through which the mining industry responds to its critics. The rise of indigenous and NGO opposition provoked a "crisis of confidence" in the mining industry in the late 1990s (Danielson 2002, 7), resulting in unprecedented collaboration among corporations that previously regarded each other as fierce competitors. The resulting forms of "audit culture" convey the message that the problems of the mining industry are being addressed while avoiding the imposition of real constraints on their operation (Power 1997; Strathern 2002a). This includes efforts to promote mining as a form of sustainable development. Mining companies creatively appropriate the tactics of their opponents, including the use of satire to discredit environmentalists. They also collaborate with conservative political organizations in the critique of NGOs and public participation in science. Finally, the mining industry has sought to increase its symbolic capital by contributing to public health campaigns and developing stronger relationships to the academy.

The last chapter of the book, "New Politics of Time," addresses efforts to focus political attention earlier in the production cycle, before new mining projects receive government approval and financing. The chapter contrasts the politics of space associated with the campaign against the Ok Tedi mine, in which building international coalitions ultimately took too long to save the river and forests, with new strategies based on the politics of time. A key strategy of the politics of time has been the establishment of international networks that seek to accelerate local learning curves by sharing information about the mining industry. These networks have also applied pressure on the multilateral organizations and international financial institutions that underwrite the mining industry to establish new policies intended to safeguard indigenous rights and the environment. I describe how pressure from international NGOs led the World Bank and the United Nations to host workshops that addressed mining conflicts, proceedings that have contributed to the recognition of the indigenous right to free, prior, and informed consent, an important resource in the politics of time. In addition, I discuss more direct efforts to accelerate the learning curve of indigenous communities that may be affected by new mining projects, which I illustrate by describing my participation in an independent review of a proposed bauxite mine in Suriname. Finally, I examine a growing social movement based on the politics of time in Latin America that uses local democratic votes (referenda, or *consultas*) to express opposition to new mining projects. The politics of time offers a potential antidote to political resignation through its contribution to more hopeful outcomes.

Despite the effectiveness of the corporate social technologies deployed by the mining industry, the social movements described here have been able to challenge the industry in a number of ways. By calling attention to the externalized costs of mining, they have radically altered public perceptions of the industry. They have forced the mining industry to reconsider some of its most destructive practices. In some cases, they have caused mining companies to incur substantial economic losses as a result of their negligent actions. They have also established legal precedents that help realign power relations between indigenous communities and mining companies. They have raised awareness of these issues among the members of communities who have the greatest exposure to harm from new mining projects. Conflicts between mining companies and communities have forced states to intervene, caused the World Bank to reconsider its investments in extractive industry, and prompted contentious debates at the United Nations. More significant reforms are still urgently needed. But these achievements illustrate the capacity of political movements and NGOs to draw attention to the problems caused by corporations, forcing their renegotiation on new terms.

CHAPTER I

Colliding Ecologies

The Ok Tedi copper and gold mine in Papua New Guinea has discharged more than two billion metric tons of tailings, overburden, and waste rock into the Fly River system since the mid-1980s, polluting the river corridor from the mine to the sea, a distance of one thousand kilometers (Tingay 2007, 5). Nearly two thousand square kilometers of rain forest and savannah along the river have been affected by flooding and die-back (OTML 2005, 4). The pollution is eventually expected to transform the entire floodplain, approximately 3,800 square kilometers, an area larger than the U.S. state of Rhode Island (Tingay 2007, 12). Until recently, the Fly River system was the site of one of the largest extant rain forests in the world and valued for its high biodiversity (Swartzendruber 1993). The project has already caused acid mine drainage at several locations, which has the potential to render large areas inhospitable to organic life for centuries (map 1).

Large-scale resource extraction projects like the Ok Tedi mine are usually dominated by distant capital and primarily responsive to international markets. Economies of scale often dictate the enormous size of hard rock mines, especially when located in remote and rugged terrain. Mining is an intensive process that focuses on a single type of resource, which it eventually exhausts. Without adequate protection, the environmental impact from these mines may extend over great distances. Yet pressure from international markets discourages mining companies from making sufficient investments in environmental controls. The absence of binding international standards for handling tailings and other mine wastes leads mining companies to pursue a "race to the bottom" for environmental standards. Mining companies lack incentive to voluntarily raise these standards, given that only those producers with the lowest costs remain profitable during economic downturns.

The environmental impacts of large-scale resource extraction projects may also pose a threat to indigenous subsistence practices, a dynamic I refer to as "colliding ecologies." When competing systems for exploiting natural resources interact, one system may limit the viability of the others. The environmental impact of the Ok Tedi mine has had significant consequences for the thirty thousand people living downstream whose livelihoods depend on access to natural resources. Until relatively recently, the diets of the peoples living in the region were entirely dependent on local subsistence production. They were also extensive, making use of a broad array of resources, combining horticulture with hunting, fishing, and the gathering of forest products. In the cloud forests of the Star Mountains, where the Ok Tedi mine is located, taro is the staple food of the Min (Barth 1983; Crook 2007; Hyndman 1994). In the lowland rain forests of the North Fly, the Yonggom and their neighbors harvest sago from the Metroxylon palm and cultivate bananas (Depew 1987; Kirsch 2006; Welsch 1994). In the savannah and lagoons of the Middle Fly, the Boazi and their neighbors rely on sago, hunting, and fishing for the bulk of their diet (Busse 1991). In the rain forest and mangroves of the South Fly, the Kiwai and their neighbors depend on sago and fish (Lawrence 1991; Ohtsuka 1983), whereas yams are the staple crop of the people living in the dry interior (Ayres 1983). These subsistence practices are compatible with a variety of other economic activities, including smallholder rubber plantations, commercial fishing, and the cultivation of cash crops. However, pollution from the Ok Tedi mine has transformed the downstream environment in ways that compromise both subsistence production and other economic opportunities.

The harsh treatment of land and other resources set aside for production is commonplace for the residents of industrialized countries, but the new landscape downstream from the Ok Tedi mine is alien to the people living there. Rivers that once ran green and clear have been transformed into muddy torrents the color of coffee with milk. Three decades of mining have transformed the verdant landscape along the river corridor into a moonscape of gray tailings. The hornbills, cockatoos, egrets, kingfishers, and birds of paradise that used to live along the

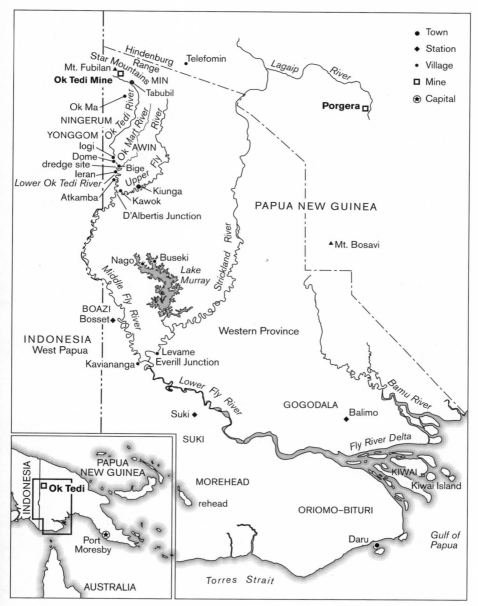

MAP I. The Fly River from the Star Mountains to the Gulf of Papua, Papua New Guinea.

river and in the forest are gone. Fish populations have been drastically reduced in number and biodiversity. Sago stands along the river and in nearby creeks have long since been choked by mud. The pollution of the river, the death of the forest along the river corridor, and the disappearance of the animals that used to live there have given rise to widespread concerns about environmental collapse. The destruction of the landscape has also evoked profound expressions of sorrow and loss from the people living along the river.

The concept of colliding ecologies suggests an alternative way of conceptualizing what economists call the "resource curse," the recognition that developing countries dependent on mining and other forms of natural resource extraction possess slower growth rates than their peers (Auty 1993; Sachs and Warner 1995; Ross 1999). The resource curse not only causes macroeconomic problems at the level of the state, but it also creates microeconomic problems for the peoples most directly affected by mining. Even though new mining projects are routinely promoted on the grounds that they will raise local standards of living, in practice, the people living in the catchment areas of these projects end up bearing a disproportionate share of their costs—in the form of environmental impacts. Instead of benefiting economically from mining, many of these communities are impoverished by pollution, an example of "accumulation by dispossession" (Harvey 2003).

I begin this chapter by examining the history of the Ok Tedi mine and the reasons why its impacts have vastly exceeded the project's original environmental impact assessment. Next, I discuss the macro- and microeconomic consequences of the resource curse. I focus on the consequences of the Ok Tedi mine's environmental impact for the Yonggom people, with whom I have carried out ethnographic research since 1986, including their perceptions of these changes. Finally, I show how these events have analogues elsewhere in the region by briefly describing several other prominent mining conflicts in Melanesia. In addition to using this exercise for its comparative value, I explain how these conflicts are interrelated.

This chapter also seeks to place the Ok Tedi mine in its proper historical context as one of the first conflicts between mining companies and communities to gain international prominence. As I argue more fully in succeeding chapters, the Ok Tedi case not only contributed to the internationalization of debate about the mining industry, but it also led to significant changes in the industry's practices, triggered a series of lawsuits against transnational mining companies, alerted multilateral banks and other international financial institutions to the problems caused by their funding of the Ok Tedi mine and other mining projects, and led to new roles for indigenous peoples and NGOs in relation to mining conflicts around the world.

PRELUDE TO DISASTER

Ok Tedi was the first mining project approved by the postcolonial government of Papua New Guinea, which acquired its independence from Australia in 1975. The flagship development project of the colonial era was the Panguna copper mine in Bougainville, which, during its operation, provided more than 16 percent of the postcolonial state's revenues (Griffin 1990, 70). After independence, Papua New Guinea continued the colonial policy of pursuing economic development through large-scale resource extraction projects (Filer and Macintyre 2006).

Kennecott exploration geologists discovered the ore body at Mt. Fubilan in 1968, nearly a century after the Australian engineer Lawrence Hargrave found copper and gold while panning in the lower Ok Tedi River in 1876 (Goode 1977, 176). Negotiations between the state of Papua New Guinea and Kennecott failed, however, in 1975, and several years later, in 1980, the Australian mining company Broken Hill Proprietary Ltd. (BHP) took the lead in establishing a consortium of investors to develop the project.[1] The Australian government was eager to see the project move forward as a means of reducing its financial obligations toward its former territory and offered BHP tax credits for exploration and other financial support for developing the mine (Pintz 1984, 56). This was the first major international venture for BHP, which had previously concentrated on domestic investments. Its participation in the Ok Tedi mine coincided with the rapid internationalization of the company, which culminated in its 2001 merger with the Anglo-Dutch mining company Billiton PLC. BHP Billiton currently operates in twenty-five countries around the world and describes itself as the "world's largest diversified resources company," producing aluminum, bauxite, coal, copper, diamonds, iron ore, lead, manganese, nickel, petroleum, silver, steel, uranium, and zinc (BHP Billiton 2006).

The Ok Tedi mine is located in the Star Mountains, eighteen kilometers from the border with the militarized Indonesian territory of West Papua. In 1982, when construction began, this was one of the least accessible areas of Papua New Guinea.[2] At the start of mining, Mt. Fubilan stood 2,094 meters high (Pintz 1984, 13), but the elevation of the mining pit will drop below sea level during the final phase of the project, which is expected to last from 2015 to 2025. The terrain is composed of rugged limestone karst. With annual rainfall in excess of ten meters, this is one of the wettest areas in the world, which proved to be a critical factor in the erosion of waste rock and overburden into the river system. The ore body is located near the headwaters of the Ok Tedi River, which runs south for about 190 kilometers to D'Albertis Junction, where it joins the Fly River, forming the largest wetland system in the country. The volume of water transported through the Fly River system per square mile of catchment area exceeds even that of the Amazon River (Townsend and Townsend 1996, 1). The river system once supported the most diverse assemblage of freshwater fish in the Australasian region, with 115 species, including seventeen endemic species (Storey et al. 2009, 428). In contrast, the Sepik River in northern Papua New Guinea, the river closest in size to the Fly, has a relatively low overall fish density, with a total of fifty-seven freshwater species (Hettler and Lehmann 1995, 15). The bird life along the Fly River was equally diverse, including tens of thousands of migratory birds that travel north from Australia during the continental dry season.

The distinguishing feature of the ore body at Mt. Fubilan was a substantial gold cap, which was expected to pay for the bulk of the project's construction costs (Jackson 1993, 168). From May 1984 until 1988, the gold cap was mined and processed, which involved the use of sodium cyanide to separate the gold from the other metals and rock; gold bars were produced at the site and flown directly out of the country. In late 1988 the mine moved to full production in the second phase of development, producing copper concentrate, which is piped 160 kilometers to the river port of Kiunga on the Fly River, where it is loaded onto ships and transported to overseas smelters in China, Germany, India, Japan, South Korea, and the Philippines.[3] During this phase of production, gold and silver are not separated from the copper concentrate, and consequently, cyanide is no longer used at the mine.

There was always a question whether the second phase of the mine would be economically viable, although the state made its contract with the mining company contingent on the continuation of the project after the gold cap was exhausted. Over the history of the mine, BHP threatened to walk away from the project several times, exercising its political leverage over the state, which had become economically dependent on the taxes and other economic benefits provided by the mine. Papua New Guinea also had a strong interest in demonstrating to the interna-

FIGURE 1. The Ok Tedi Mine, 2004. Photo: Andrew Marshall.

tional community that it was a desirable location for investment capital. BHP finally left the project in 2001, because the Ok Tedi mine's ongoing environmental impacts posed significant economic liabilities and reputational costs. However, at the insistence of the state, the Ok Tedi mine continues to operate, though without its international partners (fig. 1). Due to higher metal prices in the last decade, the most recent phase of the project has been by far its most profitable, with earnings of more than five billion dollars, a dramatic turnaround for a mine that performed so poorly during its early years of operation that BHP's original investment in the project had to be written off (Jackson 1993, 50).

Although BHP was the managing partner of the Ok Tedi mine, it initially controlled only 30 percent of the project. German interests accounted for another 20 percent of the operation. This followed the decision by the German metals industry during the 1970s to secure access to raw materials through investment in foreign mining projects, which was supported by government financing and tax incentives (IWT 1994, Mining, 60). Metallgesellschaft, the largest minerals and natural resources company in Germany, which also has substantial international interests, acquired 7.5 percent of the project. Degussa, a large precious metals and chemical company, owned another 7.5 percent of the mine, giving the company access to copper for its refinery on the Elbe River, which was operated by its subsidiary Norddeutsche Affinerie, as well as a market for the industrial chemicals it produced, including hydrogen peroxide and sodium cyanide. The German export credit agency DEG, which ordinarily provides loans to development projects, controlled another 5 percent of the project (IWT 1994, Mining, 60). Amoco (originally Standard Oil Company of Indiana) was the final international investor, acquiring 30 percent of the project. The head of Amoco's minerals subsidiary had previous experience at the Panguna copper mine in Bougainville and was instrumental in Amoco's decision to invest in the Ok Tedi mine (Pintz 1984, 59).

The Papua New Guinea state also assumed ownership of a 20 percent stake in the project. This decision was influenced by ideas about economic dependency that were prominent during the 1970s, most notably the argument that the wealthier core states of the global economy perpetuated their economic advantage by extracting raw materials from poorer and less-developed states in the periphery (Thompson and MacWilliam 1992, 170). By acquiring an ownership stake in the Ok Tedi mine, Papua New Guinea hoped to reverse this trend by reaping a greater share of the financial benefits from its natural resources (Zorn 1977). However, policy makers did not give adequate consideration to the contradictions engendered by this decision, notably that the state would have to negotiate a fundamental conflict of interest as both a shareholder and the regulator of the Ok Tedi mine. In particular, the scale of the new mining project in relation to the small size of the country's formal economic sector created a new form of dependency for Papua New Guinea on the Ok Tedi mine. Throughout the history of the project, the state has consistently made regulatory decisions that sought to minimize its expenditures and maximize its economic returns as both a shareholder in the mine and tax collector. Most of these decisions were made at the expense of people living downstream from the Ok Tedi mine.

Financing for the $1.4 billion project was supported by a number of multilateral investment authorities and state export credit agencies, the purpose of which is to promote economic activity. The Australian government backed the mine with the largest export credit ever provided by its Export Finance and Insurance Corporation (Pintz 1984, 139). The

Multilateral Investment Guarantee Authority (MIGA) of the World Bank provided guarantees that ensured lower interest rates on loans from New York–based Citicorp Bank. The U.S. Overseas Private Investment Corporation (OPIC) provided political risk insurance against the threat of nationalization (Pintz 1984, 140). The European Investment Bank and several export credit agencies in Europe also provided financial support given the German investments in the project (Pintz 1984, 140–41). In the early 1980s, these institutions lacked policies addressing the environmental impacts of the projects they funded or their consequences for indigenous rights, although this began to change in the late 1980s and 1990s as a result of lobbying and other pressure from the NGO community (Goodland 2000). Accordingly, the credit agencies and banks that financed the Ok Tedi mine lacked the legal standing or political capacity to intervene in decisions made by the mining company. Despite the large commitment of public resources to the project, civil society had little influence over the policies of Ok Tedi Mining Ltd. (OTML), even after the environmental problems caused by the mine had become pronounced and troubling.

At its independence from Australia in 1975, the legal system of Papua New Guinea was still in the process of being drafted. Consequently, the Ok Tedi project is governed under a separate act of Parliament, the Mining (Ok Tedi Agreement) Act of 1976. Despite having one of the first constitutions in the world to make reference to environmental sustainability, the bill that enforced this provision of the constitution was not passed until 1979.[4] This means that the Ok Tedi mine is exempt from the Environmental Planning Act. The original Mining Act has been modified ten times in separate agreements, each of which required parliamentary approval. The Ok Tedi mine is governed by these agreements, which have been influenced by the political concerns and often pressing economic needs of the state, rather than being regulated by the same laws as the rest of the industry. Although the transfer of responsibility for monitoring the Ok Tedi mine by the Department of Minerals and Energy, which is also charged with increasing state revenue from this sector, to the Department of Environment and Conservation in 1993 was intended to reduce the inherent conflict of interest, all of the major decisions about the mine continue to be made by the PNG Parliament, which must contend with competing priorities. In addition to repeated threats by the mining company to pull up stakes and abandon the project and the state's conflict of interest as both regulator and shareholder, these shortcomings in the governance of the project might be seen as a critical third strike in terms of undercutting the ability and motivation of the state to limit the mine's environmental impact.

The question of waste disposal from the Ok Tedi mine has dominated discussion and critique of the project. Hard rock mines produce several different waste products. *Tailings,* or *fines,* are the finely ground materials, often sand-like in consistency, that remain after the valuable metals have been extracted from the ore body. *Overburden* refers to rock and earth moved to gain access to the ore body. *Waste rock* refers to materials that have been excavated but do not contain enough metal to be processed economically. The cut-off for processing, or *head grade,* is determined by a combination of technical capacity, production costs, and market prices for metals, and can change over the life of a mining project. Historically, this figure has decreased as metals have become more valuable and new technologies have been developed to extract particles that, in the case of gold, may be so small as to be invisible to the naked eye. For the Ok Tedi mine, the tailings consist of a fine slurry of ground rock containing varying amounts of heavy metals, including cadmium, copper, lead, and zinc, as well as small quantities of organic flotation chemicals (IWT 1994). The waste rock and overburden from the Ok Tedi mine consists of soft material that breaks down easily, with a copper content of 0.2 percent or less and significant quantities of other heavy metals (IWT 1994). More than one billion metric tons of waste rock and overburden have eroded into the river over the life of the mine (Tingay 2007, 5). Another 750 million metric tons of finely ground tailings have been discharged into the river system during this time.

The initial proposal for the Ok Tedi mine included the construction of a dam in the mountains that was intended to prevent the tailings from entering the river system. But historically high gold prices encouraged the mining company to accelerate construction of the mine. Excavation for the foundation of the Ok Ma tailings dam, which was already several months behind schedule, commenced before the geological assessment of the site was complete (Townsend 1988, 113). On January 7, 1984, there was a landslide at the excavation site that destroyed the footings for the dam and prevented further construction (Townsend 1988, 114). Even though three independent reports suggested alternative sites for a tailings dam (Townsend and Townsend 2004, 13), the mining company immediately petitioned the state to begin production without a tailings dam. Anxious not to delay or jeopardize this important economic project, several weeks later the Papua New Guinea government approved an interim tailings scheme that permitted the mining company to dis-

FIGURE 2. Clean water from the Ok Mart River enters the polluted lower Ok Tedi River, 1987. Photo: Ok Tedi Mining Ltd.

charge tailings directly into the Ok Tedi River (fig. 2). Under the terms of the Sixth Supplemental Agreement, which went into effect in 1986, OTML agreed to investigate alternative plans for tailings containment and report back to the state in late 1989. The Sixth Supplemental Agreement also made an important change to the earlier agreements, redefining the river system affected by the mine as the "Fly River below the confluence of the Ok Tedi and Fly River down to and including the delta of the Fly River" (Papua New Guinea 1986), treating the Ok Tedi River as a de facto sacrifice zone (Kirsch 1989b, 58).

The predictions of the environmental impact assessment conducted for the project (Maunsell and Partners 1982), which was based on the assumption that the mining company would build a tailings dam in the mountains, were quickly rendered obsolete. Given that only a marginal amount of the tailings produced by the mine was originally expected to enter the river system, the primary impacts from the mine were anticipated to come from eroding waste rock. This was supposed to increase the volume of sediment in the river only slightly, and it was claimed that the changes would not be noticeable below Ningerum, seventy kilometers downstream from the mine. The environmental impact assessment also predicted negligible impacts in the lower Ok Tedi River and none at all for the Fly River (Maunsell and Partners 1982). Consequently, the "effects of suspended sediment loads (turbidity) on the Ok Tedi-Fly River system were never investigated" (Pintz 1984, 106). Given that there were only a handful of settlements along the upper Ok Tedi River, the report predicted that the project would have very limited social impacts on the communities downstream from the mine (Maunsell and Partners 1982; see Jackson, Emerson, and Welsch 1980).

Another key assumption made by the original environmental impact study was that the maximum rate of production at the Ok Tedi mine would be forty-five thousand metric tons per day (Pintz 1984, 73). However, the collapse of copper prices during the economic depression of the mid-1980s led the mine to increase production to eighty thousand metric tons per day in order to remain economically competitive. Significant changes in the management of waste rock and overburden were also made after production began, as more of the waste rock than originally anticipated had to be moved to the southern dump, where it quickly eroded into the river system (Pintz 1984). Due to heavy rainfall in the mountains, erosion from the so-called stable northern dump has also been much greater than predicted.

From a mine with an environmental impact assessment predicated on the construction of a tailings dam and strong controls over the volume of waste rock entering the river system, Ok Tedi morphed into a project in which thirty million metric tons of tailings and forty million metric tons of overburden and waste rock enter the river system annually, causing massive environmental degradation downstream. These impacts have also been exacerbated by the longevity of the project, which was originally expected to last for fifteen years (Pintz 1984, 35). The mine remains operational in 2013, more than twenty-five years after production began, and a proposed extension would keep the mine operational until 2025, albeit at significantly lower rates of production. The combination of discharging tailings directly into the river, accelerated erosion of waste rock into the river system, the doubling of production levels, and nearly tripling the original life of the mine have dramatically increased the impact of the project on the environment.

During the first year of gold production, there were two significant cyanide spills. On June 14, 1984, a barge transporting chemicals to the mine overturned in the Fly River delta during a storm, losing 2,800 sixty-liter drums of cyanide and several stainless-steel containers of hydrogen peroxide. Only 117 of the cyanide drums had been recovered when the search was called off. A second cyanide spill occurred at the mine on June 19, 1984, when a "by-pass valve opened for two hours and 12 minutes . . . releasing 1000 cubic meters of highly concentrated cyanide waste into the Ok Tedi River" (Hyndman 1994, 94). The people living in Dome village, about one hundred kilometers downstream from the mine, recall collecting and eating the dead fish, turtles, and crocodiles that floated to the surface of the Ok Tedi River the next day.

Ok Tedi Mining Ltd. was required to report to the national government on its new plans for tailings disposal by late 1989. Earlier that year, however, the Panguna copper mine in Bougainville had been attacked and forced to close by landowners who objected to its environmental impacts and the size of the national government's share of the mine's profits. Given the Panguna mine's contribution to Papua New Guinea's GDP, its closure dramatically increased the state's economic dependence on the Ok Tedi mine.

Although the possibility of constructing a tailings dam at the Ok Tedi mine was still being discussed as a viable option as of May 1989, in October of that year BHP reported to the Papua New Guinea government that a tailings dam was no longer economically feasible (Filer 1997b, 60).[5] BHP threatened to close the mine if it was forced to build the dam, leaving the state between a rock and a hard place. In December 1989, the state granted approval for Ok Tedi Mining Ltd. to continue discharging tailings into Fly River system, a decision described as "one of the most fateful and dangerous ever made in the history of mining in the Pacific region" (Moody 1992, 147). The failure to build a tailings dam was especially ironic for the Yonggom people, from whose language the Ok Tedi mine derives its name. Ok Tedi, or *Ok Deri*, as it is usually pronounced, is not only the name for the river along which many of the Yonggom villages in Papua New Guinea are located but also refers to fishing dams or weirs. The Yonggom use rocks, sticks, and mud to block off a section of the river, then bail out the water behind the structure to collect the fish and prawns left stranded in shallow pools. In other words, the downfall of the Ok Tedi mine was caused by the company's failure to build an *ok tedi*, a dam.

In lieu of its obligation to construct a tailings dam, OTML proposed to limit the level of suspended particulate matter in the river system. The Acceptable Particulate Level (APL) was set at approximately ten times the background level of sediment in the Fly River prior to the mine, which was aimed at preventing "unacceptable environmental damage" to the river (IWT 1994, Mining 70). But the APL was based on an arbitrary threshold established with reference to the ability of the mining company to comply. It was widely criticized for not being based on scientific evidence (IWT 1994, 7) and for "being set so as to avoid economic costs to OTML, rather than protect the environment" (Rosenbaum and Krockenberger 1993, 14; see also Mowbray 1995, 4). Allowing a mining company to set its own pollution levels is an example of the proverbial fox guarding the henhouse, as well as a staple of neoliberal economic policy that promotes the transfer of governmental powers of regulation to the private sector. The Acceptable Particulate Level became effective on April 1, 1990.

These fateful decisions—from beginning production without tailings containment to permitting the mine to continue discharging high volumes of tailings and waste rock—eventually resulted in widespread environmental degradation downstream from the Ok Tedi mine. Such slow-motion disasters are more difficult for us to perceive than catastrophes caused by earthquakes, hurricanes, or tsunamis. Sudden events also form the template for industrial disaster in the public imagination: the explosion that released a cloud of poisonous gas in Bhopal, the nuclear meltdown in Chernobyl, or the Exxon Valdez shipwreck that spilled eleven million gallons of crude oil in Alaska. It requires a different sense of time to adequately perceive the impact of slow-motion disasters as they are happening (B. Adam 1998).[6] Thomas Beamish (2002) writes about the "silent spill" in Guadalupe, California, which leaked more oil than the Exxon Valdez accident over a period of thirty-eight years before the problem was finally addressed. The threat of global climate change also fits into this category, complicating the formulation of a robust response by the international community. The slow-motion environmental disaster along the Ok Tedi and Fly Rivers was conveniently ignored by the mining company and the Papua New Guinea government even though the problems were readily perceived by the people living downstream from the mine, who are not only keen observers of the natural world but dependent on its integrity for their day-to-day subsistence and cultural survival.

This is not to say that there were no early warnings. After the original requirement to construct a tailings dam was suspended, an American engineer employed by the government of Papua New Guinea criticized the decision in a paper entitled "Giving Away the River" published by the U.N. Environment Programme (Townsend 1988). The same year, an anthropologist who contributed to the original environmental impact

FIGURE 3. Children playing in tailings deposit along the lower Ok Tedi River, 2008. Photo: Brent Stirton.

study referred to the project in the *Ecologist* as New Guinea's "disaster mine" (Hyndman 1988). The following year, I wrote an op-ed for the *Times of Papua New Guinea* that compared the Ok Tedi River to a sewer (Kirsch 1989a), and I subsequently published an extended review of the problems in a local journal (Kirsch 1989b). Four years later, the Australian Conservation Foundation described the Ok Tedi River as "almost biologically dead" (Rosenbaum and Krockenberger 1993, 9). Despite these efforts to draw attention to the pollution from the Ok Tedi mine, the mining company continued to turn a blind eye to the consequences of its operation. It also turned a deaf ear to the rising litany of complaints and demands from the people living along the river system, as I discuss in the next chapter (fig. 3). With the support of the Papua New Guinea government, the lack of any real political threat from the downstream communities, and the absence of engagement by either domestic or international NGOs during the 1980s, BHP and OTML concluded that they could safely ignore the problems caused by the mine (fig. 4). They continued to externalize the costs of production at the Ok Tedi mine onto the environment and the communities downstream rather than investing in infrastructure to reduce or eliminate riverine tailings disposal.

FIGURE 4. Ok Tedi Mining Ltd. public relations poster, ca. 1988.
The Papua New Guinea Tok Pisin caption reads: "Environment.
The company protects the river, forest, and wildlife. No harm will
come to you when the refuse from the gold and copper is released
into the river." A blue sky soaring over green fields, an orange
butterfly, and an orange and red flower, suggest that all is well.

THE LOCAL RESOURCE CURSE

The inability of the state to control or benefit from mining is generally
referred to as the "resource curse," which is usually defined as a macroeconomic problem in which investment in extractive industry inhibits
other forms of economic development, which results in the country as
a whole remaining poor rather than benefitting from the sale of its

resources (Auty 1993; Sachs and Warner 1995; Ross 1999; Sawyer and Gomez 2012). One of the problems is that investment in extractive industry contributes relatively little in the way of multiplier effects to other sectors of the economy or the diversified growth stimulated by other types of investment, such as the development of industry (Ross 1999). The promise of lucrative returns from resource rents can impede rational planning and result in the neglect of economic sectors that yield lower revenues but create more jobs, such as agriculture (Ross 1999). Richard Jackson argues that the state's dependence on resource extraction fosters the belief among Papua New Guineans that earning money does not require hard work, which he compared to popular pyramid schemes known as *moni ren*, or "money rain." (Post-Courier 2002). Jackson, a geographer and long-term consultant for Ok Tedi Mining Ltd., also attributes the lack of progress in other sectors of the economy, including commercial agriculture, to the state's reliance on revenue from the mining industry.

The contemporary mining industry is capital intensive, and its reliance on technology means that there are relatively few employment opportunities for workers from rural areas who lack the necessary technical skills. Higher wages in the extractive sector of the economy makes other forms of labor—at lower wages—less attractive to potential workers, and it may even produce negative incentives for participation in subsistence production, which becomes viewed as hard work in return for comparatively low returns. Mining projects also increase awareness of the opportunities and freedoms associated with modernity, even though access to its promises remain limited (Ross 1999; Ferguson 1999). Because of the reliance on a predominantly male workforce, mining communities are often plagued by drinking, gambling, and prostitution, which lead to increased exposure to sexually transmitted disease.

Dependence on resource rents from mining projects may also encourage other forms of rent-seeking behavior, including extortion and violence (Ross 1999). In Papua New Guinea, this takes the form of exaggerated compensation claims regarding use or damage to land and resources (Toft 1997). Criticism of unrealistic compensation claims has been exploited by the mining industry to discredit landowner concerns about pollution. They argue that landowners affected by mining exaggerate their concerns about the environment to maximize the resource rents paid by mining companies. This perspective was reflected in a joke told to the participants at a 1995 conference on investment in the Papua New Guinea minerals and petroleum industries: If Jesus were living in Papua New Guinea today, the story went, and Judas were to betray him for thirty pieces of silver, it would be nearly impossible to find a landowner who would blame him for taking the money. The crowd roared with laughter, embracing the stereotype of the greedy and immoral landowner. Legitimate concerns about the environmental impact of the Ok Tedi mine were easily assimilated into established narratives about compensation claims, impeding recognition of the problems downstream.[7]

The resource curse is also associated with undesirable trends in governance. In the parlance of the mining industry, large-scale projects like the Ok Tedi mine are known as "elephants." Because it is host to a number of large mines, miners refer to Papua New Guinea as "elephant country." The majority of government revenue comes from the mining and petroleum sector, because most of the country's population resides in rural areas and practices subsistence agriculture, paying little or no taxes. Consequently, the state can be described as riding on the backs of the elephants, on which it depends to run the country (Kirsch 1996). The interests and appetites of the elephants may be placed ahead of the needs of citizens, who only contribute a small share of the country's budget. The state is also more inclined to use force when rural populations threaten to block the elephants from their feeding troughs by interfering with mining.

The role of transnational mining companies in Papua New Guinea over the last three decades might be compared to a herd of rampaging elephants undeterred by the efforts of the state to bring them under control. But because the state is also a shareholder in these mines, its interests are more aligned with the herd of elephants than the people trampled underfoot. However, in describing the limited capacity of the Papua New Guinean state to manage its affairs, Colin Filer (1997c, 118) suggests that "we should perhaps be less inclined to represent the multinational companies as unscrupulous and dirty beasts, and think of them instead as tame elephants performing in a circus without a ringmaster."

The limited presence of the state in the rural areas in which many of these mines operate has turned these projects into new sites of governmentality that bring mining companies into closer contact with the surrounding communities (see Sawyer 2004). Many of the companies in this position assume some of the responsibilities of the state by providing support for local business development and health care. This occurs even though most people working in the mining industry see themselves as being in the business of digging holes and extracting metal, and believe that they have neither the responsibility nor the capacity to carry out these other missions. Such new forms of governmentality can engender resistance, in which mining companies are held accountable for the shortcomings of the state (Welker 2009). The failure of both the state and the mining company to meet local expectations for development can also fuel separatist ambitions, as occurred in the civil war sparked by conflict over the Panguna mine in Bougainville.

There is growing recognition of the problems associated with mining across Papua New Guinea. In an editorial titled "Mining Gains Pose Woes," the *Post-Courier* (2007) suggests that pollution from the mining industry could leave Papua New Guinea with a population of "environmental refugees." The editorial asks, "What will be the environmental cost and the cost of social-economic security for future generations" of the country's dependence on mining revenues? It concludes that "reliance on mining revenue has no exit strategy" when the other sectors of the economy continue to be neglected, an example of what Jose Carlos Orihuela and Rosemary Thorp (2012, 31) refer to as a "self-reproducing dependency." The editorial demands a populist response to the dilemma, arguing that the "policy implications of risking human survival on the increased acceleration of the exploitation of the natural environment is far too important to be left to politicians" (Post-Courier 2007).

In addition to the familiar macroeconomic problems of the resource curse (Ross 1999), mining is also responsible for a range of microeconomic problems. A more complete reckoning of the social and environmental costs of mining projects might shift their value from the positive to the negative side of the ledger, especially when accounting for the cost of replacing the resources and amenities that have been lost or damaged. A river in rural Papua New Guinea may have no market value, but the cost of providing drinking water or replacing the fish in the diet of thirty thousand people would be astronomical. Mining is also responsible for other losses, for which monetary compensation is woefully inadequate. The resource curse is not only a macroeconomic problem at the level of the state; what I call the "microeconomics of the resource curse" is also a serious concern for the communities most directly affected by mining.

YONGGOM RESPONSES TO ENVIRONMENTAL IMPACTS

From 1987 to 1989, I conducted ethnographic research among the Yonggom people living on the lower Ok Tedi River. The area is covered in lowland rain forest crosscut by narrow, swampy valleys. Their staple food is the starchy flour extracted from the sago palm *(Metroxylon sagu)*. They cultivate more than a dozen varieties of bananas and plantains in their swidden gardens along with smaller quantities of pitpit (bush asparagus), yams, and a small number of recently introduced crops, including pumpkin and cassava. They set traps in the forest and hunt cassowary, wild pig, marsupials, reptiles, and other animals with bow and arrows or shotguns, when ammunition is available. They harvest seasonal fruits and nuts from the forest, including breadfruit, lowland pandanus, and okari nuts. Until recently, they caught fish and prawns in local rivers and streams using spears, traps, nets, and hook and line. Since the 1970s, villagers have earned cash by tapping rubber trees in smallholder plots, and they sometimes sell forest and garden produce in urban markets. Other villagers have relocated to urban areas for work in local businesses and stores, the public sector, or the mining company. Circular migration between rural villages and towns is nearly universal, although most adults express a preference for living on their own land in the forest, to which they have strong historical and emotional ties.

In the early years of the project, the mining company and the state offered a steady stream of assurances about the limited impact of the project on the environment (see fig. 4). The communities lacked access to independent information about pollution from the mine. They knew very little about the consequences of open pit mining elsewhere in the region or the world. In the early 1980s, one of the councilors from Dome village visited the mine site in the mountains. On his return, he warned people about what was about to happen, as his widow, Andok Yang, recounted:

> Nandun told us that in the future, the Ok Tedi River would change:
> All the water would dry up, the fish would die, the trees would die,
> and the river would look like a highway. . . .
>
> At first we didn't understand what he was saying,
> but when the sand banks formed and the trees began dying,
> I knew the story he told us had come true. . . .
>
> [After the cyanide spill at the mine], the water was very dirty.
> There were . . . frogs, turtles, fish, and crocodiles, all dead.
> We saw all of these things.
>
> After flooding, the river left behind this mud.
> The gardens along the river were buried.
> All the small creeks became swamps.
> All the sago palms began to die.
> (Andok Yang, pers. comm., 1996)

Although the Yonggom and their neighbors initially welcomed the mine and the opportunities for development it portended, they quickly became troubled by its impact on the environment and their subsistence practices. I described these problems in the op-ed I wrote for the *Times of Papua New Guinea* in June 1989, shortly after completing my dissertation research.

One hears little of the river whose name was borrowed when the giant Ok Tedi Mining Ltd. was formed. But the Ok Tedi River has played an important role in the development of the mine, for it has been the company's dumping grounds since production began. Not only has the Ok Tedi River been devastated by pollution from the mine, but the people living along the river, the Yonggom and Awin, have never been compensated for the damage to their environment.

The sediment released into the Ok Tedi River has turned it into a sewer that runs for 200 kilometers. The water is supersaturated with tailings. Pyrite glitters in the sun on top of once-white sand banks where turtles previously came to lay their eggs. Many of these sand banks are blocked off from the river by ten- and twenty-meter-long stretches of knee-deep mud. After a heavy rain in the mountains, the Ok Tedi River overflows its banks, depositing tailings along the river floodplain.

Instead of depositing sediment along the fertile river floodplains, where crops could be grown almost continually, tailings from the mine prevent the Yonggom from planting gardens along the river at all. New gardens must be made every few years in the rain forest.

When there are heavy rains in the mountains, water from the Ok Tedi River backs up into the small creeks and streams, depositing tailings into the sago stands that provide the Yonggom with their staple food.

Other riverine life, including fish and prawns, are also impacted by the tailings, affecting local diets. The birds that depend on the fish, including egrets, kingfishers, and Brahminy kites, have left the river corridor for better hunting grounds. The entire watershed has been devastated by pollution from the mine.

The changes to the river have many practical consequences for the Yonggom and Awin living in the dozen villages along the Ok Tedi River, who can no longer drink the river water or wash clothes or swim in the river. The high volume of tailings in the river and the formation of sand banks in navigation channels have also made traveling the Ok Tedi River by motor canoe—their only means of transporting produce to local markets, rubber to buyers in Kiunga, and food and medicine back to the villages—difficult and dangerous.

The mining company and the state treat the Ok Tedi River like a sacrifice zone. However, no effort has been made to compensate the Yonggom and Awin people who live along the river and are affected by pollution from the mine.

Without construction of the delayed tailings dam in the mountains, the damage to the Ok Tedi River could be replicated further downstream. What is at stake is nothing less than the future of the entire Fly River and possibly parts of the Papuan Gulf and the Torres Straits as well. (Kirsch 1989a, 3; text abridged and edited)

The problems along the Ok Tedi River were exacerbated by the presence of four thousand political refugees from the militarized territory of West Papua living in camps along the river and below the junction of the Ok Tedi and Fly Rivers. They were part of a larger exodus of ten thousand people who crossed the border into Papua New Guinea in 1984 in response to a crackdown on separatist activities by the Indonesian military and as part of an effort by the Organisasi Papua Merdeka (Free Papua Movement) to attract international attention to their campaign for political independence (Kirsch 1989, 2006; May 1986). Given that the refugees outnumber the population of the nearby villages, their presence has greatly increased the competition for resources. Even in the case of several border camps that were abandoned after a few years of occupancy, the impact of the refugees was felt for more than a decade, given the large clearings in the forest made by the refugees for their gardens. As I noted in my op-ed, "traditional subsistence practices . . . are only suitable in areas with low population densities, and already scarce resources have become even harder to obtain" (Kirsch 1989a, 3). Pollution from the mine and competition for resources from the refugees resulted in a "destructive synergy" that crippled local food production (Kirsch 1995, 88). A former policeman who retired to one of the villages on the Ok Tedi River complained that the Yonggom had been "punished twice" (Kirsch 2006, 175).

When I returned to Papua New Guinea in 1992 to study the social impacts of the Ok Tedi mine on the villages of the lower Ok Tedi River, the environmental problems had intensified.

> Tailings from the mine have been deposited onto forest and garden land, into adjacent wetland areas, and upstream into the numerous creeks and streams that flow into the Ok Tedi River. These mine wastes have had adverse impact wherever they have been deposited, killing plants and trees and disrupting local ecosystems. The damage extends for forty kilometers along the river, with areas of dead trees that have spread two or three kilometers from the main channel. There has been little forest regrowth to date and large areas are almost completely devoid of life. This land was particularly valuable to villagers, because it is located within easy walking distance or canoe travel, and because it offered resources not readily available in the rain forest interior. The villagers living in the lower Ok Tedi area are in a state of despair, and despite the mining company's provision of some new facilities and minor benefits, feel frustrated and ignored in their efforts to obtain proper restitution. (Kirsch 1995, 50; abridged and edited)

After meeting with the people in Dome village, where I had lived for two years, I wrote:

The villagers are very upset about the mine's impact on their environment. They told me that the trees are dying, the riverbanks are eroding, and the currents in the Ok Tedi are rough when the water levels are high. The grey, sediment-laden water is causing rashes and sores. People say that some sago palms do not produce starch, only a watery substance. The small creeks are blocked off at their entrance by tailings from the Ok Tedi River, and both gardens and tree cover have been lost where the tailings are deposited. The people complain that sweet potatoes and taro grown in gardens near the river do not soften when cooked, but stay hard. They say that when banana stalks are covered by floodwaters from the Ok Tedi, their fruits open up and spoil.

Now that they have to make gardens inland, they complain of a food shortage, and they pointedly asked me who would feed them, because they do not believe they can make ends meet from ordinary subsistence practices. In part because of the refugees, there is little game in the forest to the west of the village. There are few fish remaining in the creeks and streams. These fish are small and people refuse to eat them because they do not taste good; they are described as having "no fat" and "no blood." (Kirsch 1995, 58; abridged and edited)

I also noted that

the people in Dome village are vocal about their anger towards the mine because of the impact it has had on their environment. The tenor of village life has completely changed. The river beside which the village was built is of no use to them. Instead of obtaining fresh drinking water from the creeks, they line up to collect water from a tank installed by the mining company. Instead of bathing in the river, they wait for the company to build showers. Instead of catching fish and prawns in the river, they use compensation payments from the mine to buy canned fish. Instead of looking out onto a lush tropical landscape, they see a dirty river surrounded by leafless trees [fig. 5].

The people in Dome village also question whether the chemicals used to extract the copper and gold at the mine remain toxic after being released into the river. Not surprisingly, they feel that OTML should find another means of tailings disposal and stop discharging mine wastes into the Ok Tedi River. (Kirsch 1995, 53–54; abridged and edited)

The Yonggom described the impact of the mine on the river and their forests using the Yonggom adverb *moraron*, which means "spoiled," "rotten," or "corroded," such as food that has gone bad or wood that has decayed. They referred to the pollution in the river using the Hiri Motu word *muramura*, which refers to medicine or chemicals but can also mean "poison," a common euphemism for "sorcery" in Papua New Guinea. However, they had difficulty understanding how the pollution was affecting the environment and whether it spread through the creeks and streams, came up through the ground, or fell to the earth in

FIGURE 5. Ghost forest along the lower Ok Tedi River, 1996. Photo: Stuart Kirsch.

the rain. Their inability to assess the risks posed by pollution from the mine was vividly expressed in a letter that the people from Kungim asked me to deliver to the Ok Tedi mine in 1992.

> All of these things show evidence of the mine's impact: our garden crops, dogs, pigs, fish, and even people becoming ill. Coconut trees have died. People are suffering from sores. Even our staple food, sago, is affected. The rain makes us sick. The air we breathe leaves us short of breath. And the sun now burns our skin.
>
> In the past, everything was fine. We never experienced problems like these before. But in the ten years that OTML has been in operation, all of these changes and more have taken place. Other plants in our gardens have been affected as well. We are concerned about these changes, and it seems reasonable to assume that they are signs of the impact of the Ok Tedi mine. (Letter from Kungim, dated August 11, 1992; grammar and spelling modified)

Much of what they previously took for granted about the natural environment no longer appears true. Their concerns about environmental collapse, which might be compared to the biological concept of trophic cascade, are closely related to the challenges associated with assessing the risks posed by pollution from the mine (see Beck 1992). Is it any wonder that they have come to regard the rain, the air, and the sun with suspicion?

The anger that the Yonggom feel toward the mining company, which they view as a kind of corporate person, is reflected in their view that it behaves like a sorcerer. They complained that the mining company was *inamen ipban,* or "lacking common sense," which suggests the failure to behave in a socially responsible manner. They told me that the mining company would bear responsibility (*yi dabap kandanip,* literally, "they will take the weight") for the problems they were experiencing as a result of its environmental impact. They also said that they now "live in fear" *(une doberime)* of pollution from the mine. All of these expressions are associated with sorcery, which is said to be practiced by persons who refuse to take responsibility for their actions. "Live in fear" is what people say after there has been a death attributed to sorcery. I was also told about a number of accidents and injuries for which the responsibility would previously have been attributed sorcery, but were now blamed on the mining company. These included an injury to a man's finger caused by catfish in the river, a leg broken by a tree falling on a man who was mired in knee-deep mine tailings, a drowning after a canoe overturned in the Ok Tedi River, and a death in the forest after a man had to travel a long distance from home to obtain food for his family (Kirsch 2006, 121–26).

The transformation of local landscapes has had other consequences as well. Whereas memories of past events were often associated with the places where they occurred, the destruction of local landscapes now poses a challenge to the remembrance of things past. Familiar locations like a mother's garden or the breadfruit tree where someone shot a flying fox may no longer exist. These memories have lost their moorings; pollution has erased all traces of the past. The impact of the mine not only threatens past ties between people and place but also the way that places metonymically represent personal biography and lineage identity.

These losses are accompanied by feelings of sorrow and loss, which the Yonggom call *mimyop.*[8] One woman expressed her concerns about the transformation of local landscapes in the stylized form of a lament, the speech genre associated with bereavement.

Before the river was not like this;
it makes me feel like crying.
These days, this place is ruined,
so I feel like crying.

Where I used to make gardens,
the mud banks have built up.

Where I used to catch prawns and fish,
there is an empty pool. . . .
So I feel like crying.

Before it wasn't like this.
We had no difficulty finding garden food and wild game.
We had everything we needed.
Now we are suffering and I wonder why.
(Duri Kemyat, pers. comm. 1996)

Pollution from the mine has also disrupted relationships between the Yonggom and the animals with which they previously shared the landscape. The Yonggom obtain important information about both social and natural events through these interactions. They are adept at identifying many bird species by their calls, which reveal the time of day and the seasons and demarcate sacred from profane time. Some birds are said to speak in the Yonggom language. Birds can also appear in dreams that provide insight into the future, as omens portending misfortune or signaling opportunities. The Yonggom communicate with these animals through magic spells that compel them to do their bidding. However, with the disappearance of the birds and other wildlife from the Ok Tedi River and the surrounding forests, these interactions are no longer possible, and the dialogue the Yonggom once had with these animals has all but ceased.

Yonggom rituals and myths contain multiple references to birds, fish, and other animals. Yet without being exposed to these animals in their natural habitat, their myths run the risk of degenerating to the level of amusing folk tales, known as *stori tasol* in Papua New Guinea Tok Pisin. Similarly, their rituals may lose the capacity to convey insights into the human condition or resolve the dilemmas people face. Some people have already begun to see their rituals as something that tricks people instead of enlightening them. Even though their hunting and fishing magic may still be employed away from the areas polluted by the mine, its local failure foreshadows a time in which their magic will no longer be seen as efficacious or meaningful.

These changes contribute to their profound sense of loss. They are compounded by a major shift in relationships with the environment, such that people can no longer rely on subsistence activities for their survival. People are more likely to bring home food from a trade store than parade game from the forest through the village. Their largest source of monetary income is the compensation payments they receive from the mine. Instead of living off the land, they have become dependent on these payments for survival. Not only has mining destroyed the commons, but it has also made formerly sustainable communities dependent on resource rents. Unlike ordinary resource rents, they do not receive these payments in return for the consumption of their resources by other parties, but rather for the destruction of the productive capacity of their land as the indirect consequence of activities carried out elsewhere. Local landscapes are no longer a site of productivity, but scenes of loss. They no longer provide people with security but confront them with new, indecipherable risks.

UNDERMINING THE FUTURE

The impact of the Ok Tedi mine on the environment has steadily increased as the tailings discharged by the mine make their way through the river system. In 1994, when the first lawsuit was filed against the mining company, the damage covered an area of several hundred square kilometers. In 2002, 1,300 square kilometers along the river was either dead or under stress, an area larger than New York City (Higgins 2002, 2). By 2012, the area affected by forest dieback had increased to 1,875 square kilometers (OTML 2013, 7).

Local species composition is not expected to return to pre-mine conditions; rather, savanna grassland will replace much of the lowland rain forest along the river corridor (Chapman et al. 2000, 17).[9] An independent assessment of the environmental impact of the mine conducted in 2007 predicts dramatic changes to the Middle Fly by 2050, with inundation of the floodplain for 60 to 70 percent of the year (Tingay 2007, 12). During years with higher rainfall, up to 90 percent of the floodplain will be under water—a total area of 3,800 square kilometers (12).

Water pollution has also had a severe impact on fish populations. Surveys of the fish throughout the river system indicate that "there has been a marked reduction in the diversity and biomass of fishes in most reaches downstream of the Ok Tedi mine" (Storey et al. 2009, 456). Local reductions in species diversity range from 87 percent in the Ok Tedi River to 79 percent in the Middle Fly (437). The figures for biomass have also declined precipitously, up to 96 percent reduction in the Ok Tedi River and as much as 75 percent in the Middle Fly (450).

There are serious questions about toxicity from heavy metals at both the bottom and the top of the food chain, ranging from impacts on algae to fruit bats and marsupials (Parametrix and URS Greiner

Woodward Clyde 1999, 9). While the potential health risks from exposure to heavy metals for human populations are expected to be minor (Parametrix and URS Greiner Woodward Clyde 1999, 13), reports produced by OTML consultants recommend monitoring their exposure to cadmium and lead, both highly toxic substances (Chapman et al. 2000, 14).

There are also ongoing problems with acid mine drainage, which is caused by the exposure of sulfide minerals to oxygen. The oxidation of sulfides produces sulfuric acid, which can dissolve heavy metals from waste rock, making them bioavailable. Acid mine drainage already occurs where tailings deposits are exposed to oxygen when water levels in the river are low, including both sides of the Fly River and islands in several locations. There is also acid mine drainage in the storage area for dredged tailings in the lower Ok Tedi River (Tingay 2007, 21–22). Due to higher levels of pyrites that contain sulfides in the remaining ore body, in 2008 the mining company built a pipeline to transport the pyritic fraction of the tailings to a lowland storage facility on the lower Ok Tedi River, where the acid-generating material is covered with sand to prevent oxidation. Nonetheless, the occurrence of acid mine drainage at multiple locations poses a significant threat to the future of organic life in the river system (Tingay 2007, 27).[10]

MINING MELANESIA

The Pacific Ring of Fire, which refers to volcanic activity, runs through the islands of Melanesia, resulting in significant levels of mineralization. This is particularly evident in the Indonesian territory of West Papua and Papua New Guinea, which are host to some of the world's largest copper and gold mines (map 2). The first major gold rush in Papua New Guinea began in 1921 near the town of Wau in Morobe Province. Other gold deposits were discovered in the highlands before World War II by some of the first Australians to make contact with the people living there (Connolly and Anderson 1988). There is also extensive nickel mining in New Caledonia and a new nickel and cobalt mine in Madang Province, Papua New Guinea.

In the following section of this chapter, I provide thumbnail sketches of five mining conflicts in the region to which I will make reference throughout the book: at the Panguna copper mine in Bougainville, Papua New Guinea; at Freeport-McMoRan's copper and gold mine in the Indonesian territory of West Papua; at the Porgera gold mine in the

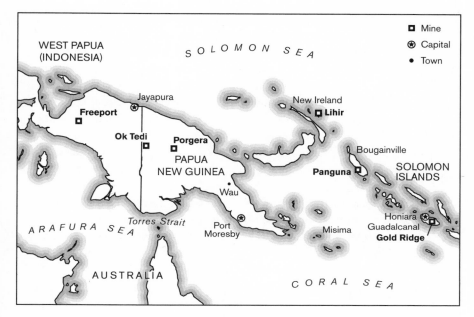

MAP 2. Major mining projects in West Papua (Indonesia), Papua New Guinea, and the Solomon Islands.

highlands of Papua New Guinea; at the Lihir gold mine in Papua New Guinea; and at the Gold Ridge mine in the Solomon Islands.

Bougainville

The Panguna copper mine in Bougainville was established by the Australian colonial administration and operated by Conzinc Riotinto (later Rio Tinto) of Australia during the 1970s and 1980s. It eventually became the largest open-pit copper mine outside of Chile. Tailings from the mine were discharged directly into the Jaba River, which travels eleven kilometers to the sea. The tailings plume from the mine extended several kilometers from the coast.

The mining project met with resistance from the outset, which was later exacerbated by both increasing environmental impacts and dissatisfaction with their share of the revenue generated by the mine. In a 1988 letter signed by Francis Ona, a former military officer who led the landowner rebellion that closed the mine in 1989, the Panguna Landowners Association asked the national government to commission an independent investigation of the environmental impacts of the mine. This document bears remarkable resemblance to the letter from Kungim village to the Ok Tedi mine cited above. It refers to soil that may have been poisoned by toxic chemicals, diseases plaguing their plant crops, shortened life spans of other garden plants, an unknown pollutant affecting cocoa harvests, introduced plant species colonizing the area, unregulated harvest of trees for timber, deforestation near the mine facilities, decline in the number of game animals, landslides, chemicals in the river system, large numbers of people suffering from illness, air pollution, and the unexplained disappearance of flying foxes from the island (Applied Geology Associates 1989, appendix 6).

The members of the landowners association agreed to abide by the findings of the inquiry but were infuriated when the preliminary results of the investigation conducted by Applied Geology Associates were made public in 1989. At a meeting held to discuss the report, representatives of the investigating team stated that

> although mining operations had resulted in extensive damage to the physical environment, they had found no significantly high levels of chemical pollution. They described as unlikely the opinion held by many Bougainvilleans that BCL [Bougainville Copper Ltd.] was responsible for the decrease in wildlife and the decline in soil fertility (except of course in the pit and waste-dump areas), or for certain illnesses then prevalent in the lease-area villages. (Oliver 1991, 208)

The findings of the study differed substantially from what landowners believed to be true based on their own experience (Connell 1991, 71). Calling the findings a "whitewash," Francis Ona stormed out of the meeting (71). John Connell concludes that the incident may have been the "catalyst for the transition to violence and the eventual closing of the mine" (72).

The rebellion against the mine, which began in 1988 and resulted in a decade of violent civil war with thousands of casualties, was unexpected, but not without warning. Relationships between Bougainvilleans and the state were complicated by powerful resentment that so much of the profits from the mine went initially to the colonial administration of the territory and later to the independent state, which fueled separatist sentiments. The resulting conflict, including the use of Australian helicopter gunships by the Papua New Guinean defense forces against their fellow citizens, may have been the inspiration for James Cameron's famous film *Avatar*, about a native uprising against an interplanetary mining company.

In 2000, lawyers representing ten thousand plaintiffs from Bougainville filed suit against Rio Tinto in the U.S. District Court in Los Angeles, charging the mining company with environmental destruction and complicity in human rights abuses and genocide perpetrated by the Papua New Guinea defense forces during the rebellion. One of the lawyers working on the case for Hagens Berman in Seattle, Washington, was Nick Styant-Browne, who previously represented the plaintiffs in the case against Ok Tedi Mining Ltd. and BHP in Australia. The case against Rio Tinto involved the controversial application of the U.S. Alien Tort Claims Act of 1789, which was originally intended to hold pirates on the high seas accountable for their actions, against transnational corporations. However, the case was dismissed in 2013 after the U.S. Supreme Court restricted the applicability of the alien tort statute.

The landowner rebellion at Bougainville had a significant impact on decisions made by the PNG state about the Ok Tedi mine. The state's need for additional revenue after the closure of the Panguna mine gave OTML important leverage when seeking permission from the state to continue discharging tailings into the river system. The landowners downstream from the Ok Tedi mine also pointed to the human costs of the Bougainville civil war as one of their reasons for taking BHP to court instead of closing the Ok Tedi mine by force.

After a decade of conflict in Bougainville, a peace process brokered by New Zealand led to a series of votes on political autonomy (Regan 2010). In seeking to enhance their economic independence, political leaders in Bougainville are, ironically, debating whether to reopen the Panguna mine, which contains reserves of 3.5 million metric tons of copper and 12.7 million ounces of gold, although the proposal has many critics. Even more controversially, Rio Tinto is seen to be the leading candidate to restart the mine, which would require an investment of several billion dollars.

Freeport

Located approximately five hundred kilometers west of the Ok Tedi mine in the highlands of the militarized Indonesian territory of West Papua (formerly known as Irian Jaya), Freeport-McMoRan's Grasberg mine is one of the largest copper and gold mines in the world.[11]

It may also be the world's largest polluter by volume, discharging up to 240,000 metric tons of tailings per day into the Ajkwa River, approximately three times the volume of the tailings from the Ok Tedi mine. In response to political pressure from the Ok Tedi court case and a concurrent Australian Council for Overseas Aid (ACFOA) investigation of the mine, the mining company began building a series of levees along the river in 1995, which were intended to contain the tailings within an area of 230 square kilometers (Leith 2003, 168).[12] Due to its lack of expenditure on environmental controls, the mine is one of the world's lowest-cost copper producers.

In 1995, the U.S. Overseas Private Investment Corporation (OPIC) cancelled Freeport's political risk insurance, the first time that support for a project was terminated for environmental reasons (Bryce 1995b). The decision was taken after the International Rivers Network set up a meeting between OPIC officials and several Indonesian activists (Emel 2002, 835). One of the officials responsible for the decision later told me that frustration with his inability to address the environmental problems caused by the Ok Tedi mine, which had previously received OPIC support, strengthened his resolve to proactively address pollution from the Freeport mine. After intensive lobbying by Henry Kissinger and others, Freeport's insurance policy was reinstated, although Freeport voluntarily cancelled its policy with OPIC in April 1996 (Fox 1997, 267).

On April 29, 1996, a $6 billion class-action lawsuit was filed against Freeport-McMoRan in the U.S. District Court in New Orleans, where the company was then based. This was the first application of the alien tort statute against a transnational mining company, setting a precedent that was repeated four years later in the suit against Rio Tinto in the Bougainville case. Amungme leader Tom Beanal alleged that the operation of the mine resulted in "the violation of human rights, environmental destruction, and cultural genocide" (Leith 2003, 112). Another Amungme plaintiff, Mama Josefa, alleged that she was beaten and held prisoner in an abandoned Freeport shipping container filled with human waste. The case was dismissed after a year of hearings, however, when the Court ruled that Beanal and his lawyers failed to provide sufficient evidence to support their allegations (Duval 1997).

Critical new information became available several years later. Transnational corporations like Freeport-McMoRan face increased scrutiny from NGOs that focus on corporate accountability and transparency, including Amnesty International and Global Witness, and the international campaign "Publish What You Pay" (Global Witness 2005). In response to the Enron accounting scandal in the United States, the Sarbanes-Oxley Act of 2002 established new reporting requirements for the U.S. Securities and Exchange Commission that compelled Freeport-

McMoRan, which trades on the New York Stock Exchange, to reveal the details of its financial relationship with the Indonesian military. In August 2004, Freeport acknowledged that the company paid the Indonesian military more than $11.4 million during the previous two years for security at the mine (Bryce 2003).[13] Critics of the mine have long argued that these transactions effectively subsidize the Indonesian military's violent repression of West Papuan political aspirations, suppressing opposition to the mine (Leith 2003, 232). Documentation of these payments may well be the smoking gun missing from the earlier claims filed against the mining company in the U.S. District Court in Louisiana.

Porgera

The Porgera Joint Venture is a large gold mine located in Enga Province, Papua New Guinea, approximately three hundred kilometers east of the Ok Tedi mine. The project was operated by Placer Dome until the company was taken over by Barrick Gold, now the world's largest gold producer, in 2006. The landowners living closest to the Porgera mine are known for their aggressive negotiation tactics, although "the precedents [for compensation] established at Porgera have not been universally adopted by other resource operators" (Banks 1998, 61).

Located at the headwaters of the Strickland River, the Porgera mine uses riverine tailings disposal like the Ok Tedi mine (Biersack 2006; Coumans 2011). The Strickland is a tributary of the Fly River, which transports tailings from both mines below Everill Junction. The commingling of tailings from the two mines affords both mining companies with protection from claims about pollution downstream from the junction. Neither mining company monitors the deposition of tailings in the South Fly or the river delta, despite two decades of evidence and testimony about the resulting problems.

The population living in the vicinity of the Porgera mine more than doubled during the first ten years of operation (Filer 1999a, 5). More than four thousand people were relocated for the expansion of the mine in 1995 (Filer 1999a, 5), and the accompanying use of force resulted in allegations of human rights violations (Amnesty International 2010). Accusations of sexual assault and rape by the mine's security forces have also been documented (Human Rights Watch 2010). Many of the anthropologists and other social scientists working near the Porgera mine have been employed as consultants for the mining company (Filer

1999a; Coumans 2011), although several of them have been prevented from publishing their findings by the threat of legal action.

Lihir

The Lihir mine is located in northeastern Papua New Guinea. Its large gold reserves are situated inside of a volcanic crater that is still geothermally active. The project was operated by Rio Tinto until 1996 and is now run by Newcrest Mining Ltd. of Australia.

The mine uses submarine tailings disposal, in which mine wastes are discharged directly into the ocean. Because of the steep drop-off and thermal cline off the coast of Lihir, the mining company asserts that the tailings will remain on the ocean floor where they are deposited rather than mix with the surrounding water. Submarine tailings disposal is prohibited in the United States, which led the U.S. Overseas Private Investment Corporation to turn down the project's request for support (Moody 2005, 202–3), although it later received backing from the Australian Export Finance and Insurance Corporation (EFIC) despite the threat to marine life.

The Lihir Landowners Association is noted for its tough bargaining over compensation, establishing the "benchmark within Papua New Guinea for such arrangements" (Banks 1998, 62). One of the mechanisms for communication between Lihirians and the mining company is the local practice of *gorgor,* the Papua New Guinea Tok Pisin name for the ginger plant used to demarcate taboo zones (e.g., gardens, an unoccupied house, one's hunting grounds) into which other people are forbidden to trespass. Tying *gorgor* onto the gates of the Lihir mine stops production, for its employees not only understand but also obey its message. By respecting this signal, the mine also legitimizes the metamessage, that the operation of the mine is contingent on the continued good will of the surrounding community (Kirsch 2001b, 156).

A common feature of the conflicts at Lihir, Porgera, and Bougainville is that they are focused on the people living adjacent to the mine. For Lihir, this is because the mine discharges tailings directly into the ocean and therefore does not have the kind of impacts on the landscape as the Ok Tedi mine. In the case of Porgera, the peoples living downstream along the Strickland River are few in number and politically impotent, and the mixing of pollution from the two mines provides ample political cover in the South Fly. The mine in Bougainville occupies a central location on the island (Filer 1990, 77). In both Porgera and Bougainville, the much larger landowner and settler groups are the primary antagonists in the conflict. This is very different from the situation at the Ok Tedi mine, where the conflict is focused on the people living downstream.

Gold Ridge

Gold Ridge is a small gold mine located in the mountains above Honiara, the capital of the Solomon Islands. It operated under Ross Mining from 1998 to 2000, when it was forced to close because of civil unrest on Guadalcanal (D. Evans 2010). In 1999, the mining company denied responsibility for a large fish kill in the Tinahula River, although a cyanide spill was thought to be the probable cause. A lawsuit regarding pollution from the mine failed to make headway in the challenging judicial environment of Solomon Islands (see D. Evans 2010, 129), despite the efforts of Slater & Gordon, which previously acted for the plaintiffs in the Ok Tedi case. The project reopened under Allied Mining in 2010 and was acquired by St. Barbara in 2012.

Although there are strong similarities across these projects, there are also significant differences in terms of the responses of the affected communities to mining, the involvement of NGOs and lawyers, and the degree to which the cases have attracted international attention. Like the Ok Tedi mine, all of these projects have had significant environmental impacts, although they have also been associated with other problems. At Bougainville, the mine discharged tailings into the Jaba River, resulting in a tailings plume that still extends several kilometers into the ocean. Pollution from the mine was one of the triggers for the rebellion, although many scholars emphasize disputes between Bougainvilleans and the state over the distribution of economic benefits (Filer 1990). The conflict at Bougainville was also exacerbated by separatist politics and conflict with highlanders who came to work at the mine.[14] In the Freeport case, concern about environmental impacts, the failure to equitably distribute the benefits from the project, and separatist politics compounded by the violence of the Indonesian military all contributed to the conflict. Like the Ok Tedi case, the conflicts at both Bougainville and Freeport ended up in foreign courts. Concerns about the environment at Lihir received less attention than negotiations over benefits, although submarine tailings disposal remains controversial. Even though the size of the Gold Ridge mine in the Solomon Islands pales in comparison to the other projects discussed here, the mine was responsible for environmental impacts that also yielded a contentious court case.

The problems associated with the resource curse are evident in most of these examples: coercive states that are intolerant of criticism or dissent, especially in their relationships to extractive industry; the failure to stimulate broader economic growth; conflict over the unbalanced distribution of economic benefits and negative environmental impacts; and state dependency on revenue from resource extraction. The problem of colliding ecologies, in which large-scale mining is incompatible with subsistence production and other economic pursuits, is present in the Ok Tedi, Freeport, and Bougainville cases, although these problems have not received much attention in Lihir or the Solomon Islands. These comparisons suggest that mining conflicts possess a family resemblance to one another, rather than simply sharing a single cause. Differences between states, environmental regimes and the degree of impact, local communities, the participation of NGOs and other actors, and the historical interactions between these conflicts combine in unique ways. Although I have limited my comparisons in this chapter to mining in Melanesia, similar dynamics are evident in mining conflicts elsewhere in the world, as I argue throughout this book.

CONCLUSION

What caused the environmental disaster downstream from the Ok Tedi mine? It might be argued it was the consequence of a perfect storm of events that no one could have foreseen, suggesting the need for caution about overgeneralizing from the Ok Tedi example. But in fact, there was an abundance of warnings from a variety of perspectives (Hyndman 1988; Kirsch 1989; Townsend 1988), all of which were ignored or rebuffed. There is also clear evidence that the mining company anticipated the increase in negative impacts—at least for the Ok Tedi River—in the changes made to the Sixth Supplemental Agreement, which treated the river as a sacrifice zone. Finally, both the mining company and the state dismissed the observations of the people living downstream about the slow-motion environmental crisis. Yonggom claims about environmental change were seen as exaggerated when they had difficulty distinguishing between pollution from the mine and environmental problems associated with higher population densities after the influx of refugees. Objections framed in the idiom of sorcery proved difficult to translate (Kirsch 1997). It was easy for the mining industry to discredit their compensation claims and even to laugh about them.

But the events leading to the environmental disaster downstream from the Ok Ted mine were more than just a series of coincidences that culminated in tragedy; they were also the direct consequence of corporate strategy. Permission to discharge tailings into the river system resulted in a slippery slope leading from a temporary reprieve from constructing a tailings dam to a perpetual license to pollute. Despite the steady stream of warnings and expressions of concern, the mining company steadfastly refused to acknowledge the severity of the threat to the river system. The mining company also failed to see the downstream communities as a political threat, even after the Bougainville civil war demonstrated that local communities retain veto power over resource extraction projects, albeit at a terrible cost. The state's ideological commitment to dependency theory led to its conflict of interest as both the regulator and a shareholder in the mine. These problems were later exacerbated when the state adopted policies that allowed mining companies to both set environmental standards and monitor their own compliance, decreasing the value of both processes. These decisions were compounded by the legal status of the project as exempt from the environmental act and the constitutional requirement of sustainability. The state's initial resolve to require tailings containment from the Ok Tedi mine was weakened by economic pressure after the closure of the Panguna copper mine in Bougainville, making the state vulnerable to BHP's threat to walk away from the project at a time when the economic needs of the country were greatest. The devastation of the Ok Tedi and Fly Rivers was not an accident; it was the outcome of strategic decisions made by a mining company that took advantage of a weak state that was economically dependent on the mining industry.

Comparison to the other mining conflicts in Melanesia suggests that Ok Tedi is not an exceptional case, even though its environmental impacts have exceeded most of the other examples. Conflicts over mining in Melanesia reveal the larger macroeconomic impacts of the resource curse on the state in terms of its recurring dependency on extractive industry and the failure to develop economic alternatives. They also illustrate the problems of colliding ecologies for communities directly impacted by mining, which can be understood as a manifestation of the microeconomics of the resource curse. For the Yonggom, this meant not only their inability to rely on subsistence production but also that much of what they previously took for granted about the environment was no longer true. It disrupted their relationships to place, including individual memories and social history. It affected their interactions with the other beings with which they once shared the land-scape, diminishing the significance of their rituals and myths. The con-sequences of colliding ecologies transcend the economic, raising existential questions about cultural survival along the Ok Tedi River.

Initially, there was very little the people living downstream from the Ok Tedi mine could do to challenge the mine and the state. They lacked political power and their traditional political institutions did not rise above the level of local kinship groups (Kirsch 1989b). But as I describe in the next chapter, the problems caused by the mine led to the emer-gence of a committed group of political activists, who were eventually able to exert a surprising degree of pressure on the mining company and the state. NGO support enabled them to internationalize their cam-paign, bringing unwanted attention to BHP everywhere it operated. They were able to draw on the discourses of environmentalism and indigeneity to enroll allies and mobilize support, although these dis-courses also rendered them vulnerable to criticism. But it was not until they turned to the Australian courts in 1996 that the Yonggom and their neighbors were able to fully challenge BHP, as I describe in chap-ter 3. Their actions also played a major role in transforming the rela-tionship between the mining industry and its critics, the focus of this book.

CHAPTER 2

The Politics of Space

The campaign against the Ok Tedi mine was one of the first protest movements against the mining industry to become an international cause célèbre. Previous anti-mining activity usually remained localized, like protests against strip-mining coal in Appalachia. But with the rapid globalization of the mining industry during the 1980s and 1990s, political opposition became increasingly international in scope. This chapter describes how the campaign against the Ok Tedi mine was able to form alliances with international NGOs in what can be called the "politics of space." Such networks are particularly effective at challenging transnational corporations because of their ability to exert pressure on corporations wherever they operate.

From its starting point in the rain forests of Papua New Guinea, the campaign against the Ok Tedi mine eventually exerted its influence around the world. The leaders of the campaign traced commodity chains from the mine site at Mt. Fubilan in the Star Mountains to copper smelters in Germany and Japan. They confronted mine managers in Tabubil and corporate executives in Melbourne. They threatened BHP's bottom line by jeopardizing its access to new mining projects, including a proposed copper mine in the Caribbean island of Dominica and a billion dollar diamond concession in the Northwest Territories in Canada. They put pressure on German and American investors in the mine as well as the multilateral organizations and international financial institutions that supported the project. By participating in a series of international conferences and meetings, including the 1992 "Earth Summit" in Rio de Janeiro, they raised the profile of their cause. It was only by taking their campaign global that they were able to force BHP and Ok Tedi Mining Ltd. to address their concerns.

The internationalization of their protests was facilitated by political alliances with NGOs on three continents. Writing about environmental movements in Indonesia, Anna Tsing (2004) emphasizes the different perspectives and assumptions of the participants, who may not fully endorse the agendas or strategies of their counterparts, limiting the possibilities for collective action. Beth Conklin (1997) describes how the political agendas of NGOs may force their partners to make significant compromises. But these alliances are also strengthened by the contributions of differentially positioned actors who employ complementary modes of access to power, discourses of persuasion, and forms of political leverage (Keck and Sikkink 1998; Kirsch 1996, 2007; Tsing 2004). For the participants in the campaign against the Ok Tedi mine, collaboration with international NGOs was a crucial turning point in what had previously been a series of uncoordinated and largely ineffective protests. These partnerships provided local activists with new opportunities to collaborate with each other, enroll new supporters, and develop new strategies. They also enhanced the legitimacy of their campaign.

Although this chapter focuses on the ethnographic particulars of the campaign against the Ok Tedi mine, I want to avoid describing these events in exceptionalist terms. Perhaps the most remarkable aspect of their campaign is how much it resembles other struggles against the encroachment of development onto the lands and territories of peoples who identify as indigenous. Some of these campaigns were also provoked by the destruction of the rain forest, including protests against logging in Indonesian Borneo (Brosius 1999). Other campaigns tried to prevent the petroleum industry from polluting the Amazon (Sawyer 2004) or addressed the threat of displacement by large dams in India (Baviskar 2004) and Brazil (Turner 1991). It is the underlying commonalities between the Ok Tedi case and these other struggles that make an accounting of the politics of space valuable. These social movements are especially worthy of study because they are diagnostic of power (Abu-Lughod 1990, 42), providing an important vantage point on the relationship between corporations and their critics.

LOCAL PROTEST, 1983–1989

The earliest objections to the Ok Tedi mine from the people living downstream focused on compensation and benefit sharing. In June 1983, protestors in Kiunga chopped down trees to block roads and lined up two hundred forty-four-gallon drums on the airstrip. They delivered a petition to the government demanding that the people living along the river system receive a larger share of the economic benefits of the project (Moses Oti, pers. comm. 1996). Roadblocks became such a regular activity that one mining company executive referred to them as "the accepted means of communicating with the Government and the Company" (Marty Bos, in 1982, cited in Burton 1997, 46). A group of Awin damaged the copper slurry pipeline that ran through their territory in 1985 in order to emphasize their demands for compensation. By the late 1980s, the mining company was receiving regular demands for compensation for damage to gardens along the Ok Tedi River floodplain, which were being covered by mine tailings (Burton 1997, 46–47).

But concerns about the environmental impact of the mine were also raised during the same period. A group of Kiwai landowners living in Port Moresby convened a meeting in 1984 to discuss concerns about the mine's impact on the environment (Gabia Gagarimabu, pers. comm. 1996). People working at the mine were alarmed by the use of cyanide and other chemicals used to process gold during the initial years of the project (Rex Dagi, pers. comm. 1996). On July 3, 1984, more than five hundred people marched in angry protest to the provincial government offices in Daru, objecting to the decision by OTML to abandon its search for the cyanide drums that were lost when the barge overturned in the Fly River delta. In December 1988, several people from Dome village on the Ok Tedi River composed the following petition about the problems caused by the mine and the refugees.

POLLUTION

When Ok Tedi Copper Mining came to full operation in 1981, every living thing—the animals and plants in the river, on the banks, creeks, and streams—it started killing them.

Now our environment is completely destroyed, and many things are lost for good, e.g. fish, prawns, crocodiles, turtles, and gardens along the riverbank. You will hardly ever find or see them. They were all completely ruined by the tailings and chemicals dumped into the Ok Tedi River.

OK TEDI COPPER ROYALTIES (COMPENSATION)

Because of all the destruction that has taken place, the Yonggom people . . . are entitled to receive compensation from the mine, but we are not. Why?

We are having more problems with copper mining than the Ningerum, Awin, and [Min]. Instead, they are getting royalties. We want the government to look into these problems.

REFUGEES

Now the [refugees from West Papua] are giving us another headache and destroying what remains of our environment. They are ruining our hunting, fishing, gardening, and sago swamps. So, we the people called Yonggom along the border of the Ok Tedi and Fly River are petitioning the government and requesting that they give us A$13.5 million. (Dome village petition, December 1, 1988; grammar and spelling modified, reproduced in Banks and Ballard 1997a, appendix 2, 221–22)

The petition focused on the destructive synergy of pollution from the Ok Tedi mine and the use of local resources by several thousand political refugees from West Papua who fled to Papua New Guinea in 1984. Yet it is worth noting that the document does not call for the mining company to build a tailings dam, as originally proposed, or to stop discharging tailings into the river. Instead, the petition demands A$13.5 million in compensation. Nor does the petition call for the mine to close, or even threaten to close the mine by force, should the company fail to accede to their demands. Although the rhetorical threat to close the mine has occasionally been deployed by the people living downstream, there has never been strong support for this option. In later years, resignation about the environmental impact of the project ironically took the form of support for the mine's continued operation, so that the people living downstream might obtain something of value in return for its negative impacts.

A year after the 1988 petition, the question whether the Ok Tedi mine should be permitted to continue discharging tailings directly into the river or compelled to construct a tailings dam had become the subject of provincial and national debates. In March 1989, the premier of Western Province and member of Parliament for the South Fly demanded that the company build a tailings dam and pay compensation for environmental damage (Post-Courier March 19, 1989, cited in Filer 1997b, 60). John Burton refers to notes taken by community relations officers from the mining company at a meeting of the Ningerum government council the same month.

As usual the councilors complained that the operation of OTML was having a very serious environmental impact on the [Ok Tedi]-Fly River Systems.

The pollution according to the councilors was very serious along the [Ok Tedi] River.... Therefore the councilors claimed that the government should establish an independent body to do a separate environmental study from that of OTML which may be bias[ed].... They also claimed a compensation package be arranged.... Mr. Tameng and I told them that the decision as to whether or not a tailings dam should be built was something for the national government to decide.

The councilors threatened to block the Kiunga-Tabubil road, Kiunga airport, and Kiunga wharf if the government and Ok Tedi Mining Ltd. do not come up with an acceptable remedy for the pollution of the [Ok Tedi]-Fly River systems. (Buhupe 1989; cited in Burton 1997, 45)

This was the situation when I completed my dissertation research on ritual and myth in Dome village on the Ok Tedi River in May 1989. I subsequently presented a post-fieldwork seminar on the political and economic problems caused by the mine and the refugee camps along the border and published an op-ed in the *Times of Papua New Guinea* under the headline "Ok Tedi River a Sewer" (Kirsch 1989a).[1] The op-ed resulted in an invitation to appear on a national radio program hosted by Roger Hau'ofa *(Tok Bak Radio)*. This was one of the most popular media outlets in the country, as I later learned when several people told me that they listened to the interview, including a colleague from the university, who told me that the grocery store where she had been shopping played the program on its speaker system. Several years later, Rex Dagi told me that he listened to the interview while working at the Ok Tedi mine. A written version of the fieldwork seminar subsequently appeared in the journal *Research in Melanesia* (Kirsch 1989b), which circulated among the managers at the Ok Tedi mine and BHP in Tabubil and Port Moresby (Burton 2000, 99).

These events overlapped with the state's recognition that the conflict in Bougainville had no easy resolution and the long-term closure of the Panguna mine would significantly reduce the state budget and negatively impact the national economy. At the Ok Tedi mine, meanwhile, the proposal to construct a tailings dam was still on the table when I conducted interviews with company executives in Tabubil in May 1989. The debate at the time was not whether to build a tailings dam, but whether it should be large enough to store both the tailings and the waste rock that was eroding into the river system at an alarming rate. Several months later, however, the state agreed to allow the mining company to continue discharging tailings directly into the river system (Filer 1997b, 60). Students from Western Province at the University of Papua New Guinea in Port Moresby protested this decision in October 1989.

Despite growing concerns about the mine's environmental impacts and the frustrations expressed by the people affected by the Ok Tedi mine, BHP did not feel the need to respond as long as the resulting protests were limited to Papua New Guinea. The petitions sent to the government and the company disappeared into file cabinets. A small group of local leaders, some of whom were involved in the earlier protests in Daru and Kiunga, were slowly finding their voices, but their actions were localized, and they did not begin collaborating with each other until several years later. Their efforts were neither effective nor sustained, and in their public statements they often failed to address the larger questions associated with the project: they focused on compensation for environmental impacts, for example, rather than challenging the use of riverine tailings disposal.[2] Consequently, it was relatively easy for both the state and the mining company to ignore them. It was only by scaling up their campaign internationally that the people living downstream from the mine were able to exert pressure on BHP.

CHARISMATIC LEADERS

The leaders of the campaign against the Ok Tedi mine attracted local support through their ability to organize opposition to the mine rather than their role in the village or by holding formal political office. This was in keeping with traditional patterns of political authority among the Yonggom, which was recognized for specific tasks like hunting, warfare, or ritual, rather than generalized across activities (Kirsch 1989b, 34). Although in the past, political authority never rose above the level of the lineage or clan, the supporters of the new political leaders were not restricted to kin or even their own ethnic group. This meant that the new leaders faced a steep learning curve, as they lacked role models for this kind of political mobilization.

The two main leaders of the campaign were Rex Dagi and Alex Maun. They grew up in different Yonggom villages on the Ok Tedi River but were members of the same *kaget won,* or initiation cohort. The Yonggom referred to Dagi and Maun as *nup korok,* "our heads." They both earned recognition for their steadfast resistance to political pressure and corruption as well as their refusal to be intimidated. For this reason, they also shared the nickname *bot-korok,* "stone-headed," for their stubborn determination (fig. 6).[3]

The emergence of this new class of political leaders and the development of new forms of political authority has parallels in comparable protest

FIGURE 6. Yonggom activist Rex Dagi raising a stone to signify his nickname *bot-korok,* "stone-headed" or stubborn. Photo: Stuart Kirsch.

movements in the Amazon. Michael Brown (1993, 320) notes that when the traditional links between political and religious authority were severed by colonialism, leadership was "reconceived as a response to the regional and global forces bearing down on Amazonian peoples." Terence Turner (1991, 302–3) describes the political resistance of the Kayapo of Brazil as "without parallel, in its scope, style, substance and achievements, in the history of Amazon native societies. Over the past half-dozen years, the Kayapo have staged a series of demonstrations against a variety of threats to their political, social and territorial integrity and their economic subsistence base." In the process, the Kayapo have become "consummate ethnic politicians: fully engaged, defiantly confrontational, articulating traditional notions with the ideas, values and causes of Western environmentalists, human rights and indigenous support groups" (Turner 1991, 311).

By 1990, Rex Dagi and Alex Maun had assumed leadership roles in the political struggle against the Ok Tedi mine. Rex Dagi quickly became

FIGURE 7. Yonggom activist Alex Maun attempts to share information about the environmental impact of the Ok Tedi mine with a participant at BHP's Annual General Meeting in Melbourne on September 26, 1995. Photo: Brett Faulkner/Newspix.

the most recognizable figure of the campaign. A natural leader and gifted orator, Dagi energized people with his charisma but sometimes became carried away by his own exuberance. Alex Maun is very different in temperament and demeanor. Quiet and soft-spoken, he often said very little at public meetings (fig. 7). In contrast to the extroverted Dagi, Maun has a tendency to internalize his emotions and often complained about feeling "under pressure." If Rex Dagi was the public voice of the campaign against the mine, Alex Maun could be described as its conscience. Despite being cousins, they are not very close, although they worked together well. Both Dagi and Maun attended school through the tenth grade before receiving vocational training and undertaking apprenticeships at the Ok Tedi mine. They later established construction companies that successfully bid for contracts with the Ok Tedi mine, the income from which ironically provided crucial economic support for their international phone calls and travel.

Dagi and Maun were soon joined by two other Yonggom men, both of whom worked for the state. Moses Oti used his clerical position in Kiunga to facilitate communication between the campaign and the provincial government. He once described their motivation to challenge the mining company in the following terms: "Our mothers whispered in our ears: 'This is your land.'" Although Oti helped organize the 1983 demonstration in Kiunga, he generally stayed in the background, making sure things happened; he rarely traveled overseas with Dagi and Maun, or spoke to the media. Robin Moken became involved in the struggle against the Ok Tedi mine after returning to the province in 1993 from West New Britain, where he worked as a patrol officer; his knowledge of how the state handles customary land tenure and his skills in navigating government bureaucracy were also strategic assets for the campaign. Moken assumed a leadership role in the second lawsuit against the Ok Tedi mine from 2000 to 2004.

The two key figures in the campaign from the South Fly were Gabia Gagarimabu and Dair Gabara. Gagarimabu is a member of the Kiwai, the largest ethnic group in Western Province. Originally from Kiwai Island in the Fly River delta, he worked in Port Moresby for a number of years and was a co-organizer of the 1984 meeting held there. He returned to the provincial capital of Daru in the early 1990s. Trained as a high school teacher, he also developed educational material for the national curriculum. A few years older and more patient than either Dagi or Maun, Gagarimabu had a calming influence on the group. A talented communicator, out of the four activists who sought to parlay their roles in the campaign against the Ok Tedi mine into elected positions, he was the only one to succeed. Gagarimabu served one term as the member of Parliament for the South Fly, from 1997 to 2002. The final member of the team was Dair Gabara, who was from the area west of the Fly River delta. Gabara is a lawyer who was serving as the acting secretary for Western Province when he became involved in the campaign against the Ok Tedi mine. Unusually reticent for a politician in Papua New Guinea, a country in which leadership is synonymous with hubris and bravado, Gabara often conveyed the impression that he was hesitant or uncertain, even though he was deeply committed to solving the problems caused by the mine. Gabara played an instrumental role in keeping the coalition of leaders from the North and South Fly together. He also used his skills as a lawyer and the resources available to him as the provincial administrator to advance their objectives. Gabara later represented the plaintiffs in the legal proceedings against the Ok Tedi mine in the courts of Papua New Guinea and played a crucial role in helping the other plaintiffs understand the legal proceedings. Many other people were involved in the campaign over the years, but these six men were the primary leaders.

NONGOVERNMENTAL ORGANIZATIONS

There was very little NGO activity in Papua New Guinea during the 1980s, apart from the work of churches and development organizations. One notable exception was the Wau Ecology Institute, which was founded as a field station of the Bishop Museum of Hawai'i in 1961 and became an independent NGO in 1973. The only other NGOs working on environmental issues or land rights during that period were the Foundation for the Peoples of the South Pacific, a regional network that focuses on village-based development projects and conservation initiatives, and the Melanesian Environment Foundation, which was established in 1986 by a mixed group of Papua New Guineans and expatriates with the support of the PNG Council of Churches; its goal was to promote a Melanesian ethic of conservation and development that blends "traditional wisdom with modern ecology." Among its other activities, the Melanesian Environment Foundation uses community theater to promote discussion about environmental and social issues in rural Papua New Guinea.

There was even less NGO activity in Western Province before the 1990s. The only NGO working on environmental issues in the province was Ecoseeds, which was established by the Montfort Catholic Mission. In the late 1980s, people living along the river corridor registered a number of landowner groups in Kiunga and Daru. Rex Dagi, Alex Maun, and Gabia Gagarimabu were among the key players, but Moses Oti and other local leaders also participated. During interviews conducted in 1992, people referred to these landowner organizations as "pressure groups" through which they hoped to influence the mining company. In other words, political action was still being organized according to groups based on customary landownership. It was not until 1993 that the first NGO to focus on pollution from the Ok Tedi mine was formed by Dagi, Maun, and several others. It was called ENECO (after *en*vironmental *eco*logy). The organization was financed primarily through the collection of dues and voluntary contributions. It played a key role in mobilizing people to participate in the lawsuit against the Ok Tedi mine.

A number of civil society organizations were formed at the national level during the 1990s as well. In 1990, the PNG Trust was formed by several youth groups and community-based organizations to focus on literacy, political awareness, and training. The Individual and Community Rights Advocacy Forum (ICRAF) was established in 1992 by two members of the law faculty at the University of Papua New Guinea to provide legal assistance on human rights, land rights, and environmental issues.[4] The Village Development Trust was formed in 1990 and Conservation Melanesia in 1993. Several international environmental organizations established programs in Papua New Guinea in the mid-1990s, including Greenpeace and the World Wide Fund for Nature (WWF) in 1995 and Conservation International in 1996. Most of these organizations focused on biodiversity conservation, which they promoted by establishing integrated conservation and development projects that were intended as alternatives to destructive forms of natural resource extraction, including mining and logging (Kirsch 1997d; West 2005). In the late 1990s, several NGOs concerned with legal rights and environmental issues were formed in Port Moresby, including the Environmental Law Centre in 1999 and the Center for Environmental Law and Community Rights (CELCOR) in 2000. The Bismarck Ramu Group (BRG), which works with communities facing threats to their land and resources, was also started in 2000. All of the events described in this chapter took place before any of these NGOs were established in Papua New Guinea, with the exception of the Wau Ecology Institute and the Melanesian Environment Foundation, although ICRAF later assisted with the lawsuit against the Ok Tedi mine.

The level of international NGO activity on mining was also very limited during the 1980s. Although international organizations came to play a key role in the campaign against the Ok Tedi mine, the early years of that struggle inspired a new generation of NGOs focused on the international context of mining. The director of the Mineral Policy Institute of Australia, which was founded in 1995, notes the failure of Australian NGOs to address the problems caused by Australian mining companies overseas prior to the Ok Tedi case: "Ok Tedi and its impacts were one of the main reasons why NGOs started addressing international mining issues in a more systematic fashion and why the Mineral Policy Institute was founded" (Harris 1997, 189). He acknowledges that "even though Ok Tedi was known about and was controversial for ten years or more, Australian NGOs for many years took little or no action on the issues" (Harris 1997, 190).

Most of the international NGOs that focus on mining issues were established in the late 1980s and 1990s. Partizans (People against Rio Tinto Zinc and Its Subsidiaries; later People against Rio Tinto and Its Subsidiaries) was founded in 1979 by journalist Roger Moody and others. The Mineral Policy Center in Washington, DC, was set up in 1988 to promote reforms in U.S. mining laws, especially the Mining Law of 1872, which established a fixed royalty rate for minerals extracted from federal property. Originally modeled after the famous lobbying firms of its K Street neighbors, the organization underwent a major rebranding exercise in 1995, reemerging as the more populist Earthworks, with stronger interests in international issues, communities impacted by mining, and consumer responsibility. One such effort is their "No Dirty Gold" campaign, which establishes strategic partnerships with retailers willing to sign a pledge restricting their purchase of gold to companies identified as practicing responsible mining.

Minewatch was established by members of Partizans in London in 1991. Minewatch Asia-Pacific was organized as a project of the original Minewatch and operated from 1996 to 2000. The Indian NGO mines, minerals & People, which describes itself as a "broad national alliance for combatting the destructive nature of mining," was formed in 1998. The Indonesian mining network JATAM was set up by WALHI, Indonesian Forum for the Environment, in 1999, the same year as Mining-Watch Canada. A number of these groups are members of the international Mines and Communities network, which was established in 2001. Christian Aid, Oxfam, and several other humanitarian organizations also initiated short-term campaigns focused on the problems caused by the mining industry around this time. The London Mining Network, "an alliance of human rights, development and environmental groups" that focuses on "the role of companies listed on the London Stock Exchange, London-based funders and the British Government in the promotion of unacceptable mining projects" was formed in 2007.

Although protests against the Ok Tedi mine began in the early 1980s, the campaign had no contact with international NGOs until the end of the decade. NGOs are often credited or blamed for instigating protest movements, but the Ok Tedi case was an important catalyst for a new cohort of NGOs that focus on mining conflicts from an international perspective. Local opposition to the Ok Tedi mine contributed to the formation of these NGOs—rather than the other way around.

OK TEDI CAMPAIGN GOES GLOBAL, 1989–1994

Protests against the Ok Tedi mine entered a new phase in 1989. The primary change was the participation of international NGOs and church groups, which helped bring these issues to new audiences, increasing the pressure on Ok Tedi Mining Ltd. and its shareholders.

Participation in these activities allowed Rex Dagi, Alex Maun, Gabia Gagarimabu, and Dair Gabara to consolidate their leadership positions and coordinate their activities for the first time. Between 1989 and 1994, the international NGOs working on the Ok Tedi case operated independently of each other. Although they often worked with the same group of local leaders, communication between them was limited or nonexistent. Despite their lack of coordination, however, they pursued similar strategies, which were focused on documenting the environmental problems downstream from the Ok Tedi mine and using this information to exert pressure on the shareholders in the project and the PNG government. These NGOs also promoted the discourses of environmentalism and indigeneity, which facilitated the ability of the leaders to raise international awareness of the problems downstream from the mine and enroll additional supporters.

Neither the provincial government nor the state played a significant role in these early debates about the mine and its impacts. John Burton (1998) argues that the funds provided by the mining company to the provincial government would have dampened criticism of the project had they been used appropriately. In hindsight, however, it is apparent that even had every last *toea* of the funds allocated to the province been well managed and wisely spent, it would still not have come close to adequately compensating the people living along the polluted river system for the spiraling environmental problems caused by the mine, although it could well have bought the mining company additional time. Although BHP has been accused of using its economic clout to influence state policy, the state's desire for revenue may have outweighed its concerns about the environment after the civil war in Bougainville increased its dependence on taxes and other economic benefits from the Ok Tedi mine. Criticism of the state's role in the Ok Tedi debacle has largely been restricted to politicians from opposition parties, with the primary exception being politicians from Western Province. There were also critics of the project within the professional ranks of government departments (Townsend 1988), but existing checks and balances on corporate practices, including the mining warden's office (Burton 1997; Filer 1997b, 66–68) and the offices tasked with reviewing the environmental reports produced by the mine, were entirely ineffective.

In 1989, Rex Dagi resigned his position at the Ok Tedi mine and began talking to people living along the Ok Tedi River about the environmental problems they were facing. In particular, he was concerned about the chemicals he had observed being used at the mine and discharged into the river system. The mining company continued to issue reassuring messages that the chemicals had been appropriately treated and would not harm the river, despite the growing evidence of impacts downstream along the river, to gardens in the flood plain, and to the forests and wildlife in the river corridor. Dagi concluded that an independent scientific review of these impacts was urgently needed.

Church groups in Papua New Guinea were also beginning to take notice of the problems downstream from the Ok Tedi mine. In 1989, Bishop Gerard Deschamps of the Sacred Heart Catholic Church in Kiunga and Daru wrote to the PNG Council of Churches, whose general secretary was Reverend Leva Kila Pat of the United Church, requesting support for an independent review of the environmental problems caused by the mine. In December 1989, a convention of United Church delegates meeting in Daru passed a resolution expressing their concerns about the environmental impact of the mine (Filer 1997b, 73). Because of the German investment in the mine, the Catholic and Lutheran members of the Council of Churches forwarded the request for assistance to two German church agencies that focus on development issues, MISEROR (the German Catholic Bishop's Organization for Development Cooperation) and EED (Evangelisch Entwicklungdienst, the Church Development Service for the Protestant Church). These organizations contacted the Starnberg Institute in Germany, which focuses on the study of global structures, development, and crises, and funded Dr. Otto Kreye and Dr. Lutz F. P. Castell to conduct the requested research. During their visit to Papua New Guinea, Kreye and Castell met with Rex Dagi and Moses Oti in the North Fly and Gabia Gagarimabu in Daru.

Dair Gabara refers to another event in mid-1989 as a key turning point for his involvement in the campaign against the mine. While serving as acting secretary for Western Province, he was invited to attend a meeting in Port Moresby to discuss OTML's response to the Sixth Supplemental Amendment to the Mining (Ok Tedi) Act. The company proposed the acceptable particulate level for suspended matter in the Fly River but did nothing to stop the mine from discharging tailings into the river system.[5] The meeting was boycotted by representatives from Western Province and several government departments, because they felt the elected government was making decisions that would adversely affect the people living along the Fly River. Gabara decided that he needed to protect the interests of the people of Western Province from the state (pers. comm. 1996).[6]

Another investigation into the impact of the Ok Tedi mine on the environment resulted from a collaboration between the Wau Ecology Institute and the International Water Tribunal in the Netherlands. In 1990, Rex Dagi and Harry Sakulas, the director of the Wau Ecology Institute, teamed up to develop background materials on Ok Tedi, which were later presented at the hearings of the second International Water Tribunal in early 1992 (Sakulas and Tjamei 1991). The International Water Tribunal was founded in 1982 to draw attention to the "widely recognized inadequacy of existing mechanisms for overseeing water management" (IWT 1994, Background and Results, 18); the first tribunal addressed water pollution in Europe and the second was focused on pollution, mining, and dams in the developing world. The Wau Ecology Institute made field trips to collect data in Western Province in June and October 1991. During the second trip, the lab technicians traveled with Rex Dagi to collect water, fish, and soil samples from the lower Ok Tedi River. The complaint produced by the Wau Ecology Institute against Ok Tedi Mining Ltd. states that

> OTML is accused of showing disregard for the environment of PNG; taking advantage of low environmental standards in a Third World country; operating a mine without waste retention facilities, which would not be permitted in any of the shareholders' home countries; taking advantage of economic pressures on PNG to avoid cost-effective environmental protection measures. The Department of Minerals and Energy is accused of repeatedly bowing to pressure from OTML; failing to implement environmental protection measures to protect the PNG environment; being unable to fulfill its duties as an impartial regulator due to a conflict of interests arising from its double function as both OTML shareholder and monitoring body. (IWT 1994, Programme, 28)[7]

On December 12, 1990, Rex Dagi and Alex Maun organized a protest march of six hundred to eight hundred people to present a petition to OTML and the government demanding K50 million in annual compensation "for our destroyed environment," with the payments backdated to include the early years of the project (Burton 1997, 45–46). They also sought an investment of K50 million in local infrastructure and a 20 percent equity share in the mine. The petition ended with the following threat: "If our demand is not met to our satisfaction, we will take further actions. This may jeopardize Company (OTML) normal operations" (reproduced in Banks and Ballard 1997a, appendix 3, 223–24). With the expectation that the Ok Tedi mine would continue operating until 2006, their demands exceeded one billion dollars. As before, their demands fell on deaf ears. The government's failure to respond to the petition has been cited as a turning point for the protesters, leading them to recognize that they required external assistance to successfully bring about change (Gordon 1997, 148).

By mid-1991, several executives at OTML recognized that growing social unrest downstream from the mine had the potential to disrupt the project. The manager for the environment and public relations at the Ok Tedi mine, who had previously worked at the ill-fated Panguna mine in Bougainville, commissioned a series of reports from Unisearch PNG Pty. Ltd., the business arm of the University of Papua New Guinea (Filer 1997b, 72; 1999b). Although the official remit of the project was limited to monitoring the economic impact of the Lower Ok Tedi/Fly River Trust, which was established in 1989 to provide small-scale development projects and token cash payments to the people living in the areas affected by the mine, in practice, most of the final reports resembled full-scale social impact studies (Filer 1997b, 72–73; 1999b). The project ran from May 1991 until late 1995, delivering a dozen reports to OTML, the first systematic data collection by the company on these communities. Not all of the mine management supported the project. Kipling Uiari, a successful Papua New Guinean politician and businessman who became deputy manager of the Ok Tedi mine and was later promoted to BHP's corporate general manager for Papua New Guinea, expressed concern that social scientists—and anthropologists in particular—posed a risk to the company by inciting local resentment.

In October 1991, the report from the Starnberg Institute was published by the Melanesian Institute, and it was serialized in the *Times of Papua New Guinea* during the following month. It combined environmental and economic data in the following critique of the Ok Tedi mine.

> It is well known that mining operations at Ok Tedi have imposed massive burdens on the environment. What is controversial is whether these burdens will lead to permanent environmental damage and whether they represent an enduring threat to the natural foundations of human life. . . .
>
> There are good grounds for fearing that mining operations at Ok Tedi will initiate long term, that is centuries of ecological, cultural, health and economic damage far exceeding the short-term economic gains. . . .
>
> The Ok Tedi project appears to have fallen far short of fulfilling the hopes originally pinned on it. Should it prove impossible to adequately eliminate the . . . extremely high burden on the environment and secure an appropriate participation for the country in economic gains from the project, then only

one recommendation can be plausible: that mining operations should be stopped without delay, and the project wound up in an orderly fashion. (Kreye and Castell 1991, 8–11)

The report concludes by calling on Papua New Guinea to rethink its "development model" so that the "country [can] . . . make the most of its natural riches" (Kreye and Castell 1991, 11).

BHP quickly produced an exhaustive rebuttal of the Starnberg report, addressing everything from shortcomings in data collection and interpretation to flaws in presentation, including typographical and citation errors (Allen and Mugavin 1991). The International Union for Conservation of Nature was also commissioned to review the Starnberg report by OTML's German shareholders (Filer 1997b, 74); they concluded that "the objectivity of the report is open to serious question given the emotive and emotional language contained in various sections and the scientific validity of the report is dubious given the woefully inadequate scientific data upon which the conclusions are based" (IUCN 1992, 4).[8] Despite being somewhat crude in terms of data collection, analysis, and presentation, the Starnberg report proved to be more accurate in its predictions than contemporaneous reports produced by the mining company. In reaction to the critical assessment by the Starnberg report, OTML subsequently encouraged two additional reviews of the mine's impacts by the Great Barrier Reef Marine Park Authority (Filer 1997b, 75; see Lawrence and Cansfield-Smith 1991) and the Australian Conservation Foundation (Rosenbaum and Krockenberger 1993), which the company hoped would be more positive.

Also in October 1991, two young volunteers for a German development organization visited Western Province. Christoph Meyer and Joseph Neiteler met with Gabia Gagarimabu in Daru before traveling to Kiunga, where they met Rex Dagi and Alex Maun. Dagi and Moses Oti took them to visit several of the Yonggom villages on the lower Ok Tedi River by canoe. A month later, in Port Moresby, the two German volunteers introduced Gagarimabu to Dagi and Maun, all future plaintiffs in the lawsuit against the Ok Tedi mine, for the first time. Their involvement in the political aspects of the campaign against the mine eventually earned Meyer and Neiteler a stinging rebuke from the German ambassador to Papua New Guinea (Meyer, pers. comm. 2011).

The hearings of the International Water Tribunal were held in Amsterdam on February 18, 1992. In its findings, the tribunal called on foreign investors in the Ok Tedi mine to ensure that the company complies with environmental standards comparable to those "enforced in their home countries and appropriate to the geographical characteristics of the Ok Tedi region" (IWT 1994, Mining, 84). The tribunal criticized BHP for using its foreign earning power to coerce the Papua New Guinea government into violating its own environmental standards by permitting riverine tailings disposal (84). It also criticized the PNG government for allowing the mining company to monitor its own impacts and called for a public audit of the assessments produced by the mine (84–85). The tribunal recommended early closure of the mine if it could not identify a safe alternative to riverine tailings disposal (85). Given that the International Water Tribunal is unable to enforce its decisions, it pointed out that the Ok Tedi case was "a good example of the need for establishing liability of shareholding foreign companies for damage caused by the national counterpart" (85). The findings of the International Water Tribunal provided international credibility to the environmental concerns of the people living downstream from the Ok Tedi mine. It also made the crucial suggestion that the case was judiciable in a foreign court.

After attending the hearings of the International Water Tribunal in Amsterdam, Rex Dagi and Dair Gabara traveled to London to meet Roger Moody, a campaign t-shirt–wearing journalist turned mining activist.[9] Moody first became involved in anti-mining activities when writing about conflicts over uranium mining in Australia during the 1970s. He later cofounded Partizans and has been a key contributor to London-based NGOs and networks focused on mining issues.[10] Moody gave Gabara a recently published copy of *The Gulliver File,* a phone book–sized compendium of financial information about the mining industry (Moody 1992).[11] He also alerted Dagi and Gabara to the U.N. Conference on Environment and Development scheduled for Rio de Janeiro that June, which they resolved to attend.

In April 1992, the findings of the Starnberg report were discussed at a conference at the Tutzing Evangelical Academy in Germany, which was attended by several representatives from Papua New Guinea, including Alex Maun. The proceedings for the seminar, including several dissenting chapters, were subsequently published by the Melanesian Institute in Papua New Guinea (Schoell 1994a). A chapter submitted by Murray Eagle (1994, 80), the manager of environment and public relations at the Ok Tedi mine, concludes, "the Ok Tedi case study provides an example of an approach to achieving high standards of environmental management tailored to specific Papua New Guinea environmental and economic standards." The official representative of the Papua New Guinea government to the conference angrily denounced the Starnberg report as "an example of irresponsible intrusion into [the] sovereignty of responsible governments, not only in Papua New Guinea, but similarly in other parts of the Pacific Islands. Such reports create problems for Pacific Island countries and do not contribute to resolution of development problems" (Lepani 1994, 57). Both of these responses to criticism—by the mining company claiming that it operates according to appropriate standards, and by the state that national sovereignty interests are paramount—continued to shape debates about the Ok Tedi mine over the next decade.

Alex Maun stayed in Germany for several weeks after the Tutzing conference, traveling part of the time with Christoph Meyer of the Pacific Action Network, whom he had previously met in Kiunga, and reporting to church groups and environmental organizations on the impact of the Ok Tedi mine. With assistance from members of the German Green Party, Maun met with several members of the German Federal Parliament in Bonn, who asked Parliament to require German shareholders in overseas corporations to apply the same environmental standards as in Germany. The strategy of focusing on the foreign shareholders in the mine was subsequently expanded to include BHP in Australia and Amoco in the United States.

As a result of lobbying by environmental and church groups, a resolution was proposed and accepted by the German Parliament on January 14, 1993. It called on the Federal Government to influence German shareholders and the government of Papua New Guinea through diplomatic links. It sought to reduce pollution to German standards and, in particular, to find better solutions for tailings containment, as well as to increase compensation and financial participation in the project by the communities affected by the mine. The resolution also called on the Federal Government to provide increased NGO assistance to Papua New Guinea, including environmentally appropriate forms of development in agriculture and forestry (Finau 1994, 113). Six months later, however, it became apparent that the resolution had not been acted upon (Schoell 1994b, 14). Nonetheless, subsequent pressure led to the decision by the German government to sell DEG's 5 percent share in the mine to Metallgeschaft in 1993.[12]

While these events were taking place in Germany, there was also some progress in Australia. In April 1992, the Australian Conservation Foundation (ACF) independently conveyed its concerns about the impacts of pollution from the Ok Tedi mine in a letter to the Australian prime minister, Paul Keating (Rosenbaum and Krockenberger 1993, 1).[13] The letter claimed that "BHP would not be prepared to operate in Australia with the same lax standards it employs in Papua New Guinea." It continued: "The Ok Tedi mine sets a dangerous precedent" by favoring profits over "minimum standards of environmental protection" and should therefore be closed (cited in Connell 1997, 163). Keating, who had not previously shown support on environmental issues, surprised ACF by publicly presenting the letter to his counterpart, Papua New Guinea prime minister Rabbie Namaliu, instead of privately conveying the message (Rosenbaum and Krockenberger 1993, 1). Namaliu responded by inviting the Australian Conservation Foundation to send a delegation to visit the Ok Tedi mine, which it did in December 1992.

There was increasing unrest in the province in 1992 concerning both the environmental impact of the mine and the distribution of benefits. In May, the premier of Western Province, Isadore Kaseng, threatened to close down the mine unless the national government agreed to renegotiate the provincial share of benefits from the project; the government responded by sending a police riot squad to Tabubil and arresting the premier (Filer 1997b, 76). In October, there were riots in the provincial capital of Daru over the failure of the provincial government to make appropriate use of the funds provided by the mining company. Gabia Gagarimabu was involved in the organization of the protests, which were intended to address the problems caused by pollution as well as the misappropriation of funds, but ended up "out of control" (Gagarimabu 1996, pers. comm.). The government was forced to send the police riot squad to Western Province for the second time in six months.

In July 1992, I returned to Papua New Guinea to study the social impact of the mine in the villages of the lower Ok Tedi River, part of a larger project organized by Colin Filer at the University of Papua New Guinea that was funded by Ok Tedi Mining Ltd. (see Filer 1999b). My report systematically documented many of the claims on which the lawsuit against the mine was subsequently based. The consensus among the people in the lower Ok Tedi River area was that the mining company should stop discharging tailings into their river system and should compensate them for the damage to their environment (Kirsch 1995). They told me that they planned to seek a political solution to these problems by enlisting members of local "pressure groups" rather than resorting to violence like the people from Bougainville. In one village, the people I interviewed complained that the mining company "does not know what we are feeling down here. We are hungry, we are angry, and we are unhappy about the pollution. We do not want to shut down the mine, we just want them to build a tailings dam." I was also told that the mining company should not have begun production before devising a way to safely dispose of the tailings from the project, a perspective equivalent to the precautionary principle. Other people told me that they felt the pollution had already "spoiled" (*moraron*) their land, but they wanted the mine to continue operating so that the mining company could compensate them for the damages to their environment. It was during this visit that the people from Kungim presented me with their letter listing the environmental problems they had experienced: "Garden crops, dogs, pigs, fish and even people becoming ill. Coconut trees have died. People are suffering from sores. Even our staple food sago is affected. The rain makes us sick. The air we breathe leaves us short of breath. And now the sun burns our skin." Because I was collecting data for the corporate-sponsored research project, they threatened me with violence if the company did not meet their demands. It was clear from the letter and the manner in which it was presented to me that they were feeling overwhelmed by these transformations.

Although the mining company executive who commissioned the social impact studies characterized my final report as "gripping," he later remarked to a colleague that it would "never see the light of day." In a roundtable discussion of the reports held in Port Moresby in 1993, Kipling Uiari, who had grown up in a sago-producing village on the north coast of Papua New Guinea, denied the villagers' claim that pollution from the mine was responsible for the failure of their sago palms to bear edible starch, arguing that this was a natural phenomenon.

In June 1992, Rex Dagi, Dair Gabara, Gabia Gagarimabu, and several delegates from the provincial government attended the U.N. Conference on Environment and Development (UNCED) in Rio de Janeiro, Brazil. The Rio meetings were a follow-up to the U.N. Conference on the Human Environment held twenty years earlier in Stockholm, which first expressed the need for sustainable forms of development (Ward and Dubos 1972, xiii). The 1992 Rio Earth Summit, as the meetings were later called, "gave unprecedented publicity to the issues of the environment and development and popularized the term 'sustainable development' to such an extent that its use is now *de rigueur* among NGOs, governmental bodies and the private sector" (Reed 2002, 206). Several influential documents were produced at the Rio Earth Summit, including the Forest Principles, the U.N. Framework Convention on Climate Change, and the U.N. Convention on Biological Diversity. The Earth Summit is equally famous for being the "coming out party" of the global NGO community. The official meeting included representatives from 172 nations, while a parallel NGO forum included 2,400 representatives from nongovernmental organizations and was attended by 17,000 people.

Rex Dagi was invited to present on the impacts of the Ok Tedi mine at a press conference held on board the Greenpeace ship *Rainbow Warrior II*, with hundreds of people watching from the shore. When I later asked Dagi what he said, he told me that he read aloud from one of my papers. Dair Gabara, whose trip was sponsored by the Papua New Guinea law firm Warner Shand, met with a number of NGOs regarding potential support for a legal case against the corporate investors in Ok Tedi Mining Ltd. One of the people he met was Glen Prickett from the U.S. Natural Resources Defense Council (NRDC), who invited him to come to New York for further discussion.

Gabara, Gagarimabu, and Dagi traveled to the United States after Rio. In New York City, they met with Prickett at NRDC about the possibility of bringing suit against Amoco, although Pricket concluded that such a case would fail on questions of jurisdiction. They met with Stephen Zorn, the legal advisor for the U.N. Centre on Transnational Corporations. Zorn had previously helped to negotiate the original Ok Tedi agreement while serving as Assistant Director of the Office of Minerals and Energy for the government of Papua New Guinea (Zorn 1977). They also met with Stuart Waugh, a metals trader on Wall Street who had become alarmed by reports about the environmental impact of the Ok Tedi mine and had previously traveled to Daru, where he met Gagarimabu. With Waugh's assistance, the three Papua New Guineans went to Washington, DC, for a meeting organized by the staff of *Multinational Monitor,* a publication founded by Ralph Nader, who had become concerned about the Ok Tedi mine while traveling in Australia on behalf of the Australian Green party. The purpose of the meeting was to discuss Amoco's 30 percent share in the Ok Tedi mine and the possibility of sponsoring a campaign against or boycott of the company. However, the NGOs cited the difficulty of enrolling public support for an action focused on a minority shareholder of a copper and gold mine located in a distant country that is largely unfamiliar to most Americans. After meeting with Meg Taylor, the Papua New Guinea ambassador to the United States and the United Nations, about their concerns, she helped fund their trip home.

Amoco sold off its other investments in mining in 1985, but retained its shares in the Ok Tedi mine until October 1993, when it sold 10 percent of OTML to BHP and the remaining 10 percent of its stake in project to the government of Papua New Guinea (Wall Street Journal 1993). The terms of the sale were not disclosed, but were said to include a waiver of environmental liability. The reconfiguration of shares in the project left BHP with a controlling 52 percent share in the mine, increasing its vulnerability to legal action.

In August 1993, the University of Papua New Guinea sponsored the national follow-up meeting to the Rio Earth Summit in Port Moresby, which I was able to attend (see Gladman, Mowbray, and Duguman 1996). Heated debate about the Ok Tedi mine ended up being one of the focal points of the conference. Governor General Sir Wiwa Korowi, who had also been in Rio, raised the issue of pollution from the mine in his opening remarks, "Think of our children, who will ask: 'What have you done to us? Why are there no fish in our rivers? Why are there no trees in our forest?' What will we say to them? There has been horrible damage done to the Fly River by development. We have the best studies, we have spent millions of kina to protect the environment, but it doesn't matter.[14] We have failed the people."

The Honorable Parry Zeipi, member of Parliament from Western Province and minister for the environment and conservation, added the following thoughts on the problems caused by development, invoking the situation downstream from the Ok Tedi mine: "Traditionally we were constrained by the limits of what would grow in our gardens. With technology, markets, and capital, people start to believe that there are no limits. We believe that fish come from tin cans and [imported] rice is replacing our crops. The river is no longer bringing life, but killing our crops instead." Ambassador Meg Taylor expressed her shame as a member of the generation responsible for Papua New Guinea's seventeen years of independence, calling on the participants to speak honestly about the problems faced by the country, "not to talk more bullshit like the last twenty years," a comment that made headlines in the next day's newspapers.

Discussion about the Ok Tedi mine became even more vitriolic as representatives from the mine and the downstream communities were granted the opportunity to speak. Kipling Uiari responded to the questions raised by the previous speakers.

What has Ok Tedi done for PNG, for Western Province, for the Star Mountains people who claim Mt. Fubilan? People told me that: "We want development, we want schools, we want hospitals," and those changes have taken place. We have produced useful developments beyond the mine, sustainable business and industry. People say: "There are also negative impacts." Well, of course there are negative impacts, but in the main they are temporary, they are reversible, and they will go away. . . . People ask: "Do we need development?" I want to wear shoes, put a tie on, put a shirt on and be like the white man. In order to gain that, we have to sacrifice something. There are beneficial and there are negative aspects, most of which, we believe, are temporary. What will be left will be positive change. That change will be sustained. We are positively engaged in sustainable development.

Uiari's speech was disrupted by catcalls. A Greenpeace representative from the Solomon Islands yelled out that the only reason a real Melanesian would need a necktie would be to hang himself. During the question and answer period, Rex Dagi spoke out, "This will lead to the next Bougainville. I don't think there is proper sustainable development [from the mining project]. To use the Ambassador's word, this is 'bullshit.' The national government has made a mistake on Bougainville and also on Ok Tedi." Uiari interrupted Dagi at that point: "I know Rex well," he told the audience. Then, addressing Dagi, he said, "Let's not fool ourselves. I hope that your business is helping the people downriver," before turning back to the audience: "Rex has a contract with us. That money is percolating down. [That is how] we will achieve something. Do not expect more from us than what a good citizen can do." Alex Maun had the last word in the debate when he presented his paper, in which he argued, "Mining is threatening the lives of the people who live along the river. Subsistence farmers depend on the environment. The destruction has been covered up." In Tabubil, he said, the "landowners are enjoying the life of the mine, while the affected people downstream are directly exposed to damage from the mine. People are living in fear. Even if Ok Tedi says it is safe to drink the water and eat the fish, people live in fear."

In November 1993, the Australian Conservation Foundation (ACF) released its report on the Ok Tedi mine, which was scathing in its critique (Rosenbaum and Krockenberger 1993). It noted that pollution was no longer being monitored above the Fly River, effectively treating the Ok Tedi River as a "sacrifice zone" (Rosenbaum and Krockenberger 1993, 10; see Kirsch 1989, 58). The authors continued, "Pollution from the mine has rendered the first 70 kilometers of the Ok Tedi River *almost biologically dead,* and species diversity in the next 130 kilometers . . . has been dramatically reduced" (Rosenbaum and Krockenberger 1993, 9; emphasis added and references omitted).[15] The report rejects the company's "in-house" approach to monitoring, which "means that OTML is not publically accountable for its environmental performance," because there is "no independent verification of the monitoring, nor of the interpretation of the data" (15; references omitted). The authors of the ACF report also refer to this arrangement as a "parody of environmental management" (Rosenbaum and Krockenberger 1993, 7). The report calls for an independent investigation of the options to reduce the volume of tailings discharged into the river system, including the possibility of reducing the production rate at the mine by half (35).

Much like its response to the Starnberg report, OTML issued a swift and condemnatory rebuttal accompanied by a press release titled "ACF Distorting the Facts" (OTML 1993a, 1993b). The twenty-page commentary from OTML compares the "style" of the Australian Conservation Foundation report to the 1992 Starnberg report "in that it uses data and information selectively in an attempt to discredit the company's environmental monitoring programs and present the monitoring data in the worst possible light" (OTML 1993a, 19). The press release quotes Kipling Uiari's view that the report is "a distortion of the facts based on selective use of information" (OTML 1993b, 1), because it failed to take the project's economic benefits into account. Uiari also criticized ACF for ignoring the role of the sovereign state in determining the best outcome for Papua New Guineans. Uiari expressed his disappointment with the framing of the report. He felt that OTML was "entitled to expect fair treatment" from ACF, given the cooperation extended by the mining company and the assurances from ACF that the report "would be properly balanced" (OTML 1993b, 1). The press release also presents a new script for how the company should respond to criticism of its environmental record by trumpeting the economic benefits provided by the mining project, including jobs, taxes, and foreign exchange earnings.

The chief significance of the ACF report, which added to the criticism in the Starnberg report and the findings of the International Water Tribunal, was that it exposed BHP to criticism of the Ok Tedi mine for the first time, signaling that the environmental problems downstream from the mine could affect the parent company. In contrast to the Starnberg Report and the International Water Tribunal, both of which focused on Ok Tedi Mining Ltd., the Australian Conservation Foundation report led to the first significant reputational risks to BHP from the Ok Tedi mine.

By the end of 1993, several aspects of the campaign against the Ok Tedi mine were well established. There was a small cadre of vocal, charismatic, and capable leaders, especially Rex Dagi, Alex Maun, and Gabia

Gagarimabu, who were committed to working together. They had the assistance of Dair Gabara, whose training as a lawyer helped them navigate potential legal challenges to the mine. Despite these developments, nothing was changing on the ground. As indicated by the people I interviewed for the social impact study, people were frustrated: "We are hungry, we are angry, and we are unhappy about the pollution" from the mine. The people living along the Ok Tedi River were also becoming increasingly aware of the deteriorating environmental conditions, though they were hard pressed to distinguish between the problems caused by the mine and other changes to the landscape, including population pressure from the refugee camps along the border. The pollution was also steadily spreading downstream.

Yet OTML remained defiant. The mining company continued to deny the significance of the environmental impacts from the mine or that their duration would have to be measured in decades, if not centuries. Its refusal to take responsibility for these impacts allowed the mining company to continue externalizing the social and environmental costs of production. Although BHP was directly exposed to criticism for the first time by the Australian Conservation Foundation report, it was content to defer questions about tailings containment to the state, despite the company's role as the managing partner of the mine and, by the end of 1993, the majority shareholder in OTML as well. The next step was for the activists from the Ok Tedi and Fly Rivers to follow up on the suggestion by the International Water Tribunal to pursue litigation, either in Papua New Guinea, or as the tribunal suggested, in BHP's home court. Dair Gabara had already initiated these conversations through his connections to the Port Moresby legal community, and by mid-1993 Gabara and Dagi were in discussion with several law firms, including Slater & Gordon in Australia, about how to take OTML and BHP to court.

CONCLUSION

By forging alliances with international NGOs, the people living downstream from the Ok Tedi mine were able to expand the horizons of their campaign. This allowed them to enroll new supporters, mobilize new discourses in support of their actions, and advance their claims. In some cases, these new collaborations also imposed constraints on their campaign.

The leaders of the campaign collaborated with European NGOs and church groups that provided valuable resources and raised the profile of their campaign. They explicitly targeted the countries where investors in the mine were located. They had some success in Germany, where the state sold its shares in the mine, though their effort to persuade the Parliament to regulate the other German investors failed. In the United States, the corporate connection to the mine via Amoco was considered too remote for an effective campaign.

Several NGOs also documented the environmental problems along the river, verifying local concerns. Reports from the Starnberg Institute in Germany and the Australian Conservation Foundation were criticized by OTML and BHP for their emotive presentation and their failure to consider the economic benefits from the mine. The International Water Tribunal gave the campaign additional credibility. The report by the Australian Conservation Foundation also created reputational risks for BHP that steadily intensified throughout the legal proceedings, until the company was forced to concede that the cost of its association with the mine exceeded the economic benefits it received.

In the early years of the campaign against the Ok Tedi mine, there were no relevant NGOs in Papua New Guinea and international NGOs had not yet become involved. When international NGOs began working with the leaders of the campaign, these were often novel engagements for both sides. The broader NGO community had only recently begun to recognize its need to play a more active role in monitoring corporate activity. In contrast to the popular assumption that indigenous protests are instigated and orchestrated by outside NGOs, the campaign against the Ok Tedi mine was a catalyst for the development of new international NGOs focused on mining, including the establishment of the Mineral Policy Institute in Australia.

Some of the tactics used by other anticorporate social movements were not available to the people protesting the Ok Tedi mine, because mining companies do not sell directly to consumers and therefore protestors cannot organize boycotts or other actions based on consumer preference. The closest analogue to this strategy for the Ok Tedi campaign involved the efforts of the German NGO *Rettet die Elbe* (Save the Elbe), which protested against the Norddeutsche Affinerie, which processes copper from the Ok Tedi mine at a refinery on the Elbe River. However, when a representative of Norddeutsche Affinerie visited the Ok Tedi mine in November 2000, he told the media that if his company stopped purchasing copper from the Ok Tedi mine, another company would simply take its place (Post-Courier 2000). He said that by maintaining its relationship to the Ok Tedi mine, Norddeutsche Affinerie could continue to exert pressure on BHP to reduce its environmental impact (Post-Courier 2000). The Uniting Church of Australia, which was also under pressure to divest its shares in BHP, reached a similar conclusion, deciding that it would have more influence over the company if it continued to be a shareholder.

The horizontal relationships between the participants in these alliances greatly expanded the campaign against the Ok Tedi mine. Jeffrey Juris (2008) and David Graeber (2013) extol the democratic potential of network organization in Occupy Wall Street and other movements against corporation globalization. But as Malcolm Gladwell (2010) points out, without some form of centralized organization or hierarchy, it is difficult for the members of horizontal networks to make decisions quickly or achieve specific goals. Although Dagi, Maun, and the other leaders of the campaign against the Ok Tedi mine were actively engaged in all of the initiatives described here, there was limited communication or coordination among the different organizations participating in the campaign. In contrast to the democratic politics ordinarily associated with horizontal networks, the campaign against the Ok Tedi mine more closely resembled a distributed mode of action in which the participants were not always informed about each other's activities.

Collaboration with international NGOs also exposed the participants in the campaign to new political discourses. Although the term *indigenous* had not entered the vocabulary of most Yonggom speakers when I began working with them in 1986, it is increasingly used by the Yonggom and other Papua New Guineans to refer to important distinctions between themselves and Euro-Americans, including significant linguistic, cultural, and economic differences.[16] Perhaps most importantly, they invoke the discourse of indigeneity rather than class to explain Euro-American control over the dominant means of production, including mines and factories, which results in the economic marginalization of rural Papua New Guineans.[17] The state of Papua New Guinea, however, rejects the claim that its citizens are indigenous. Yet indigenous rights have become as integral to international campaigns against transnational mining companies as the organized labor movement is to a collective bargaining regime (see Szablowski 2007, 292).[18] Similarly, academic writings that reduce indigenous politics to the "savage slot" (T. M. Li 2000) run the risk of undermining hard-won gains, much as Marilyn Strathern (1998, 127) observes when she warns against the hasty deconstruction of claims that operate in a "world of already existing inequalities, where . . . it is hard to make one's voice heard."

The Yonggom and their neighbors also invoke the discourse of environmentalism and the language of science to convey their concerns about pollution from the Ok Tedi mine, but in doing so, they face a double bind. If they address environmental problems using their own terms and concepts, as when the Yonggom describe the Ok Tedi mine as a corporate sorcerer, they risk being misunderstood and having their views treated as irrelevant to scientific or technocratic decision making (Burton 1997, 41–43). Conversely, people claiming indigenous rights risk having their testimony judged as inauthentic if they use the language of science when speaking about environmental issues (see Banks 2002), much as Laura Graham (2002) argues that indigenous leaders in Latin America are discredited when they express their political concerns in the language of the state.

But people facing environmental challenges may require new vocabulary and concepts to describe problems that lack precedent, including pollution, chemical toxicity, acid mine drainage, and trophic cascade.[19] Consequently, it is not surprising that the participants in the campaign against the Ok Tedi mine regularly drew on scientific language in expressing their concerns about the environment, as illustrated by the following letter from the people of Levame village in the Middle Fly, which gracefully combines scientific explanation of the threat to local food chains with a discussion about the interconnectedness of all living things and the value of nature:

> What we have been complaining about the Government and Company has now admitted. We now know that the government and the company have found out that they are guilty of serious environmental impacts along the Fly River System.
>
> Since the beginning of the mine, the company and the government have been denying the fact that the river system was highly contaminated and that every life along the river was affected.
>
> For a brief detail on environmental impact we will touch on only one key point contributing to life: In science under the section of biology and the subsection of ecology, the study of living organisms and their environment. These are topics such as biotic factors, food factors/food chain. Plants are the ultimate source of organic food for all animals. Plants are eaten by herbivores, which are, in turn, eaten by carnivores.
>
> It makes us sad to see that the environment around us that once supported us on this earthly lives of ours has lost its beauty and is gone forever, which money will not bring back, and that it has become history for our children and grandchildren. Once nature is changed it is changed forever.
>
> We are appealing to defend and protect the basis of the food chain that contributes to our lives. . . . Along the Fly River System, every life is in danger

because of the destruction of this dependency of one life upon one another. (Written submission from Levame village, reproduced in ICRAF 2000, 11–12, modified spelling and grammar)

Although the people living downstream from the Ok Tedi mine chose not to follow Bougainville's path from civil disobedience to civil war, rumors circulated about an organization called the Fly River Army, or FRA, modeled after the Bougainville Revolutionary Army (BRA), which was responsible for the uprising against the Panguna mine. The people in Bougainville turned to violence in part because they lacked NGO allies and the political alternatives available to the people affected by the Ok Tedi mine. The leaders of the Ok Tedi campaign decided to take their case to court rather than turn to violence, as Moses Oti (pers. comm. 1996) explained to me: "We want to prove to the world that we have savvy [intelligence]. If we [fight] like Bougainville, we are not civilized, we are nothing. We are fighting legally and mentally. This problem will be sorted out before the eyes of the world: no bloodshed, no fighting. The world will recognize that Yonggom can sort out problems at the international level. [We want to] tell the whole world. The Yonggom will be somebody in the eyes of the world. If we took up arms, it would just make problems worse."

The campaign against the Ok Tedi mine also raised important questions about capitalism. These events overlapped with the fall of communism, which made it difficult to imagine alternative economic arrangements. The campaign drew attention to corporate harm in a neoliberal era in which the state fails to prioritize the rights of its citizens or environmental protection over economic activity. It raised questions about whether it is possible to limit capitalism's destructive capacity and whether capitalism and the environment can coexist (Jameson 1994, xii). The Euro-American participants in the campaign were also concerned about the negative role of their countries in development contexts as well as their personal responsibilities as consumers. For Australians and Germans, in particular, national connections to the Ok Tedi project justified their involvement in the campaign. And for many of the Euro-American supporters of the campaign, the rise of indigenous politics also signified the possibility of alternative relationships to nature they wanted to protect. In this sense, anticorporate campaigns ask whether capitalism, left unfettered, will erase all cultural differences, and whether it is still possible for people to live differently, should that be their desire, in other places. They demonstrate the need and the potential capacity to reign in the virtually unrestricted activity of capital and tame the most destructive aspects of the market. These questions—on the need to place limits on capital and markets, the fate of the natural environment, and the cultural survival of indigenous peoples—are central to understanding the consequences of globalization, including whether it is possible to achieve better outcomes.

The communities living along the Ok Tedi and Fly Rivers faced a steep learning curve when they set out to challenge the Ok Tedi mine. They needed new leaders with skills appropriate to the challenges they faced. Their alliances with international NGOs allowed them to put pressure on BHP wherever it operated. But their invocation of the discourses of indigeneity and environmentalism provoked criticism that threatened to undermine their legitimacy. Despite the best efforts of the participants in the campaign against the Ok Tedi mine, the mining company continued to deny that real problems existed and moved quickly and aggressively to discredit any independent reporting or analysis. Yet by 1993, the environmental problems from the mine had become widely recognized and acknowledged. A small number of activists and their allies had been able to transform the public profile of a mine located in an "out of the way place" (Tsing 1993) in a relatively short period of time. But they were still unable to stop the mine from discharging tailing into the river system. Consequently, the next step in their campaign was to take the mining company to court, as I discuss in the following chapter.

CHAPTER 3

Down by Law

On May 5, 1994, Rex Dagi filed suit against BHP in the Supreme Court of Victoria in Melbourne, Australia. The complaint represented Dagi and the other members of his clan from Iogi village on the Ok Tedi River against the mining company. The plaintiffs alleged that BHP, as the majority shareholder and managing partner of the Ok Tedi mine, was responsible for polluting the Ok Tedi River, the floodplains, and the surrounding rain forest. BHP was alleged to have committed a private nuisance, a public nuisance, trespass, and breach of a duty of care in their operation of the mine. The writ sought injunctions to stop the defendant from polluting the river and to compel the construction of a tailings dam. The lawyers for the plaintiffs informed the media that they had signed writs representing thirty thousand people living downstream from the mine. The case sought up to A$4 billion in compensation and exemplary damages, the largest monetary claim in Australian history (Pheasant 1994, 15; Callick 1994) and one of the largest environmental claims ever made. The case was also exemplary in that BHP was being sued under the laws and in the courts of Australia, where the company was incorporated, rather than in Papua New Guinea, where the mine was located and the damage occurred.

The Ok Tedi case was a pioneer in efforts to use the law to hold corporations accountable for their international operations. Since then, there have been a number of international legal cases in which indigenous peoples have sued corporations engaged in resource extraction on environmental grounds.[1] The defendants in these cases are not rogue corporations but some of the largest and most powerful companies in the world. BHP, commonly known as "The Big Australian," is not only a blue chip stock, but is also a popular investment vehicle for organizations sensitive to ethical concerns, including churches and teachers' unions. ChevronTexaco, Rio Tinto, and Shell, all of which are regarded as industry leaders, have also been the targets of international litigation concerning indigenous peoples, environmental degradation, and human rights violations.

These legal actions offer strategic resources to communities and social movements that otherwise lack the ability to alter corporate practices. In particular, the cases against mining companies have contributed to significant changes in corporate policy and practices, including the ways in which mining companies interact with the communities affected by their operations. The threat of litigation may be one of the few sources of regulatory power available in a neoliberal world order. In practice, however, these court cases are complex undertakings, and their legacies have been mixed. They stimulate fierce opposition. They can take years to deliver results. Settlement agreements may falter in their implementation. Favorable judgments tend to be reduced on appeal. The cases also acquire a social and political life that often exceeds the legal proceedings themselves.

A key issue raised by these cases is the challenge of adequately representing indigenous plaintiffs who may be unfamiliar with legal language and court proceedings. The plaintiffs may reside in remote areas that make communication difficult. They may also be vulnerable to pressure from transnational corporations and the state in the form of incentives or sanctions. The host states, in which the resource extraction takes place, may regard international legal proceedings as an infringement on their national sovereignty and seek to block intervention by foreign courts. The relationships among the plaintiffs in these cases may be affected by these actions, and their commitment to the proceedings may wax and wane. Increased scrutiny of the corporation and its operations may threaten its reputation. Litigation against transnational corporations can be hugely expensive, and the resulting financial constraints may affect the strategies of law firms representing the plaintiffs. All of these factors were significant in the Ok Tedi case.

These cases often have important interconnections. Not only do the developments and judgments in one case influence strategies and outcomes in the others, but the participants may also exchange information or become involved in multiple cases. The Ok Tedi case was an important precursor to legal claims against Freeport-McMoRan in the U.S. District Court in New Orleans regarding its Grasberg mine in West Papua and against Rio Tinto regarding its Panguna mine in Bougainville in the U.S. District Court in Los Angeles. In 1996, the Komoro and Amungme people from West Papua brought suit against the American company over the environmental impact of the mine and its alleged complicity in the violence of Indonesian armed forces against critics of the project, including accusations of "cultural genocide." Prior to filing suit against Freeport, the American attorney Martin Regan sought advice from Slater & Gordon, the solicitors in the Ok Tedi case. The 2000 case against Rio Tinto charged the company with environmental damage and alleged complicity in the Bougainville civil war. The case against Rio Tinto was mounted by Nick Styant-Browne, the lead attorney in the Ok Tedi case, who relocated to the United States from Australia to pursue the claim.

Both the Freeport and Rio Tinto cases were based on the previously obscure U.S. Alien Tort Claims Act of 1789, which was enacted to provide the United States with jurisdiction "over violations of safe conduct, infringement of the rights of ambassadors, and piracy" (Koebele 2010, 32). These cases assert that the American courts are an appropriate forum in which to adjudicate claims regarding the violations of international law by transnational corporations (Joseph 2004; Koebele 2010). Dozens of cases against transnational corporations have been filed in the United States under the alien tort statute, including an important case against Unocal regarding forced labor on its gas pipeline in Burma that resulted in a confidential settlement in 2005. However, in a 2013 ruling on a case against Royal Dutch Petroleum concerning pollution and alleged human rights violations associated with its oil operations in the Niger Delta, the U.S. Supreme Court restricted the applicability of the alien tort statute, which led to the dismissal of the case against Rio Tinto regarding the Panguna mine and civil war in Bougainville. A similar lawsuit against ChevronTexaco, for pollution caused by petroleum extraction in the Amazon, although not an alien tort case, has moved back and forth between the courts in the United States and Ecuador since 1993.[2]

The turn to the courts by social and political movements is viewed with skepticism by "hegemony theorists," who argue that the law privileges the interests of powerful elites, including transnational corporations (Santos and Rodríguez-Garavito 2005, 5). This perspective relies on "structuralist conceptions of power as well as 'populist views' of law and society that draw a stark contrast between powerful actors . . . and powerless 'victims'" (Santos and Rodríguez-Garavito 2005, 7–8). These scholars treat the law as a mode of depoliticizing conflict, as suggested by regulations that prevent labor from engaging in militant action or provoking radical change (Eckert et al. 2012a, 4). Other authors describe how the "rule of law" is invoked to protect the "sovereign authority of the state" against violence and disorder (Comaroff and Comaroff 2006, 20). Similarly, postcolonial scholars argue that the law alienates subalterns from their own language and experience (Das 1989, 316, but see Kirsch 2012).

However, these critiques may underestimate the potential for mobilizing law from below as a means of democratizing power. Julia Eckert (2012, 149–50) quotes an informant in Mumbai, India, who speaks poignantly of this possibility: "We need the law. We want to use law. But we do not know enough. We need information. The powerful break the law. We also have rights in law. . . . We want to use the law against them." Not only did the plaintiffs in the lawsuit against the Ok Tedi mine share this view of the law, but so did their attorneys, who sought to "advance agendas that stand in explicit contrast with those of hegemonic actors" (Santos and Rodríguez-Garavito 2005, 11). Instead of treating the law as a closed system that inevitably reproduces political power, the legal practitioners in these cases regard the law as open-ended and consequently a resource for promoting political and economic transformation. This perspective has particular significance for the mining conflicts discussed here given the "regulatory fracture" between state law and the global economy (Sassen 1998, 155), as challenging the conduct of transnational corporations requires new strategies for bridging the resulting gap. The failure to consider how the law might be used to bring about change also runs the risk of reproducing a "deterministic image of globalization in which there is virtually no space for resistance and change" (Santos and Rodríguez-Garavito 2005, 12).

THE OK TEDI CASE

The Supreme Court of Victoria was considered an appropriate forum for the Ok Tedi case because major decisions about the project were made at the corporate headquarters in Melbourne. The initial case against BHP was not a class action, which was unavailable under Victorian law in 1994.[3] Dagi's complaint was the first test case filed in

Melbourne. Two additional writs were subsequently filed with modified claims, as I describe below, and a fourth writ represented the claims of an Australian fisherman who worked commercially in the lower Fly River. An additional 1,056 writs were lodged in the Papua New Guinea courts against Ok Tedi Mining Ltd. in September 1994.

The case was inspired by the findings of the 1992 International Water Tribunal (1994), which called on OTML to identify and implement an alternative means of tailings containment or close down the mine. The tribunal's inability to enforce its decisions led Rex Dagi and Dair Gabara to consider filing a lawsuit against the mining company. Initially they intended to bring their case to court in Papua New Guinea, but preliminary discussions with lawyers in Port Moresby led to the conclusion that none of the firms based in Papua New Guinea had the resources or the capacity to pursue litigation against a corporation as wealthy and powerful as BHP. In the process, Warner Shand lawyer Greg Sheppard contacted John Gordon, a friend from law school in Australia, about the case. Gordon was working for Slater & Gordon, a prominent plaintiffs law firm based in Melbourne, which immediately expressed an interest in the case.

Nick Styant-Browne, a brash but brilliant young lawyer at Slater & Gordon, assumed responsibility for the case and became certified to practice law in Papua New Guinea in 1993. John Gordon, who had established his reputation in a successful case against the Wittenoom asbestos mine, moved to Melbourne from Slater & Gordon's Perth office for the Ok Tedi case. His powers of deduction and recall were essential to the conduct of the case. Peter Gordon, head of the firm's major projects division, added strategic acumen as the third member of the team. They were motivated by concern for the people downstream from the mine, the quixotic challenges posed by the case, and disdain for BHP's arrogance. They also believed in the leveling power of the common law to redress harm (Gordon 1997, 166).

Dair Gabara began collecting instructions and depositions from the people affected by the Ok Tedi mine for Slater & Gordon in 1993, in what the media and the mining company came to refer to as "litigation patrols" (Cannon 1998, 248).[4]

> Agreements setting out the terms upon which Slater & Gordon would accept instructions to run test cases and pursue claims for injunctive and declaratory relief were drawn up, translated into appropriate [languages], and distributed to villages along the entire river system. Meetings of villages, and clans within those villages, were then held to discuss whether or not they

would join in the legal actions. A series of major meetings was then convened in regional centres along the river. Under the supervision of the government-appointed Administrator of the Western Province, these meetings were addressed by several landowner leaders. The agreements were again read in full, in English, Tok Pisin, and Motu, and a question and answer session was held. Then, any clans who wished to instruct Slater & Gordon to act for them were invited to talk with the lawyer and the landowner leaders individually, and if content to do so, execute the agreements by way of instructions. As a result of this process, some 500 clans representing nearly 30,000 people along the river systems instructed us to act for them. (Gordon 1997, 149–50)

The decision to file a test case against BHP in the Supreme Court of Victoria took the mining company by surprise. BHP had expected Slater & Gordon to file suit in Port Moresby, where the company was confident of its standing under PNG law. Styant-Browne originally intended to try the case in the Papua New Guinea courts, but was persuaded by Peter Gordon to run the test case in Melbourne. They both expected BHP to challenge Dagi's writ on the basis of forum non conveniens, arguing that the case should be heard by the courts in Papua New Guinea rather than Australia.[5] However, during the ensuing media frenzy, Styant-Browne challenged BHP to defend itself at home, and the company accepted his dare, announcing that it was prepared to fight the claim in Melbourne. Styant-Browne later referred to BHP's reaction as its biggest mistake in the legal proceedings (Cannon 1998, 249).

Slater & Gordon was one of the few Australian law firms with the resources to conduct a case of this magnitude, which eventually exceeded A$7 million in costs and fees. Plaintiffs law firms use earnings from previously successful cases to fund new ones. Slater & Gordon was able to draw on earnings from settlements obtained on behalf of asbestos miners in Western Australia and persons with medically acquired HIV. In taking on the Ok Tedi case, they assumed an enormous financial risk, because they would not receive compensation or reimbursement of their expenses unless the case succeeded. Running cases on a contingency basis like this can affect legal strategies, as lawyers representing the plaintiffs need the case to progress while they still have sufficient funds. In contrast, lawyers for corporate defendants continue to be paid as long as their clients remain solvent, and having clients with deep pockets provides them with a significant advantage. The ability of corporate lawyers to outspend their opponents is an important dynamic in such cases, as it was in the Ok Tedi lawsuit, which never moved beyond procedural hearings to a discussion of the evidence.

Despite the financial risk assumed by Slater & Gordon, the media and politicians in Papua New Guinea accused the law firm of taking the case solely for monetary gain. They pointed to agreements signed by the plaintiffs indicating that legal costs could be deducted from any award up to a maximum of K950 ($750) per plaintiff. The leader for the political opposition in Papua New Guinea famously referred to Slater & Gordon as "foreign spivs, crooks, and carpetbaggers" (Filer 1997b, 78). On the eve of the lawsuit, one of the executives from the Ok Tedi mine sought to persuade me in a phone call that Slater & Gordon would take the money and run, whereas the mining company would do a better job protecting the long-term interests of the downstream landowners. However, John Gordon (1997, 141–42) later pointed out that there were much easier ways for Slater & Gordon to earn a living, listing the following challenges posed by the Ok Tedi case:

- Your clients are impecunious.
- There are many thousands of them similarly affected.
- They live in another country.
- That country's government is opposed to their claim.
- They live in villages without phones, television, or newspapers, four hours by plane and many hours by boat from the capital.
- Your opponent is the biggest company in Australia. They engage one of the country's biggest law firms to act for them, and up to 50 lawyers and paralegals are working on the case.
- The litigation is vigorously contested and is likely to run for years.
- You have to fund it yourself.

The claim that the lawyers were only interested in the money was reminiscent of the mining industry's attempt to stigmatize landowners in Papua New Guinea as greedy and corrupt.

From day one, the lawsuit against BHP earned regular headlines in the business section of Australian newspapers. Given the close association of the mining industry with Australian national identity (D. B. Rose 1999), the story received considerably more attention from the media than comparable lawsuits in the United States (fig. 8). On television, the Australian version of the news show *Sixty Minutes,* the investigative news program *Four Corners,* and a popular Friday evening comedy show all addressed the Ok Tedi case. The media coverage often portrayed the case as a modern-day struggle between David and Goliath (Banks and Ballard 1997b; Filer 1997b; Jackson 1998). Images broadcast of the polluted Ok Tedi River on Australian television were especially compelling.

FIGURE 8. "It's Chirac . . . protesting at our polluting the South Pacific . . ." Editorial cartoon from the *Sydney Morning Herald* linking pollution from the Ok Tedi mine to Australian concerns about President Jacques Chirac's plan to resume testing nuclear weapons in Mururoa Atoll, French Polynesia. September 26, 1995. Courtesy of Alan Moir.

Negative publicity from the case led BHP to sponsor its own media campaign on the Ok Tedi mine in September and October 1995 (BHP 1995a, 1995b, 1995c). BHP emphasized the social benefits of "improved health, education and infrastructure for the local people," even though these benefits are disproportionately enjoyed by the relatively small number of people who live near the mining township of Tabubil rather than the people living downstream from the mine. The ads also sought to naturalize the impact of the mine by arguing that the tailings discharged into the Ok Tedi River were "virtually identical" to the material already in the river system. It conservatively estimated that only "20 km of the 100 km river system" had been affected. It optimistically claimed that eventually "the river should revert to its natural condition" and that "fish numbers seem to be increasing again" (Cannon 1998, 254). In a television commercial that included images of children laughing, Kipling Uiari was shown saying, "We would rather have [economic] growth, send our kids to school, have the health facilities" (Cannon 1998, 254). The written materials from the mining company concluded: "Ok Tedi is helping our children grow up in a better world" (BHP 1995b).

However, the mining company was unable to persuade the Australian public to accept the kind of economic trade-offs that allowed the Ok Tedi mine to discharge millions of tons of tailings into the river system, which not only had negative environmental impacts but also disrupted the lives and livelihoods of thousands of indigenous peoples. It took BHP several years to realize that the Ok Tedi mine was irrevocably associated not only with environmental disaster but also with corporate indifference to the plight of the people living downstream from the mine.

During the early phase of litigation, both BHP and Slater & Gordon sought expert advice from social scientists who previously worked in the region. Richard Jackson, a regular consultant for the mining industry and the author of a book on the Ok Tedi mine (Jackson 1982), and Ron Brunton, an Australian anthropologist known in part for his conservative political views, agreed to work with BHP. I began working with Slater & Gordon after meeting Nick Styant-Browne and John Gordon during their 1994 visit to the United States. None of the other anthropologists with relevant ethnographic knowledge participated in the case, although several of the anthropologists who previously conducted social impact studies commissioned by Ok Tedi Mining Ltd. remained in contact with the mining company during the initial years of litigation.

Slater & Gordon sought to increase pressure on BHP by bringing notice of the case to other locations where BHP operated or had potential interests. At the invitation of the Dene First Nation in Canada's Northwest Territories, Nick Styant-Browne accompanied Alex Maun on a trip to Yellowknife in February 1996 to testify at public hearings concerning BHP's bid to acquire a billion-dollar diamond concession. Kipling Uiari from BHP and Ian Wood, the manager for the environment at the Ok Tedi mine, arrived a few days later to rebut Maun's testimony. Environmentalists also helped to deter the prospect of a new BHP copper mine in the Caribbean island of Dominica by disseminating information about the company's track record in Papua New Guinea (R. Nader 1996). Meetings were arranged with the owners of a copper smelter in Japan to request that they seek an alternative source of raw material and stop importing copper from the Ok Tedi mine. These initiatives ratcheted up the international pressure on BHP and dramatically increased the cost of the litigation to them.

Slater & Gordon also established back-channel communication with members of the Papua New Guinea government. Given the doctrine of sovereign immunity, the state was not a party to the case, despite being a shareholder in the mine.[6] Lawyers from Slater & Gordon sought support from the PNG government for an amicable settlement, meeting with several government ministers, including the minister for the environment, Parry Zeipi, who was from the Suki area in the South Fly.

With the exception of Zeipi, long an outspoken critic of the Ok Tedi mine, the dominant political opinion in Parliament was that the legal action in Australia violated that state's sovereign right to manage its own national resources. This perspective was articulated most forcefully by the prime minister, Julius Chan, during a speech to an Australian audience in which he criticized those persons "who presume to tell the people of Papua New Guinea how to run their country" (Baker 1996, 50). The prime minister argued that Western countries had achieved their long life expectancies "by centuries of raping their forests and polluting their Rhines, their Thameses, and their Murray-Darling river systems to the brink of extinction." For Papua New Guineans to live as long as Australians, he continued, "We must exploit our forests and our minerals and fisheries just as your forefathers did" (Baker 1996, 50). Papua New Guinea was under economic stress due to the 1989 closure of the Panguna copper mine in Bougainville, which had been responsible for 16 percent of the country's earnings, and was consequently willing to fight even harder to ensure continued access to revenue from the Ok Tedi mine by avoiding costly expenditures on environmental controls, a key issue in the case.

PROPERTY AND SUBSISTENCE

The major claims and allegations in the Dagi proceedings included the following:

1. Dagi (and other members of the Miripki clan)
   a. are the possessors and occupiers of land adjacent to the Ok Tedi River;
   b. are the owners of the land;
   c. are riparian proprietors by custom and/or entitled to the use of water from the river and surrounding floodplains; and
   d. live on the land and floodplains and traditionally use the water from the river and floodplains.
2. BHP and OTML, as owners and operators of the Ok Tedi mine, have knowingly breached duties of care owed to Dagi (and others) by
   a. polluting and contaminating the Ok Tedi River, land, and floodplains;
   b. disposing of waste products so as to interfere with the use of the river, land, and floodplains;

    c. causing the waters to become detrimental to the health, safety, and welfare of Dagi (and others) who traditionally rely thereon; and

    d. interfering with the said possession, occupation, use, enjoyment, ownership, and customary rights of Dagi (and others).

3. By reason of those breaches, Dagi (and others) suffered loss and damage, including

    a. flooding and degradation of land used for gardens;

    b. loss of soil due to erosion;

    c. disturbance of local creeks and sago swamps;

    d. reduced levels of fish and animals as food sources.

Although BHP did not contest hearing the case in Melbourne, it did challenge the court's jurisdiction over the statement of claims.[7] Lawyers for BHP invoked the nineteenth-century Moçambique principle, which prohibits a court from adjudicating a cause of action relating to land or other immovable property located in another jurisdiction (Gordon 1997, 153). This threatened the legal proceedings, which were based on claims that Rex Dagi and the other members of Miripki clan are the "owners of the land" and consequently suffered loss and damages as property owners.

Ethnographic information proved crucial to resolving the impasse, as land ownership was not the most salient variable in the case. Only a fraction of the people impacted by pollution from the mine own land in the affected areas. The Yonggom recognize two categories of rights with respect to land. Landowners are known as *ambip kin yariman,* "the persons responsible for the land."[8] Most of the villages along the Ok Tedi River were established in the 1970s. People moved there from smaller, lineage-based settlements located closer to the Indonesian border. The migrants were granted use rights to the land along the river by its owners. They are known as *animan od yi karup,* "the people who obtain food *(animan)* and wealth *(od)* from the land." Both the landowners and the migrants make use of resources affected by pollution from the mine, which deprives them of access to the subsistence resources they need to survive.

In response to BHP's challenge of the original writ, which relied on claims about property ownership, Slater & Gordon reformulated their case to claim damages from the Ok Tedi mine on local subsistence practices. New writs were filed for Alex Maun and Gabia Gagarimabu that claimed negligence and loss of amenity as a consequence of being deprived of their subsistence rights by pollution discharged by the mine. The new claim was argued by Julian Burnside, QC, on October 24, 1995.

> What distinguishes these claims from the usual claims that come before courts is that these plaintiffs are people who live a subsistence lifestyle. They live substantially, if not entirely, outside the economic system which uses money as the medium of exchange. But to say that does not alter the fact that if they are deprived of the very things which support their existence, they suffer loss. Of course it is a loss which appears in an uncommon guise because typically the courts have dealt with claims that are rooted in a society's adherence to the monetary medium of exchange. . . . It simply cannot be right that because people exist outside the ordinary economic system, they therefore do not have rights where their lives are damaged by the negligence of others. (Supreme Court of Victoria 1995, 59)

Burnside countered BHP's argument that the villagers had not suffered economic loss because their subsistence practices were not part of the formal cash economy.

> Now, the lifestyle of the Papua New Guinea natives in gathering food, fishing and game and the like and using it to eat or sell is no less an economic activity because it is not translated through the medium of money. It is economic loss to be deprived of your source of food, and it doesn't matter whether you are deprived of it because somebody takes away your abilities to pay for it or hunt for it or because they kill it before you can hunt for it. It is all ultimately economic loss, whether measured in money or not. What Mr. Myers [for BHP] says really precedes from the unstated assumption that a thing is only economic if it is passed through the system of monetary exchange, and there is simply no reason in theory or in law for that to be so. (Supreme Court of Victoria 1995, 60)

Burnside continued, questioning the equity of excluding certain claims from consideration simply because the plaintiffs participate in a different kind of economic system:

> The question is: can it fairly be said that you haven't been damaged if you are a subsistence dweller whose lifestyle is destroyed, where in the same circumstance a person who deals in the money economy would be able to prove damage on identical facts? It is just unthinkable. The notion of damage is not confined to those who deal in the orthodox money economy, and the notion of economy isn't confined to money. (Supreme Court of Victoria 1995, 62)

Justice Byrne replied to Burnside, conveying his reluctance to break new legal ground in the proceeding:

> Well, until very recently that argument would have been addressed and rejected by counsel saying, well, economic loss should be the subject of a

claim and that loss in negligence should not be limited to property damage or personal injury damage. The law has to draw lines, doesn't it? It may well be that this is where the line is drawn. (Supreme Court of Victoria 1995, 62–63)

Burnside responded, pressing his claim on the judge:

With respect, Your Honour, we would find it surprising if the law drew the line in such a way that the same facts giving rise to the same consequences was actionable or not depending on whether the person who suffers participates in a money economy or is a subsistence dweller on the other hand. It would be a distinction which the law would strain against, in our submission. (Supreme Court of Victoria 1995, 64)

Burnside went on to acknowledge the novelty of the claim and the absence of a legal precedent for treating subsistence rights as analogous to property rights. He emphasized the historical nature of the question, suggesting that colonialism may be characterized in part by the inability or refusal to recognize indigenous property rights (see McLaren et al. 2005; Pocock 1992; Rose 1994), echoing important debates in Australia at the time concerning Aboriginal land rights.[9] The debate about jurisdiction and the fate of the case depended on convincing the judge to recognize the subsistence rights of the plaintiffs. Burnside argued:

Now, you say is there any authority on it? The short answer is no, not that we are aware of, and that is not very surprising because for a long time, for practical reasons, people who don't participate in the money economy have not had the practical ability to vindicate their rights in court, and so it is a relatively rare occurrence, and one which is not welcomed by BHP. That people who operate outside the money system do try to assert their rights, and they should not be less entitled to assert them simply because they don't use money as the medium of exchange or the foundation of their lives. (Supreme Court of Victoria 1995, 63)

Finally, in his judgment of November 10, 1995, Judge Byrne ruled positively on the question of subsistence rights.

It was said that to restrict the duty of care to cases of pure economic loss would be to deny a remedy to those whose life is substantially, if not entirely, outside an economic system which uses money as a medium of exchange. It was put that, in the case of subsistence dwellers, loss of the things necessary for subsistence may be seen as akin to economic loss. If the plaintiffs are unable or less able to have or enjoy those things which are necessary for their subsistence as a result of the defendants' negligent conduct of the mine, they must look elsewhere for them, perhaps to obtain them by purchase or barter or perhaps to obtain some substitute. . . .

It is sufficient that I conclude, as I do, that, on the facts alleged in the October proposed Statements of Claim in each of the proceedings, the plaintiffs' cases are not so clearly untenable that they cannot possibly give rise to a cause of action in negligence. (Byrne 1995, 16–17)

The decision affirmed the right of the Alex Maun, Gabia Gagarimabu, and Rex Dagi (in a revised statement of claim) to continue their action against BHP for negligence, public nuisance, and loss of amenity. It established an important legal precedent for both the subsistence rights of indigenous peoples, confirming the commensurability of subsistence rights and the economic rights associated with property ownership. It also concluded that a corporation that deprives others of their subsistence rights may be held accountable by the law.

In addition to challenging the jurisdiction of the Supreme Court of Victoria, BHP asked the court to require the villagers or their lawyers to pay into the court sufficient funds to cover the costs of the case should it fail; judgment on the motion was deferred. Finally, the judge decided in November 1995 that while the court possessed jurisdiction to impose an injunction on the mine from discharging tailings into the river system, it lacked jurisdiction to impose a specific remedy, such as compelling OTML to construct a tailings dam.

STATE OF OPPOSITION

The Papua New Guinea government also sought to stop the Australian legal proceedings, which it viewed as an infringement on state sovereignty. Lawyers for BHP helped the PNG Parliament draft legislation to unilaterally settle the outstanding claims against OTML by paying K110 million in compensation to the downstream landowners.[10] The value of the compensation package was established by the managing director of OTML based on his estimation of what the company could afford (John Grub, pers. comm. 1996). The bill was presented to the Parliament as the eighth in a series of agreements between the state, BHP, and OTML. However, the proposed Eighth Supplemental Agreement was hardly an olive branch to the 30,000 plaintiffs; it also criminalized their participation in the Australian legal proceedings. It would impose fines of up to K100,000 or a five-year prison term for anyone participating in the litigation against BHP, plus additional fines of K10,000 for every day the legal action continued (Papua New Guinea 1995a). These penalties extended to all persons who provided assistance or evidence in the legal proceedings against the mine. The bill also prohibited additional litigation against the mine concerning damages, compensation, or any other claims resulting from its operation. Further, it prohibited any challenge to the Eighth Supplemental Agreement that claimed that its provisions were unconstitutional, and it applied the same penalties to this offense.

The proposed legislation was widely condemned, including criticism from the International Commission of Jurists and the Council for Civil Liberties (Gordon 1997, 158). When Slater & Gordon received a copy of the agreement, John Gordon recognized that the word-processing code on the document belonged to Allens Arthur Robinson, the lawyers representing BHP. In presenting this information to the Supreme Court of Victoria, Julian Burnside QC argued that BHP sought to deny his clients their legal rights by criminalizing their access to the court. The prime minister of Papua New Guinea was forced to acknowledge on August 17, 1995, that BHP's lawyers had prepared the legislation (Cannon 1998, 252). On September 15, Slater & Gordon introduced a formal motion against BHP for contempt of court, which resulted in a ruling on September 19 that BHP "had interfered with the administration of justice by cooperating with the PNG government in drafting its legislation barring villagers from access to foreign courts" (Cannon 1998, 252). BHP's actions were found to be in contempt of court, although the conviction was subsequently overturned on technical grounds (Cannon 1998, 252). The finding of contempt raised the profile of the case to another level.[11]

Following the citation for contempt, BHP issued an apology and advised the prime minister of Papua New Guinea that it was no longer able to consent to the agreement (Gordon 1997, 159). The Papua New Guinea government wasted little time in reissuing the bill, dividing it in two. The Mining (Ok Tedi Restated Eighth Supplemental Agreement) Act of 1995, between the Independent State of Papua New Guinea, OTML, and BHP, addressed the question of compensation. It established a general fund of K110 million for the people impacted by the mine, including back-payments of K15 million to the affected landowners and a minimum of K4 million per year in payments for the remainder of the mine life.[12] However, the revised agreement forced the thirty thousand plaintiffs to choose between monetary compensation and continued participation in the Australian legal proceedings.

Ok Tedi Mining Ltd. promoted the bill with a full-page newspaper advertisement claiming that the agreement protected their "rights to compensation for direct economic loss" by providing "a choice between two new systems of compensation," referring to the payment of general compensation by OTML or the filing of individual claims through the PNG courts. The advertisement also indicated that the plaintiffs could continue to pursue compensation in the Australian courts even "though it may take years before there are any results, and the result may not be what people want." However, the claim that their access to the courts in Australia was protected turned out to be false when the Parliament subsequently passed a second bill criminalizing participation in foreign legal proceedings. The ad also claimed that the mining company "supported a government proposal for an independent inquiry into disposal of tailings from the mine" and that "the company has also made a commitment to reduce the environmental impact of sediment on the river," but offered no concrete guarantees that anything would be done. Finally, the mining company acknowledged that the payment of general compensation could be reduced by the cost of any new spending on tailings containment (OTML 1995).

There was vigorous debate in the PNG Parliament about the restated eighth supplemental agreement, which one member of Parliament initially identified as the bill "drafted by BHP" (Papua New Guinea 1995a, 25). Several MPs were concerned that the agreement did not address tailings containment, although the sponsor of the bill indicated that OTML had expressed its willingness to address the issue separately. Other MPs made reference to mining projects in their own districts and wanted the Parliament to devise a general solution to the question of compensation. They also expressed concerns about the environmental impacts of mining, oil, and gas projects in Papua New Guinea, given the country's dependence on resource extraction. But there was general support for separating the provision of compensation to the people living downstream from the Ok Tedi mine, which was seen to be urgent and desirable, from the larger and more complex question of reducing environmental impacts. Several of the MPs raised concerns about the relatively low value of the compensation payments, which, after being divided up among the number of people affected by the mine, amounted to annual payments of only K125 ($95) per person. But other MPs pointed out that the total value of the compensation package was larger than any other group in Papua New Guinea had received (Papua New Guinea 1995b).

In their discussion of the restated eighth supplemental agreement, several of the MPs observed that the Australian court case infringed on the sovereignty of Papua New Guinea. The prime minister objected to decisions about compensation being made by the courts in Australia, the former colonial power, asking, "If we allow that, we will lose our sovereignty. What is the use of having independence?" (Papua New Guinea 1995a, 37). However, another MP disagreed, arguing that since the problems were caused by an Australian company, it was appropriate for the Australian courts to intervene. Even though several MPs declared their opposition to the bill, and others expressed reservations, the Restated Eighth Supplemental Agreement received overwhelming support, passing sixty to two (Papua New Guinea 1995b, 34).

The second piece of legislation was the Compensation (Prohibition of Foreign Legal Proceedings) Act of 1995. It prohibited "the taking or pursuing in foreign courts of legal proceedings in relation to compensation claims arising from mining projects and petroleum projects in Papua New Guinea" (Papua New Guinea 1995d, 1). The Individual and Community Rights Advocacy Forum published a full-page critique of the act in the *National* that identified ten reasons why members of Parliament should vote against it (ICRAF 1995). The ad pointed out that the bill has "no provision to stop pollution," that it "does not allow fair and just determination of compensation claims," that it criminalizes landowners "whose environment and livelihood has been destroyed or severely affected by companies involved in resource extraction when they take their claims to court," and that it leaves these landowners "defenseless against big companies who make profits at the expense of the environment and peoples' livelihood." The ad also noted that the bill "sets a dangerous precedent" and that members of Parliament could "one day face similar problems in their own districts" (ICRAF 1995).

On December 15, the Compensation (Prohibition of Foreign Legal Proceedings) Act of 1995 was brought to a vote.[13] In addition to restoring some of the criminal penalties against participants in foreign legal proceedings, it also sought to render judgments in foreign courts unenforceable in Papua New Guinea. The legislation passed in a close vote. Under the terms of the act, the plaintiffs had sixty days to withdraw from the Australian proceedings or face criminal charges. Rex Dagi immediately issued a press release saying that he would not be deterred by the proposed legislation and was ready to go to jail for the case. After an appeal from the Australian foreign minister, Gareth Evans, the PNG government agreed to defer gazettal of the legislation (Cannon 1998, 255). When Evans fell from power, however, along with the Keating Labor government, the new Liberal foreign minister, Alexander Downer, withdrew Australia's objection to the bill, concluding, "In the final analysis, the

PNG Parliament has the sovereign right to decide what law should be applied to PNG citizens and activities within its borders" (cited in Cannon 1998, 256). The legislation subsequently came into effect on April 11, 1996, although Slater & Gordon immediately filed a constitutional challenge to the bill in the Papua New Guinea Supreme Court.

Meanwhile, the Papua New Guinea government began to exert pressure on the lead plaintiffs to drop the case. While on their way to Australia to consult with their lawyers, Rex Dagi, Alex Maun, Dair Gabara, and Gabia Gagarimabu were pulled aside at Jacksons International Airport in Port Moresby and encouraged to abandon their case in Melbourne. They were told that the K110 million in compensation would be paid only if Slater & Gordon were excluded from the settlement. Recognizing that the case was in jeopardy, Slater & Gordon chartered a plane to bring the plaintiffs to Australia, where, several days later, they filed another claim, charging BHP with contempt of court for using "threats and improper inducements" to deny Dagi and Maun access to their lawyers (Cannon 1998, 255).[14]

SETTLEMENT

By April 1996, BHP had begun to make compensation payments to the people living along the Ok Tedi and Fly Rivers who opted out of the Australian legal proceedings under the Restated Eighth Supplemental Agreement. Slater & Gordon was managing multiple writs, injunctions, constitutional challenges, and contempt and conspiracy proceedings against BHP in both PNG and Australia. Both John Gordon and Nick Styant-Browne had been detained at Jacksons International Airport in Port Moresby and prevented from entering the country. The firm was running low on cash and concerned about additional defections of its plaintiffs.

Down the street, at BHP headquarters, the company was facing pressure from the legal proceedings, on which they were spending several million dollars a month. They had been battered by the media and in public opinion and were receiving unwelcome scrutiny of their international operations. They faced another round of contempt and conspiracy charges, allegations that a number of BHP directors and officers found deeply troubling (Cannon 1998, 257). According to veteran PNG correspondent Rowan Callick (1996), "BHP had little choice but to settle." The company had "underestimated the impact of the action on BHP's public profile" (Hextall 1996) and "could not contemplate a 15-year mine life of constant litigation and argument" (Callick 1996).

The constitutional challenge to the PNG Compensation (Prohibition of Foreign Legal Proceedings) Act of 1995 was scheduled for June 24 in Port Moresby. But in early June, Jerry Ellis, head of BHP Minerals, decided to settle the case, reportedly instructing his lawyers to "fucking fix it" before kicking over a chair and storming out of the room.[15] According to Nick Styant-Browne, once BHP agreed to settle the case, they were "not to be diverted." Toward the end, after negotiating for twenty-seven hours straight, Styant-Browne broke off the talks. But after a late-night phone call from BHP's lawyers, the terms of the settlement were agreed upon, and the document was signed the following morning at Styant-Browne's house in Melbourne. The settlement was released to the public on June 11, 1996. As part of the settlement, all of the remaining proceedings in Melbourne and Port Moresby were withdrawn, including the contempt and conspiracy hearings and the constitutional challenge to the prohibition of foreign legal proceedings.

The settlement augmented the earlier agreement between the PNG state, BHP, and OTML to pay K110 million in compensation to the people affected by pollution from the mine.[16] Another K40 million was earmarked for the communities along the lower Ok Tedi River, where the damage was the greatest, including the Yonggom villages of Iogi and Ieran, where Rex Dagi and Alex Maun grew up, and Dome, where I lived from 1987 to 1989.[17] All of these payments were now guaranteed by BHP (rather than just OTML) and could no longer be reduced by expenditures on tailings containment. The government of Papua New Guinea also agreed to acquire a ten percent equity share in the mine on behalf of Western Province. The centerpiece of the settlement was BHP's agreement to implement the most viable tailings containment option as determined by studies to be carried out by the mining company and approved by the government in an independent inquiry. The most promising option at the time of the settlement was held to be a pipeline—at an estimated cost of $350 million—to transport tailings to a lowland storage facility.[18] The settlement included A$7.6 million in legal costs and fees paid directly by BHP.[19] The total value of the settlement was estimated at $500 million in compensation and commitments to tailings containment (Tait 1996, 19).

The settlement was widely hailed as a great success for the plaintiffs and a strong reproach to the mining industry. Writing under the headline "Ok Tedi Win for Villagers and a Lesson for All Miners" in the *Australian Financial Review*, Callick (1996) opined, "The Ok Tedi case is not over. It will remain a watershed in corporate dealings with developing countries. . . . Every other mining company operating, exploring, or considering investing in PNG and other developing countries will also have built files on Ok Tedi." He also highlighted the role played by environmentalists in the case: "And the reach of the anti–Ok Tedi lobby—as far as Canada's Yellowknife, where BHP is establishing a diamond mine—demonstrates the globalization of the environment movement" (Callick 1996).

The NGO community concurred in its judgment of the settlement. A media release from the Australian Conservation Foundation, which played an important role in critically asserting the Ok Tedi mine's impact on the environment, announced, "We believe this is a lesson for all Australian mining companies operating overseas that they are not 'out of sight, out of mind.' . . . BHP has suffered much damage to its reputation by initially defending its practices at Ok Tedi. The message for all mining companies is: *No More Ok Tedis*" (Krockenberger 1996; emphasis in original).

The settlement also raised a red flag for the mining industry. Rio Tinto was apparently furious with BHP's decision to settle out of court, out of concern that this would encourage additional litigation against the industry. Its fears were prescient, as the company subsequently became the target of legal action regarding the operation of its Panguna copper mine in Bougainville and its alleged misconduct during the island's decade of civil war. Gavin Murray and Ian Williams (1997, 99) from Placer Pacific Ltd., at that point the owner and operator of the Porgera gold mine in Papua New Guinea, characterized the industry response to the settlement as "disappointment, annoyance, and a feeling that BHP had let the industry down. There were concerns that such a compromise would open the floodgates to compensation through litigation and polarize community views on mining and its impact." They concluded:

> The Ok Tedi debate will be acknowledged as a major driver of change within the Australian mining industry. . . . While many critics would argue that a confrontation of this scale was required to bring the industry to its senses, some in the Australian minerals industry were already promoting the need for strategic repositioning. The Ok Tedi debate drew industry's attention to the need for change and therefore is now recognized as a major turning point in stimulating a strategic industry response to public opinion. (Murray and Williams 1997, 200)

Significantly, their statement focuses on corporate strategy and public relations rather than the need to alter the relationship between mining and its environmental impacts, perhaps by calling for new industry standards.

The Ok Tedi case is also frequently cited as an exemplar of international litigation against corporations, especially for extractive industry (e.g., Gao, Akpan, and Vanjik 2002; Prince and Nelson 1996). John Gordon emphasized the environmental aspect of the case in comments reported by the *Age:* "I think it's quite clear that multinational companies are to be measured in terms of their environmental standards by the same sorts of standards which prevail in their home country," and "I think it's fair to say that the attitude amongst the mining industry that you could get away with minimal environmental standards offshore is now a thing of the past" (Kaye 1996). In other words, the Ok Tedi case put the mining industry on notice that abiding by the laws of the host country may not be sufficient protection from criticism and that mining companies may face litigation in their home courts, where environmental standards are often higher.

As for BHP, its stocks climbed 16 cents to A$18.74 on news of the settlement (Trueman 1996, 32). The head of BHP Minerals, Jerry Ellis, described the lawsuit as a learning experience for the company. He argued that the settlement demonstrated BHP's willingness to accept responsibility for the project: "I think though in the longer term our ability to recognize that we have got things wrong and do something about it; the fact that we haven't quit; and the fact that this really is a very demanding project and *we don't propose to walk away from it or walk away from our obligations in respect of it,* might in the longer term be seen more positively" (Jamieson 1996, emphasis added). In hindsight, however, BHP's commitment to solving the environmental problems downstream from the Ok Tedi mine proved to be largely rhetorical.

COMMUNITY WRITS

At first, we didn't say anything to the company or the government.
We were worried about our gardens and the river,
but we had no idea how to fight against the mine,
because we are not educated people.

Initially, I questioned Rex and Alex:
"What are you going to do about our land and our river?"
I asked them that.
They answered me: "We'll take them to court."
So we really supported the lawsuit.

I was opposed to the government's attempt
to make us accept the [compensation package]
because of the damage to the environment.
We backed the lawsuit instead.

I'm very proud of the lawsuit and I praise Rex and Alex
for taking the matter to court and winning the case.

—Andok Yang, Dome Village, 1996

FIGURE 9. Slater & Gordon lawyer Ikenna Nwokolo looks on as a plaintiff in the first lawsuit against BHP signs the settlement agreement. July 18, 1996. Kiunga, Papua New Guinea. Photo: Stuart Kirsch.

In July 1996, I joined the lead plaintiffs and their legal representatives as they explained the terms of the settlement and collected signatures from clan representatives to approve the withdrawal of their legal action from the court (fig. 9). When Nick Styant-Browne presented the terms of the settlement to a large crowd in the town of Kiunga, he began by acknowledging that they had been fighting for much longer than the two years of the legal proceedings and praised their leaders for their role in the struggle. He described how they fought together against the many challenges they confronted along the way. He explained how the settlement represented negotiations with OTML and BHP, and that Rex Dagi, Alex Maun, Moses Oti, Robin Moken, Gabia Gagarimabu, and Dair Gabara all consented to the terms of the settlement. He thanked everyone for their patience and their trust.

Styant-Browne also summarized the major achievements of the settlement. The first was OTML's obligation to stop discharging tailings into the river, and he indicated that they must do so as soon as possible. He emphasized that this would be the first time a mining project in Papua New Guinea would not discharge tailings into rivers or the sea, and he credited their efforts for making this possible. He identified compensation as the second achievement, in particular BHP's guarantee of the

K110 million, which could no longer be reduced by expenditure on tailings containment, and the additional K40 million for the people living
on the lower Ok Tedi River, because they had suffered the most. He
explained that some of this money would be set aside for business development; some would be held in trust for the next generation; some
would be used to relocate their villages, if that was what people wanted;
and the remainder of the funds would be used to lease the dieback area
of the forest from its owners. He also announced that the ten percent
equity share in the mine would benefit everyone in Western Province,
the largest equity share held in trust for the local community by any
mining project in Papua New Guinea. Styant-Browne pointed out that
there was still a great deal of work to be done, including consultation
between OTML and local leaders to implement these agreements.
Finally, he announced that none of the legal costs for the case would
come from the landowners, but would be paid directly by BHP, which
received the largest applause of the afternoon. He emphasized, "this is
a great settlement," and he told them, "you should feel proud." He
concluded by thanking all of the people involved in the case. Turning to
Rex Dagi, he told the crowd, "Rex is a great leader," who always
cheered him up when he became discouraged by telling him, "Nick, it's
ok, we're going to win." To Alex Maun, he acknowledged, "We talk.
Sometimes we argue with each other. But after talking, we come to the
right decisions." He also thanked the other local leaders for their help
and support and for their participation in the case.

The questions from the audience in Kiunga were largely procedural
and focused on the financial aspects of the settlement agreement rather
than tailings containment. They asked questions about who should sign
the releases (everyone who signed the original agreement); whether
public servants would benefit from the settlement (yes, from the 10 percent equity share in the mine); how to ensure that the money would be
used appropriately (a committee composed of their leaders would negotiate with the mining company); how to ensure that the money would
be spent fairly (there would be an annual public accounting of expenditures); what would happen to the Restated Eighth Supplemental Agreement (part of the agreement was included in the settlement package);
and how the money for the lower Ok Tedi River would be spent (there
was still a lot of work to be done in deciding how to manage these
resources).

The team also traveled to the other urban areas and larger villages
where the plaintiffs resided. Styant-Browne returned to Australia, but

Ikenna Nwokolo from Slater & Gordon and Dair Gabara ably answered questions about the settlement. In the presentation at Kawok village on the Fly River, Gabara made the following observation: "We traveled to many countries and spoke to many NGOs to get their support. This case was not just fought in PNG and Melbourne, it was fought all over the world, and so we would like to thank them for their contributions." He also described the sacrifices they had made: "I have resigned from the government. . . . I did not think about my three children and their mother, but I was thinking of you people." About their relationship to the mining company, Gabara added, "The manager of OTML has written to tell us that his doors are open. We will work together to ensure that the benefits will be delivered. We are no longer enemies."

In Atkamba on the lower Ok Tedi River, the village councilor addressed the team: "When the case started in 1994, we didn't know whether we would win or lose. Now it is 1996 and we won the case. OTML didn't listen to us. The government didn't listen to us. BHP was corrupt and so was the government. But we had a good plan. They offered us K110 million, but they were playing politics.[20] They sought our approval of the [Restated] Eighth Supplemental Agreement, but we refused. They were tricking us, so we broke away. We didn't lose; we won the case.[21] After the agreement is signed, we can start to work."

During an emotional visit to Alex Maun's home village of Ieran on the Ok Tedi River, Maun described the relief he felt after presenting the agreement in Kiunga. He explained that the damage from the mine had first been felt by the people living in Ieran. Dair Gabara explained how he had been concerned that the kind of violent conflict that occurred in Bougainville could have happened on the Fly River, which is why he pushed Dagi and Maun to take the matter to court. Someone from the village commented, "We are a Christian community, so we have been praying for this case, and now our prayers are answered. My land and river have been destroyed; thank you for fighting hard on our behalf!" Another person from Ieran identified himself as one of the primary landowners from the village: "When our land and resources were destroyed, we were crying. But Rex and Alex took up our case." Because we were in his village, Maun thanked all of us for our contribution to the case. He singled out Gabia Gagarimabu, telling him, "Like an older brother, you kept me calm."

I looked forward to the meeting in Dome village, where I had lived for two years. However, Dome had been split by the decision whether to accept compensation through the Restated Eighth Supplemental

Agreement, even though this meant that some of them had opted out of the lawsuit. Rex Dagi spoke first in a mixture of Yonggom, Papua New Guinea Tok Pisin, and English:

Nup ku kanaka ban, nup ku bot-korokman.
The Ok Tedi is our life.
Deri ku moraron kowe ye pay geran.
Inamen mimo ambagiwen.[22]

We're not backward, we're determined.
The Ok Tedi is our life.
The Ok Tedi River is polluted, so [the company] must pay.
We worked together as one.

We received compliments and thanks for our efforts. But people were skeptical of the mining company's commitment to follow through on its obligations. At Dome, someone asked, "What happened to the $4 billion [in compensation] mentioned in the media?" Dair Gabara responded, "That figure was not brought to the courts; this was the best settlement that could be reached."

We were greeted by Rex Dagi's elderly aunt on our arrival to Ambaga village, west of the Ok Tedi River. She danced toward us carrying a stalk of bananas, singing, "You fed on this; you fed on bananas. From there, you went and helped us. Hallelujah!" She danced a circle around us several times, saying that she had prayed for the settlement, because of the difficult conditions there. Her gardens along the river had been destroyed, and she had to walk for several hours carrying her heavy string bag of produce back to the village. At the meeting in Ambaga, they thanked us for bringing them all together (*helpim mipela kamap wanbel* in Tok Pisin), which may have been a reference to the division caused by the Restated Eighth Supplemental Agreement, which split the plaintiffs in the lawsuit. One of the villagers stood up to tell us, "Thank you very much for your hard work; we fought this hardship for a long time. . . . God will bless you. As a spokesman and supporter of the lawsuit, I would like to thank you all." At Ningerum, where the road from Kiunga to the mining township of Tabubil crosses the Ok Tedi River, Dagi told them, "They told us we were crazy. They called us *bus kanakas* [backward], but . . . we beat Papua New Guinea. We won the struggle." Here Dagi was referring to the effort by the state to scuttle their court case in Melbourne.

We were also greeted with support in the Middle Fly. After the group presentations in Bosset, one of the Boazi leaders responded to our call for questions by saying, "Everything is clear. We don't have any questions. We want to sign." In nearby Kaviananga village at Obo station, the pastor presented the following blessing in Tok Pisin, "Thank you, God. You gave Rex Dagi the insight to help us. God, you were the one who put gold and silver and copper in the ground. They don't belong to us; they belong to you. We only use them. The Fly River doesn't belong to us; it belongs only to you."[23]

Dair Gabara spoke to the people in Kaviananga, saying, "You depend on the river for food, gardening, water, and washing, and these things have been destroyed. When someone destroys your property, you want to get it back to the way it should be. We chose the democratic way of acting. Going to court rather than fighting has worked for us. This was a politically sensitive case and we went through some hard times. . . . So it is a great victory for you and me." People responded by saying, "we understand" and "it's a good package." Others expressed concern about how the settlement might treat the landowners in the village differently from others who lived there but did not own land.

Finally, in the former provincial capital of Daru, an island west of the Fly River delta, we were greeted by the following words of welcome: "No man has the right to take away the environment of others. This was our objective: Let justice be done. . . . It will be remembered for many generations to come." Dair Gabara, who is from the area, responded, "We've been together, we've fought, we've sweated, and our families have suffered, but the reward we have achieved will benefit all of the people of Western Province. This has been a struggle for all of us; thank you for your patience and your trust."

AN INCOMPLETE VICTORY

Concerns about the terms of the settlement agreement were raised almost immediately after it was made public. Ralph Nader presciently warned that the agreement failed to guarantee that the necessary infrastructure for tailings containment would be constructed (R. Nader 1996). Nader (1996) also objected to the withdrawal of the constitutional challenge to the prohibition of foreign legal proceedings. Alex Maun, despite being one of the original signatories to the agreement, expressed similar concerns about the constitutional challenge. Maun also stressed the need for long-term economic development in contrast to short-term monetary compensation (Maun 1997, 11). I warned that OTML might delay the implementation of tailings containment by continuing to call for additional research and engineering studies, as they had in the past, or by hiding behind the government's reluctance to pay its share of the costs (Kirsch 1997b, 139). I expressed concern to Nick Styant-Browne that there were no provisions for settling disputes on the implementation of the settlement short of returning to court in Melbourne and suggested the need for intermediate mechanisms for arbitration. Finally, I also asked why the compensation agreements were indexed to the Papua New Guinea kina rather than being linked to the dollar, the currency in which copper and gold are traded. Styant-Browne explained that the Papua New Guinea government stipulated that the terms of the settlement had to be calculated in its national currency. The value of the kina had historically been kept artificially strong, but shifted to a floating exchange rate before the settlement. The kina subsequently declined to one-quarter of its previous exchange rate, greatly diminishing the value of the compensation payments.[24]

The lead plaintiffs also expressed ambivalence about the settlement process. Dair Gabara acknowledged that it had been difficult to convince the other plaintiffs that a settlement was in their best interest, because they wanted to face BHP directly in court. The plaintiffs recognized, however, that Slater & Gordon had done a good job representing their interests. They also realized that the case had to be settled out of court, because of the number of plaintiffs who opted out of the lawsuit in order to receive payments under the Restated Eighth Supplemental Agreement. However, they were upset about the pressure on them to sign the agreement on behalf of the other plaintiffs in the lawsuit, even though the settlement was not legally binding until the other plaintiffs signed the releases themselves. Some of their discomfort about settling the case might be compared to the feeling of "buyer's remorse" associated with making a large purchase, such as a house, when positive sentiments about the transaction are diminished by anxiety about whether one could have obtained a better deal. Alex Maun expressed his concerns to me this way: "Nick [Styant-Browne] goes away, but I am here all my life. The Yonggom are the ones who have to live with the deal."

The plaintiffs had other concerns about the settlement as well. Some people were critical of the settlement because the compensation fell far short of the original A$4 billion figure reported by the media. As Gabia Gagarimabu explained to me, "because their loss has been so catastrophic, they seek something that will change their lives again in an equally comprehensive way, not just small payments."[25] Given the high cost of commodities in Papua New Guinea, people living in the communities affected by the mine were dissatisfied with the size of the compensation payments, which averaged K125 (US$95) per person annually. Dagi and Maun decided to run for political office in the wake of the settlement and were upset when their opponents claimed that they had "lost the case," because the compensation payments were so low. Dagi and Maun had also solicited contributions from people to help cover their expenses during their campaign against the mine, both before and during the lawsuit, and were expected not only to reimburse their sponsors but also to reciprocate with an incrementally larger amount, which they were unable to do. Finally, Dagi and Maun were concerned that BHP and OTML would belittle them and thwart their requests during the implementation of the settlement. They thought that having the court in Melbourne as the ultimate sanction was insufficient and sought additional support in negotiating with OTML.

Other problems emerged during the implementation of the settlement. The plaintiffs were concerned when the specific compensation payments, which were based on a combination of factors, including forest dieback area and population size, were higher for one village than another, generating resentment. Some of the villages that participated in the campaign or contributed to its expenses were now categorized as outside of the impact zone and therefore ineligible for compensation. The lawyers for BHP initially wanted to restrict the compensation payments to landowners, even though the case focused on subsistence practices rather than property—although eventually it was agreed that everyone affected by pollution would receive compensation from the mine. There were also disputes about whether people who held land rights in the village but no longer lived there were entitled to compensation. Ultimately, this dilemma was resolved by allowing each community to decide how the compensation would be divided, a culturally appropriate solution, given that land rights in Papua New Guinea must be maintained through exchange relations (Gewertz and Errington 1991). Nonetheless, there was considerable tension in the villages as people fought over the distribution of compensation.

These problems frustrated the former plaintiffs, who sometimes felt abandoned by Slater & Gordon in their dealings with OMTL. In 1998 Alex Maun called a press conference at which he announced his intention to "rewind the case" and return to the courts. Gagarimabu expressed similar frustrations at the time, telling me that "the lawyers told us lies, fooled us, took the money and ran away; we were cheated by the lawyers." Such frustrations may not be uncommon in dealings with lawyers, who move on to their next case after a settlement. There was also residual anger among the plaintiffs regarding the withdrawal of the challenge to the prohibition of foreign legal proceedings, as stipulated by the settlement agreement, which they felt had deprived them of an important right. Slater & Gordon, however, continued to monitor the implementation of the settlement, even though they were not involved in the day-to-day negotiations.

There were also rising concerns about the failure to advance toward a solution to the environmental problems caused by the mine. The initial step taken by OTML was to install a dredge in the lower Ok Tedi River, which helped to lower the riverbed and reduce flooding into the surrounding forest. However, the dredge removed less than half of the tailings discharged into the river every day, and only 20 percent of the total volume of waste material entering the river system. Nor did it reduce the volume of tailings and other mine wastes already in the river system. OTML also commissioned a series of waste management studies intended to determine how best to manage tailings disposal. The completion of these studies was delayed by the year-long El Niño weather cycle, which resulted in droughts across Western Province and generated false expectations for the recovery of the deforested areas. When the rains finally returned, overbank flooding and forest dieback continued as before. New concerns about acid mine drainage emerged as the portion of the ore body being mined had higher levels of pyrites, which oxidize into sulfuric acid. OTML began to mix limestone with the tailings to buffer their acid-generating potential. This caused the river to change color again, from muddy brown to gray.

By 1998 the damage along the Ok Tedi River was so great that many people living there concluded that it was "too late to save the river." "Even if they build the pipeline," I was told in Dome village, "it will take two or three years, and the damage will continue." In 1998 the projected closure date for the mine was 2010, leading people from the Ok Tedi River to question the value of additional investment in environmental controls. For them, the rationale for protecting the river was no longer valid: "What is growing there now: pitpit, elephant grass, softwood trees. Why protect them? They can grow anywhere. If we were talking about [hardwood] forest and wildlife, that would be different. But now? It's not worth protecting what is there."[26] However, these comments failed to take the larger picture into account, that the problems they faced would continue to spread downstream unless they were able to stop the mine from discharging tailings into the river system.

The lead plaintiffs in the lawsuit against the Ok Tedi mine had largely given up on the settlement by 1998. Despite their frustration with Slater & Gordon, they wanted to return to court to enforce the original agreement. Two years had passed since the settlement and the mining company had not produced the required reports on waste management. The delay was attributed to the El Niño event, even though the company already had two decades of environmental data to work with.

The preliminary results from OTML's waste management studies were finally announced in June 1999, three years after the out-of-court settlement. OTML (1999) reported that the impacts of the mine would be "significantly greater than expected in earlier studies." The release of the final reports, in August 1999, generated a firestorm of controversy. BHP began to distance itself from the Ok Tedi mine, indicating that the project was "incompatible with its environmental values" (Barker and Oldfield 1999). The reports, which I discuss in more detail in chapter 4, concluded that none of the proposed strategies for tailings containment would substantially mitigate the environmental impact of the mine. These conclusions were subsequently challenged by the World Bank (2000), which concluded that the mining company reports were more concerned with the risks to investors than to the PNG state or the environment. The peer review group assembled by the mine also argued that the corporate reports systematically underestimated the environmental benefits of potential intervention strategies (Chapman et al. 2000, 14–15).

By 2000 it had become clear that BHP and OTML had no intention of making the additional investment required for tailings containment as stipulated by the 1996 settlement. Under the provisions of that agreement, the only way to challenge BHP's inertia was to return to the Supreme Court of Victoria in Melbourne. On April 11, 2000, the plaintiffs returned to court.

SUING BHP, TAKE TWO

The 2000 lawsuit charged BHP with breach of contract. The goal was to enforce implementation of tailings mitigation. At issue was whether BHP had complied with the terms of the 1996 settlement agreement, which required the company to "commit as soon as practicable to the implementation of any tailings option recommended by the independent enquiry or review to be conducted by the State (the tailings option) providing BHP bona fide considers that option to be economically and technically feasible" (Ok Tedi Settlement Agreement 1996; reproduced in Banks and Ballard 1997a, appendix 1, 216–17).[27] The plaintiffs needed to demonstrate that BHP had either prevented or interfered with the government's conduct of the appropriate inquiry, or if such an inquiry had taken place, that BHP ignored its findings.

There was widespread support among the plaintiffs for the new proceedings, which also sought additional damages resulting from the mining company's failure to stop discharging tailings into the river system. The new writs represented forty-six thousand people, including plaintiffs in areas recently affected by pollution from the mine. The proceedings were organized according to new provisions for class actions in the Australian state of Victoria. Gabia Gagarimabu, who had been elected to the PNG Parliament after the first case, was chosen as the representative plaintiff for the case.

The second case had a very different feeling than the first. Instead of charging ahead with bravado, as they had done in 1994, Slater & Gordon reluctantly returned to court out of professional responsibility to their clients.[28] Both John Gordon and Nick Styant-Browne left the firm during the course of the second lawsuit, turning over its prosecution to colleagues who lacked their passion and experience. BHP may still have been licking its wounds from the first case, but its lawyers seemed keen to avenge their earlier loss. BHP had learned from what had worked in the first case, notably the offer of additional compensation to reduce the number of plaintiffs. They also continued to challenge the legitimacy of the legal proceedings, this time by questioning whether it was possible to adequately inform plaintiffs living in remote villages about the case—although that motion was not favorably received by the court, which objected to its undemocratic implications. But most importantly, BHP eventually recognized that the case presented them with a double bind: even a finding that they had not violated the settlement agreement would not convince the pubic that the company had done everything in its power to solve the environmental problems downstream from the mine. Consequently, the legal action played a key role in accelerating and helping to define the terms of BHP's subsequent exit from the mine.

THE COMMUNITY MINE CONTINUATION AGREEMENTS

Soon after the plaintiffs returned to court in 2000, OTML offered additional compensation to the people affected by the mine in return for their commitment not to disrupt its operation. The public rationale for the Community Mine Continuation Agreements, or CMCAs, was to allow the people living along the polluted river corridor to decide whether the mine should continue to operate. This was in keeping with the PNG government's perspective on the future of the Ok Tedi mine: "The National Government wants the people to have a voice in the decision about the future of the mine, and their future. The Government's first objective is to ensure that people are properly informed about the advantages and disadvantages to them of mine continuation and mine closure" (Letter from the Office of the Minister for Mining to the Presidents, Councilors and Village leaders in Western Province, February 15, 2000).

The language of political choice, however, can be used to mask dilemmas in which people lack desirable options. In this case, the people affected by the Ok Tedi mine were being asked to choose between being poisoned and being poor.

The third option available to the people living downstream from the Ok Tedi mine—to continue their court case against BHP and OTML in Melbourne, with the objective of stopping the mine from discharging tailings into the river—was excluded by the CMCAs, although this was not always made clear to the signatories. However, once the documents were signed, OTML told people they were not permitted to "stay in two canoes," and that signing the CMCAs meant they had to opt out of the legal proceedings. Thus the CMCAs replicated the company's strategy in the first court case: offering compensation in return for opting out of the litigation.

The manner in which people were asked to commit to the CMCAs was also problematic in two other ways. The documents authorized any "person representing or purporting to represent a Community or clan" to bind its members to the agreement "notwithstanding . . . that there is no express authority for that person to sign or execute the Community Mine Continuation Agreement on behalf of the members of the Community or clan concerned." This means that an individual could legally obligate the other members of the village or community to the agreement without having secured their consent. It deprived them of the right to object to the agreements, and it committed the members of future generations to the agreements as well. An independent study of the CMCA process by Oxfam Community Aid Abroad (Australia) concluded that the process was incompatible with the principle of prior, informed consent, given that there was only "partial or selective" disclosure of information and that the provisions of the act concerning the binding of multiple persons through a single signature "are inconsistent with the notion of prior informed consent," which is, by definition, an individual or personal matter (Kalinoe 2003, 41, 42).

Slater & Gordon moved to challenge the CMCAs in court and asked me to compose an affidavit addressing my views on their legitimacy. I argued that because the CMCAs are fundamentally concerned with environmental impacts, they must comply with customary land rights, which are protected by law in Papua New Guinea. PNG law requires that in circumstances in which land is collectively owned, all of the landowners must be consulted prior to making a decision about the disposition of their land.[29] Consequently, I argued that individual signatories to the CMCAs lacked the authority to commit the other members of their village or community to the agreement.

A related concern was that land ownership in Western Province is often independent of village residence. Many of these villages were first established during the colonial period (Welsch 1994, 88). My affidavit included a map drawn for the social impact study that I conducted in 1992, which depicted the distribution of land ownership for the people living in Kawok village on the Fly River. All of the land in the village is owned by the members of two lineages. The other residents in the village are members of eleven other lineages, some with land rights adjacent to Kawok, others with land rights close to the border with West Papua, and yet others with land rights in West Papua or near Lake Murray, about forty kilometers to the south. I argued that the members of these lineages should not be permitted to make decisions about land rights in Kawok.

In affidavits secured by OTML, the counterargument was presented that it has become common practice in Papua New Guinea for villages to elect or appoint representatives with the authority to make decisions on their behalf, and that these decisions are binding on the community. However, I argued that elected officials are not empowered to make decisions about customary land rights, which requires consent from all of the landowning groups.

The CMCA process had divisive consequences for the communities located downstream from the mine. Critics of the agreements accused the signatories of acting without their consent and against their interests. Some of the people who signed the agreements subsequently became *persona non grata* in their home villages and were forced to resettle in urban areas. In other cases, violence was directed at the signatories and their homes (Cavadini 2010). These conflicts were also the catalyst for sorcery accusations, which reflected the level of tension within the body politic (Kirsch 2008, 292–93). Some of the communities were united in favor of accepting additional compensation payments through the CMCAs, and other villages were united in support of the lawsuit—and therefore opposed to the CMCAs—but most of the villages were divided.

BHP BILLITON EXIT STAGE RIGHT

Additional complications in the second lawsuit against the Ok Tedi mine arose as a result of BHP's merger with Billiton to become the world's largest mining company, BHP Billiton, in June 2001. Resolving the Ok Tedi case was one of the pressing issues on the agenda after the merger, both in terms of future liabilities and the desire for the new company to present itself as environmentally responsible. By August 2001, BHP Billiton publically indicated its intention to withdraw from the Ok Tedi mine by the end of the fiscal year (Post-Courier 2001).[30]

BHP Billiton's preference was to close the Ok Tedi mine early. However, its partners in the joint venture—the State of Papua New Guinea, which controlled 30 percent of the project, and the Canadian company Inmet, a spin-off from the original German investment in the project, which controlled another 18 percent of the shares—were committed to keeping the mine operational for as long as possible. Prior to the merger, BHP briefly considered selling its shares in OTML to another mining company, and Atlas Mining in the Philippines had expressed strong interest. However, the threat of ongoing environmental impacts and liabilities complicated any potential deal, especially if the company operating the mine had limited assets.

In the end, instead of selling its stake in the Ok Tedi mine, BHP Billiton established an independent development trust in Singapore to manage its 52 percent share in the project.[31] The transfer of its assets did not end the legal proceedings, but raised questions about the feasibility of imposing environmental controls on the project. BHP Billiton's subsequent exit from the mine, in January 2002, was ratified in an agreement in which the company and the state were "indemnified by the Sustainable Development Program Ltd." for any future environmental liabilities (Papua New Guinea 2001).

The PNG Mining (Ok Tedi Mine Continuation (Ninth Supplement) Agreement) Act of 2001 approved the transfer of BHP Billiton's shares in the Ok Tedi mine to the Papua New Guinea Sustainable Development Program Ltd. in Singapore, where the funds are independently administered (Papua New Guinea 2001). Two-thirds of all revenue from what had been BHP Billiton's share of the mine are set aside for expenditures after mine closure. Although not under the control of the Papua New Guinea government, the trust has nonetheless provided an important subsidy to the state budget, as the remaining third of the funds have been used to support everything from highway maintenance and bridge construction to investments in commercial enterprises, and have even paid for programs seeking to enhance governance of the mining industry. Only one-third of these funds, or one-ninth of all the funds received by the program, is earmarked for the people affected by pollution from the Ok Tedi mine.

Dividing the revenue of the Sustainable Development Program Ltd. in this way was clearly intended as a sweetener for the government in return for its support for BHP Billiton's departure, although the state opposed locating the fund in Singapore beyond its control. The people living downstream from the mine have no say in how the funds are distributed, which they think should be used primarily to benefit the communities affected by pollution. The diversion of these funds away from the people affected by the mine is reminiscent of the way that funds earmarked for public health and education in the settlement of U.S. litigation against the tobacco industry are commonly used for other purposes. The Mineral Policy Institute in Sydney described the Sustainable Development Program as a "poisoned chalice," because it relies on the continued operation of the mine and additional environmental destruction to pay for development (G. Evans 2002).

The Mining Act of 2001 also granted legal force to the CMCAs, leading Slater & Gordon to file a constitutional challenge in Papua New Guinea. They filed an injunction against the CMCAs in the Australian proceedings as well, the hearing for which was scheduled for February 4, 2002. Slater & Gordon planned to introduce evidence in the form of affidavits from eight landowners who signed the CMCAs without being aware that the documents obligated the members of their community to opt out of the court case in Melbourne, and other affidavits from landowners who declared that they had been pressured into signing the agreements. Also at issue was my affidavit arguing that the CMCAs violated customary land rights. After an initial day of hearings, the two parties reached a compromise wherein BHP Billiton agreed to refrain from enforcing the CMCAs without giving Slater & Gordon thirty days' notice. Slater & Gordon agreed to the compromise because its constitutional challenge to the CMCAs was pending in the Papua New Guinea Supreme Court. Since the passage of the Mining Act of 2001, Ok Tedi Mining Ltd. operates independently of BHP Billiton. BHP Billiton continues to influence the decisions of the Sustainable Development Program Ltd., however, as it appoints three of the six board members, the board continues to report to BHP Billiton, and the rules and constitution of the trust company can only be changed with BHP Billiton's approval. The Mining Act also granted the operators of the Ok Tedi mine unprecedented authority to set the environmental standards for its operation, as well as the procedures for monitoring and compliance, which has been described as an extraordinary transfer of rights from the public to the private sector (Divecha 2001). Inmet, which was the last publically traded company to own shares in OTML, sold its interest in the mine to OTML in 2010. This left the PNG Sustainable Development Program Ltd. as the only party with legal liability for the mine and its environmental impacts past, present, and future.

The Australian public relations firm engaged by BHP Billiton to mitigate negative publicity associated with the company's departure from Papua New Guinea described its intervention in the following terms:

> Our client had on its hands 25 volumes of scientific reports that told a story of widespread environmental damage to one of Papua New Guinea's largest river systems. The damage would be worse than previously told to the public by the company's majority shareholder. The challenge was to release the results of the risk assessment into a highly sensitised and critical public arena in a way that minimised damage to the corporate reputations of each of the company's shareholders. At the same time, it needed to respect the people whose environment and lives would be changed by the increased damage. . . . We delivered a tightly controlled and highly strategic public release to diverse and often aggressive stakeholders in PNG, Australia and the US. Media coverage was limited because direct engagement over the complexity of the issues meant few critics were prepared to provide media comment. As a result of the release strategy, there was no civil unrest in PNG and the company's two listed shareholders contained potentially damaging media coverage. (Offor Sharp 2006)

BHP Billiton not only avoided liability for the environmental impact of the mine, but it also evaded public debate concerning its responsibility to the people affected by the project.

The irony of the transfer was that the Ok Tedi mine had finally turned the corner financially, earning its first significant profits. Throughout the 1990s, the state had to be content with tax receipts and other indirect economic benefits from the mine. In 2001, the project paid its first dividends to its shareholders. However, no one predicted that copper and gold prices were about to go sky high. It is not clear whether BHP Billiton would have walked away from the project had it known that its share in the mine would earn more than two billion dollars over the ensuing decade, or that the project would become so lucrative that its current operators would seek to extend the life of the mine beyond 2014 to 2025.

SLATER & GORDON EXIT STAGE LEFT

In December 2003, Slater & Gordon agreed to an out-of-court settlement in the case against BHP Billiton and the Ok Tedi mine. The settlement was ratified by the Supreme Court of Victoria on January 16, 2004. The case had been substantially weakened by the exclusion of plaintiffs who were disenfranchised by the CMCA process. Even though the legal status of the CMCA process remained undetermined, BHP Billiton had filed opt-out notices representing the majority of the plaintiffs. The company being sued by Slater & Gordon was no longer operating the mine in question, making it difficult, if not impossible, to enforce any decision regarding the implementation of tailings containment. More fundamentally, Slater & Gordon was unable to find documentary evidence demonstrating that BHP Billiton prevented the PNG government from reviewing potential tailings containment options, as stipulated by the 1996 settlement agreement. To the contrary, the state had shown little interest in conducting such a review, because it opposed additional spending by the mining company on environmental controls. It reasoned that it would end up paying twice for any increase in spending by the mining company, once in terms of lost revenue as a shareholder, and a second time in decreased tax revenue (Warren Dutton, pers. comm. 1996). In the settlement, Slater & Gordon indicated that they "now acknowledge and accept that BHP B[illiton] and OTML have at all times been in compliance with the 1996 Agreement, have not breached the 1996 Agreement and in their considered opinion there are no unresolved claims, outstanding obligations or disputes under the 1996 Agreement" (Grech 2004, paragraph 21).[32] In return for these admissions, BHP Billiton agreed to pay Slater & Gordon's costs associated with their challenge to the CMCAs.

Because this was a class action, the members of the class were bound by the settlement, including plaintiffs who objected to the agreement, although Judge Bongiorno expressed concern about the legitimacy of this order: "Let's hope that clause . . . never needs to be litigated" (Supreme Court of Victoria 2004, 11). Nonetheless, a number of the plaintiffs conveyed their objections to the settlement in notices sent to the Supreme Court of Victoria. "Can your Honour tell us who will be responsible for the environmental damage that has been caused?" asked one group of plaintiffs represented by Paul Katut, who played an active role in the proceedings (Katut et al. 2004, 2). Another group challenged the basis of the settlement, asking, "Where is the evidence that the Companies have complied with all [of the] environmental standards of the State of Papua New Guinea and international standard[s]? . . . Where is the evidence that the water is safe to drink? Where is the evidence that there is no factual or scientific proof of environmental degradation?" (Dakop et al. 2004, 2). Robin Moken wrote on behalf of his clan, denying that the case was simply about gaining additional compensation from the mine: "BHP/OTML has . . . diverted the minds of the people and the Papua New Guinea government from the real issue— the effects of the mine pollution and the cleaning of the river system" (Moken 2004, 1). They pleaded with the courts for sympathy: "Your Honour, we pray that this Honourable Supreme Court may save our lives in the type of decision or verdict that is favorable to us" (Katut 2004, 2), but they remained defiant: "We will not be intimidated by the Company nor succumb to their bully tactics" (Dakop et al. 2004, 2). However, in its approval of the settlement, the court rejected the plaintiffs' final plea for justice from the Australian legal system.[33]

The lack of significant expenditure on environmental controls at the Ok Tedi mine allows the project to continue operating "with profit margins running at an astonishing 60 percent" (Garnaut 2004). In 2012, the reserves accumulated by the PNG Sustainable Development Program Ltd. totaled $1.4 billion after expenditures of $600 million (PNGSDP 2013, 3). Additional compensation continues to go to the villages affected by the Ok Tedi mine through the CMCAs, which were renegotiated in 2007 and 2012.[34] With the proposed extension of the mine life to 2025, the total financial cost to BHP Billiton for walking away from the Ok Tedi mine may eventually reach $3 billion.[35] It is doubtful that this unprecedented transfer of wealth would have occurred without significant pressure from the second court case in Melbourne.

Perhaps most importantly, it is clear that any of the proposed tailings containment systems could easily have been paid for by the mining project, with substantial revenue to spare. The failure to stop discharging tailings into the river system means that the damage to the environment continues to increase. Whereas the original legal proceedings had widespread support, subsequent maneuvers by the state and the mining company left the people downstream from the Ok Tedi mine divided, confused, and angry: recipients of monetary compensation, yes, but at a level incommensurate with their losses. The people living along the river corridor, and any of their descendants who choose to remain in the area, will have to cope with the continued deterioration of the environment for several centuries.

CONCLUSION

Litigation is one of few available remedies for corporate harm, as well as a potential form of regulatory power. The kinds of legal claims discussed in this chapter face steep hurdles, however, and may end in failure for reasons that have very little to do with the substance of their claims. Yet they can also provide legitimacy for grievances, leverage social movements, reach new publics, and enroll new allies. They can focus international attention on the harms caused by corporate actors. Litigation can also expose the vulnerabilities of an entire industry. It can radically transform the playing field in which corporations and their critics interact. In recent decades, international legal proceedings have become a key component of relationships between transnational corporations and their critics (Joseph 2004; Koebele 2010; Tzeutschler 1999).

The lawsuit against BHP and the Ok Tedi mine resulted in important legal debates about corporate social responsibility and the subsistence rights of indigenous peoples. It also generated thousands of documents, declarations, and affidavits from the plaintiffs, the defendants, and experts chosen by both sides on everything from customary land tenure to the measurement of copper levels in the river. The case demanded attention at the highest levels of the state in both Papua New Guinea and Australia. BHP so acutely felt its vulnerability from the legal proceedings that it instructed its solicitors to draft legislation for the Papua New Guinea government that criminalized access to the Australian courts, resulting in a verdict of contempt. The apparent victory in the first legal proceedings against BHP suggested that the company was down by law. However, at the conclusion of the second proceedings, the results were reversed, leaving the plaintiffs down by law. One might also say that, in the long run, the environment was also let down by the law.

The law is commonly supposed to be a domain in which there are clear verdicts: guilty or not guilty in criminal cases; winners or losers in civil claims. However, the cases described in this chapter are far more complicated. As Gregory Tzeutschler (1999, 418), writing about international legal proceedings, observes:

> The suits are inevitably second-best alternatives to actual processes of reform of the judiciary, labor-management relations, and land use and planning processes in the countries where the violations occur. Reforms in the latter two areas might allow the victims of these violations, who have typically had no control over the processes that result in abuses, a greater say in these processes, thus preventing abuses from happening in the first place.

However, despite their limitations, he concludes:

> These suits do offer victims a much-needed forum to voice their interests and may hold out the possibility of compensation. In all of the . . . cases discussed, a verdict against the defendants would articulate an authoritative finding of wrongdoing. A damages award would provide a measure of compensation to the victims and serve as a deterrent to the defendants and others. In environmental cases, such compensation can actually be used for restoration to remedy the damage caused, although this is not possible where the damages are physical or psychological harms to humans. Finally, [international legal proceedings] may be able to prompt settlements between plaintiffs and their governments and corporations that will have long-term preventive effects. . . . Most importantly, they provide hope that the plaintiff may at last obtain the recognition, the hearing, and perhaps even the righting of wrongs from those who have disrupted their lives and abused their rights. (Tzeutschler 1999, 418–19)

The ramifications of these cases also tend to be greater than the immediate verdicts. Despite its failure to progress in the courts, the litigation against Freeport-McMoRan in New Orleans clearly put the company on the defensive. Having to defend itself against charges of human rights violations and genocide was a public relations nightmare for the company. The decision by the Overseas Private Investment Corporation (OPIC) to cancel the company's political risk insurance also tarnished the company's public profile. Nevertheless, Freeport-McMoRan was successful in fighting back against its critics. The court case was dismissed, and high-profile lobbying by the company overturned the OPIC decision. In a full-page ad in the *New York Times,* James R. Moffett invoked Mark Twain's aphorism "a lie can travel halfway around the world while the truth is putting on its shoes" in his defense of the West Papua mine, which he describes as a "model venture" that is "bringing modern science and technology to bear to make certain we minimize environmental impacts associated with the mining process." Efforts to promote reform through shareholder actions have also been unsuccessful (Emel 2002, 836–41), but the company remains vulnerable to future legal action after disclosing its payments to the Indonesian military.

After more than a decade before the courts, the case against Rio Tinto in relation to the Panguna mine and the civil war in Bougainville was dismissed in 2013. Rio Tinto presumably learned a valuable lesson from its observation of the Ok Tedi case in Melbourne: that it should not rush to settle. However, in contrast to the attention paid by the Australian media to the Ok Tedi case, the distance between Bougainville and the U.S. District Court in Los Angeles and Rio Tinto's limited presence in the United States ensured that relatively few people followed the case closely beyond the participants in the case and lawyers interested in the alien tort statute.[36] Despite the ultimate failure of the litigation, the fact that Rio Tinto was forced to defend its actions in the civil war has the potential to limit human rights abuses by transnational mining companies, though there are no guarantees on that front. The lawsuit against Rio Tinto does not seem to have slowed the rush to exploit the coltan, tantalum, and other valuable minerals used in mobile telecommunications at the epicenter of the conflict zone in the Democratic Republic of Congo, regardless of the risk of complicity in human rights violations.

In contrast to the horizontal relationships in the political campaign against the Ok Tedi mine, the hierarchical organization of the litigation facilitated decision making but restricted political participation, reducing local commitment to the lawsuit, as evidenced by the plaintiffs who opted out of the original court case to receive compensation under the Restated Eighth Supplemental Agreement. The same vulnerability was exploited by BHP Billiton when the plaintiffs returned to court. The complexity of the litigation—involving multiple proceedings and courts—also made it difficult for the lawyers to keep track of the case, let alone the lead plaintiffs. All of these processes were carefully explained to them, but the information that reached the other plaintiffs living in the towns and rural areas of Papua New Guinea was necessarily simplified. The court proceedings also required that some decisions be made very quickly. The lead plaintiffs found it alienating to make decisions on behalf of everyone represented by the case, even though the settlement agreement had to be ratified by the clan representatives who signed the original writs. The legal proceedings also had opportunity costs in terms of their failure to pursue other courses of action—by collaborating with the mine workers union at the Ok Tedi mine, for example, or through novel political avenues, such as the creation of a Green Party in Papua New Guinea that could press for the enforcement of higher environmental standards.

In all three of these cases against mining companies in Melanesia, damage to the environment was one of the primary causes of action. Although state law for environmental protection has gradually become more robust since the 1970s, environmental claims in international law remain poorly developed (Verschuuren 2010).[37] The primary exceptions address international commons, such as treaties and laws protecting the ocean. In the case against ChevronTexaco regarding its oil operations in Ecuador, the judge presiding over the original claims in the U.S. District Court in New York City invoked the Rio Declaration on Environment and Development (1992), which recognizes that although states have "the sovereign right to exploit their own resources pursuant to their own environmental and development policies," they also have "the responsibilities to ensure that activities within their jurisdiction or control do not cause damage to the environment of other States or areas beyond the limits of national jurisdiction." Judge Broderick observed that the "Rio Declaration may be declaratory of what it treated as pre-existing principles just as was the Declaration of Independence," providing support for trying the case in the United States rather than Ecuador (Broderick 1994, 16; cited in Koebele 2010, 158). However, when the same argument was proposed in the Freeport case, Judge Duval did not challenge Broderick's opinion about forum but concluded that it remains unclear which norms regarding the treatment of the environment have risen to the level of customary obligations (Duval 1997, 43–48). These cases compel the judiciary to make decisions about international environmental law. In particular, these cases have the potential to identify emerging "soft law" standards, such as those employed by the World Bank, as examples of international norms, allowing them to be treated as "hard law" that is regulatory and binding (Pring, Otto, and Naito 1999, 41). This raises the possibility of not only the receipt of a fair hearing for grievances, the potential for receiving compensation, and meting out punishment of corporations for their misconduct, but also further development of the law as a means of regulating corporations.[38]

The Ok Tedi case was a bellwether for recognition of the relationship between mining companies and indigenous communities—specifically in terms of subsistence rights, but also, more generally, in terms of holding corporations legally accountable for their social and environmental impacts. This is in contrast to the situation only a decade earlier, when it was taken for granted that the state was the proper body to negotiate with mining companies on behalf of its citizens (Ballard and Banks 2003, 298). By actively seeking to block the Ok Tedi litigation in the Australian courts through the Prohibition of Foreign Legal Proceedings Act, which remains in effect, the state of Papua New Guinea continues to deny the legal relationship between corporations and the persons they have harmed.

As George Akpan (2002, 77) notes, "The success of [international legal claims] against host states and [transnational corporations] must be viewed not only from the narrow spectrum of financial benefits, but also from the pressure mounted on both governments and [transnational corporations] and the personal satisfaction of bringing these actors to court." These cases demonstrate that the actions of transnational corporations are increasingly subject to public scrutiny, as Akpan (2002, 77) optimistically concludes: "Conduct that was previously accepted may no longer be tolerated. Adopting a higher standard for operations in the developed world and a lower one in the developing countries would only expose the [transnational corporations] to more problems. There can be no more pollution havens or countries that are more receptive to human rights abuses. What this requires is the adoption of common or higher standards that would not discriminate against areas where natural resource projects are sited."

Although it may be salutary for the plaintiffs to have "a public forum in which to articulate their grievances and the opportunity to seek official recognition that they have been harmed" (Tzeutschler 1999, 363), in the long run, the potential to "bring about a change in business practices" may be the more practical result (Akpan 2002, 76). To this end, recourse to international courts remains a valuable, albeit imperfect, resource in the relationship between corporations and their critics.

The limits of legal intervention, however, suggest the need for what I call the politics of time, which focuses intervention earlier in the production cycle, before mining projects are able to cause harm, as I discuss in chapter 6. The environmental devastation downstream from the Ok Tedi mine also raises the question of how the engineers and scientists working for the mining company could have failed to predict the environmental consequences of discharging two billion metric tons of tailings, overburden, and waste rock into the river system. This is the starting point for the next chapter, which examines how science is used by corporations to manage their relationships with their critics.

CHAPTER 4

Corporate Science

How is it possible that despite spending tens of millions of dollars on environmental research and monitoring, the scientists employed by Ok Tedi Mining Ltd. failed to predict the impending environmental catastrophe or even to accurately report on it while it was occurring? Their failure calls into question the way that science is deployed by mining companies, and by extension, how corporations strategically exploit science. I begin this chapter by presenting material from two comparative examples. Scientific research conducted by the tobacco industry has been thoroughly discredited (Brandt 2007; Proctor 2012). Yet given the ethical responsibilities associated with research on human health and medicine, it is surprising to learn that recent studies of the pharmaceutical industry identify comparable concerns (Angell 2005; Kassirer 2005; Petryna et al. 2006). These similarities suggest that the problems associated with corporate science may be intrinsic to contemporary capitalism rather than restricted to particular firms or industries. Consequently, this chapter examines how corporations manipulate science in order to limit critique, how such strategies circulate within and across industries, and how corporations adapt them to their needs.

These issues are central to the analysis of the scientific practices of mining companies, which incorporate many of the strategies initially developed by the tobacco and pharmaceutical industries. I argue that the predictions made by the department of environment and public relations at the Ok Tedi mine were systematically biased, and that they consistently refused to acknowledge anything but the best possible outcomes. Next, I examine the strategies employed by OTML and other mining companies to delay recognition or conceal evidence of their environmental impacts. This includes efforts to naturalize these impacts through misleading comparisons of natural and industrial systems. They make systematic measurement errors by ignoring background rates and presenting averages that conceal significant variations. Mining companies also misrepresent their environmental impacts in order to reassure skeptical or concerned stakeholders. They strategically manage the politics of time to gain regulatory and public approval. They also control information in ways that limit the effectiveness of their critics. Drawing on the literature from organizational studies, I consider how these corporate strategies become institutionalized and legitimized. In conclusion, I argue that the strategic manipulation and deployment of science has become a central feature of the relationship between corporations and their critics.

SMOKE SCREENS

Allan Brandt's (2007, 153) history of the Tobacco Industry Research Council describes how "powerful economic and industrial interests . . . deploy their resources to influence, delay, and disrupt normative scientific process." He shows how the tobacco industry "responded [to criticism] with a new and unprecedented public relations strategy. Its goal was to produce and sustain scientific skepticism and controversy in order to disrupt the emerging consensus on the harms of cigarette smoking. This strategy required intrusions into scientific process and procedure" (160).

When independent researchers and physicians first publicized their findings on the harms of tobacco and cigarette smoking, industry CEOs dismissed their activities as "misguided" (Brandt 2007, 164). However, once the mainstream media began to report on the health concerns raised by these new studies, industry leaders realized that they would have to respond to their critics by defending their products and the integrity of their companies (165). Despite being fierce competitors for customers, tobacco companies joined together in a novel collaborative effort (165). They recognized that public relations alone would not suffice to win over a skeptical public, so they decided to appropriate the authority of scientific research, which the public viewed as disinterested and therefore objective (166–67).

The rise of tobacco industry science has an unexpected connection to the university where I teach. The strategies of the Tobacco Industry Research Council were devised by Clarence Cook Little, who was president of the University of Michigan from 1925 until 1929, when his unpopular views on eugenics and other opinionated behavior cut short his tenure (Brandt 2007, 175–77).[1] One of the science buildings on campus still bears his name.[2] Little, who has been described as "the ultimate skeptic concerning the harms of smoking," directed the Tobacco Industry Research Council for two decades and was the leading industry spokesman on the science of tobacco and health (175). Described as "gregarious, charming, combative, and arrogant," his opinions on the relationship between smoking and health problems never wavered during his career; "he steadfastly refused to acknowledge the growing evidence, repeatedly confirmed, that smoking was a cause of lung cancer" (175, 181). Smoking was responsible for the deaths of several hundred million people in the last century, and Little contributed to this outcome by reassuring smokers that there was no proven link between smoking and mortality (Brandt 2007). As Brandt notes, the "seemingly obvious epidemiological conclusion [that cigarette smoking causes disease and death] was delayed by decades of medical and public debate, largely fueled by the tobacco industry" (106).

A key strategy of the tobacco industry was to cast doubt on the relationship between smoking and cancer. The tobacco companies reasoned that they did not need to convince the public of the validity of their case; they only needed to demonstrate that there were two sides to the debate (Brandt 2007, 167). This recognition led to the establishment of the Tobacco Industry Research Council, which was initially run by a public relations manager with no scientific training. Once Little was hired as the organization's scientific director, in 1954, the council began to sponsor scientific research. These investigations were intended to demonstrate that existing studies were flawed or inadequate and that there was "more to know" about the links between smoking and health problems (167). Despite claims about their independence, researchers were reminded that continued funding "depended on not rocking the boat of Big Tobacco" (236). The strategy was to "utilize 'science' in the service of public relations" (168). The Tobacco Industry Research Council emphasized four principles: "insist that there is no proof that tobacco causes disease; disparage and attack all studies indicating such a relationship; support basic research on cancer largely unrelated to the hypothesis that smoking and cancer are linked; and support research on alternative theories of carcinogenesis" (230). These studies contributed to the tobacco indus-try's goal of promoting "scientific controversy and uncertainty" (230).

In short, when independent scientific research linking smoking to health problems threatened the tobacco industry, it began to produce its own defensive brand of science (Brandt 2007, 170). By leveraging pop-ular assumptions about science, including "the fact that science valued knowledge and honored skepticism," the industry was able to stave off a potential crisis of legitimacy (72).

The strategic promotion of uncertainty and controversy has become central to corporate manipulation of science (Michaels 2008; Markow-itz and Rosner 2002; Oreskes and Conway 2010), most prominently in oil industry claims that sought to refute the relationship between fossil fuel consumption, the production of greenhouse gases, and global cli-mate change. Other industries have denied the harmful effects of asbes-tos (Brodeur 1985), lead (D. Davis 2002), and a wide range of risky consumer products (Singer and Baer 2008). The tobacco industry also pioneered other strategies to divert attention from the consequences of smoking, including the sponsorship of research on alternative etiologies for lung cancer. More generally, the tobacco industry has been credited for developing "seminal tactics for co-opting the prestige of academic science on behalf of corporate interests" (Greenberg 2007, 3). It also played a shell game with funding, obscuring its support for various research programs and organizations, including political action groups that reject government regulation in favor of the individual's right to smoke (Benson and Kirsch 2010a; Brandt 2007). All of these practices have become mainstream corporate strategies for responding to cri-tique, including by the mining industry.

Even though legal action against the tobacco industry during the 1980s allowed for the continued production and sale of cigarettes, it forced disclosure of particularly damning evidence of the misuse of sci-entific practice. As one judge in a tobacco case concluded, "The [goal of the] tobacco industry's so-called investigation into the risks [of smok-ing] was not to find the truth and inform their consumers but merely an effort to determine if they could refute the adverse reports and maintain their sales" (Judge Sarokin, cited in Brandt 2007, 344).[3]

DRUG DEALS

Recent studies of the pharmaceutical industry reveal concerns about scientific practice that are remarkably similar to those of the tobacco industry (Krimsky 2003; Angell 2005; Kassirer 2005; Petryna et al. 2006). A central concern is how university research has been co-opted by the drug companies, a strategy pioneered by the tobacco industry (Greenberg 2007, 3). Before the 1980s, clinical research on drugs was largely independent of pharmaceutical companies (Angell 2005, 100). "Now, however, companies are involved in every detail of the research— from design of the study through analysis of the data to the decision whether to publish the results. . . . Researchers don't control clinical trials anymore; sponsors do" (100).

There are a number of concerns about how clinical trials are conducted. New drugs that are modifications of medicines about to lose patent protection are strategically compared to competitors or placebos rather than to the original medication, which is the only way to determine whether the modified drug delivers new benefits (Angell 2005, 75–76; Kassirer 2005, 167). Bias is commonly built into the design of these studies, which may enroll predominantly young subjects, who will experience fewer side effects in drug trials (Angell 2005, 107). The trials themselves may be of insufficient duration, especially when the medication is intended to be taken long term (108).

Other problems are associated with the presentation of research results. Studies show that corporate-funded research is much more likely to recommend pharmaceuticals produced by the sponsor than research supported by nonprofits (Angell 2005, 107). Pharmaceutical companies may suppress results from clinical trials that are negative or prejudicial to the company's economic interests (109). Even independently contracted research may be subject to corporate pressure regarding the publication of results from clinical trials, and corporate lawyers have invoked their proprietary rights to prevent the disclosure of negative findings. Another strategy is the selective publication of only the portion of the study with favorable results, while ignoring data that does not support the drug or publishing multiple versions of the positive results to drown out the negative (112). These strategies are aided by the practice of ghostwriting, in which science writers are hired to compose research articles for influential scholars, who are then paid to publish the work in their names. While the nominal authors are encouraged to make whatever changes to the text they want, they frequently do not. If too many changes are made, the company may not publish the article (Healy 2006, 68–69; Kassirer 2005, 31–33).

Like the tobacco industry, pharmaceutical companies have become adept at establishing productive relationships with professionals who have expertise relevant to their products by providing them with research funds and other benefits. In 2007, the *New York Times* published a confession titled "Dr. Drug Rep," in which the author, a psychiatrist, described his experience conducting paid workshops on the benefits of a particular medication (Carlat 2007). Pressure from the company to stay on script eventually led to the author's resignation. The medical profession has become increasingly concerned about conflicts of interest in research and the ethical dilemmas posed by its relationship to the pharmaceutical industry. Drug companies have established such dense networks of financial patronage among medical professionals that it is often difficult to find independent reviewers for pharmaceutical research (Angell 2005; Kassirer 2005, 21). The strategy of buying up all of the available expertise, imposing confidentiality agreements, and limiting the access of independent scholars to basic data has become a standard corporate practice, as illustrated most recently by British Petroleum's management of its oil spill in the Gulf of Mexico (Kirsch 2010).

In addition to funding clinical research, financial ties between the pharmaceutical industry and medical researchers have proliferated. Faculty researchers have lucrative financial stakes in drug companies as consultants and paid members of advisory boards, and they also own shares in patents and equity interests in companies. Pharmaceutical promotions also influence the medications doctors prescribe; Jerome Kassirer (2005, 72) cites a study showing that only 39 percent of respondents believed these promotions influenced their own prescribing habits, although 84 percent thought it affected the prescribing habits of others. He interprets these results by invoking the logic of the gift, noting that "we tend to reciprocate in some fashion, even for small favors" (Kassirer 2005, xvi).

Like the tobacco industry, pharmaceutical companies also play a shell game with funding by setting up industry-sponsored research projects and organizations (Angell 2005, 152). Not even the doctors who participate in these programs necessarily know the source of the funding, although the companies may continue to dictate research strategies and control the rights to publication. In another strategy borrowed from the tobacco industry's playbook, drug companies identify special interest groups that already express a message that benefits their interests and increase the influence of the group through direct funding, a practice Joseph Dumit (2005, 12) refers to as "amplification."

In contrast to tobacco industry research, which has been so widely criticized that the industry no longer has a significant financial role in academic research, critics of the pharmaceutical industry remain confident that the academy has the capacity to solve most of the problems identified here, primarily through mechanisms to enhance disclosure and transparency. They trust that the normative ethics of science can be harnessed to reform the practices of the pharmaceutical industry.

As I have suggested, the critique of the pharmaceutical industry is more disconcerting than similar findings about the tobacco industry, because the field of medicine and the pharmaceutical industry are held to higher ethical standards than the tobacco industry, which produces the only legal commodity that is lethal to the consumer when used as intended (Benson and Kirsch 2010a). The replication of tobacco industry practices by the pharmaceutical industry suggests the need to reconsider whether the tobacco industry is really the outlier and exception rather than the pioneer and paradigm for corporate science.[4]

A CONSPIRACY OF OPTIMISM

To return to the question with which I began this chapter: how could the scientists and engineers employed by Ok Tedi Mining Ltd. have failed to anticipate the magnitude of harm that would be caused by discharging more than two billion metric tons of mine tailings, overburden, and waste rock into local rivers? In what elsewhere has been described as a "conspiracy of optimism" (Hirt 1994), mining company employees steadfastly refused to acknowledge the steady accumulation of negative impacts on the environment.[5] This differs from the hubris associated with modernist practices of remaking nature for our own purposes without adequately weighing the consequences (Worster 1992) or high modernist ideology that exhibits unwarranted confidence in rational, scientific planning despite past failures (see Scott 1999). The extraordinary failure of the Ok Tedi mine was the direct consequence of corporate strategies that intentionally delayed recognition of the severity of the slow-motion environmental disaster. The mining company ignored the early warnings of the crisis that were obvious to the people living along the river (e.g., Kirsch 1989a, 1995) and other observers (Hyndman 1988; Townsend 1988; Kirsch 1989b).[6] This involved blind spots in research and reporting that can only be described as reckless disregard for the environment, for the affected communities, and for the truth. The mining company's defense of its environmental management programs involved systematic manipulation of scientific processes from data collection and analysis to the presentation of the results.

FIGURE 10. Progress and tradition. From *Ok Tedi 24:00*, published by the mining company, with the caption "A villager is dwarfed" (Fishman, Brown, and Cooke 1983, 88). A man from the Star Mountains poses in traditional attire in front of a mine haul truck at the Ok Tedi mine. Photo: John Lamb/Ok Tedi Mining Ltd.

For mining company executives, confidence that new projects will not repeat the mistakes of their predecessors is always the starting point. No one wants a project to fail. Thus the rallying cry for the Ok Tedi mine was "Not another Bougainville"—the copper mine that spawned social and environmental problems leading to a prolonged and deadly civil war—much as the Porgera gold mine in the highlands of Papua New Guinea subsequently adopted the slogan "Not another Ok Tedi." These expressions of confidence are also examples of the way people working in the mining industry seek to legitimate their actions through narrative devices that promote the optimistic view that they will be able to overcome previous errors, "to believe that this time they've gotten it right," without first "providing an ideological critique of the institutions themselves" (Povinelli 2002, 155, 159).[7] Given the movement of personnel from one mining project to the next, it was often the same people who had worked on the earlier projects who vowed to do better the next time.

Modern mines are enormously complex and risky endeavors. The size and value of the ore body may not be fully known until after the project has been under way for many years. Determinations about whether a project is economically viable require economic projections about global supply and demand for minerals, as well as the resulting commodity prices, many years into the future. The remote location of most new mining projects in developing countries exposes them to risks associated with weak governance and potentially volatile fiscal and legal regimes.[8] Despite these uncertainties, there is enormous pressure on these projects to succeed given the scale of the investment: construction of a large-scale mine can cost three or four billion dollars and sometimes as much as ten or twelve billion dollars, and it is not unusual for relatively small mines to cost several hundred million dollars. There are also powerful incentives to reduce the costs of these projects as much as possible. The mines that continue to operate when metal prices decline are the lowest-cost producers, a status that can only be achieved by limiting spending on environmental controls, regardless of the long-term consequences of this strategy.

Despite pledges to the contrary, serious mistakes are regularly made from the very outset of new mining projects. In a masterful study, mining engineer James R. Kuipers, the hydrologist Ann S. Maest, and others compared the environmental impact assessments for 183 hard rock mines in operation in the United States since 1975 to their actual impacts on water quality (Kuipers et al. 2006). They found that the initial assessments systematically underestimated their eventual impacts. Thus even in the United States, where the U.S. Environmental Protection Agency has responsibility for oversight and regulation of the industry, the actual impacts of mining projects regularly exceed the predictions of environmental impact assessments, which are the basis on which permits for new projects are issued. These assessments are conducted by consultants who are not held accountable for the accuracy of their predictions but rather are beholden to industry for future contracts, despite the obvious conflict of interest (Szablowski 2007, 301).[9] As long as pollution levels remain below legal limits, mining companies are not generally held accountable for these discrepancies.

The original environmental assessment for the Ok Tedi mine included the construction of a tailings dam in the mountains. However, the structure was never built because of the landslip that destroyed its footings (Townsend 1988). Ok Tedi Mining Ltd. subsequently obtained permission from the state to discharge tailings directly into the Ok Tedi River and the Fly River system. A team of hydrologists designed a series of computer simulations to predict changes to the river system, a task that has been described as "one of the world's most difficult sediment modeling challenges" (Pickup and Cui 2009, 259). The original simulations predicted riverbed aggradation but evidently failed to include a variable representing riverbank overflow (Kirsch 1995, 64). It was left to a team of anthropologists working on a social impact study to alert the mining company that the rivers were regularly overflowing their banks into the surrounding forest (31). Backflow from the river into feeder creeks and streams after heavy rainfall in the mountains, which transports mine tailings deep into the surrounding forests and swamps (60–61), was also missing from the computer simulations. By neglecting these variables, two of the most significant impacts from the Ok Tedi mine were completely ignored. Deforestation caused by riverbank overflow and backflow from the main river channel into the larger network of creeks, streams, and swamps affects nearly two thousand square kilometers and is expected to increase significantly in the future.

Even more damning than the failure to predict the impact of mine tailings on the rain forest was the mining company's refusal to acknowledge the problem or undertake the necessary steps to stop it from spreading downstream. This was not due to the absence of environmental monitoring. The mining company had permanent monitoring stations at strategic intervals along the river system. It outfitted a ship to travel up and down the Fly River collecting samples. It established one of the largest and most sophisticated environmental laboratories in Papua New Guinea, in the remote mining township of Tabubil (Burton 1997, 50). The lab was reputed to have produced more pages of information than any commercial publisher in Papua New Guinea during the 1990s. Yet as I noted in the conclusion to my 1992 social impact study, "Monitoring must involve feedback, so that when a problem is discovered, a strategy of mitigation can be devised. In the present case, the feedback loop . . . is faulty, involves too long a delay, or is proven not to exist. . . . What purpose does monitoring serve when there is no effective response?" (Kirsch 1995, 89). Comprehensive monitoring is useless unless corrective measures are undertaken to address the problems it identifies; this requires a strong feedback loop between monitoring and controls over production.

Despite an extensive program of monitoring and predictions by external observers that the environmental impact on the Ok Tedi River was likely to be replicated downstream along the length of the Fly River

(Kirsch 1989a), the mining company claimed to be surprised by the results of a new study of waste management practices, which was stipulated by the 1996 settlement agreement and released to the public in 1999. The admission that the impact of the mine "will be significantly greater than expected" (OTML 1999) corresponds with Ulrich Beck's (1992, 60) observation that "the very people who predict, test, and explore possibilities of economic utility with every trick of the trade always fight shy of risks and then are deeply shocked and surprised at their 'unforeseen' or even 'unforeseeable' arrival." The 1999 studies indicated that even if the mining project were to close immediately, the problems would continue for another fifty years as the tailings already in the river system cascade downstream, spreading deforestation in their wake. The public acknowledgment of the full extent of the problems downstream from the mine put BHP's subsequent economic divestment from the project into motion.

These issues were compounded by the shortcomings identified in two external appraisals of the environmental reports produced by the Ok Tedi Mining Ltd. In 1999, the prime minister of Papua New Guinea asked the World Bank to review the environmental data produced by the mine. The World Bank, which provided loan guarantees to the project during its initial capitalization, criticized the waste management studies produced by the mine for focusing exclusively on the risks posed to shareholders and profit rather than the risks to the state, which is financially dependent on revenue and taxes from the mine. The World Bank also noted that the corporate reports evaluated only a limited set of potential solutions to the problem, some of which were not feasible, such as closing the mine immediately, which would have destabilizing social and economic consequences at both local and national levels, while ignoring other legitimate options, such as substantially reducing production rates. Ultimately, the World Bank (2000) recommended that the mine should close early—as soon as it implements programs to facilitate the social and economic transition to life after mining.

However, the World Bank (2000) review failed to examine how corporate self-interest affected the studies produced by the mining company. It also declined to assess BHP's financial liability for the long-term environmental problems caused by the mine. These omissions cast doubt on the sincerity of the World Bank's promotion of neoliberal reforms that transfer regulatory responsibilities from the state to the corporation. Although the World Bank criticized the mining company for neglecting the interests of the state, it was equally myopic in its failure to address corporate responsibility for the impact of the mine on the communities living downstream.

The mine reports were also submitted for peer review to a group composed of Australian and North American scientists chosen by the mining company. The authors of the peer review report disputed the corporate explanation for deforestation, that the trees along the river and in the floodplains were dying of hypoxia because their roots were covered by tailings and water rather than chemical toxicity from the heavy metals in the river system (Chapman et al. 2000, 7). They rejected long-standing corporate claims about the absence of toxic material in the tailings released into the river system, raising concerns about the toxicity of heavy metals from the bottom to the top of the food chain (Chapman et al. 2000). They identified a range of indigenous fauna that may be vulnerable to the high concentrations of heavy metals in the ecosystem (Chapman et al. 2000). The peer review group was also critical of the mining company for systematically underestimating the potential benefits of the various tailings containment options (Chapman et al. 2000, 3), consistent with its reluctance to pay for these costly interventions. According to their report, the mining company also underestimated the difference that early mine closure would make to the extent and duration of the impacts downstream (Chapman et al. 2000, 14). In addition, the peer review expressed concerns about the substantial threat from acid mine drainage (Chapman et al. 2000, 8–9).[10]

Although both the World Bank and the peer review were critical of the studies produced by the mining company and its consultants, they fell short of calling for independent research. Despite the systematic failure of the mining company to predict the environmental impact of the mine or modify its handling of tailings and waste rock in response to its extensive program of environmental monitoring, until recently the mining-company reports were the sole scientific basis for evaluating the environmental impact of the mine. That these reports are problematic at best is obvious given the company's track record. However, as I argue in the remainder of this chapter, the shortcomings of these reports are representative of the systematic problems associated with mining-company science.

NATURALIZING IMPACTS

One of the rhetorical strategies employed by mining companies to defend themselves from criticism is to invoke comparisons that "naturalize" their environmental impacts (McEachern 1995). During the 1990s, Ok Tedi Mining Ltd. regularly compared the Ok Tedi River, which once ran green and clear but later turned brown from mine tailings, to the Strickland River to the east, which descends much more rapidly from the mountains than the Ok Tedi River and carries a much heavier sediment load (Pickup and Marshall 2009, 13).[11] By invoking the Strickland River, the mining company sought to discount its impact on the Ok Tedi River by suggesting that its new sediment load is comparable to that of other "natural" rivers in Papua New Guinea. For instance, in writing about the tailings discharged by the mine into the Ok Tedi River, the manager for the environment and public relations at OTML argued, "These increased sediment concentrations represent just 50% of the natural sediment loading of the Strickland and are within the ranges measured in other natural river systems in Papua New Guinea" (Eagle 1994, 63). The same spokesperson also argued that river bed aggradation and the formation of sand banks at various locations along the river "can mostly be attributed to the landslide which occurred in the upper Ok Tedi catchment in 1989 resulting in 160 million [metric tons] of material washing to the river" (Eagle 1994, 66; see also Burton 1997, 40), even though these problems were documented prior to the landslide (Kirsch 1995, 66). Such rhetoric suggests that the "actions of the mining companies, while not themselves natural, are fully compatible with natural processes, and the resulting damage is either slight, irrelevant, or self-correcting if left to 'natural' processes" (McEachern 1995, 59).[12]

Mining companies' "claims about nature and naturalness as the grounds of their defense" (McEachern 1995, 59) draw, in part, on the ways in which "seeing like a mining company" entails viewing time like a geologist—that is, in relation to millions of years rather than the decades, centuries, or millennia in which human history is ordinarily conceptualized. For example, during the 1990s, Freeport regularly argued that discharging 150,000 tons of tailings into the Ajkwa River every day was simply accelerating the natural process of erosion, or "speeding up geological time," as Denise Leith notes (2003, 167). Regarding the environmental impact of the Grasberg mine, Freeport CEO James R. Moffett, a geologist by training, famously said "[It's] the equivalent of me pissing into the Arafura Sea" (Bryce 1996, 69).

Another example of how mining companies make inappropriate comparisons between natural and industrial systems is OTML's comparison of copper levels in the Ok Tedi River to the standards for copper in the municipal water supply in Sydney. The mining company claim that the copper levels in the Ok Tedi River were lower than the legal limits for copper in drinking water was accurate but misleading. The Ok Tedi River is part of a living ecosystem and the suppression of algae by elevated copper levels in the river system has the potential to disrupt local food chains. In contrast, public water supplies are intended to be sterile. The Freeport mine also compares copper levels in the Ajkwa River to international standards for drinking water (WALHI 2006, 36). Humans have a higher tolerance for ingested copper than some aquatic organisms, and the level of copper in these rivers may be toxic to these organisms (36). Freeport may have borrowed the strategic comparison to drinking water standards from the manager for the environment and public relations at the Ok Tedi mine, who began his career working for a municipal water system in Australia, following a meeting of the environmental staff for the two companies in the early 1990s.

Strategic comparisons to natural or background rates were also used by the tobacco industry in combating reports concerning the health risks of secondhand smoke (Brandt 2007). The industry called attention to the problems associated with radon, wood and gas stoves, formaldehyde, and asbestos, yielding a "general indictment of the air we breathe indoors" (Brandt 2007, 294). They established a new scientific research center to address these issues so the studies would not be seen as emanating from the tobacco industry. The Center for Indoor Air Research was intended to draw attention to background levels of pollutants in indoor air, reducing the blame on secondhand smoke. The tobacco industry strategy is similar to mining industry use of the rhetoric of nature to downplay the responsibility of mining companies for their environmental impacts, including elevated copper and sediment levels downstream.

MEASUREMENT ERRORS

Mining companies also regularly commit measurement errors in how they collect and report data, with the intended consequence of obscuring or minimizing their environmental impacts. An important example of measurement error is the inappropriate reporting of means, or average values, rather than reporting data points at multiple intervals, which allows for attention to variability. As the Commonwealth Scientific and Industrial Research Organization points out in a review of environmental data from the Porgera mine in Papua New Guinea, "it is not the average concentration of a pollutant that is biologically or environmentally important—it is the frequency of exceedence of a threshold or 'critical' value with which we should be most concerned" (CSIRO 1996, 6.16). For example, during the 1990s, Ok Tedi Mining Ltd. only released the monthly averages for copper levels in the river system rather than the daily or hourly levels, both of which were also available. This is problematic, because there are sharp peaks and valleys in the volume of dissolved copper in the river system (Apte 2009, 340). When copper levels peak, the metal is more likely to become bioavailable, entering the food chain, where it accumulates in particular organisms, including prawns, which are consumed by the people living along the river system. By only presenting the monthly averages, the mining company reports flatten out these spikes and thereby misrepresent both the degree to which copper is bioavailable and its potential impact on the environment and human health (Apte 2009, 343).[13] Another example of the misleading use of averages is the claim that the acid-generating potential of a mine can be buffered by adding ground limestone into the river system, as both the Ok Tedi and Freeport mines do; acid generation can still occur even if the average pH of the entire river system is neutral, because the materials do not necessarily travel together.

A second type of measurement error is caused by ignoring the background levels of toxic chemicals. This can lead to the underreporting of potential harmful effects. For example, there are elevated levels of mercury in Lake Murray, downstream from the Ok Tedi mine. However, when Ok Tedi Mining Ltd. reports the level of mercury in its tailings, it does not acknowledge the background levels of mercury in Lake Murray. Nor does OTML acknowledge that tailings from the Porgera gold mine, some of which are transported into Lake Murray via the Strickland River (CSIRO 1996, ES-9), also contain significant mercury levels. Mercury is a dangerous neurotoxin that readily moves up the food chain to affect humans. With high background levels of mercury already present in local ecosystems, the addition of even a small amount of mercury may be sufficient to produce clinical effects in human populations. The crucial variable from a public health perspective is not the volume of mercury released by the Ok Tedi mine, but the cumulative exposure to mercury of the people living near Lake Murray. Disaggregating pollutants in this manner can obscure important thresholds or tipping points for harm. It is also important to consider the exposure of vulnerable populations, including pregnant women and children, in contrast to averages for the general population.

A third type of measurement error is caused by overflow from mine sites. When extreme weather events occur, the catchment areas or storage ponds at mining or processing sites may not be able to handle the volume of water. The overflow usually enters local rivers or the sea. Although companies are generally required to report these events, they often lack instrumentation to measure how much water leaves the facility under these conditions. In some cases, mine operators may manually open sluice gates to avoid flooding the facility. There may not be any reporting of these events at all. This means that some mining companies underreport the volume of waste material from catchment areas and storage ponds that enters local waterways. Mining companies are required to predict how often such conditions are expected to occur—such as with design specifications for a storage pond that can withstand "once every ten years" rainfall events—but these events may occur more frequently than originally predicted. For example, heavy rainfall and subsequent flooding from an open-pit copper and zinc mine may have been the cause of a fish kill that extended for seven kilometers and affected five coastal villages near the Rapu-Rapu mine in the Philippines in 2007 (Aguilar 2007). The mine, which uses cyanide to process ore, received a substantial fine after a similar fish kill occurred two years earlier (Aguilar 2007). These extreme weather events presumably occurred at greater frequency than originally predicted by the mine.

A fourth type of measurement error involves the claim that a mining project will only impact a small area. For example, a proposed bauxite mine in the Bakhuis Mountains of Suriname had a catchment area of 2,800 square kilometers, of which BHP Billiton proposed to mine only 3 percent. However, the total area affected by the project would be much larger (Kirsch 2009). The bauxite deposits are not contiguous, but distributed throughout a significant portion of the concession area. Vibrations and noise from regular blasting and heavy vehicle traffic are likely to affect wildlife over a large area. All of the river systems that pass through the concession are vulnerable to run-off from mining activities. New roads for the project will provide access for legal and illegal logging and other forms of resource extraction. Migrants moving to the area in search of employment are likely to set up squatter settlements along the roads and engage in illegal hunting and fishing. The impact of the mining project would be greater than the concession area rather than limited to a fraction of it.

Such relationships hold true for most other mining projects as well. In the past, mining required enormous volumes of timber to shore up underground mines and provide fuel for smelters, denuding huge forest areas in the process (Studnicki-Gilbert 2010). Air pollution from smelters may also spread over wide areas. In regions with heavy rainfall, the tailings from a project may be dispersed over hundreds or even thousands of square kilometers, as in the Ok Tedi case. In dry climates, the impact from tailings and waste rock may be localized, but these mines often compete for water supplies with other users, especially agriculturalists, sometimes across very large catchment areas. The immediate, localized impact from a mine is often dwarfed by its impact on the surrounding countryside.

Some of these measurement errors, including the presentation of means rather than reporting on variability, ignoring background levels and other sources of pollution that might provide critical information about cumulative impacts and tipping points, and the overflowing of existing measurement systems, might be attributable to budgetary constraints or the sheer complexity of the task entailed in modeling and monitoring large-scale mining projects. However, all of these measurement errors underestimate environmental impacts, presenting mining projects in a more favorable light. The underlying bias is clearly directional.

DEMONSTRATION EFFECTS

Mining companies also strategically misrepresent their environmental impacts in other ways. One technique used by corporate personnel to reassure the people living downstream from a mine that the water is safe to drink or that it is safe to consume fish caught in the river is through literal demonstrations to this effect. In the past, when mining company representatives visited the villages downstream from the Ok Tedi mine to give a presentation, they would occasionally fill a clear plastic bottle with river water, and after the presentation, when the sediment in the water had settled, they would drink some of the water.[14] The exercise was intended to demonstrate that the river water was clean enough to drink. On other occasions, mining company employees who set up nets to monitor local fish populations would, after paying for their catch, cook and eat some of the fish. But even though these actions prove their willingness to drink the water or eat the fish caught in the river, these demonstrations are misleading.

The problem with the demonstrations is that they conflate short-term and long-term exposure to pollutants. The important question is not whether it is safe to drink small quantities of water or occasionally consume fish from the river. It is the cumulative exposure to pollutants that is the critical variable for health risks. Studies about the levels of heavy metals downstream from the Ok Tedi mine conclude that "potential risks to humans are uncertain at this time," but they recommend continued monitoring for potentially hazardous levels of cadmium and lead (Parametrix and URS Greiner Woodward Clyde 1999, 14). Consequently, these symbolic acts of consumption are a fraudulent charade. They depend on sleight-of-hand rather than scientific evidence to falsely reassure the communities exposed to pollution from the mine. The demonstrations are especially problematic because they are directed at people who lack the means to independently assess the risks of chemical pollutants (Kirsch 2006, 199–200).

The logic underlying these demonstrations has also been invoked by scholars seeking to downplay environmental problems and concerns associated with mining in Papua New Guinea. Glenn Banks (2002, 49) points to the occasional purchase of fish from Lake Murray by the Porgera Joint Venture for consumption by workers at the company mess as a "symbolic . . . display of confidence" that pollution from the mine is harmless. Yet the willingness to consume fish caught in a large freshwater lake several hundred kilometers downstream from the mine says little about the pollution of the Lagaip River, which runs red from pollution and has been designated a "sacrifice zone" (Biersack 2006), or even the pollution upstream from Lake Murray on the Strickland River. Nor does it mean that it is safe to base one's diet on fish caught in Lake Murray, as several thousand people living there do. Similarly, Banks (2002, 48) reports that people living in the vicinity of the Porgera mine pan for gold while standing directly beneath the tailings outflow from the mine. Other people pan for gold in the upper Ok Tedi River. Banks argues that their actions illustrate the general lack of concern about potential health risks from mine tailings. He also notes that these men earn more than unskilled laborers at the mine (Banks 2002, 48). It is hardly surprising that in a capitalist economy there are people willing to perform dangerous work in return for higher rates of compensation. One cannot infer general attitudes toward pollution from their actions.

Corporations may even claim that pollutants provide unexpected benefits, as Stauber and Rampton lampoon in their book *Toxic Sludge Is Good for You* (1995). Consultants for the Freeport mine in West Papua argued that tailings from the mine would have "beneficial" impacts on the mangrove forests in the Ajkwa River estuary (Parametrix 2002, cited in WALHI 2006, 85). The executive summary of the Parametrix (2002) report describes how the deposition of mine tailings will expand the estuary into the shallow Arafura Sea, creating additional habitat for many species, for which the forests serve as a nursery. However, as I suggested to the authors of a critical report on the Freeport mine produced by the Indonesian NGO WALHI (Indonesian Forum for the Environment), more detailed evidence in the body of the Parametrix (2002) report indicates that the expansion of the estuary is unlikely to keep pace with the destruction of existing mangrove forests through sedimentation. The WALHI report concludes that the "ecological role and function of the mangrove habitat which will be lost cannot be adequately replaced. The newly formed outer estuary deposits are unlikely to be colonized quickly enough or with the same biodiversity to replace the lost mangrove habitat" (WALHI 2006, 85). The claim that tailings from the Freeport mine will expand the mangrove forests lining the estuary incorrectly attempts to claim benefits from what will actually be a net loss of mangroves along the coast.

THE POLITICS OF TIME

Mining companies benefit from the latency period between the onset of mining and public recognition of the project's long-term environmental impacts, as the delay facilitates the externalization of the costs of production onto the landscape. Mining companies also strategically manipulate scientific research to extend this period of time, practices I refer to as the "politics of time."

One strategy employed by mining companies to reduce their accountability for environmental impacts is to limit the collection of background data. The failure to conduct proper baseline studies for new mining projects results in "honeymoon" periods, during which environmental impacts cannot be measured, because there is no basis on which to make comparisons. For example, the Porgera gold mine has been criticized for producing incomplete baseline data for the Strickland River (CSIRO 1996, 6.15). The period of data collection was insufficient given the variability in rainfall and the sediment load transported by the river. In particular, there was missing data from periods when water levels in the river were low. In some cases, median discharges were "estimated from only seven months of daily flows collected over two years." Consequently, the water quality baseline data is "too sparse to allow statistically valid 'before-and-after' mine operation comparisons" (6.15).

Without adequate background data, it is impossible to assess the impact of pollution on the river system. Although the shortcomings in data collection might be explained in financial terms, since mining companies seek to defer non-production-related expenses until after the project is operational and generating revenue (Gerritsen and Macintyre 1991), the failure to collect comprehensive baseline data is nonetheless an example of the politics of time.

Mining companies also strategically manage information about the operational life of a mine. The duration of a mining project can only be estimated. Mining companies continually update their knowledge of the ore body through drilling and core sampling. Higher metal prices can extend the life of a mine by making it economically feasible to mine lower-grade ore deposits. Technological developments can have similar consequences. In contrast, reduced demand and lower commodity prices during an economic downturn can lead to a temporary shutdown or early mine closure. Changes to the policies of the host country regarding environmental regulation or taxation can also lead to early mine closure, especially for projects that are only marginally profitable. The life of an ore body is therefore as much of a social as a natural fact.

Mining companies can exploit the flexibility in the life of an ore body for political purposes, especially to extract concessions from the state. The Ok Tedi mine, which was originally projected to operate for fifteen years, from 1984 to 1999 (Pintz 1984), has repeatedly used the threat of early mine closure in its negotiations with the Papua New Guinea government. BHP threatened to walk away from the project after the initial phase of mining, which involved extraction of the rich gold cap on the top of Mt. Fubilan. In return for the company's commitment to the second phase of mining, which focused on the lower-value copper ore, in 1986 the government temporarily granted the mining company's request to discharge tailings directly into the river system. The permission was renewed in 1989, after the Bougainville rebellion closed down the Panguna copper mine, a major source of revenue for the state. After the first lawsuit against Ok Tedi Mining Ltd. was settled out of court in 1996, the company took three years to report on its tailing containment options. It argued that investment in tailings containment was impractical given the impending closure of the mine, which at that point was scheduled for 2010. However, after a new round of compensation agreements were signed with the downstream communities in 2000, the mining company extended the closure date for the project until 2015. After another round of negotiations and a revised compensation agreement, the mining company announced a proposal to continue operating at a reduced rate until 2025. The last two extensions of the mine life were driven by very high prices for both copper and gold, which have generated windfall profits.[15]

The systematic manipulation of announcements to extend the life of the project, like the earlier threat of mine closure, is more political than geological. By gradually lengthening projections of the life of the mine, the company forced the other stakeholders in the project to make short-term decisions. In particular, this has influenced decision making about whether to invest in tailings containment. With the threat of mine closure permanently on the horizon, it has been easier for the mining company to argue that the cost of building a tailings dam or a pipeline to a lowland storage area was not economically feasible. Similarly, the expectation that mine closure was imminent discouraged some people living downstream from continuing to demand that the mining company address the problem of tailings containment. In the domain of environmental impact assessments, it is generally illegal to review the different components of a project separately, because this makes it more difficult to evaluate its cumulative impacts. Yet this is comparable to the way that Ok Tedi Mining Ltd. forced the other stakeholders to make short-term decisions about the project instead of allowing them to weigh the costs and benefits over the extended life of the mine.[16]

The politics of time is also evident in how Ok Tedi Mining Ltd. has tried to perpetuate doubt and uncertainty about the fate of the fish living in the Ok Tedi and Fly Rivers, which have been described as the "most diverse freshwater fish fauna in the Australasian region, . . . [including] over 115 freshwater and marine vagrant species . . . [of which] 17 are endemic to the Fly Basin, and over 30 are known only from the Fly and one or more of the large rivers in central-southern New Guinea" (Storey et al. 2009, 428). The mining company has monitored local fish populations throughout the life of the project, documenting a decline in both species diversity and population sizes since production began (Storey et al. 2009). The negative impacts of riverine tailings disposal for fish populations include "increased sediment loads, mobile bed loads, smothering of habitats, loss of food resources, and possible issues such as chronic toxicity to eggs/larvae" (436, 438). However, until recently the mining company consistently argued that feeder streams and off-river water bodies provide refuge areas for fish species that avoid the polluted river corridor. Consultants for the mining company asserted that after mine closure, these fish would recolonize the main river (448). However, their claim does not account for the transport of mine tailings into these refuge areas following heavy rainfall in the mountains, which forces polluted water upstream. The argument was also premised on the recovery of the river system after mine closure, which has been repeatedly and extensively delayed. Impacts from the mine are now expected to last for 150 years in some places. There are also several invasive species living in the rivers, with which any returning fish species will have to compete.

Only in their most recent studies has the mining company finally admitted what most independent observers have long surmised, that "fish lost from riverine sites are not using floodplain habitats as refuges against adverse conditions in the Ok Tedi and Fly Rivers. This perhaps implies the loss of species from parts of the Fly River system" (Storey et al. 2009, 449). The fiction that the fishery will eventually replenish itself can no longer be sustained. By invoking the deus ex machina of the refuge areas, the mining company was able to persuade state regulators that fish populations in the Ok Tedi and Fly Rivers were not in danger of permanent reduction or extinction. The mining company manipulated the politics of time by delaying recognition of the mine's impact on the local fishery until it was too late to do anything about it.

INFORMATION CONTROL

The final set of corporate strategies I describe here show how mining companies benefit from their ability to control information. These strategies take several forms, including the promotion of doubt and uncertainty (Brandt 2007; Michaels 2008; Oreskes and Conway 2010). An example of this strategy comes from my work in the Solomon Islands. In 1998, on the day that I arrived in the capital of Honiara to consult for the plaintiffs in a lawsuit against the Gold Ridge Mine, the local media reported a cyanide spill in the Tinahula River downstream from the mine. The effects of the spill were still evident when I visited the area two days after the incident occurred: both sides of the river were littered with thousands of dead fish and prawns. The mining company claimed that the cyanide used at the mine site was contained within a closed system and therefore could not have been the cause of the fish kill. Instead, the company sought to naturalize the problem by suggesting it may have been caused by low levels of oxygen in the river. It is not uncommon for short sections of slow-moving tropical rivers to temporarily undergo deoxygenization, but it is rather unlikely that this would occur along such a long stretch of a steadily flowing river. A local news-paper known for its pro-business slant even asked whether the lawyers suing the mining company might have played a role in the accident. When I subsequently met the man who had been responsible for environmental management at the Gold Ridge mine, he was employed in a similar capacity at the Ok Tedi mine. When I asked him what happened to the Tinahula River that April, he shrugged his shoulders and replied, "It's a mystery." He continued to promote doubt and uncertainty, even though he no longer worked at the mine and the project had undergone a change in ownership.

Mining companies have also used legal means to restrict access to information about their environmental impacts. This became a matter for debate after the U.S. Overseas Private Investment Corporation (OPIC) cancelled the political risk insurance of the Freeport mine on environmental grounds in 1995 (Bryce 1995), although the policy was later reinstated after intense pressure by corporate lobbyists, including the consulting firm directed by Henry Kissinger. Two journalists in the United States filed a Freedom of Information Act request for the documents on which the OPIC decision was based, and their lawyers asked me to provide a deposition commenting on Freeport's *amicus curiae* brief, which claimed that the information provided by the mining company to OPIC was legally protected from disclosure (Kirsch 1997b). This included data about pollution downstream from the mine. Freeport argued that data about potentially toxic substances in the river, including arsenic, cadmium, copper, and lead, should be treated as proprietary business information, even though the Ajkwa River is in the public domain. The claim that data about pollution from the mine should be confidential can be compared to the way tobacco industry scientists reported internally on the carcinogenic consequences of smoking cigarettes but were not permitted to publish their findings (Brandt 2007, 498).

In my affidavit, I argued that the people living downstream from the Freeport mine are primarily subsistence agriculturalists who, by necessity, rely on the river for a variety of uses. Consequently, it is in their interests to know the chemical composition of the water so that, for example, they can decide whether it is safe to drink the water or consume fish caught in local rivers. The fact that their water is polluted is already public knowledge. But the release of detailed information about the pollution is a matter of considerable significance to local residents, and withholding that data conceals potential health risks posed by heavy metals and other chemicals in local rivers (Kirsch 1997b, 1). I also argued that the level of privacy claimed by Freeport was higher than that enjoyed by other mine operators. In other countries, independent public authorities are able to assess water quality and potential health risks from exposure to polluted rivers and water bodies. But given that the mine is located in the militarized Indonesian province of West Papua, access to the area downstream from the Freeport mine is restricted. Critics of the regime or the mining company are prevented from visiting the area. Consequently, there are no independent assessments of water quality or pollution levels. Freeport benefits economically from its ability to restrict access to basic environmental data (Kirsch 1997b, 2–3).

I also expressed my opinion that the attempt by Freeport and OPIC to expand the laws of confidentiality beyond the ore deposit and manufacturing facility at the mine to the surrounding ecosystem was inappropriate. Water quality tests and observations by environmental consultants should not be secret or proprietary when it affects people whose primary connection to the mining project is their exposure to the pollutants it discharges. I argued that the level of confidentiality about potential public health risks to the people living downstream from the mine violates the company's scientific and ethical responsibilities to make such information public (Kirsch 1997b, 4).[17] In July 1999, U.S. District Judge James Nowlin ordered the Overseas Private Investment Corporation to release a number of the requested documents, including a 1995 environmental report by an independent consulting company and some of OPIC's internal working papers (Nowlin 1999). However, the documents were heavily redacted before their release, in some cases to the point of illegibility.

I wish to mention two additional strategies of information control used by mining companies to limit critique. Variations of the first strategy—buying up the available expertise, imposing confidentiality agreements, and restricting the access of independent researchers to basic data—have already been noted for the pharmaceutical (Angell 2005; Kassirer 2005) and petroleum industries (Kirsch 2010). Similarly, the mining industry in Papua New Guinea employs anthropologists with expertise in the local area but then imposes restrictions on what they are able to publish or present (see Kirsch 2002; Coumans 2011).[18] In many cases, these restrictions have been enforced with the threat of legal action. Yet the majority of the anthropologists who consult for the mining industry in Papua New Guinea deny that the corporations influence their work, much like doctors assert that receiving benefits from pharmaceutical companies does not influence their clinical decisions—even though they are far less confident about its effects on their colleagues.

The ability to restrict the information that is released to the public provides mining companies with a strategic advantage over their critics. However, the sheer volume of data produced by mining companies and the level of technical expertise in multiple scientific disciplines needed to interpret that data may also limit the ability of the state, NGOs, and independent researchers to assess their impacts. The advantage this provided Ok Tedi Mining Ltd. was emphasized by the public relations firm representing the company in its dealings with the media and the public in the wake of the second lawsuit (Offor Sharp 2006).

In terms of technical expertise, resources, and access to information, the capacity of mining companies to report on their operations almost always exceeds that of their critics. Mining companies frequently exploit these resources when challenging criticism. For example, OMTL produced exhaustive rebuttals of the first detailed, independent studies of the environmental impacts from the Ok Tedi mine. BHP's response to the 119 pages of the original Starnberg report (Kreye and Castell 1991) was 143 pages long (Allen and Mugavin 1991). The OTML Environmental Department (1993a) also produced a condemnatory response to the Australian Conservation Foundation report (Rosenbaum and Krockenberger 1993). These rebuttals index the degree to which the mining company was concerned by the content of the NGOs reports; they can also be seen as attempts to intimidate future critics.

The two-page press release "ACF Distorting the Facts" from Ok Tedi Mining Ltd. (1993b) also introduced a new strategy for responding to criticism of its environmental record, arguing that the report should have paid greater attention to the economic benefits of the project. The argument that a conservation organization should consider both the economic benefits and the environmental impacts of the project is an example of the strategy pioneered by the tobacco industry to insist that the public is entitled to hear "both sides" of every story (Brandt 2007, 167). This has become familiar in relation to the media's practice of including skeptical views in response to evidence about global climate change or the creationist response to stories about evolution. As Brandt (2007, 167) observes, from a corporate perspective, there is no requirement that both sides present comparable data or even that one side directly challenge or disprove the claims made by the other; it is sufficient to demonstrate that there are alternative points of view.

ORGANIZATIONAL CULTURE AND INDUSTRIAL HARM

This chapter raises questions about the complicity of mining company personnel in corporate strategies that systematically underestimate and conceal negative environmental impacts through data collection strategies that fail to record adequate baseline data and present misleading averages, naturalize industrial impacts, conduct deceptive demonstrations, manipulate the politics of time, and strategically manage information. These practices occur at every phase of the life cycle of mining projects. Comparative evidence from the tobacco and pharmaceutical industries suggest that the structural problems of corporate science are the result of calculated decision making by executives.[19] However, research by sociologists who study the organizational failures responsible for industrial accidents indicate that participants in these organizations have been socialized into a larger set of norms and practices that shape their behavior (Perrow 1994, 1997).[20] For example, writing about the "conspiracy of optimism" in the U.S. Forest Service, Hirt (1994, xxxii–xxxiii) argues, "this was not a conscious, manipulative conspiracy of self-servers. Most foresters were well-meaning, public-spirited individuals doing what they were trained to do. Most, no doubt, felt that any failures of management were due to uncontrollable natural contingencies or to shortcomings in knowledge or to a lack of institutional support. But blaming external forces for management failures simply obscured the agency's own contribution to the problem." Like their corporate counterparts, the forest service employees were strongly constrained by organizational practices that limited alternative actions apart from completely opting out.[21]

Tom Beamish (2002), who describes the response to a chronic oil spill in Guadalupe, California, provides a concrete example of how corporations discipline the response of their employees to environmental concerns. Over a period of thirty-eight years, an oil pipeline slowly leaked into the surrounding area, spilling more oil than the sinking of the Exxon Valdez. When evidence of the slow-motion oil spill finally became public, "some 50,000 documents were confiscated, along with maps depicting more than 200 leaks of more than a barrel—spillage Unocal managers had claimed to know nothing about" (Beamish 2002, 95). Beamish notes that the enforcement of federal regulations concerning the petroleum industry is largely contingent on corporate self-reporting. This system encourages oil companies to weigh the costs of stopping leaks and reporting them to the federal government against the option of doing nothing. Oil companies may find it more expedient to ignore the problem and avoid the costs of cleanup, at least in the short term. Beamish (2002, 55) cites the sociologist Diane Vaughan's (1999, 274) observation that "much organizational deviance [from larger norms or standards] is a routine by-product of characteristics of the system itself." In other words, organizational norms encourage participants to ignore any "noise" in the system that requires substantial intervention or modification, especially if this would attract attention from those higher up in the hierarchy.

A key factor in the Guadalupe case was that the "normalcy of spilling oil . . . worked to blunt perceptions of the leaks as problematic" (Beamish 2002, 59). Negative feedback from the management reinforced this attitude. When the problem became too large to ignore, oil workers felt vulnerable in reporting it, because they had been complicit, initially as a matter of ordinary operations and subsequently as a result of more deliberate efforts to cover up the spill. Beamish explains the contradictory attitudes of workers—who were aware that there was a serious problem and knew that ignoring the action was wrong but took no action—in terms of the hierarchical workplace, in which workers and managers each felt that the other had responsibility for addressing the problem. Following Vaughan (1999), Beamish refers to this as the "dark side" of organizational culture.

> None of the individuals who knew about the field's pervasive (albeit undramatic) petroleum contamination responded until it was an established and incontrovertible disaster. When the danger the spillage presented was recognized, the workers did not turn to remedy, but to secrecy and coverup. The ability of workers to keep information inside field operations is attributable to the field's social organization and cultural milieu and its structural isolation. These factors (along with Unocal's corporate "disposition", which did not stress environmental compliance) explain the long-term continuation of the leakage even after the workers recognized the leaks and spills as a significant problem. (2002, 138)

When corporate employees and consultants perceive a gap between what they observe and the standards for best practice, they may assume that the inconsistency is sanctioned and that the company is not interested in hearing about its shortcomings. Similarly, mining companies may actively discourage employee concerns by denying that there are problems or by acknowledging that problems exist but confidently asserting that they are under control or being addressed. These organizational practices favor the status quo over intervention and reform.

They suggest that the strategies of corporate science production described in this chapter are intended not only to influence public opinion but also to convince employees that the corporations they work for are doing their best and, furthermore, that their best is adequate.[22] This highlights the importance of external critics in provoking reevaluation of the practices of the mining industry.

It is important to note that employee attitudes regarding the social and environmental impact of the Ok Tedi mine varied widely. Once, during a conversation about the mine, a corporate executive raised the question of his personal legacy. He was about sixty years old and had spent most of his life in remote mining townships, far from his family in Australia. Given the project's notoriety, he wondered how his grandchildren would come to regard his long-term association with the Ok Tedi mine. He hoped they would view his accomplishments positively, in light of the development opportunities the mine helped to bring to Papua New Guinea. Like most of the expatriate employees of the mine with whom I discussed these issues, he believed in the development paradigm and was proud that the mine contributed to improved standards of living and increased life expectancies. However, his calculations failed to account for the way pollution from the mine has impoverished thousands of people living downstream. Other expatriates employed by the mining company left their jobs because of their concerns about the environmental impact of the mine.

There were also differences among the Papua New Guineans employed by the mine. Until his death in 1996, Kipling Uiari remained a die-hard skeptic about the harm caused by the mine, asserting the "lack of any clear evidence of permanent environmental damage" (Uiari 1995, 6; cited in Burton 1997, 49). Most of the other Papua New Guinean employees at the mine, many of whom grew up in subsistence-based communities in rural areas, were sympathetic to the people living downstream. When an Australian NGO distributed bumper stickers in Kiunga that read, "Clean up Ok Tedi. BHP, it's not O.K.," some employees of the mine even put them on company vehicles until the company mandated their removal. When I encountered company employees during the lawsuit, they never seemed angry or threatening; in contrast, most of them grudgingly recognized the value of the lawsuit as a means of finally getting the company to take the pollution downstream from the mine seriously. Concern among the mine workers did not, however, result in the mobilization of their union to exert pressure on the company to reduce its environmental impact.

CONCLUSION

This chapter describes the strategies through which mining companies manipulate and present the results of scientific research. Their primary objective is to continue externalizing the costs of production onto communities and the environment by delaying recognition of their destructive environmental impacts. They also seek to avoid reputational risks and the threat of external regulation. The mining industry has followed the lead of the tobacco industry by promoting uncertainty and doubt, making it difficult for independent observers to accurately predict the environmental impact of mining projects, assess the damage that occurs, evaluate the alternatives, and determine whether or not the impacts can be remediated. The emphasis on delaying recognition, forestalling critique, and avoiding regulatory intervention suggests that these strategies are also examples of how corporations manipulate the politics of time.

The practices described in this chapter run counter to standards of "civic science that is intended to serve public interest" (Fortun and Fortun 2005). Yet it seems unlikely that the mining industry will ever experience the delegitimization of the tobacco industry, which markets lethal commodities directly to consumers. Nor does it seem possible that the mining industry will be subject to the kinds of reforms being undertaken in the academy and the medical establishment with regard to the pharmaceutical industry. But scholars from the natural and social sciences can make constructive interventions into these processes. In addition to assessing the scientific claims made by mining companies and their consultants (e.g., Kuipers et al. 2006), they can analyze and critique the ways that the mining industry strategically manipulates and deploys scientific research. They can promote open access to information about the impacts of mining on the environment and public health, as illustrated by the Freedom of Information Act case against the U.S. Overseas Private Investment Corporation and Freeport-McMoRan. Scientists can also make their expertise available to the communities most vulnerable to the impacts of mining rather than to the mining industry. An example of this is the independent, interdisciplinary review of an environmental and social impact assessment for a proposed bauxite mine in Suriname that I discuss in chapter 6.

As the examples from tobacco industry science and the pharmaceutical industry suggest, however, the strategic management and presentation of scientific information by corporations is not limited to the mining industry. There are abundant examples of the corporate misuse of science across a wide array of industries, corresponding with a stunning range of environmental problems that loom over the modern world like a dark cloud. Research from organizational studies indicates that these practices are institutionalized throughout all levels of the corporation. The examples discussed here suggest that these strategies are intrinsic to contemporary capitalism rather than restricted to particular corporations or industries. Recognition of the way that corporations manipulate science is a valuable starting point for the critique of the corporation as the aggressive purveyor of misleading utopian visions, including the claim that every environmental problem has a practical solution.

The ubiquity of these concerns suggests the need to catalogue and analyze how these corporate strategies operate, how they travel within and across industries, and how they are deployed by different industries. Learning how to identify and unpack these strategies is essential to understanding how corporations protect themselves from scrutiny and critique, promoting resignation and forestalling reform. Corporate science exhibits measurement errors and strategic blind spots in which pressing problems are conveniently ignored. Other strategies prolong the latency period between the onset of production and the recognition of problems. Background rates are also disregarded, obscuring potential tipping points that may result in irreversible harm. Corporations make use of inappropriate comparisons, whether to "natural" settings or artificial contexts. There are also several strategies of information control that seek to limit the effectiveness of critics: whether fighting to keep information out of the public domain, arranging for the selective presentation of data, amplifying favorable views, or overwhelming potential critics with the sheer volume and complexity of the data. Through a variety of deceptive techniques, corporations seek to reassure various publics about the safety of their products or processes of production. The feedback loop between monitoring and the processes of production responsible for causing harm is often lacking, resulting in the failure to institute reforms. While some of these shortcomings might be attributed to the complexity of the problems or the limitations of scientific knowledge and procedures, the clear directional bias of the information presented suggests that the defense of the corporation is the primary goal.

Greater involvement by citizens groups and NGOs in the production and analysis of science threatens the monopolization of science by capital and industry. Consequently, public involvement in science has become a threat to corporations and the target of counterattacks, as I discuss in the next chapter. It also raises questions about the ways in which scientific authority has become a political resource in the relationship between corporations and their critics. There are a number of ways that corporations mobilize scientific authority in response to criticism from scientists, the state, and NGOs. A common response to critique is to challenge its objectivity by protesting the use of "emotive and emotional language," as illustrated by the review of the Starnberg report commissioned by the German shareholders of OTML. Another response is to challenge the adequacy of the scientific data produced by the critics, which takes advantage of the corporation's ability to amass and control access to data. A third response—not evident in the cases discussed here, but deployed in conflicts over genetically modified crops and in other debates, is to accuse the critics of being antiscience, suggesting that they refuse to accept the legitimacy of scientific methods. This naked appeal to the authority of science ignores the degree to which scientific research has been captured by capital and industry, as well as the relevance of social and political concerns. A fourth response entails shifting the frame of the debate. In the Ok Tedi case, when scientific evidence could no longer be used to conceal the impact of the disaster, the mining company began to promote the project's value on economic grounds. The tobacco industry pursued a similar strategy when the argument about scientific uncertainty was no longer persuasive; instead, it promoted the view that smoking was a matter of individual choice. A final, somewhat surprising response to critique has been to undermine the authority of science. Although this strategy has not been deployed by the mining industry, it has been pursued by the petroleum industry and its conservative allies in the argument that the scientific evidence documenting global climate change is a hoax. Challenging the legitimacy of science is obviously a risky strategy for corporations to pursue, as belatedly recognized by the petroleum industry, which, after decades of funding climate change denialism, is now promoting its use of science and technology to address the challenges of developing new sources of energy.

This chapter also demonstrates the value of making the relationship between corporations and their critics a subject of ethnographic inquiry, both the strategies through which corporations manipulate and present science and their mobilization of scientific authority as a political resource. It suggests that the dialectical relationship between corporations and their critics has become fundamental to the contemporary production of science. This holds true for the mining industry and can also be seen in more prominent debates about the pharmaceutical industry, the petroleum industry's relationship to climate change scientists and activists, and the relationship between Monsanto and the critics of genetically modified organisms (GMOs). Finally, this chapter illustrates how science has become a critical resource for contemporary corporations in managing their relationship to their critics.

The manipulation of science is only one of many strategies corporations use to respond to their critics. As indigenous political movements and NGOs have become more successful in challenging the environmental impacts of mining, the industry has responded through the application of corporate social technologies that seek to neutralize their critics, including novel forms of collaboration among companies that previously viewed each other as fierce competitors and the promotion of the virtuous discourses of responsibility and sustainability, as I discuss in the next chapter. The politics of time, which appears in this chapter as an example of corporate strategy, has also become central to new strategies employed by the critics of the mining industry, who increasingly focus their protests earlier in the production cycle, with the aim of preventing harm from occurring rather than addressing it after the fact, as I discuss in the final chapter of the book.

CHAPTER 5

Industry Strikes Back

In July 1997, the London-based consulting company Control Risks, which advises Fortune 500 companies on political risk management, published the report *No Hiding Place,* describing how transnational corporations face unprecedented pressure from NGOs to adopt "the highest environmental, labor, and ethical standards" (Bray 1997, 1). Using case studies from the extractive industries, the report argues that criticism from NGOs poses a significant risk to corporate reputations, that legal activism has become a standard component of NGO repertoires, and that international NGOs are as much a part of corporate risk profiles as the communities with which they interact (Bray 1997, 39, 42, 45). Control Risks instructs its corporate subscribers to take their NGO critics seriously and seize the initiative, whenever possible, by finding common ground on standards, codes of practice, and their implementation. However, the report warns that where disagreements remain, corporations "must be prepared to justify their policies, even in regions once considered remote" (Bray 1997, 2). Control Risks concludes that interactions between NGOs and corporations are "part of a long-term process of political and social change" and that "heightened scrutiny means that perceived transgressors truly have 'no hiding place'" (Bray 1997, 70, 72).

Sustained attention from NGOs and increasingly effective tactics of resistance by indigenous peoples provoked a "crisis of confidence" among mining industry executives in the late 1990s (Danielson 2002,

7). As one industry observer noted, "It is hard to identify any industrial sector (with the possible exception of nuclear power) that features such low levels of trust and such a history of division, strife and anger as the extractive industries," and added that "some polls showed the [mining] industry as being held in lower public esteem than the tobacco industry" (Danielson 2006, 26, 52). At the 1999 World Economic Forum in Davos, and in subsequent meetings in London, executives from the world's largest mining companies met to discuss these issues. They identified their strained relationship with indigenous peoples as their greatest challenge (Mining Journal 2001, 268). They reluctantly conceded that "despite the industry's best efforts . . . [its] message had failed to get through," leaving them "too often on the defensive" (267).

This chapter examines the "corporate social technologies" (Rogers 2012) through which the mining industry has responded to indigenous resistance and NGO criticism. Mining companies pursue strategies of engagement that divide their opposition. They co-opt the discourse of their critics, including the language of responsibility and sustainability, transforming the terms of the debate. They appropriate the tactics of their opponents, including the production of a satirical film about environmental activism, turning the tables on liberal exposés of corporate behavior. The industry's loss of credibility also provoked cooperation among corporations that previously viewed each other as competitors. In challenging the legitimacy of their NGO critics, the mining industry has found allies and support not only on the right but also on the left, in the academy, and from the state. The industry also collaborates with conservative political organizations that challenge public participation in science. Finally, the mining industry has sought to increase its symbolic capital by directing resources to public health campaigns and by developing stronger ties to the academy.

THE POLITICS OF ENGAGEMENT

One of the responses of the mining industry to increased pressure has been to selectively engage with its critics. This strategy was promoted by a new genre of corporate manuals with titles like *Industry Risk Communication Manual: Improving Dialogue with Communities* (Hance, Chess, and Sandman 1990) and *Managing Activism: A Guide to Dealing with Activists and Pressure Groups* (Deegan 2001). The first handbook encourages corporations to engage in an ongoing dialogue with community members. The authors argue that corporations have a responsibility to educate the public about their operations. They also acknowledge that activists play a valuable role in pressuring companies to reduce risk. They contend that dialogue with communities cannot succeed unless corporations commit to more effective risk management: they encourage companies to set their own standards higher than existing regulations in order to enhance trust and improve their standing in the community.[1]

In contrast to the conciliatory tone of the first book, *Managing Activism,* by Denise Deegan, is assertive and even combative, encouraging corporations to "get to know the enemy" (Deegan 2001, 3). For Deegan, "learning to manage activists involves learning about activists. Who are they? What do they want? What will they do to achieve their objectives? And most importantly of all—what is the best way to deal with them?" (3).

Deegan describes many of the popular strategies and tactics employed by activists and NGOs. She argues that activists try to seize the "moral high ground" in their interactions with corporations by emphasizing emotions over facts. She contends that it makes little difference to the damage inflicted on corporate reputations whether the accusations made by activists are substantiated. In contrast to the authors of the *Industry Risk Communication Manual,* Deegan focuses on the management of public relations rather than the responsibilities of corporations to the public. But both manuals encourage corporations to engage in "relationship building, negotiation, and conflict resolution" with NGOs (Deegan 2001, 73).

The mining industry engages with its NGO critics in a variety of ways. Some corporations hold regular briefings for NGOs. Others invite NGO members to join advisory panels or even serve on corporate boards.[2] In the wake of negative publicity from the Ok Tedi case, the Australian mining industry invited several prominent environmental groups, including Oxfam Australia and the Australian Conservation Foundation, to participate in regular roundtable meetings. The discussions were governed by Chatham House Rules, which stipulate confidentiality when addressing sensitive topics in order to facilitate candor. However, their participation in the confidential proceedings prevented the NGOs from openly criticizing their mining company partners in public, undermining their autonomy and effectiveness while enhancing the standing of the mining industry through its public association with these prominent environmental organizations. The meetings divided the NGO community in Australia into two groups, those organizations willing to engage with the mining industry and other groups opposed to these relationships. It also disrupted communication among the members of civil society because of concerns about NGOs sharing confidential information with their industry partners. Thus mining industry strategies of engagement effectively operated like a policy of divide and conquer.[3]

The mining industry also praises some NGOs for their "reasonableness" while criticizing others for being "rigidly anti-mining" or even "dangerously radical" (Chadwick 2002). Industry journalist John Chadwick divides opposition NGOs into three categories according to their willingness to engage with the mining industry. The first group is comprised of the large, northern conservation NGOs, including Friends of the Earth, Greenpeace, and the World Wide Fund for Nature (WWF), which he identifies as playing "a valuable role in trying to keep mining companies 'honest' in their dealings with communities and their environmental management." The middle group is comprised of smaller NGOs willing to "engage discreetly" with the mining industry. Chadwick characterizes the remaining NGOs as "strong to very strong in their condemnation of mining" and not "receptive to logic or science" (20). He suggests that they refrain from engaging with corporations because "it might jeopardise their funding" (22).[4]

Critics of the mining industry have also been subject to political harassment that draws on the language of national security. For example, no one challenged a commentator who identified NGO critics of the mining industry as "ecoterrorists" after the screening of an antienvironmentalist film at the conservative Heritage Foundation in Washington, DC (Heritage Foundation 2007). A similar comparison was made in an article published in the industry newsletter *Mineweb* after a screening of the same film at a meeting of the Prospectors and Developers Association of Canada: "The NGOs, like terrorists, do not seem to abide by the rules of the game. They do need to be brought into account in some way or another" (Williams 2007). Proponents of the mining industry have even invoked the post-9/11 global war on terror by spreading rumors about the involvement of prominent environmentalists in armed terrorist groups. For instance, the director of WALHI, the Indonesian Forum for the Environment, who previously oversaw JATAM, the Mining Advocacy Network of Indonesia, was falsely accused of being a terrorist by a mining company executive, a charge that was subsequently repeated to the media by an Australian senator.[5]

Mining companies have also recruited and hired prominent members of the NGO community, who offer valuable insider knowledge that helps their corporate employers counter negative publicity and thwart NGO actions. One former environmentalist, who started a public relations firm that works with many of the same corporations he previously criticized, confided to me during an interview that environmentalists refer to their turncoat colleagues as "greenies who have cashed in their chips." He justified his new career and clientele by arguing that activism is a young person's game, a transitional status between college and the workforce. He asked rhetorically how long adult men and women can be expected to wear old clothes, live in group houses, eat brown rice, and have no retirement plan. Corporate "flipping" of activists can have negative consequences for NGO campaigns. In another case, the executive director of a major environmental organization took a position with a consulting firm that had a contract with BHP. He later conveyed information from confidential NGO discussions about the Ok Tedi mine to BHP, including updates from a former colleague with whom he had remained friendly, essentially spying on the NGO community on behalf of his new employer.

Mining companies have also cultivated close relationships with conservation organizations that might otherwise be critical of their environmental impacts. These relationships have largely displaced previous efforts by conservationists to form alliances with indigenous peoples. In a controversial essay published in a prominent conservation magazine, Mac Chapin, an anthropologist with four decades of experience working with indigenous peoples in Latin America, rebukes major conservation organizations for "partnering . . . with multinational corporations— particularly in the business of gas and oil, pharmaceuticals, and mining— that are directly involved in pillaging and destroying forest areas owned by indigenous peoples" (Chapin 2004, 18). He notes the irony that Conservation International, the Nature Conservancy, and the World Wide Fund for Nature are "allying themselves with forces that are destroying the world's remaining ecosystems, while ignoring or even opposing those forces that are attempting to save them from destruction" (26). These relationships have led indigenous peoples in many parts of the world to regard conservation organizations as a threat to their land, territories, and environment, as well as their political autonomy and cultural survival.

Partnerships between the mining industry and conservation organizations have proliferated since the 2002 World Summit on Sustainable Development in Johannesburg, at which new agreements between Rio Tinto and Bird Life International, and between the International

Council on Minerals and Mining (ICMM) and the International Union for Conservation of Nature (IUCN) were announced—although IUCN later backpedalled on its commitment after receiving criticism from its members. The mining industry also funds conservation projects designed to offset the environmental impacts of new mining projects (BBOP 2009; Rio Tinto 2008; Seagle 2012). These projects may doubly disenfranchise indigenous peoples through the loss of lands to resource extraction and reduced access to other lands set aside for conservation.[6]

CO-OPTING THE DISCOURSE OF ITS CRITICS

Another key strategy through which the mining industry responds to its critics is by appropriating the terms of their critique. The promotion of the discourse of corporate social responsibility by the mining industry has overtaken its use by activists seeking to expose industry shortcomings (Welker 2009; Rajak 2011a). This is especially obvious in public tournaments of virtue in which mining companies receive awards from industry associations for being responsible, sustainable, and transparent (Rajak 2011b). The symbolic capital associated with these claims is central to corporate efforts to reclaim the moral high ground from their NGO critics. The discourse of corporate social responsibility also provides support for the view that solutions based on the market can replace regulation (Shamir 2010).

Corporate claims about social responsibility are driven in part by transformations to capitalism that have increased the significance of reputational risks to the corporate bottom line. These changes are an unintended consequence of the rise of shareholder capitalism, which emphasizes share value at the expense of corporate relationships to labor, consumers, and communities (Ho 2009). Shareholder capitalism is closely associated with the financial collapse of the last decade, during which attention to share value took precedence over economic performance. Shareholder capitalism is also linked to increased participation in the stock market by individual investors, which has been spurred by the dismantling and privatization of pensions and retirement plans. Managing shareholder confidence has become an essential component of doing business for publically traded companies. Consequently, corporations seek to reassure shareholders and potential investors by adopting policies on corporate social responsibility. Mining companies also invoke the awards they have received from industry associations when seeking inclusion within green and social-choice investment funds.[7]

In reaction to widespread concern about its environmental impacts, the mining industry aggressively promotes its contribution to sustainable development. Sustainability and sustainable development are hybrid concepts that combine economic interests with environmental concerns. The definitional careers of these concepts are particularly interesting for having been progressively shaped in a series of multilateral conferences, much like the recognition of indigenous rights. The definition of *sustainability* has its roots in the 1972 U.N. Conference on the Human Environment in Stockholm, which first expressed the need to "maintain the earth as a place suitable for human life not only now but for future generations" (Ward and Dubos 1972, xiii). The emphasis was on human activities that result in environmental degradation, especially pollution and resource depletion (W.M. Adam 2001, 55).[8] When the International Union for Conservation of Nature (IUCN) published the *World Conservation Strategy* in 1980, it applied the concept of sustainability to development: "For development to be sustainable, it must take account of social and ecological factors, as well as economic ones; of the living and nonliving resource base; and of the long term as well as short term advantages and disadvantages of alternative actions" (IUCN 1980, 1). This approach to sustainability sought to balance the demand for growth and development with environmental concerns.

The 1987 World Commission on Environment and Development, now known as the Brundtland Commission, addressed questions of equity in relation to sustainable development (Reed 2002, 206). Responding to concerns that imposing environmental restrictions on southern-hemisphere countries would impede their ability to catch up to northern-hemisphere economies, the commission placed greater emphasis on the economic needs of people living in developing countries, including their requirements in the future. The Brundtland commission formulated the definition that remains in popular parlance, that sustainable development "meets the needs of the present without compromising the ability of future generations to meet their own needs" (Brundtland 1987, 15).

The discourse of sustainable development underwent further modification during the 1990s. The 1992 United Nations Conference on Environment and Development in Rio de Janeiro, widely known as the "Earth Summit," promoted a "growth-centered" approach to development that advocated the preservation of biodiversity through the establishment of small, relatively pristine sites as conservation areas, while avoiding restrictions on the industries responsible for environmental degradation (Reed 2002, 206). It remains unclear, however, whether protecting 1 percent of the planet is the most effective strategy for preserving biodiversity in the long run, in contrast to raising environmental standards to protect the other 99 percent. This is especially the case given the specter of global climate change, which raises the question of whether the species these projects are intended to preserve will be able to survive in the areas set aside for them.

The mining industry's use of the discourse of sustainability follows the growth-centered approach promoted by the 1992 Rio Earth Summit and reinforced a decade later during the 2002 World Summit on Sustainable Development in Johannesburg, South Africa. The contributions made by mining projects to sustainable development are presented in terms of royalties and taxes that can be used to create economic opportunities that will continue to benefit local populations after mine closure (Crook 2004; Welker 2009). One of the first mining companies to integrate sustainability into corporate accounting was the Canadian firm Placer Dome, which began to issue annual sustainability reports for its major projects in 1999.[9] These reports identify the primary objective of sustainability as the "capacity to maintain profitability for the shareholders," although they also seek to "develop closer integration as a partner and contributor to community development," and "to leave an environment that offers no loss of opportunities to future generations after mine closure" (Placer Dome Asia Pacific 2000). Less than a decade later, all of the major mining companies had enacted policies on sustainability. For BHP Billiton, "sustainable development is about ensuring our business remains viable and contributes lasting benefits to society" (BHP Billiton 2009). Similarly, Rio Tinto asserts that "our contribution to sustainable development is not just the right thing to do. We also understand that it gives us business reputational benefits that result in greater access to land, human, and financial resources" (Rio Tinto 2009). These corporate definitions of sustainable development emphasize institutional and economic stability.

Although the original definition of sustainable development emphasized the need to balance economic growth with the protection of the environment, this relationship has shifted over time, culminating in the elision of biology and ecology in how sustainability is currently defined by the mining industry.[10] This redefinition has been facilitated by the shift from "strong sustainability" to "weak sustainability" (Daly 1996, 76–77; see Danielson 2002, 22). The two competing notions of sustainability differ with respect to the relationship between natural capital and human or manufactured capital. *Weak sustainability* refers to the argument that natural capital and manufactured capital are interchangeable and that sustainability is achieved when the total value of capital remains constant or increases. According to this formula, a mine that pollutes a river and causes extensive deforestation may be considered sustainable if the profits from the project are successfully converted into manufactured capital with an economic value that equals or exceeds the value of what has been consumed or destroyed in the process. From this perspective, a mine is considered sustainable as long as the "total stock" of capital remains the same or increases. In contrast, the definition of *strong sustainability* acknowledges the interdependence of human economies and the environment, without treating them as interchangeable. From this perspective, the position of weak sustainability to which the mining industry subscribes is a category error. The economist Herman Daly (1996, 77) illustrates his critique of weak sustainability by pointing out that the complete replacement of fishing stock (natural capital) with fishing boats (manufactured capital) is a recipe for a tragedy of the commons.

Sustainable mining is an example of a corporate oxymoron in which a harmful practice or commodity is camouflaged by a positive cover term (Benson and Kirsch 2010b).[11] Another example of a corporate oxymoron promoted by the mining industry is "clean coal," which is intended to alleviate concern about the environmental impacts of burning coal (Kirsch 2010). Although there are technologies to scrub sulfuric acid from the emissions of power plants that burn coal, preventing acid rain, there are no economical technologies for burning coal without releasing carbon dioxide, the greenhouse gas most responsible for global climate change, into the atmosphere. Yet the reassuring phrase "clean coal" implies that such technology is already available, or at least within reach.[12] The objective is to limit criticism of the coal industry by promoting the illusion that it is possible to produce energy from coal without exacerbating global climate change. Similarly, the corporate oxymoron of sustainable mining is intended to reassure the public that the mining industry shares their environmental values.

Another rationale for appropriating the discourse of one's critics is to turn it against them. The discourses of transparency and accountability, which NGOs have used to challenge the collaboration of mining companies with authoritarian and military governments, have been deployed against NGOs by conservative political organizations. The NGOs Global Witness and Transparency International and the Extractive Industries Transparency Initiative, as well as the global campaign "Publish What You Pay," have promoted the discourses of transparency and accountability. Freeport-McMoRan's disclosure of its payments to the Indonesian army (Bryce 2003) is but one example of how these efforts have affected the mining industry. But in 2002, the conservative American Enterprise Institute turned the discourse of accountability back on NGOs by setting up a website called NGO Watch, which tracks the funding and activities of NGOs. NGO Watch quickly spawned offspring called Greenwatch and Activist Cash. These campaigns are part of the larger critique of NGOs by the right, as I discuss below.

AUDIT CULTURE

Like the tobacco industry during its own crisis of legitimacy (Brandt 2007), nine of the largest mining companies reached an agreement in 1999 to establish a new industry body that would represent their collective interests. The primary undertaking of the Global Mining Initiative was to commission a two-year multi-stakeholder analysis of the challenges facing the mining sector. Working through the World Business Council for Sustainable Development, the International Institute for Environment and Development (IIED) was chosen to direct the Mines, Minerals and Sustainable Development project, known by the acronym MMSD. The $10 million budget for the project was provided largely through corporate subscription. The project was tasked with investigating a set of challenges to the mining and minerals sector identified by its corporate sponsors, including disputes concerning land tenure, environmental management, and relationships to communities (IIED 2001). The remit of the project extended to issues of production, consumption, governance, and standards for best practice (IIED 2001). Many of the NGOs working on mining issues declined invitations to participate in the project, which they viewed as an extended public relations exercise rather than an independent investigation. According to José de Echave, head of the Mining and Communities Program at the Peruvian NGO CooperAcción, "The MMSD, however much good work has gone into it, is still an attempt to set an agenda from the top down, to limit the debate, and to define who the legitimate actors or stakeholders are. [In contrast], the role of NGOs is to support processes that are built from below, to construct a new social agenda, and to support communities' struggles to recuperate their economic, social, and cultural rights" (cited in Chadwick 2002, 22).

In retrospect, even staunch critics of the mining industry conceded that the MMSD project provided an "objective" overview of the problems facing the industry (Moody 2007, 160). The MMSD project did very little, however, in the way of providing solutions. David Szablowski (2007, 84) concludes that the MMSD report "represents a particular snapshot of contemporary debates without attempting to settle them." The 440-page report paid special attention to the sites of conflict—including Ok Tedi, Freeport, and the Panguna mine in Bougainville—that led to its commission (Danielson 2002). For the Ok Tedi mine, it referred to my presentation at a workshop convened by the U.N. Office of the High Commissioner for Human Rights (Kirsch 2003) in which I described the need for more robust international mechanisms to address community grievances about the negative impacts of mining projects, including the ability to mandate reduction in environmental impacts (Danielson 2002, 349). The report also referred to my argument that "mining companies need to assess their responsibilities in terms of longer time frames commensurate with the longevity of their environmental impacts" (Danielson 2002, 349, paraphrasing Kirsch 2003). This discussion, however, was presented in a text box labeled "an alternative view," which was juxtaposed with a more conventional overview of the problems caused by the Ok Tedi mine (Danielson 2002, 348), rather than integrating my recommendations into the larger report.

One of the directors of the MMSD project subsequently described its three major accomplishments (Danielson 2006, 83). In his view, the first was the recognition that mining projects need to provide economic benefits directly to local communities rather than rely on the state to deliver them. This argument became the basis on which mining was identified as a contributor to sustainable development. The second contribution was the recognition of the need to address the problems that occur after mine closure. The third was based on the Ok Tedi case: the recognition that rivers should not be used for tailings disposal. BHP Billiton adopted the new standard, although it hedged its commitment by pledging that "we will not participate in any *new* project that puts tailings into rivers" (Gilbertson 2002, emphasis added). (This loophole subsequently triggered media chatter during BHP Billiton's unsuccessful takeover bid for Rio Tinto, which owns a significant stake in Freeport-McMoRan's Grasberg gold and copper mine in West Papua, which employs riverine tailings disposal.) However, BHP Billiton's major Australian competitor, Rio Tinto, rejected the new standard proposed by the MMSD report, arguing that decisions about tailings management should be made on a case-by-case basis. The MMSD report offers similar contextual justification for the controversial practice of submarine tailings disposal, as used by the Lihir gold mine in Papua New Guinea.[13]

Critics of the MMSD project question whether the exercise was ever intended to change industry practice. Darryl Reed (2002, 218) argues that the primary goal of the Global Mining Initiative was to preempt civil society from demanding stricter regulations on the industry during the 2002 World Summit on Sustainable Development in Johannesburg.[14] From this perspective, the MMSD project was part of a major rebranding exercise intended to emphasize the industry's contribution to sustainable development. At the Johannesburg meetings, the mining industry touted its role in poverty reduction. BHP Billiton's CEO, Brian Gilbertson (2002), invoked John F. Kennedy's call to "abolish all forms of human poverty" and Nelson Mandela's comments on the need to fight against "poverty and lack of human dignity" in describing the contribution that the mining industry makes to sustainable development. He also argued that "the real challenges of Sustainable Development arise when a major project goes awry, when one stares into an environmental abyss. For BHP Billiton, that abyss was Ok Tedi. . . . Those of you familiar with the history will know of the complex trade-offs that had to be made. The final result has not, I think, fully satisfied everybody, but most will concede that it represents the best trade-off that could be made in very complex circumstances, by parties acting in good faith, and with the best of intentions" (Gilbertson 2002).

Gilbertson praised BHP Billiton for transferring its ownership stake in the mine to the PNG Sustainable Development Program Ltd., even though the company failed to redress the environmental problems downstream from the mine. His self-congratulatory rhetoric was particularly ironic given that the public relations firm engaged by the mining company subsequently bragged about limiting the damage to BHP Billiton's corporate reputation after its exit from the Ok Tedi mine (Offor Sharp 2006). Gilbertson concluded his speech by commending the Global Mining Initiative and the MMSD project for having "brought much self-examination throughout the industry" (Gilbertson 2002).

The Global Mining Initiative and MMSD are examples of managerial interventions known as "audit culture" (Power 1994, 1997; Strathern 2002a). Audit culture reinforces the premises of neoliberalism: that the market is the most efficient means of solving problems and that effective management by the corporation can substitute for regulation.[15] According to Marilyn Strathern, "audit regimes accompany a specific epoch in Western international affairs, a period when governance has been reconfigured through a veritable army of 'moral fieldworkers' (NGOs), when environmental liability has been made an issue of global concern (after the Rio convention), when the ethics of appropriation has been acknowledged to an unprecedented scale in respect of indigenous rights, and when transparency of operation is everywhere endorsed as the outward sign of integrity" (2000b, 2).

Audit culture "encourages ritualization of performance and tokenistic gestures of accountability . . . to the detriment of real effectiveness" (Shore and Wright 2002, 81). Like all rituals, audit "tries to persuade participants of the way the world is without acknowledging its own particular perspective" (Strathern 2002c, 285).

As Michael Power, the accounting professor who pioneered the study of audit culture, notes:

> What is subject to inspection is the auditee's own system for self-monitoring rather than the real practices of the auditee. What is audited is whether there is a system which embodies standards and the standards of performance themselves are shaped by the need to be auditable. In this way, the existence of a system is more significant for audit purposes than what the system is; audit becomes a formal "loop" by which the system observes itself. (1994, 28)

Claims of improvement are not calculated with reference to external standards, but in relation to criteria that corporations have established for their own evaluation. In other words, audit culture simulates reform in order to avoid the imposition of real constraints on its operations (Szablowski 2007, 99–100).

One of the more popular technologies of audit culture is the certification regime, which includes codes of conduct, voluntary initiatives, and other forms of self-regulation. Certification consists of a set of rules or guidelines and a mechanism for monitoring or self-reporting that indicates compliance (Szablowski 2007, 63). However, participation is voluntary, compliance is not enforceable, and the sanctions that do exist tend to be informal, including dialogue, peer pressure, and the threat of expulsion (Szablowski 2007, 63–64). Despite these limitations, some industry observers—including Jared Diamond (2005, 449) in his book *Collapse: How Societies Choose to Fail or Succeed*—argue that mining and petroleum companies should compete for public approval through voluntary adoption of higher environmental standards.

In the case of the mining industry, however, the presence of free riders—competitors that fail to adhere to voluntary standards—makes self-regulation unlikely. Free riders are able to extract minerals at lower cost and consequently have higher profit margins; these are also the projects that continue operating when supply exceeds demand and mineral prices fall. The mining industry has largely avoided participation in certification regimes because of the problem of free riders. The primary exception has been the Kimberley Process for the diamond industry, which blocks the export of diamonds from conflict zones. This benefits the major participants by restricting supply and thereby keeping prices artificially high.[16] Even the Kimberley Process faces criticism, however, because of the continued ability of free riders from conflict zones to bypass these restrictions and market their diamonds.

At the conclusion of the MMSD process in 2001, the mining industry established the International Council on Mining and Metals (ICMM), which replaced the temporary Global Mining Initiative. One of the goals of the ICMM is "to act as a catalyst for performance improvement in the mining and metals industry" (ICMM 2013). It is possible that some of the primary sponsors of the organization are committed to raising the bar for performance through incremental change. For example, a colleague who studies mining in Africa was told by representatives of the major mining companies operating there that they recognized the need for higher industry standards in order to maintain their legitimacy. Despite this, the drive to reduce operating costs and remain competitive with free riders poses significant challenges to reform. There are limited ways to solve such collective action problems short of external regulation. Thus the jury remains out on whether the ICMM is capable of slowly bootstrapping industry standards higher or whether the industry will continue to engage in meaningless acts of audit culture, signifying much but accomplishing little or nothing.

APPROPRIATING TACTICS

Billed as the first antienvironmentalist film, *Mine Your Own Business* borrows tactics from the popular filmmaker Michael Moore in its satirical treatment of environmentalists critical of the mining industry.[17] Filmed in 2006, it was funded primarily by Gabriel Resources, the Canadian mining company whose plan to build an open-pit gold mine in Roşia Montană, Romania, has faced lengthy delays due to environmental considerations (Vesalon and Creţan 2013). The filmmakers, Phelim McAleer and Ann McElhinney, showed the film to audiences at conservative political organizations, mining conferences, and on college campuses in the United States, Europe, and Australia from 2006 to 2007. The film was also shown in mining countries like Ghana, where it appeared on prime-time television on four consecutive nights.

Mine Your Own Business criticizes Western environmentalists for opposing mining projects that offer valuable employment opportunities to poor people living in developing countries. It challenges the legitimacy of NGOs that purport to speak on behalf of communities affected by the mining industry but know little about their lives or living conditions. The film focuses on the people of Roşia Montană who support the proposed gold mine. The town is historically linked to the mining industry, as it was founded by the Romans as a gold-mining outpost. There were also state-operated mining operations at Roşia Montană during the socialist period, although Romanian membership in the European Union required that they be modernized and privatized.[18] In order to build the $340 million project, several hundred people from the town would have to be relocated, although the mining company promised to preserve the historic town center. The company also promised to employ 1,200 people during the construction phase and 600 workers during the mine's seventeen-year operational life (Gabriel Resources 2008).

The film succeeds in embarrassing several Western environmentalists whose comments reveal their ignorance about the people living near proposed mine sites. In one case, the World Wide Fund for Nature representative in Madagascar arrogantly suggests that the people of Fort Dauphin are better off being poor, because money does not guarantee happiness, and even if they had more money, they would not handle it responsibly. The filmmaker also interviews a scholar known for his iconoclastic view that environmentalism is a form of Western imperialism that deprives people living in the developing world of the benefits of development and economic opportunity. Despite the film's criticisms, there is growing evidence that the poor are especially vulnerable to environmental degradation, and, consequently, poor people's movements have become increasingly vocal about environmental issues, including protests against mining (Martinez-Alier 2003).

To deliver its polemical message, the film relies on the selective presentation of evidence. Although the people interviewed in Roşia Montană suggest that there are "only a few" local opponents of the mine, other sources indicate that the community is divided (Smith 2007). Even though some people willingly sold their houses to the mining company, other houses in town bear protest signs reading, "This property is not for sale" (Smith 2007). Local support for the mine is based on the promise of employment for the residents of Roşia Montană. One of the film's central characters is a man from Roşia Montană named Gheorghe

Lucian, who points out that "Greenpeace [does not] ask what you need or what you do, what you eat today, what you eat tomorrow. People don't have money to eat, don't have money for clothes. . . . I know what I need. I need a job, work." However, capital-intensive mines like the one proposed for Roşia Montană offer limited employment opportunities for people without a high level of technical skills.

There is exaggeration on both sides of the debate. Although anti-mining campaigners have emphasized the pristine nature of the area surrounding Roşia Montană, the filmmakers depict a landscape that is historically scarred by gold mining. There are empty pits from state-run mines less than two kilometers from the center of town, and a local stream runs fluorescent orange, the result of acid mine drainage. From this perspective, the new project, which "will grind down several hills, leaving four deep pits in their place, and slowly fill an entire valley with waste water and tailings that will take years to solidify" (Smith 2007), will not necessarily be out of place. Lucian's sister Ela describes the environmental trade-offs of the mining project in the following way: "It is beautiful here, but we can't live on that." Gabriel Resources pledges to operate a state-of-the-art facility that poses no risk to the environment. It also promises to spend $70 million to clean up environmental problems left behind by the abandoned mining projects of earlier eras. Yet opponents of the proposed Roşia Montană mine inevitably draw comparisons to the Baia Mare gold project 150 kilometers to the north, which accidently discharged large volumes of cyanide into the Tisza and Danube Rivers in 2000, killing 1,240 metric tons of fish (Vesalon and Creţan 2013). The cyanide plume traveled into Hungary, through the former Yugoslavia, and into the Black Sea (Csagoly 2000). The Baia Mare cyanide spill has been described as the worst environmental disaster in Europe since Chernobyl (Batha 2000).

The film then follows McAleer and his Romanian sidekick, Lucian, as they travel to two other prospective mine sites, in Africa and Latin America. The accounts of Rio Tinto's titanium sands project in Fort Dauphin, Madagascar, and Barrick Gold's Pascua Lama gold mine in the Andes mountains between Chile and Argentina follow the same narrative as the portion of the film in Romania: that opposition to mining by outside environmentalists prevents people from acquiring the jobs they need to escape poverty. However, the opinions of the people interviewed at the two locations are pragmatically balanced. One man in Madagascar says, "I am afraid about the possibility of damage to the environment, but the mining company will work to resolve that problem," while another observes, "It is a very hard life here and we need money." In Chile, one man argues, "It is important to get the best technology, to try to not cause contamination, not to be against work or development." All of the mining projects profiled in the film are stalled at the review phase, and, consequently, the risks of pollution and competition over access to water remain matters of conjecture.[19] Whether it is possible to rely on the mining companies to follow through on their commitment to protect the environment may be the most significant variable in public opinion about these projects.

The film's central argument is that local communities should be empowered to decide whether these mining projects proceed. As a dentist living in Roşia Montană opines, "We don't need foreign advocates. We are smart enough to take our own fate in our own hands." But as the Baia Mare cyanide spill suggests, people living elsewhere in the mine's catchment area also have an important stake in the project. Similarly, Barrick Gold's proposed mine in Pascua Lama will affect several large glaciers that provide water to thousands of agriculturalists in the surrounding valleys, who greatly outnumber the few hundred people who will end up with long-term employment at the mine. Nor does the framing of the film's central dilemma in terms of local choice address the fact that the people of Roşia Montană lack experience negotiating with foreign mining companies.

When *Mine Your Own Business* was screened at the conservative Heritage Foundation in Washington, DC, on May 30, 2007, McAleer acknowledged that the film had failed to promote dialogue with environmentalists, which he identified as his original objective (Heritage Foundation 2007). However, the film's core message that "the poor need and desperately want development," and that "we owe it to the poor to allow them to have economic dignity," struck a chord among the conservative audience members. Aligning themselves with a moral good like poverty reduction through development provides conservatives with a new reason to oppose environmental regulation. The audience members even appeared to embrace the film's invocation of the "human right of a job and decent housing" despite ordinary conservative resistance to expanding the canon of human rights. Like Brian Gilbertson's speech at the World Summit on Sustainable Development in Johannesburg, championing the rights of the poor enables mining companies and political conservatives to reclaim the moral high ground from their critics.[20]

THE CRITIQUE OF NONGOVERNMENTAL ORGANIZATIONS

The mining industry has also joined the widespread effort to discredit NGOs. In an editorial preface to an issue of the industry journal *Mining Environmental Management,* Terry Mudder (2002) asks whether the NGO movement has outlived its usefulness. While acknowledging the contribution made by NGOs to raising awareness about the environmental impacts of mining, he questions whether these organizations still have a constructive role to play, given that the mining industry has already conceded the need for change. This is a common refrain of the business community, that the institutionalization of environmental values has rendered environmental NGOs obsolete (Hoffman 1997, 180).[21] An example of this dynamic is the assertion that the mining industry has learned from the mistakes of its predecessors (e.g., "Not another Ok Tedi") and consequently has nothing further to learn from the NGO community. A variation on this theme is the claim by the manager of OTML after the settlement of the 1994 lawsuit that whereas NGOs and communities were justified in not trusting his predecessors, their continued skepticism is no longer warranted.

The response of the mining industry to NGOs is part of a larger critique of NGOs from the right. The ability of NGOs to influence corporate behavior was the subject of a conference sponsored by the conservative American Enterprise Institute held in Washington, DC, in June 2003.[22] The conference organizers asserted that

> NGOs have created their own rules and regulations and demanded that governments and corporations abide by those rules. Many nations' legal systems encourage NGOs to use the courts—or the specter of the courts—to compel compliance. Politicians and corporate leaders are often forced to respond to the NGO media machine, and the resources of taxpayers and shareholders are used in support of ends they did not intend to sanction. The extraordinary growth of advocacy NGOs in liberal democracies has the potential to undermine the sovereignty of constitutional democracies, as well as the effectiveness of credible NGOs. (American Enterprise Institute 2003)

The conference participants made similar claims, arguing that the social investment movement, in which shareholders choose stocks on the basis of their performance on key social and environmental indicators, enables NGOs to operate like a "Trojan Horse" that forces corporations to "shift their priorities away from the profit motive that was formerly their governing ideology" (Entine 2003). They also complained that advocacy NGOs wage campaigns that enable organizations that are unelected and unaccountable to the people they purport to represent to impose their values on independent corporations (Manheim 2003, 2004).[23] This is similar to mining company executives and consultants who view NGOs as the problem rather than pollution or social conflict. For example, a senior executive for Rio Tinto once told me, "it isn't the environment I'm worried about, it's the environmentalists!"

The American Enterprise Institute conference first came to my attention when the media reported the claim that NGOs were responsible for "putting Papua New Guinea on the road to bankruptcy" by forcing out the mining industry (Lobe 2003; Nahan 2003, 12).[24] This allegation presumably referred to BHP Billiton's decision to withdraw its investment from the Ok Tedi mine in 2001. Mike Nahan (2003) is not the only observer to suggest that problems associated with the mining industry have left Papua New Guinea on the verge of becoming a "failed state" (see also Windybank and Manning 2003), although most of them would attribute the problems to the resource curse rather than the radical activism of NGOs. In any case, the mining industry in Papua New Guinea subsequently rebounded from the civil war in Bougainville and the lawsuit against the Ok Tedi mine. Five years after the American Enterprise Institute conference, there were a number of midsize mines at various stages of development in Papua New Guinea, and several established projects, including the Ok Tedi mine, were seeking ways to extend their operational life (PNG Industry News 2008). The rumor that NGOs killed the goose that laid the golden egg was greatly exaggerated.

The mining industry and the right are not alone in their critical assessment of NGO politics. In recent years, academics have shifted from valorizing NGOs for creating new forms of politics outside of stalemated or exclusionary political arenas to more negative, cynical, and even dour assessments of their capacity for "doing good" (Fisher 1997). A common academic criticism is that NGOs have more in common with the institutions they purport to critique than is acknowledged. Paul Rabinow (2002, 14; see also H. Moore 2004, 82) argues that despite claims by NGOs to occupy opposing positions on the political spectrum from transnational corporations, they operate in terms of the same fundamental understandings of the person, life, and ownership. NGO debates about property rights also tend to reproduce Euro-American conceptions of the body, nature, and culture (Kirsch 2004). Annelise Riles (2000) points out that the knowledge practices of NGOs rely on the same categories and modes of documentation as the organizations they criticize. Drawing on new institutional economics, Cooley and Ron (2002) show how NGOs operate according to the dictates of the market with respect to funding and competition with their peers in ways belied by their commitment to liberal values.

Indeed, NGOs have become so thoroughly discredited in the academy that everything they report is vulnerable to dismissal as "NGO speak," as though truth and reason were the exclusive province of the state, science, and capital. There is no doubt that even well-intentioned NGOs get a good many things wrong. In my work on the Ok Tedi campaign, I have heard NGOs criticize the people living on the Ok Tedi River for developing a "supermarket culture," ignoring the fact that pollution from the mine has made it very difficult to produce enough food to survive and even the reasons why purchasing food from a store might be more convenient and desirable. I have heard other NGOs criticize Papua New Guineans by invoking the pejorative expression "cargo cult mentality," which suggests that they expect NGOs to solve their problems instead of taking responsibility for them. I have also argued with indigenous advocates who claim that indigenous property regimes are always collective or communal, in contrast to the centrality of private property in Euro-American political and legal traditions, even though anthropologists since Malinowski (1935, 280) have pointed out the reductive nature of this opposition. NGO arguments about indigenous rights also tend to rely on claims about underlying similarities, despite the diversity of peoples included in the category and the ways in which rhetorical opposition to the West can result in the "inversion of tradition" (N. Thomas 1992).

NGOs have also lost friends on the left due to concerns that they operate as the "left hand of empire" (Nina Glick Schiller, pers. comm., 2006). From this perspective, NGOs have become too beholden to their donors to be capable of radical action. Like the classic rites of rebellion described by anthropologists, NGOs channel the expression of resistance and opposition in ways that not only fail to challenge the underlying structures of power but end up reinforcing them (Hardt and Negri 2000, 312–13). Their actions are said to fall somewhere between therapy and false consciousness.

Finally, NGOs are also increasingly under pressure from states seeking to reassert authoritarian control over civil society, although the crackdown is often justified in terms of the threat posed by foreign funding of NGOs to their political sovereignty. Two prominent examples of states that have recently moved to restrict NGO activity are Russia and Egypt, although the problem is widespread (OBS 2013).

The poor, beleaguered NGO: Where else has the right, the left, the academy, and the state come together to reach a consensus? This alone bears examination. Before passing judgment on nongovernmental organizations, it is important to remember the role they have played in the campaign against the Ok Tedi mine and similar political struggles. In his speech to landowners in the town of Daru after the settlement of the first lawsuit against the mine, Gabia Gagarimabu said, "international help was the very thing that let us succeed; it was NGO help that made the company settle." It is also crucial to recognize how corporations benefit from the multipronged attack on their most potent critics, especially during a neoliberal era of deregulation.

ACQUIRING SYMBOLIC CAPITAL

Finally, the mining industry is trying to repair the damage to its reputation from mining conflicts by increasing its symbolic capital (Bourdieu 1977) through philanthropy, especially donations to public health campaigns and universities.

Corporations have long made important charitable contributions at the local level, which were generally seen as demonstrations of the corporation's role as a good neighbor (Marchand 1998). However, such donations are not readily visible in the era of globalization. Raising the profile of corporate giving requires new forms of philanthropy, leading transnational corporations to identify targets for corporate giving that can enhance their international stature. In particular, global public health has become a key focus for corporate donations. Dinah Rajak (2011a, 18) argues that these contributions help corporations "gain access to new kinds of moral and social resources" that can be mobilized "in pursuit of their economic goals." In the last decade, the companies comprising the Fortune 500 have made regular contributions to campaigns against some of the major global public health threats, including HIV/AIDS, malaria, and tuberculosis, which are often announced in newspaper advertisements. Examples include a two-page ad in the *New York Times* from Chevron on Wednesday, June 1, 2011, with the caption "Fighting Aids Should be Corporate Policy. We Agree" and a similar ad from the Global Business Coalition on HIV/AIDS, tuberculosis, and malaria with the headline "Fighting AIDS, TB and Malaria is Our Business," which lists a number of mining companies as sponsors.

The mining industry's attention to malaria is of particular interest. At the 2003 American Enterprise Institute conference, NGOs were criticized not only for their influence on corporations but also for blocking the use of DDT in fighting malaria in Africa (Bate and Tren 2003). Public concern about DDT can be traced back to the publication of Rachel Carson's 1962 book *Silent Spring,* which describes the threat posed by the use of chemical pesticides in industrial agriculture. Criticism of the chemical industry inspired by Carson's work led to the establishment of the U.S. Environmental Protection Agency, which subsequently banned DDT manufacture and use. As historian James McWilliams makes clear in *American Pests* (2008), much of the evidence presented by Rachel Carson about the harmful effects of DDT was already well established in the scientific community. But the toxic effect of DDT on songbirds provided the evocative image of a spring in which "no birds sing," which captured the imagination of Americans who were already becoming disenchanted with corporate America's disregard for its environmental impacts (Hoffman 1997, 56–57).

Carson's book is widely celebrated for its enrollment of supporters in what became the environmental movement. *Silent Spring* was also an important crossover point for public involvement in scientific decision making. Her work helped to inaugurate a new relationship between science and society that recognizes both the public's right to participate in decision making and the social responsibility of scientists, rather than treating scientists as neutral technicians independent of society (Nowotny, Scott, and Gibbons 2001). This transition was central to the efflorescence of environmental NGOs during the 1980s and 1990s, which helps to explain why Carson's work remains a target for the conservative movement so long after its publication.

The critique of the ban on DDT can be seen as an attempt to put the genie of public involvement in science back in the bottle, returning policy making to scientists and their corporate employers. If it were possible to demonstrate that NGO opposition to DDT use in controlling malaria was misguided, it would discredit NGOs on the very grounds through which they claim legitimacy: the protection of vulnerable populations. The assertion that millions of people have needlessly died as a consequence of Rachel Carson's work seeks to reverse the tide of public participation in scientific decision making. It also represents an effort to reclaim the moral high ground in the struggle between corporations and their critics.[25] This helps to explain why the American Enterprise Institute supports the NGO Africa Fighting Malaria, which seeks to overturn the ban on DDT use, and why two of the most prominent funders of the organization are the mining companies Anglo American and BHP Billiton (Africa Fighting Malaria 2008).

The mining industry also seeks to acquire symbolic capital by cultivating relationships with the academy. For example, in 2005, the new institute for sustainability at the university where I teach invited BHP Billiton to join its external advisory board. Other companies with controversial environmental records appointed to the board included Dow Chemical, Shell Oil, and Duke Energy. The acting director of the institute defended the decision to include BHP Billiton on the board to the *Chronicle of Higher Education:* "'There's no pure company out there,' he says. 'I have no reason to doubt that this company has really screwed a lot of people,' just as nearly every other company is 'unjust to people' at one point or another. . . . 'These organizations are part of the problem, and they're also part of the solution'" (Blumenstyk 2007).

This is not the only connection between the mining industry and the University of Michigan. For a number of years, the BHP Billiton logo was prominently displayed on the College of Engineering's solar car, an important symbol of the university's commitment to environmental issues. The School of Natural Resources and Environment at the University of Michigan is also the North American partner of the Alcoa Foundation, established by the world's largest miner of bauxite and producer of aluminum, which supports fellowships in conservation and sustainability.

Nor are the ties between the University of Michigan and the mining industry unique. Freeport-McMoRan has donated millions of dollars to universities in New Orleans and Austin (Bryce 1996, 69; Fox 1997). After OPIC cancelled the company's political risk insurance for its mine in West Papua, Louisiana State University took out a full-page ad in the *Times-Picayune* expressing its support for the company (Bryce 1996, 69). Freeport CEO James R. Moffet's donations to the University of Texas at Austin, including fellowships for geology students to prospect for copper in the militarized Indonesian territory of West Papua, were denounced by faculty and students. After Freeport threatened legal action against professors critical of the company, the chancellor of the university was forced to resign his lucrative position on the company's board of directors (Bryce 1996, 69). The Munk School of Global Affairs at the University of Toronto, which is named after the chairman and founder of Barrick Gold, which operates the Porgera mine in Papua New Guinea, has also been the target of criticism. In 2012, faculty responsible for the university's long-running interdisciplinary seminar on development ended its affiliation with the Munk School, noting the contradiction in using funds earned by the controversial mining company for this purpose (Vukosavic 2012). Similarly, in Australia, Kristen Lyons and Carol Richards (2013) express concern about industry support for the Centre for Social Responsibility in Mining at the University of Queensland, a relationship that might be compared to the Tobacco Industry Research Council's sponsorship of academic research during its heyday in the 1960s and 1970s.

CONCLUSION

Elsewhere, Peter Benson and I outline the three phases of corporate response to critique (Benson and Kirsch 2010a). Phase 1 involves the denial that the critique is valid or that a legitimate problem exists. An example of a phase 1 response in the Ok Tedi case is the public relations poster from the late 1980s that provides the reassuring message: "The company protects the river, forest, and wildlife. No harm will come to you when the refuse from the gold and copper is released into the river" (see fig. 4). The goal of phase 1 is to avoid engagement with externalities that have the potential to erode profitability and raise questions about legitimacy that may threaten the corporation or industry's ability to continue operating. A key strategy of this phase is the proliferation of doubt. As I argued in chapter 4, this often entails the establishment of industry counterscience that supports their claims. Phase 1 is the status quo for most relationships between corporations and their critics.

When problems become too great to deny and the opposition too effective to ignore, companies may shift to phase 2, which involves acknowledgment that a problem exists, that something is harmful or defective, and that the critique has some scientific validity or ethical merit. In phase 2, the response to critique is generally limited to symbolic gestures of accommodation, such as the payment of compensation or small-scale improvements.

The shift from phase 1 to phase 2 for BHP can be seen in the pair of corporate images reproduced as figures 11 and 12. The first of these images has the caption "Leaving our environment the same way we found it," denying that the mining industry has long-lasting environmental impacts. However, what appears to be a bucolic natural scene is actually the mine pit of the Island Copper mine in Vancouver Island, Canada, which has been filled with salt water. Instead of restoring the

LEAVING OUR
ENVIRONMENT THE
SAME WAY WE FOUND IT

BHP is one of the world's largest diversified resources companies, with operations
and offices in more than 59 countries and more than 100 years of experience in the
resources industry. It has four main businesses—Copper, Minerals, Petroleum and
Steel—and specialized support provided by its Service Companies Group.

 **BHP**

We aim to achieve leadership in our performance in every aspect of our business.
Safety and environment are our highest priority and our most serious commitment.

600 Bourke Street   550 California Street
Melbourne Vic 3000   San Francisco CA 94101
Australia   United States

FIGURE 11. "Leaving our environment the same way we found it." BHP advertisement, *Engineering and Mining Journal*, February 1997. This optimistic assessment of BHP's environmental impacts was published less than a year after the settlement of the first Ok Tedi case.

FIGURE 12. "There's no question our business has an impact." BHP Environment and Community Report, 1999. Published several years after the settlement of the first Ok Tedi case, it acknowledges the environmental impact of the mining industry by depicting the use of explosives at the Gregory coal mine in Queensland, Australia.

pre-mining environment, the company created a sterile inland lake (see Keeling 2004).[26] In contrast, the second image, from a BHP Environment and Community Report, depicts the use of explosives at the Gregory coal mine in Australia, acknowledging that mining transforms the environment with the caption "There's no question our business has an impact. . . ." The first image was published in 1997, shortly after the settlement of the original Ok Tedi case, but before its lessons had been internalized throughout the corporation. The second image appeared in 1999, after the corporation realized that the Ok Tedi conflict was not an isolated incident. It illustrates a phase 2 response, in which corporations recognize the need to engage with their critics.

Phase 2 corporate responses to critique take many forms. One strategy is the institution of audit culture, the development of regimes of monitoring and accountability that avoid the imposition of significant structural change. Corporations may also attempt to assimilate their critics within corporate structures by forming partnerships with NGOs or by recruiting activists to join corporate boards, reducing their ability and motivation to promote radical restructuring and change. Conversely, other critics may be portrayed as radical and impractical, a strategy of divide and conquer that can have disruptive consequences for NGOs and civil society. Corporations also co-opt the discourse of their critics, using the virtuous language of responsibility, sustainability, and transparency to influence shareholders and the market. For example, the concept of sustainability has undergone progressive redefinition, "emptying out the meaning" of the term (Negri 1999, 9)—its original reference to ecology and biology. Industries may also promote corporate oxymorons that attempt to conceal intractable problems. They align themselves with conservative political organizations in the critique of NGOs and public participation in science. They also seek to increase their symbolic capital by participating in global public-health initiatives and enhancing their ties to the academy. These responses to critique seek to spare corporations and industries the full cost of addressing the problems they cause.

Whereas in phase 2 the threats posed to the corporation are limited, phase 3 is defined by the risk that the problems facing the corporation or industry will become financially and socially too great to manage. The threat of catastrophic loss, bankruptcy, industry collapse, or the complete loss of legitimacy motivates corporations to shift to phase 3. These problems force the corporation to actively engage with its critics and participate in the shaping of politics that lead to the regulation and management of industry-related problems. For example, after it was established that exposure to asbestos causes lung cancer and other respiratory ailments, legal action against the industry led to bankruptcy proceedings. Paint manufacturers faced similarly catastrophic costs due to the effects of lead on children's nervous systems. However, the threat of financial insolvency posed by the costs of cleanup and compensation resulted in the negotiation of novel agreements that allowed corporations to continue operating so that they could make partial restitution for the harms they caused. Other costs from asbestos and lead were socialized by their transfer to the government or the affected individuals, including consumers made responsible for cleaning up properties affected by these toxic materials (Brodeur 1985; Warren 2001).

The core of phase 3 is the strategic management of critique and the establishment of a new status quo. Corporations may also envision the possibility of competitive advantage and the achievement of a new kind of legitimacy through their participation in regulatory processes. The mining industry has thus far been able to avoid a phase 3 crisis, except in the case of individual mining projects like Ok Tedi with catastrophic impacts, to which the standard response is to sever ties, transferring environmental liabilities to a third party. In the Ok Tedi case, the damage to BHP's corporate reputation and threat to its legitimacy forced the company to transfer its shares in the mine to the PNG Sustainable Development Company Ltd., which indemnified BHP Billiton against any future environmental liabilities. The costs of environmental remediation in these cases are typically borne by the public, as illustrated by the estimated $15 billion cost to clean up the abandoned hard rock mining sites in the United States.

Corporations and industries move back and forth through the different phases of response. Particular corporations within a given industry may respond differently to critique and thus may be located in a different phase than their competitors, and all three phases coexist across capitalism at the same moment. In general, phase 1 is the most profitable position for corporations to occupy, because it allows them to avoid financial liability for costly externalities. Corporations generally resist the move to phase 2, because of the transaction costs associated with engaging with one's critics. In some cases, however, it may be strategically advantageous for corporations to move preemptively into phase 2 in order to manage their critics. This strategy is promoted by the public relations industry, which encourages corporations to meet with and educate their critics before conflicts arise. Corporations can then achieve positive recognition for being responsible citizens without engaging in more confrontational relationships that might require them to modify production or undertake other actions that might reduce their profitability. Phase 3 is typically the last resort for corporations, in which the possibility of bankruptcy or illegitimacy threatens the viability of the corporation or the industry.

The ingenuity with which corporations have been able to neutralize or appropriate critical discourse, as well as their ability to co-opt and divide their critics, suggests that even successful strategies of opposition will not necessarily be effective in other campaigns. Industry adapts quickly to the challenges posed by its critics. A recent example of this dynamic comes from two campaigns against sulfide copper mining in the Great Lakes region of the United States. In northern Wisconsin, Native American groups and sport fishers—who previously had antagonistic relations—found common ground in blocking the development of a proposed zinc and copper mine (Gedicks and Grossman 2005; Grossman 2005). When Rio Tinto came to the Upper Peninsula in northern Michigan to open a controversial sulfide mine at Eagle Rock several years later, they sought to preempt a similar alliance by cultivating support among local hunters, fishers, and lovers of the outdoors. Corporations are adept at responding to the strategies and tactics of their critics, which requires activists to engage in continual strategic innovation. This is the starting point for the final chapter, which examines new strategies based on the politics of time.

CHAPTER 6

New Politics of Time

This chapter compares political strategies employed by critics of the mining industry. The first strategy is the politics of space, which links actors in multiple locations. The resulting networks are comprised of individuals, communities, nongovernmental organizations, experts, lawyers, and others. They benefit from the complementary mobilization of resources, discourses of persuasion, access to power, and forms of leverage deployed by their participants (Keck and Sikkink 1998; Kirsch 1995, 2007; Tsing 2004). The ability to enroll members in multiple locations makes these networks especially effective in challenging transnational corporations wherever they operate. The accomplishments of these networks, however, may be limited by their lack of coordination and the potential for conflicting strategies and agendas. Nevertheless, the politics of space has enabled the participants in these networks to mobilize support, gain recognition, foster new debates, and achieve many of their goals. The campaign against the Ok Tedi mine, like many other environmental movements during the 1990s, was organized according the politics of space.

The Ok Tedi case reveals both the strengths and weaknesses of the politics of space. By scaling up their opposition from the local to the global, the campaign was able to exert significant pressure on one of Australia's largest corporations. Their lawsuit against BHP was a pioneering example of litigation that seeks to hold transnational corporations accountable in their home court for their international operations

(Koebele 2010), another manifestation of the politics of space. The campaign against the Ok Tedi mine helped to usher in a new era, in which mining companies recognize the need to negotiate directly with the communities affected by their projects, trumping the state's claim to be the sole representative of its citizens (Ballard and Banks 2003, 298). The litigation also served notice to the mining industry that it could no longer afford to ignore its critics, leading to unprecedented collaboration among the world's largest mining companies.

But the campaign against the Ok Tedi mine also illustrates a crucial shortcoming of the politics of space: the length of time required to diagnose a problem, enroll a network of supporters, and stage an effective intervention. Margaret Keck and Kathryn Sikkink (1998, 161) describe the effectiveness of transnational action networks in gaining "seats at the bargaining table for new actors," including previously excluded indigenous peoples, but they have less to say about the steep learning curves these communities face in order to become effective political actors. It took years before the Yonggom and their neighbors recognized the full extent of the threat posed by the mine to their environment and even longer before they were able to effectively challenge the mining company. The delay allowed the mining company to continue polluting the river system with impunity. By the time the Yonggom and their neighbors filed suit against BHP and Ok Tedi Mining Ltd. in 1994, the project had already caused substantial environmental damage. During the decade in which their claims were being adjudicated in the Australian courts, the mine continued to operate as before, discharging seventy million metric tons of tailings, waste rock, and overburden into the river system annually. By the time they returned to court for the second case against BHP in 2000, many of the people living along the Ok Tedi River had concluded that the river was no longer worth saving. The opportunity to protect the Fly River from a similar fate eventually slipped through their fingers as well (fig. 13).

The ghost forests along the Ok Tedi and Fly Rivers attest to the limitations of the politics of space. So do the rivers themselves, which now run thick with grey tailings, the color and consistency of concrete poured at a construction site. The few plant species able to take root and grow in the tailings deposited along the floodplain have no value to the people living there. It is difficult to imagine that the birds and other animals that once lived along the river corridor will ever return. The presence of acid mine drainage at multiple locations poses a significant threat to organic life in the river system (Tingay 2007, 27).[1]

FIGURE 13. Yonggom activist Robin Moken makes a point while Middle Fly activist Barnabus Uwako (seated immediately to his left) looks on at a meeting held in Kiunga, Western Province. On November 7–9, 2005, more than three hundred people representing the communities downstream from the Ok Tedi mine met to plan a new political strategy after the precipitous end to their legal proceedings (see Kirsch 2007). Photo: Stuart Kirsch.

The failure of the politics of space to protect the Ok Tedi and Fly Rivers suggests the need for new political strategies to prevent future mining disasters from occurring. In contrast to earlier social movements organized through the politics of space, more recent protests against the mining industry increasingly make use of the politics of time. These new forms of politics seek to prevent the negative environmental impacts of mining by shifting their attention to the period before mining begins. A key strength of the politics of time as an activist strategy is that it avoids contesting mining projects that are already operational. The huge financial investments required to build a new mine generate almost insurmountable political inertia; these projects become even more firmly entrenched once they begin to produce revenue for the state. Political movements rarely have enough leverage to stop a mining project after production has commenced. Consequently, political pressure may be most effective when targeted at the planning stage of new projects, which can make it difficult for the mining company to raise the necessary capital or receive government approval. In contrast to the outcome of the campaign against the Ok Tedi mine, which was ultimately too late to save the river, new approaches based on the politics of time represent a more hopeful political turn.

To succeed, campaigns based on the politics of time must change the way people perceive the impacts of mining. Slow-motion environmental disasters rarely capture the public's attention until they reach a tipping point. By that time, however, the damage may already be irreversible. It took years before the pollution from the Ok Tedi mine was adequately acknowledged by political actors in the capital of Port Moresby. These problems are exacerbated by the way mining companies manipulate the politics of time to delay recognition of their environmental impacts. This makes it easier for these companies to issue reassuring messages to their stakeholders, make optimistic assessments about the future, or argue that problematic trends have been stabilized or reversed, all of which occurred in the early years of the campaign against the Ok Tedi mine. Even when the impacts from mining are obvious to the people living downstream, as they were in the Ok Tedi case, mining companies are often able to use the scientific data they have collected to rebut their observations. Challenging these corporate claims requires comparative knowledge about the mining industry and its track record.

This chapter describes how the politics of time is increasingly mobilized by environmental activists and other critics of the mining industry. My discussion of the politics of time augments the way other anthropologists have written about the subject, focusing on the means by which elites extend their power over the body politic through their control over the social construction of time, including encounters with the "bearers of nonwestern or non-capitalist temporalities" (Rutz 1992; Verdery 1992, 37).[2] The politics of time is also central to contemporary environmental debates (B. Adam 1998), especially the contradiction between the short-term interests of capital and corporations and the longue durée of industrial impacts on the environment. New strategies invoking the politics of time must bring these longer temporal horizons into public consciousness and make them subject to political and economic calculation. This requires paying greater attention to the production of environmental risks and hazards rather than deferring their diagnosis and solution to the future (B. Adam 1998; Melucci 1998, 428).

In this chapter, I examine several strategies based on the politics of time that seek to prevent mining projects from causing harm. The first example involves the formation of international networks of NGOs that share information and coordinate responses to the mining industry. One of the goals of these networks has been to accelerate local learning curves through both vertical and horizontal sharing of information. Another strategy of these networks has been to exert pressure on multilateral organizations and international financial institutions to address problems in the mining sector. I describe two pivotal workshops on indigenous peoples and extractive industry sponsored by the United Nations and the World Bank in 2001 and 2003; the extraordinary confluence of interest in these issues was prompted by the rising levels of conflict between mines and communities in the late 1990s, including the examples from Melanesia described in this book. I focus in particular on the contribution of these workshops to the recognition of indigenous peoples' rights to free, prior, and informed consent, an important resource in the politics of time. Next, I address some of the complexities that may arise when seeking to accelerate the learning curve of indigenous peoples facing the prospect of a new mining project by drawing on my participation in the independent review of the environmental and social impact assessment of a proposed bauxite mine in Suriname. Finally, I examine a growing social movement based on the politics of time, the *consulta,* or referendum, movement in Latin America, in which communities vote on whether to permit mining or other development projects on their lands and territories. The success of the *consulta* movement depends on both greater awareness of the social and environmental impacts of mining and recognition of their right to determine whether these projects should go forward.

NETWORKING POLITICS

One of the key strategies of the politics of time has been to accelerate the learning curve of communities facing the prospect of a new mining project. Given their limited knowledge and experience of mining, these communities are initially at a disadvantage in interactions with their industry counterparts. Even where there is history of mining in the region, knowledge drawn from past experiences may be challenged. The mining industry may claim to have undergone significant reform, whether through the development of new technologies purported to overcome the problems caused by previous mining projects, or through new commitments to social responsibility and sustainability. Such claims are difficult to evaluate without access to comparative information about the mining industry. For example, even though people living in rural Papua New Guinea are familiar with the conflicts associated with the Ok Tedi mine and the Panguna mine in Bougainville (Halvaksz 2010), they generally remain optimistic about the prospect of new mining ventures. Reactions to the proposed Ramu nickel mine in northeastern Papua New Guinea provide an illustrative example: the first protests about the mine were directed at the national government for delaying approval of the project, because the people living nearby were keen to benefit from the economic opportunities promised by the developers. Protests against the Ramu mine's proposed use of submarine tailings disposal, in which tailings and other mine wastes are discharged directly into the ocean, affecting coral reefs and other marine life, did not begin until several years later.

NGOs have employed a variety of means to reduce the disparity in access to information between mining companies and local communities. The most common strategy for achieving this goal is the vertical transfer of information from metropolitan NGOs to rural communities by sharing materials about comparable mining projects or the track record of the relevant mining company. NGOs also facilitate horizontal information sharing between communities facing similar challenges (Appadurai 2002); this may involve sponsoring visits by local leaders or community representatives to comparable mining sites or attendance at conferences where they can learn about the experiences of other communities affected by mining. Alex Maun's 1995 trip from Papua New Guinea to meet with members of the Dene Nation in Yellowknife, Canada, where BHP Billiton sought to obtain the concession for a billion dollar diamond mine, exemplifies this strategy. NGOs also exploit new opportunities provided by the Internet to share information with people from communities affected by mining, although these efforts are constrained by both the problems of translation and the persistence of the digital divide. Nevertheless, NGO reports are generally more accessible to the public than academic publications, the digital forms of which are ordinarily locked behind expensive paywalls. And the information gap is shrinking as a result of increased attention to mining conflicts by traditional news media, as well as by new social media, including electronic mailing lists, websites, and online video.

The desire to increase access to information about the mining industry led to the establishment of two international networks of NGOs that focused on mining conflicts. These networks were also intended to keep pace with the globalization of the mining industry, including transformations to companies like BHP Billiton, which since the 1980s has rapidly expanded beyond its original economic base in Australia to become the world's largest resource company, with significant operations in every region of the world. In addition, these international networks were meant to compete head-to-head with parallel organizations formed by the mining industry, including the International Council on Mining and Metals, which was established in 2001.

The first international network of NGOs working on mining issues, organized in 2001 by the Mineral Policy Center in Washington, DC, was short lived. The Global Mining Campaign involved NGOs and individuals from forty countries (Young and Septoff 2002). However, the Mineral Policy Center's top-down efforts to coordinate the network clashed with the commitment of its members to horizontal politics (see Graeber 2013; Juris 2008). Concern among the participants in the network initially flared up in relation to policy positions independently adopted by the Mineral Policy Center, including its decision to participate in the industry-sponsored Mines, Minerals, and Sustainable Development (MMSD) project, which had been condemned by many of the network members for being a vehicle for industry propaganda. Disagreement spilled over into discord when the director of the Mineral Policy Center optimistically endorsed the prospects for collaboration between the NGO community and the mining industry in a plenary speech delivered at the industry-sponsored conference held to announce the findings of the MMSD project in May 2002. Despite the subsequent dissolution of the network less than a year later, the Mineral Policy Center, which rebranded itself as Earthworks in 2005, has contributed to a number of the signature mining campaigns of the last decade, including protests against proposed mining projects in Tambogrande, Peru; Esquel, Argentina; and the Pebble gold mine in Alaska. All of these campaigns are examples of the politics of time in that they seek to block the approval of new mining protects.

A second international network of NGOs working on mining issues, with a specific focus on indigenous communities affected by mining, was founded in the United Kingdom in 2001, shortly after the establishment of its American counterpart. The Mines and Communities network has been more resilient than the Global Mining Campaign.[3] The hub of the network is London, home to both the London Stock Exchange, which includes listings of many of the world's largest mining companies, including Anglo American, BHP Billiton, Glencore Xstrata, Rio Tinto, and Vedanta, and the London Metal Exchange, the primary market through which the trade in nonferrous and nonprecious metals is carried out, including aluminum, copper, lead, nickel, tin, and zinc. The founding members of the Mines and Communities network included NGOs and individuals from Canada, Colombia, Ghana, India, Indonesia, Peru, the Philippines, Sierra Leone, the United Kingdom, and the United States. The members were invited to join in part because of their prior working relationships with London-based organizations and activists. The NGO members of the network are also among the most prominent organizations focused on mining, indigenous rights, and the environment in their home countries. Individual members of the network have also organized and participated in a variety of regional and international networks addressing related problems, contributed to the leadership of the U.N. Permanent Forum on Indigenous Issues, and helped organize key multilateral meetings examining the relationship between extractive industry and indigenous peoples.

The first policy decision made by the participants—at the inaugural meeting of the Mines and Communities network in May 2001—was to reject efforts by the mining industry to engage with the NGO community, most notably the industry-sponsored Mines, Minerals, and Sustainable Development project. This position was articulated in the London Declaration of 2001, which became the charter for the network and the basis on which new members and supporters were subsequently recruited (Mines and Communities 2001). The London Declaration also expressed the views of the participants on a number of issues. It condemned neoliberal reform of national mining legislation, which has weakened or eliminated existing regulatory statutes in dozens of countries. It challenged several common assumptions about mining: that the demand for metal will increase exponentially, which fails to consider the potential for increased recycling and the substitution of alternative materials; that mining catalyzes development despite the problems of the resource curse; that new technologies can be developed to mitigate the ongoing environmental impacts of mining, known as the fallacy of ecological modernization theory (Buttel 2000; York and Rosa 2003); and that critics of the mining industry are opposed to all forms of development. The London Declaration called for a moratorium on new mining projects on previously undeveloped lands, known as greenfield sites. It also directed the mining industry to pay for the remediation of landscapes polluted by abandoned mines, known as brownfield sites. The declaration called on the World Bank and the International Monetary Fund to stop promoting voluntary codes of conduct, which are neither sufficiently specific nor robust enough to bring about significant change (see Szablowski 2007, 63–64). It also called for stricter international standards for mining; recognition of indigenous rights to both surface and subsurface minerals; and support for the right of indigenous peoples to free, prior, and informed consent, including the right to veto projects they regard as unacceptable.

The purpose of the London Declaration was to establish a collective agenda for NGOs campaigning on mining issues, but the horizontal politics of the network also acknowledged the autonomy and differences of the NGOs that comprise its membership. For example, although the London Declaration opposes NGO participation in industry-sponsored forums, the NGO CooperAcción in Peru helped organize a multistakeholder forum with BHP Billiton that addressed the problems associated with the Tintaya copper mine, which resulted in a compensation plan for farmers whose land had been expropriated and agreements on human rights protections, environmental issues, and community development (Keenan, de Echave, and Traynor 2007, 189–92). Mines and Communities members have also participated in workshops sponsored by the World Bank, the United Nations, and other organizations that included corporate participants. These decisions have not generated friction, because none of the organizations purport to speak on behalf of the network. On the other hand, the horizontal structure of the network, including its reliance on a deliberative model of consensus building, has diminished its capacity to respond to events in a timely fashion.

The signature contribution of the Mines and Communities network has been its ability to track and analyze the strategies of the mining industry, information that is posted on its website (www.minesandcommunities.org). Other mining websites tend to focus on specific mining projects, companies, or countries; technologies such as mountaintop removal; or particular commodities, such as coal, diamonds, or gold. The Mines and Communities website provides a more comprehensive overview of the mining industry by drawing on regional materials submitted and reviewed by its members, who contribute important contextual information and analysis. Participation in the editorial process for the website has been a two-way street for network members, enhancing the content posted on the website while providing the editors with a valuable comparative perspective on the mining industry. Although the original objective of the website was to provide information that could be used by indigenous communities affected by mining projects, it largely failed to reach its target audience. Instead, the most frequent users of the site tend to be researchers, journalists, and students, though it has also proven to be a valuable resource for NGOs working on mining-related issues.[4]

A second meeting of the Mines and Communities network was held in conjunction with the 2004 World Social Forum in Mumbai, and a third was held three years later in London. The participants at the 2007 meeting discussed the continued use of voluntary rather than legally binding mechanisms to address the problems caused by mining companies. The participants objected to state protection of transnational mining companies through the criminalization of social protest and listened to concerns about these practices in Indonesia, India, Peru, and the Philippines, including the disturbing rise in acts of violence against mining activists by both the state and private security forces employed by mining companies. Other issues addressed at the meeting included the ability of transnational corporations to defeat efforts to raise taxes and royalty rates; the lack of state capacity to monitor and regulate large mining projects; and the expansion of mining into ecologically sensitive areas, including protected forests and marine environments through submarine tailings disposal.

The 2007 meeting of the Mines and Communities network also updated the London Declaration, calling for a halt to multilateral support for the mining industry and the cancellation of contracts and licenses that provide unfairly low rates of return. It acknowledges the passage of the U.N. Declaration on the Rights of Indigenous Peoples, which mandates recognition of the indigenous right to free, prior, and informed consent. The revised declaration also calls on larger humanitarian NGOs that have undertaken independent campaigns on mining to refrain from negotiating on behalf of communities affected by mining or representing their interests unless invited to do so, to advocate and assist other forms of development as alternatives to mining, to reject funding from the mining industry, and to refuse to collaborate with or employ consultants who are affiliated with the mining industry. It challenges the uncritical promotion of the discourse of corporate social responsibility and its entry into the public sphere and the academy. Finally, it rejects collaborations between the mining industry and conservation organizations that infringe on the rights of indigenous peoples. Although the Mines and Communities network is not unique in its attention to these concerns, it is one of the few political and intellectual spaces in which they are comprehensively examined.

The Mines and Communities network is currently in a transitional phase, including a proposed shift in management from the Global North to the Global South and potential changes in the way that it shares information. Some members of the network would prefer a broader mandate to campaign internationally against the mining industry, although the more centralized or vertical forms of organization this would entail might clash with the network's ethos and practice of horizontal politics.[5] The desire to expand membership in the network also poses challenges of scale, including the dilution of the strong personal ties among its current members. But like many other NGO networks, the majority of the participants have full-time obligations to other organizations, which limits their ability to implement these changes. There is also a shared sense of diminishing returns from the network, and its continuity into the future is less than assured.

The transformation of the Mines and Community network after a decade of operation is hardly unprecedented. The recent history of mining activism can be roughly divided into three overlapping periods, each lasting about a decade. The first generation of NGOs to focus on mining issues emerged in the 1970s and 1980s. Most of these groups were short-lived coalitions organized around specific problems, such as uranium mining in Australia. The NGO Partizans (People against Rio Tinto Zinc and its Subsidiaries), founded in 1979, was one of the first groups to target a specific mining company. The second wave of mining activism took place during the late 1980s and the 1990s. It involved the creation of national organizations focused on mining, including the Mineral Policy Center in the United States in 1988; the Mineral Policy Institute in Australia and JATAM in Indonesia in 1995; mines, minerals & People in India in 1998; and MiningWatch Canada in 1999. The third phase involved international networks. A relatively short-lived organization called Project Underground, which was based in San Francisco, adopted an international perspective on the problems caused by extractive industry, operating from 1996 until 2004. The two international networks discussed here both began in 2001, although the Global Mining Campaign was short-lived and the future of Mines and Communities is uncertain. The different organizational forms represent adaptations to rapidly changing circumstances, including initiatives by the mining industry.

The next generation of anti-mining activism may already be emerging in the form of virtual networks that operate primarily through the Internet. New forms of social media make it possible to attract a wider range of participants than before. These new networks share information, recruit academic expertise, raise funding, research and promote reports, and influence the public and policy makers almost entirely through social media. Like hunter-gatherers of the virtual world, these new groups form through the fusion of like-minded activists and settle their disputes through fission, avoiding the political infighting that notoriously affects many "brick-and-mortar" NGOs. One example of such an Internet-based network is a campaign opposing the use of submarine tailings disposal by the Ramu nickel mine in Madang, Papua New Guinea, although a legal challenge mounted late in the construction phase of the mine failed to stop the completion of the tailings pipeline (see chapter 3, n. 13). The campaign website received more than fifty thousand hits in its first nine months, before expanding to cover the entire mining sector in Papua New Guinea. Another virtual campaign opposes the use of deep-sea (or sea-bed) mining near Papua New Guinea, which is jointly coordinated by two veterans of mining and environmental NGOs in Australia. The capacity of these new organizational forms to take the lead in responding to pressing concerns can be seen in the response to the online campaign against seabed mining by a more traditional NGO, Greenpeace, which followed suit by producing its own report on the subject. Another virtual collective uses art and music produced by its anonymous members to draw attention to political violence in West Papua and throughout Southeast Asia, including conflicts over mining and other extractive industries.[6]

These new virtual networks enroll participants who might not participate in more conventional forms of NGO politics. However, some forms of Internet activism, such as signing a petition, charging a donation to a credit card, or sending a form letter to a politician, ask very little from participants. As climate change activist Tim DeChristopher (pers. comm. 2009) argues, "Aren't we diminishing the importance of the problem if the solution demands so little of us? Aren't the problems big enough that we should be demanding more from activists, not less?" Changing the status quo is likely to require more extensive commitment than token forms of online participation. Nonetheless, new forms of social media activism increasingly supplement and may in some cases supplant conventional NGOs.

MULTILATERAL CONDITIONALITIES

One of the more productive strategies involving the politics of time has been to persuade multilateral organizations to establish new policies.

For instance, NGOs have lobbied international financial institutions such as the World Bank and regional development banks to impose stricter conditions on the projects they support. Corporate regulation has historically been treated as the responsibility of the state in which the activity takes place, even when the firm is incorporated elsewhere (J. P. Davis 1961). However, recognition that the economic clout of the world's largest corporations eclipses the resources of many states reveals a key shortcoming of this system, an example of what Saskia Sassen (1998, 155) refers to as "regulatory fracture." Since the 1980s, NGOs have exerted pressure on the financial institutions that invest, guarantee loans, and provide political risk insurance to transnational corporations to ensure that their projects meet minimum performance standards. The gradual inclusion of social and environmental standards for new loans has turned international financial institutions into de facto regulatory gatekeepers for future mining projects.

Over time, the World Bank has adopted a series of "safeguard policies" that address environmental impacts, resettlement, and indigenous peoples. As Robert Goodland notes (2000, 3; reference omitted; see also Goldman 2005), these structural changes did not arise independently, as a result of internal pressure to reform, but were hard-won through external intervention.

> From 1984 to 1986, criticism of projects causing much environmental damage increased, a series of US congressional hearings warned the Bank to improve its environmental capacity, member governments and NGO pressures became more difficult for the Bank to ignore, and the US voted against a project for the first time on environmental grounds. Even so, the Bank did not budge. It took a concerted threat by member governments and NGOs to vote against replenishment of [International Development Association] grant funds, and change in World Bank presidents for the Bank to strengthen its environmental capacity.

The conditionalities imposed by international financial institutions on new mining projects are among the most significant regulatory requirements currently faced by the industry. However, some mining companies have devised ways to bypass these restrictions. Although many international financial institutions follow the benchmarks established by the World Bank, their implementation varies by institution, which allows corporations to shop for a more favorable regulatory regime. When the U.S. Overseas Private Investment Corporation rejected a request to guarantee the loans for the Lihir gold mine in Papua New Guinea because the project planned to discharge mine tailings directly into the ocean, violating U.S. environmental policy, the mining company was able to turn to the Export Finance and Investment Company of Australia for support (Moody 2005, 202–3). The investment of sovereign wealth funds in new mining projects may also avoid the new restrictions altogether. For instance, Chinese and South Korean sovereign wealth funds have invested in nickel and copper mines that will provide access to raw materials needed for their strategic manufacturing sectors, but because these projects are financed by the state, they are not subject to the rules of the international financial institutions. Another way to avoid the restrictions is through the investment of private sector capital in the mining industry, including capital from the hedge funds that were partially to blame for the recent global economic crisis (Moody 2012). The controversial coal and bauxite projects in India owned by Vedanta Resources PLC, a private equity company that is based in London and trades on the London Stock Exchange, are not subject to review or restrictions imposed by international financial institutions (Das and Padel 2010; Moody 2012). Projects financed by sovereign wealth funds and private equity capital have a distinct economic advantage in terms of their lower regulatory costs, effectively becoming free riders in the mining industry. They also threaten to weaken the reforms of the international financial institutions achieved by NGOs and civil societies during the last two decades of lobbying.

By the late 1990s, criticism from civil society of multilateral organizations had raised their awareness of the problems between the extractive industry and indigenous peoples. As a result of pressure from a campaign run by Friends of the Earth, in 2000 the World Bank promised to undertake a review of its investment in the extractive industries sector (Caruso et al. 2003, 19; MacKay 2004, 43). There was concurrent discussion at the United Nations as to whether that organization could play a constructive role in reducing conflict between extractive industry and indigenous peoples, including human rights violations. Both the World Bank and the United Nations subsequently convened workshops to address these issues between 2001 and 2003, bringing unprecedented international attention to the problems caused by transnational mining, oil, and gas companies. These workshops invoked the politics of time by emphasizing policy reforms that would diminish future conflicts.

The World Bank's extractive industry review was driven by two fundamental questions: whether the bank's investments in the extractive industries fulfilled its long-standing mandate on poverty reduction given the economic problems associated with the resource curse, and whether these investments were in keeping with the bank's more recent commitments to sustainable development. However, the World Bank's involvement in the extractive industry sector is complicated by the fact that the bank has historically treated these investments as "a key opening wedge in the process of attracting foreign investment" (Danielson 2006, 16). Mining is seen to "create attractive opportunities where there were few other investment possibilities, and be enticing enough to cause governments to 'open up' in ways that would make other kinds of investment more likely" (16). To achieve this goal, the bank has promoted the restructuring of national mining laws to attract foreign investment while simultaneously dismantling regulatory regimes that previously controlled how the industry operated (Colchester et al. 2003; Moody 2005, 19).

As part of the World Bank extractive industry review, a special event was organized by several of the NGOs affiliated with the Mines and Communities network. An April 2003 workshop at Oxford University focused on the consequences of World Bank investments in mining, oil, and gas projects for indigenous peoples (Colchester et al. 2003). The case studies presented at the workshop addressed the impoverishment of *adivasis* in India relocated for a coal mine (Mundo 2003); the failure to limit corruption associated with an oil pipeline in Cameroon and Chad (Nouah et al. 2003); and the social and environmental problems caused by the Lihir gold mine in Papua New Guinea (Koma 2003), all of which received financial support from the World Bank. The participants at the workshop argued that despite covenants intended to protect indigenous peoples, labor rights, and the environment, many of the mining, oil, and gas projects supported by the World Bank ultimately fail to meet these standards. They suggested that investment in these industries contravened the bank's public commitment to poverty reduction and treated negative social and environmental impacts as externalities that did not need to be addressed. When the question was raised as to whether the recipients of World Bank investments were required to comply with principles of human rights, the representatives of the bank responded that human rights standards were binding on states but not on multilateral organizations like the World Bank or the corporations to which they provided financial support. When the participants at the workshop argued that the implementation of free, prior, and informed consent should be a condition of project support, the bank representatives also demurred.

The World Bank extractive industry review was chaired by a single eminent person, Dr. Emil Salim, who previously served as the Indonesian minister for population and the environment under Suharto. His appointment was initially opposed by civil society groups, who had expressed the desire for a multi-stakeholder review process, akin to the twelve-member World Commission on Dams, which was cosponsored by the World Bank and the International Union for Conservation of Nature (World Commission on Dams 2000).[7] During the meeting in Oxford, Dr. Salim sat attentively in the front row asking questions but never betrayed his views. One of the discussions that may have piqued his curiosity was prompted by my question whether free, prior, and informed consent was possible in countries like Papua New Guinea, where people often lacked the experience needed to imagine both the scale and scope of the impacts from a large-scale mine on their society and environment. I compared the process of obtaining free, prior, and informed consent to a greyhound chasing a stuffed rabbit on a racetrack, only to find out, if it indeed manages to catch the lure, that it is not real. The resulting debate encouraged the participants to explain their rationales for supporting the right to free, prior, and informed consent, including their views on how it could be successfully operationalized. During one of the coffee breaks, Dr. Salim asked me how to account for the recent proliferation of claims to indigeneity; in response, I suggested that the promotion of stronger standards for the protection of indigenous rights at the World Bank was partially responsible for this development.

Given their low expectations for the extractive industry review, the NGOs working on these issues were taken by surprise when Salim's (2003) final report was deeply critical of the World Bank's involvement in the extractive sector. The extractive industries review called on the World Bank to stop investing in coal immediately, given its contribution to global climate change, and to phase out its investment in oil and gas projects, because financial support from the bank was unneeded: if these projects were economically sound, they would go forward regardless of the bank's investment. The report also called on the bank to use its own resources to address problems caused by pollution from its previous investments. New mining projects should be supported by the bank only if they benefit local communities and guarantee them an equitable share of the revenue, and these projects should follow the precautionary principle with regard to their environmental impacts. Ecologically sensitive areas should be off-limits to projects supported by the bank. Destructive practices like the use of riverine tailings disposal should be banned, along with submarine tailings disposal, which is used by the Lihir gold mine and by a number of mines in Salim's home country of Indonesia. Salim also agued for greater transparency in World Bank funding of the extractive industry, in contrast to the proprietary claims to confidential business information that are common in industry dealings with international financial institutions. Finally, in what was the greatest surprise to the NGO community, the final report of the World Bank extractive industry review endorsed the right of indigenous peoples to free, prior, and informed consent (MacKay 2004).

The World Bank management group moved swiftly to reject the most sweeping reforms proposed by Salim, arguing that the bank should still support resource extraction projects "as these will continue to be an essential part of the development of many poor nations. . . . Bank group capital and expertise can help ensure such projects meet high environmental, social and governance standards" (cited in A. Thomas 2004, 5). Remarkably, the reforms achieved as a result of NGO pressure were now being touted by the bank to justify its continued investment in extractive industry (see Goldman 2005). Some of the proposals in the extractive industry review, however, will be implemented gradually, including increased support for renewable energy and projects to improve energy efficiency, and ending support for mining in ecologically sensitive habitats. However, the call for the World Bank to recognize the right to free, prior, and informed consent for indigenous peoples was reduced to recognition of the importance of "informed consultation," a much weaker standard. Salim (2004) subsequently published his rebuttal under the title "Business as Usual with Marginal Change."

In another important discussion examining many of the same issues, in December 2001 the U.N. Office of the High Commissioner for Human Rights sponsored an expert workshop on indigenous peoples, the extractive industry, and human rights at the former headquarters of the League of Nations in Geneva. The participants included representatives from indigenous groups, NGOs, and private-sector resource extraction companies. Ecuador was one of the few states to send a delegate. The purpose of the meeting was to "provide mutually beneficial guidance for future actions," including the 2002 World Summit on Sustainable Development in Johannesburg. The mining industry had an economic interest in participating in the United Nations forum, because of its concern that the Johannesburg meetings might result in the tightening of international regulatory standards on mining (Reed 2002,

218). Instead, the industry hoped to strengthen its position that voluntary principles and agreements are preferable to mandatory rules. Similarly, the NGOs and indigenous participants at the U.N. forum were
interested in pursuing a collective strategy vis-à-vis extractive industry.
Case studies on the Ok Tedi mine and Freeport-McMoRan's Grasberg
mine in West Papua were focal points for discussion at the workshop.
Other important presentations addressed oil and the distribution of
benefits in the Amazon, anomie and teen suicide among First Nations
peoples in Canada affected by mining projects, and the environmental
impacts of logging.

I was invited to present an expert report on the Ok Tedi case, but
the recently established International Council on Mining and Metals
(ICMM) objected to my participation in the workshop. The organizers
from the United Nations proposed a compromise, that I could attend
the meeting as an observer rather than deliver my paper, which would
nonetheless be included in the final proceedings. However, I decided
not to attend the workshop if the mining industry had veto power over
the presentations. When I explained my decision to withdraw from the
meeting to my NGO colleagues, they decided not to participate in the
workshop unless the United Nations agreed to reinstate my original
invitation, which forced the mining industry to back down. In my presentation, I used the Ok Tedi case to show that the political and legal
remedies available to indigenous peoples affected by mining were
insufficient and should be strengthened (Kirsch 2003). BHP Billiton
opted not to contest my presentation, sending only a single representative to the meeting, a staff lawyer with limited knowledge about the Ok
Tedi case, whose only contribution to the discussion was to make
minor technical corrections to my summary of the 1996 settlement
agreement between the company and the people living downstream
from the mine.

In contrast, Freeport-McMoRan was represented by the largest group
of delegates at the workshop, including an established anthropologist
who was the senior social advisor for Rio Tinto, an important investor
in Freeport's West Papuan mine. His sarcastic opening comment about
my presence at the workshop had the unintended consequence of enhancing my credibility among the indigenous participants whom I had not
previously met. The primary spokesperson for Freeport-McMoRan at
the workshop was CEO James R. Moffett's former pastor, whom Moffett had appointed chief public relations officer of the company. He
reported on the advances made by the company since being accused of

human rights violations in the U.S. District Court in New Orleans, charges that had already been dismissed. Also representing the company was an American judge who had previously served on the International Criminal Tribunal, under the auspices of the United Nations. The judge was revered by the staff of the Office of the High Commissioner for Human Rights for her past work. In the ensuing discussion about Freeport-McMoRan's human rights record in West Papua, the judge aggressively defended the company. The contingent from Freeport-McMoRan denied allegations that the company had an improper relationship with the Indonesian military, although subsequent corporate filings with the U.S. Securities and Exchange Commission under the Sarbanes-Oxley Act revealed payments to the Indonesian military totaling $4.7 million in 2001, the same year as the U.N. workshop, and additional payments of $5.6 million the following year (Bryce 2003). Also in attendance at the workshop was a West Papuan political exile based in the Netherlands who was a regular participant at U.N. proceedings but said very little during the discussion. I subsequently heard rumors that Freeport had hedged its bets during the so-called Papuan Spring after Suharto's fall from power in 1998 (Chauvel 2005) by providing financial support to the political arm of the West Papuan independence movement, which may have accounted for the dignitary's silence.

Workshops at the United Nations usually conclude by producing a set of resolutions that summarize the discussion (Merry 2006, 38–44; Riles 2000, 78–91). These texts begin by citing established principles from previous declarations and reports that form the starting point or baseline of the new resolutions. For example, the text produced at the U.N. workshop on indigenous peoples and extractive industry in Geneva "affirmed the relevance to the discussions of existing and emerging international human rights norms and standards." The text also acknowledges the different positions of the participants, recognizing that while "indigenous peoples are suffering negative impacts due to the practices of extractive and energy developments on their lands and territories," "efforts [are] being made by a number of companies to address these issues." When differences in opinion or alternative wordings arise during the discussion, they are bracketed off, where they remain sequestered until the differences can be satisfactorily resolved; the anthropologist and lawyer Annelise Riles (2000, 86) brilliantly refers to the bracketed-off text as political "rabbit holes."

The most controversial resolution at the December 2001 workshop referred to the standard of free, prior, and informed consent promoted by the indigenous participants and NGO representatives. The draft resolutions, compiled by several of the workshop participants the previous evening, included the following statement, which was presented entirely within brackets: "[The Workshop recommended that consultation between indigenous peoples and the private sector should be guided by the principles of . . . free, informed and prior consent of all parties concerned]." However, during the discussion, I proposed a related resolution about indigenous rights to veto unwanted developments, which was subsequently paraphrased in combination with two established principles: "[the right to development means that indigenous peoples have the right to determine their own pace of change, consistent with their own vision of development, including the right to say 'No'.]" The wording of the new resolution was based on earlier discussion at the workshop, during which I expressed concern that participation by indigenous peoples in meetings about proposed projects should not be taken as an indication of their approval or consent. However, the proposal to affirm the right of indigenous peoples to veto proposed development projects was swiftly and decisively blocked by the judge representing Freeport-McMoRan, illustrating how power relations continue to operate in U.N. workshops despite the presumption of a level playing field among the participants. Ironically, the discussion of indigenous veto power may have inadvertently forestalled criticism of the bracketed resolution concerning free, prior, and informed consent, which was ultimately included—unbracketed—in the final version of the text. Moreover, the right to say no was included in the final version of the text compiled by the Office of the High Commissioner for Human Rights after follow-up emails from workshop participants objected to its deletion.

The failure to schedule another workshop, as originally proposed, might have been the result of what a veteran participant of such meetings later described as the "rather tense" discussions between mining companies and NGOs, especially the arguments about Freeport-McMoRan's track record on human rights. But given the intertextuality of U.N. documents, the workshop report continues to influence discussions at the United Nations. For example, the following summary of our discussion about the right to say no appeared in a U.N. document on free, prior, and informed consent (FPIC) produced several years later:

> 13. UN Workshop on Indigenous Peoples, Private Sector Natural Resource, Energy and Mining Companies and Human Rights, held in Geneva from 5–7 Dec. 2001 discussed the principle of FPIC and recognized the need to have a

universally agreed upon definition of the principle. The participants reached a basic common understanding of the meaning of the principle, as the right of indigenous peoples, as land and resource owners, to *say "no"* to proposed development projects at any point during negotiations with governments and/ or extractive industries. (E/CN.4/Sub.2/AC.4/ 2002/3, para. 52). (Tamang 2005, emphasis in original)

It was not a coincidence that the issue of free, prior, and informed consent ended up as the focal point of the U.N. workshop. The principle of free, prior, and informed consent was first established in binding international treaty law by the International Labour Organization (ILO) Convention No. 169 in 1989 (McGee 2009, 585). At the time of the Geneva workshop in 2001, however, the principle was still being fiercely contested. For example, writing about indigenous resettlement in 2001, World Bank president James Wolfensohn argued that the bank

> does not incorporate provisions requiring prior, informed consent of indigenous peoples to resettlement. Instead it calls for meaningful consultations with and informed participation of all potentially displaced persons. . . . The reasons for not including such a provision are the following: the concept of prior, informed consent is very difficult to operationalize; it is not reflected in the legal framework of any country, whether developing or developed; it is contrary to the principle of eminent domain in effect in most countries. (Cited in Downing 2001, 23)

Employing the same acronym, but representing a much weaker standard, the World Bank adopted a policy of free, prior, and informed *consultation* (FPIC), a formulation that was subsequently applied by many international financial institutions and transnational mining companies (McGee 2009, 600–602). Free, prior, and informed *consultation* has been described by critics as the obligation to inform people that their human rights are about to be violated.[8]

Lobbying at the United Nations by indigenous peoples and NGOs subsequently led to the passage of the U.N. Declaration on the Rights of Indigenous Peoples in 2007, which mandates the principle of free, prior, and informed consent. As a declaration, rather than a treaty, it is not a direct source of law, but recognition of such "soft law" standards can gradually give rise to new international norms. Even the World Bank has begun to take heed; in May 2011, it announced a new policy recognizing the higher standard of consent for certain projects affecting the rights of indigenous peoples (Bridge and Wong 2011, 15). BHP Billiton's (2010, 9) recent statement of operating principles also stakes out a position in the middle ground: "New operations or projects must have broad-based community support before proceeding with development. Free Prior Informed Consent (FPIC) is only required where it is mandated by law." According to one pair of industry observers, although "the debate over FPIC will continue . . . the realization that the game has changed is sinking in. The goal posts are shifting" (Bridge and Wong 2011, 15). As a result of these changes, the mining industry is currently engaged in a series of public (Doyle and Cariño 2013) and privately facilitated discussions on how to implement the standard of free, prior, and informed consent.

Some of the participants in the mining sector prefer the notion of a "social license to operate," which refers to the existence of "broad-based community support." The expression was previously used by the American pulp and paper industry to indicate its need to gain the trust of the public and thereby avoid "costly new regulations" (W. H. Moore 1996, 23). It first entered conversations about the mining industry in 1997 (Thomson and Boutilier 2011, 1179; Filer, Banks, and Burton 2008), at the time when mining conflicts in Melanesia were receiving considerable international attention. It is treated as a kind of shorthand for those aspects of the relationships between mines and communities that are not directly addressed by government contracts and permits (Colin Filer, pers. comm., 2012). A key difference between the concept of a social license to operate and free, prior, and informed consent is that the purpose of the former is to reassure potential investors that a project meets certain baseline criteria, reducing their exposure to risk, whereas the latter is based on the recognition of indigenous rights and addresses the interests of those communities. The notion of a social license to operate also fails to recognize the special rights of indigenous peoples to their lands and territories.

At a May 2013 workshop on free, prior, and informed consent and extractive industry held at the Middlesex University School of Law in London, indigenous and corporate representatives discussed their views on the subject (see Doyle and Cariño 2013). In general, the mining company representatives viewed FPIC in terms of the costs of compliance rather than the rights of indigenous peoples, and some regarded FPIC as a kind of tax. It is not only the costs of these agreements that concern the mining industry, however, but also how the time-consuming process of obtaining FPIC affects the scheduling of proposed mining projects. In contrast, the indigenous representatives at the workshop argued that discussions of free, prior, and informed consent were part of a larger process of defining and pursuing long-term community goals rather than just a tool to facilitate agreements with mining companies. There was also disagreement at the meeting as to whether FPIC entails potential veto power over proposed mining projects, although the recognition that local consent is necessary for a project to proceed increasingly approximates the right to say no. It was also clear from the discussion that mining companies do not all share the same views on the subject: some companies recognized the advantages to be gained in terms of their corporate reputations by respecting the indigenous right to free, prior, and informed consent, while others saw the costs and uncertainty involved as too great.

The emergence of free, prior, and informed consent as a standard for best practice bodes well for the politics of time, as it has the potential to strengthen the political position of the peoples most directly affected by mining projects. Its inclusion as a standard component of discussions about new mining projects is the result of long-term efforts by indigenous organizers and critics of the mining industry. However, there is also a corresponding risk that the protocols for implementing the new standard may result in the transfer of political authority from communities recently empowered to speak on their own behalf to the private-sector consultants who conduct assessments on behalf of their corporate sponsors, potentially turning free, prior, and informed consent into the check-box compliance of audit culture.

Unresolved questions about corporations and human rights from the World Bank extractive industry review, including whether corporations are obligated to comply with international human rights standards, also resurfaced in subsequent discussions at the United Nations.[9] One of the first attempts by the United Nations to address these issues resulted in the 2003 document widely known as the "U.N. Norms," which identified the responsibilities of corporations (United Nations Economic and Social Council 2003). The report was universally criticized: corporations opposed being held accountable for human rights violations in countries in which they have limited control over the state; NGOs objected to the voluntary nature of the norms and the lack of binding obligations; and states were concerned about potential infringement on their sovereignty (Mongoven 2007). These discussions subsequently evolved into a U.N. process led by John Ruggie, the U.N. Secretary-General's special representative for business and human rights. The framework produced by Ruggie has three parts: (1) the duty of the state to *protect* against human rights abuses by third parties, including businesses; (2) the corporate responsibility to *respect* human rights; and (3) the responsibility of both the state and businesses to provide effective *remedies* to the victims of human rights violations (United Nations 2011). Significantly, the responsibilities articulated by the Ruggie report remain aspirational and do not establish any new legal obligations on the part of corporations or states.

The discussions at the 2001 and 2003 meetings of the World Bank and the United Nations and their subsequent developments have resulted in incremental gains. When they recognize the indigenous right to free, prior, and informed consent, they add leverage to the politics of time. They have also established new norms for corporations and financial institutions with respect to international human rights. But these achievements have been weakened or bypassed in a number of ways: by corporations that avoid the conditionalities imposed by international financial institutions or that use concepts like the "social license to operate" that lack legal definition; by the World Bank in rejecting the conclusions of its own review process; and by the establishment of a new cohort of corporate social responsibility consultants with greater fealty to their employers than to the indigenous peoples these processes were intended to protect.

ACCELERATING LOCAL LEARNING CURVES

In addition to indirect efforts to reduce the negative impacts of mining through the establishment of networks that share information and lobby international financial institutions for higher standards, other NGOs work directly with indigenous communities that may be affected by new mining projects. In 2008, I participated in a project to provide independent information about a proposed bauxite mine to several Lokono (Arawak) and Trio communities in Suriname (Goodland 2009). The project was organized by the Association of Indigenous Village Leaders in Suriname (VIDS) and two international partners, the North-South Institute in Canada and the Forest Peoples Programme in the United Kingdom. The organizations had already worked with these communities for several years, providing information about mining and indigenous rights, helping the communities carry out participatory mapping of local resources, conducting documentary and oral history projects, and strengthening the political capacity of the communities and their elected leaders.

BHP Billiton, the corporation responsible for the Ok Tedi mine, planned to construct a $307 million bauxite mine in the Bakhuis

Mountains of west Suriname. The project included a fifty-year contract to strip mine for bauxite ore within the boundaries of a 2,800 square kilometer catchment area (SRK Consulting 2008). The indigenous communities living closest to the concession were initially supportive of the mine given the promise of economic development, although they also had reservations about its potential social and environmental impacts (Kirsch 2009). Until they began working with VIDS and its partner organizations, the mining company was their only source of information about the project. Their knowledge about the long, environmentally destructive history of bauxite mining in east Suriname was also limited.[10] I worked with an interdisciplinary team of experts to provide an independent review of the environmental and social impact assessment of the Bakhuis mine produced by a South African consulting firm under contract to BHP Billiton (SRK Consulting 2008).[11] Social and environmental impact assessments have become standard practice for new mining projects in most countries since the 1980s, although they almost always conclude that the risks associated with development can be effectively mitigated or managed (F. Li 2009). However, comparative research on the accuracy of these assessments indicates that the environmental impacts of mining projects are systematically underestimated and the efficacy of mitigation practices are systematically overestimated (Kuipers et al. 2006).[12]

As part of my contribution to the review process, I conducted interviews and organized focus groups with members of the Lokono and Trio communities in west Suriname. Although the Lokono people I spoke with recognized that modern mines provide relatively few jobs, they hoped that the project would stimulate the local economy. They spoke about economic development in terms of its ability to enhance their freedom (see Sen 1999).[13] However, their views differed from Georg Simmel's (1978) classic assessment of the relationship between money and modernity. Simmel describes how the universal form of value created by money is a vehicle for realizing new forms of the self that are freed from prior attachment to particular people, places, and things. Thus access to money has generally been taken to signify the negation of tradition, which is replaced by the modern project of self-realization (Maclean 1994). But when young men from the indigenous communities of Suriname spoke about their hopes for the future, their answers always emphasized living in their own villages. They did not dream of the bright lights of the city, but of economic opportunities that would allow them to stay at home. They did not think of money as the path to individualization and modernity, but as the means to protect their values (see Sahlins 1999).

The women I spoke with in west Suriname also invoked the discourse of freedom in relation to money, albeit differently from the men. Women supported the mining project for their own reasons. They objected to the fact that the men in their communities had gained privileged access to money through wage labor. The women whom I interviewed explained that traditional gender roles were complementary: in their gardens, the men cleared the forest and wove the *matapi* strainers for processing cassava, while the women planted, weeded, harvested, and prepared their staple root crop for consumption. They each depended on the labor of the other in contrast to their current circumstances, in which women are dependent on their husbands for money. For the women, gaining access to their own sources of income would enhance their freedom. They saw development associated with the mine as the means to earn the money they needed to overcome their unwanted dependence on their husbands and fulfill their responsibilities to their children.

My initial reception in west Suriname was less than welcoming. The village leaders, known as captains, trusted the corporate social responsibility officer from BHP Billiton, a young woman from Suriname who had been working closely with them for the previous year, much more than me, a complete stranger, even though I arrived with one of the staff members from VIDS with whom they had a longstanding and congenial relationship. The captains were under pressure from the other members of the community to support the bauxite mine and consequently were ambivalent about the review process. Two weeks before my arrival, the captains had unexpectedly signed an impact-benefit agreement with BHP Billiton, even though the rush to complete the agreement before the independent review was carried out could hardly be considered best practice on the part of the mining company. The captains felt compelled to sign the agreement because their communities were beset with rumors that their refusal to do so would jeopardize the project, angering their constituents.

The failure of the captains to consult with VIDS and the other organizations coordinating the review before signing the impact-benefit agreement called the continuation of the review process into question. In our deliberations on how to proceed, I pointed out that in the highly charged circumstances accompanying economic transactions on this scale, local commitments and relationships are likely to be vulnerable to pressure.

We also discussed the possibility that the specter of the independent review may have prompted BHP Billiton to push through an agreement with the indigenous communities. I expressed my opinion that the review was not being undertaken solely for the benefit of the captains but rather for the entire community. We agreed to complete the review with the proviso that the captains sign a memorandum of understanding indicating that they would consult with the NGOs working with the communities before signing additional agreements with BHP Billiton. The captains readily agreed to these terms, pointing out that the memorandum of understanding would protect them against pressure from the other members of the community.

Shortly before I completed my research in west Suriname, BHP Billiton announced that it was pulling out of the Bakhuis project due to the global economic downturn. Given the possibility that the project may eventually be revived, the team completed the review, the results of which were subsequently presented at a meeting of the indigenous communities on the Corantijn River in west Suriname and at a public venue in the capital, Paramaribo, in October 2009. We identified a number of problems that were not well documented in the original environmental and social impact assessment, including the potential for long-term impacts on wildlife populations, negative social impacts from migration to the area, and the increased likelihood that the construction of the Bakhuis project would lead to the implementation of a long-standing proposal to build a dam and hydroelectric power plant on the nearby Kabelebo River, to which the indigenous communities strongly object, as a source of cheap electricity for a new bauxite refinery.

One of the challenges in presenting this information to the people living in the indigenous communities was to explain the technical findings in accessible terms. For example, when describing how the removal of the bauxite layer, which absorbs water during the rainy season and slowly releases it during the dry season, would affect the plateau, I illustrated the process by pouring water onto a sponge, which I then squeezed dry, explaining that bauxite mining would change the micro-climate of the concession area, causing it to dry out. When discussing how five decades of mining would affect local wildlife, much of which would migrate away from the explosions and heavy vehicle traffic, I was helped by a question from a community member about where the animals would go and the answer from someone else in the audience, who jokingly suggested that the animals would cross the border into Brazil, Suriname's enormous neighbor to the south, which was already resented for encroaching on its resources. Everyone laughed, but no one liked the image of Brazilians barbequing their precious tapirs and peccaries. Although BHP Billiton informed the communities that it planned to implement a state-of-the-art rehabilitation process developed for a nickel mine in Brazil—and even paid for several community members to tour the mine and observe the process in operation—at the eleventh hour, the company revealed that the process could not be used in Suriname due to differences in soil conditions, eliminating the only compelling reason to expect that the project would not repeat the failure of the other bauxite mines in Suriname to rehabilitate the rain forest.

My experience in Suriname suggests some of challenges associated with efforts to accelerate the learning curve of indigenous communities about the social and environmental impacts of mining projects. The captains were initially reluctant to learn more about the potential risks and hazards of the Bakhuis project. My ability to gain their trust was compromised by the short-term nature of my intervention, in contrast to the long-term relationship that I developed with the Yonggom and their neighbors in Papua New Guinea. However, the disappointment that the community members felt when BHP Billiton pulled out of the project eventually gave way, at least in part, to a sense of relief. At a meeting with the community leaders after the review team made its presentation, one of the leaders opined that whereas they had previously thought about the development in terms of its ability to solve their problems, they subsequently realized that it could also lead to new problems. Whereas they initially anticipated that the economic opportunities presented by the bauxite mine would enhance their freedom, they learned that its social and environmental impacts would impose new kinds of constraints that had not been immediately apparent to them.

Although the captains do not necessarily oppose mining for bauxite in the Bakhuis Mountains, they felt that the review process helped inform them about the risks it entailed and the kinds of questions they should ask before granting their consent to any future project.[14] They also came to recognize the importance of having independent information and counsel when navigating such processes, which prompted an invitation for me to return in the event that a new developer for the project emerges. Despite the initial challenges, the experience in Suriname suggests that the independent review process can be an effective means of educating indigenous communities about the potential impacts of mining projects, contributing to the politics of time.

THE POLITICS OF TIME AS A SOCIAL MOVEMENT

There is also a burgeoning social movement based on the politics of time in Latin America, in which communities undertake popular votes—known as *consultas,* or referenda—that express their support or opposition to proposed development projects, especially new mines (map 3). In many cases, these votes are also intended to contest the authority of the state to grant mining licenses or otherwise promote large-scale development projects in rural areas. The organizers of these events do not necessarily see themselves as participants in a regional social movement; they view community referenda as the expression of local rights to self-determination and sovereignty over their lands and territories. However, they are generally aware of the history of these actions across the region. A recent tally identifies sixty-eight *consultas* on mining projects in Latin America over the last decade, including votes in Argentina, Colombia, Ecuador, Guatemala, Mexico, and Peru (Fultz 2011).

The first *consulta* on a major mining project in Latin America was held in the town of Tambogrande in northwest Peru in 2002 (McGee 2009, 604–10). Located in land reclaimed from the desert with the help of a World Bank–funded irrigation scheme, the region generates $150 million in annual export earnings from agriculture. When the Manhattan Minerals Corporation applied for a license to construct a $315 million open-pit gold mine in Tambogrande, the residents of the valley objected, because the project threatened their livelihood: growing lemons, limes, avocadoes, and mangoes. After three years of protest by citizens' groups, the town held a municipal referendum in which 98 percent of the eligible voters rejected the mine.[15]

In contrast to other mining conflicts in Latin America, the majority of the participants in the Tambogrande *consulta* were *mestizo* farmers rather than indigenous peoples. One of their campaign slogans was "¿Se imagina el ceviche sin limones?" ("Can you imagine *ceviche* without limes?"), referring to a popular seafood dish. Another campaign slogan referred to the *pisco sour,* a popular drink made from limes, grape brandy, and egg whites. The campaign did not promote identification with *mestizo* farmers in the manner of international campaigns focused on indigenous peoples living in the rain forest, but instead invoked nationalist pride in Peruvian cuisine. Even though the Peruvian government refused to acknowledge the legitimacy of the vote, the project's failure to acquire a "social license to operate" prevented the mining company from obtaining sufficient international funding, lead-

UNITED STATES

MEXICO

San Luis Potosí

Sipacapa
Santa Cruz del Quiché

GUATEMALA

Chocó
COLOMBIA

ECUADOR

Victoria del Portete
Tambogrande
Ayabaca and **Huancabamba**

PERU

ARGENTINA

Esquel

✔ Votes

MEXICO
San Luis Potosí (2006) against the
Cerro San Pedro project owned by New
Gold, which has been operational since
2008.

GUATEMALA
Sipacapa (2005) against the Marlin mine
owned by Goldcorp, which has been
operational since 2005.

Santa Cruz del Quiché (2010) against
transnational development.

COLOMBIA
Chocó (2009) against the Mandé Norte project
owned by Muriel Mining. Development was
suspended by the Colombian Constitutional Court in
2009, but is being pursued by Rio Tinto.

ECUADOR
Victoria del Portete (2011) against the proposed
IAMGOLD mine in Quimsacocha. IAMGOLD subsequently
transferred its shares to the junior mining company
INV Metals, in which it owns 47%.

PERU
Tambogrande (2002) against the Manhattan Minerals
project, which failed to attract adequate investment.
Other companies are pursuing the project.

Ayabaca and **Huancabamba** (2007) against the
proposed Rio Blanco mine. Project development has
been suspended until 2015.

ARGENTINA
Esquel (2005) against Meridian Gold.
The project was not developed.

MAP 3. Key referenda on mining and development in Latin America.

FIGURE 14. A woman from Ayabaca casts her ballot at a referendum on the proposed Rio Blanco mine in northern Peru on September 16, 2007, which was modeled after the 2005 referendum in Tambogrande (Bebbington 2012b, 77–78). Approximately 60 percent of the eligible voters in three districts participated, 93 percent of whom voted against the $1.44 billion project (Fultz 2011). Opposition to the project continues to delay its development. Photo: Stephanie Boyd/Guarango.

ing the state to withdraw the company's permit to develop the project (McGee 2009, 609; see fig. 14).

Another important referendum was held three years later in Esquel, Argentina (McGee 2009, 616–18). Meridian Gold from Reno, Nevada, proposed the construction of an open-pit gold mine using cyanide-leaching technology seven kilometers upstream from the town. The environmental impact assessment for the project was heavily criticized by an independent reviewer and professors from a local university. In 2005, the members of the largely middle-class community voted overwhelmingly against the mine, blocking its development (616). The provincial government also passed a law banning open-pit mining and the use of cyanide in mining operations, which was challenged by the state but subsequently upheld by the courts. By 2008, five other Argentine provinces had passed similar laws (617), although in many cases these laws are largely symbolic, as there are no known mineral deposits.

In 2005, the first of many *consultas* about mining projects in Guatemala was held in the town of Sipacapa (McGee 2009, 618–26; Revenga

2005). The vote differed from the referenda in Peru and Argentina, because the Marlin mine in neighboring San Miguel Ixtahuacán was already operational. Thirteen indigenous communities voted against the open-pit gold mine, with only a handful of votes in support. When Gold-corp challenged the referendum, the Constitutional Court of Guatemala ruled that the results were informational rather than binding on the state (McGee 2009, 625). The Marlin mine continues to operate and remains controversial. In 2010, after a study conducted by the activist group Physicians for Human Rights determined that the mine poses serious health risks to the communities living downstream (Basu and Hu 2010), the Inter-American Court of Human Rights called for the suspension of its operations. Although the state initially indicated that it would comply with the precautionary measure, it subsequently petitioned the court to allow the mine to continue operating. However, the circulation of video images depicting the environmental impact of the Marlin mine have been influential in the proliferation of anti-mining referenda in Guatemala (Katherine Fultz, pers. comm., 2012; see fig. 15).

Since 2005, there have been referenda on mining, hydroelectric power, and other transnational development projects in fifty-four municipalities in Guatemala, the results of which have been almost all negative (Fultz 2011). The votes clearly reject mining as a legitimate option for develop-ment. However, they also reflect the political complexities of post–civil war Guatemala, including Guatemalans' lack of confidence in the state to protect indigenous rights and ensure the equitable distribution of benefits from development. The votes also seek to limit state intervention in local affairs, which is in keeping with strong sentiments about political auton-omy that resonate across the region (e.g., Escobar 2008; Speed 2008).

The *consultas* of Latin America can also be understood as a form of communication between rural communities and the state (see Bebbing-ton and Bury 2009), although the response by the state has been largely negative. Some states regard the votes as informational but nonbinding, others challenge their legality, and at least one state has sought to crim-inalize participation in community referenda altogether. Although the organizers and participants in these *consultas* do not see themselves as members of a unified social movement, their actions are connected by a shared politics of time. They seek to protect the environment and their land by blocking the approval of new mining projects. They build on the growing recognition of the rights of rural communities and indige-nous peoples to make fundamental decisions concerning their lands, livelihoods, and resources—including water—especially when these

FIGURE 15. Referendum on development in Santa Cruz del Quiché, Guatemala, on October 21, 2010. The consultation was carried out in ninety-three voting centers in eighty-seven rural communities and six urban zones in the municipal capital. Ninety-eight percent of the eligible voters participated, casting their votes unanimously against mining, hydroelectric power, and other forms of large-scale development. The photo depicts Lolita Chávez, coordinator of the K'iche' People's Council, reading the municipal act ratifying the plebiscite. The banner overhead reads: "Yes to life. No to transnational corporations. For the defense of life, mother nature, land and territory." Photo: James Rodríguez/mimundo.org.

decisions have implications for their health and well-being. The *consultas* are also taking place at a historical moment in which these communities have greater access to information about mining and the problems associated with the resource curse than in the past, both as a result of NGO interventions and by the way that mining conflicts have become central to political debates across Latin America during the last decade (Bebbington 2012a).[16] These conflicts and debates have not only influenced electoral outcomes at the highest levels of the state, but have also led to extended delays and the potential cancellation of several multibillion dollar mining projects proposed for the Andes.

CONCLUSION

The campaign against the Ok Tedi mine was a signal event in the rise of international organizing against the mining industry. The use of the law in holding BHP accountable for its actions enhanced the legitimacy of concerns about the impact of large-scale mines and served as a catalyst in changing the industry. But suing after the damage is done ultimately reinforces the politics of resignation. In contrast, the politics of time is a more hopeful strategy given its potential to prevent harm from occurring.[17]

These new developments involving the politics of time lead me to ask the following question: what would it take to write in a more hopeful vein about the relationships between corporations and their critics, especially with regard to mining conflicts? More than two decades of research and practical experience in seeking reforms tempers my optimism. There are sound reasons to question the virtuous language of corporate social responsibility, sustainability, and transparency. Yet there is a corresponding risk of being dismissed as closed-minded or chided for "low-minded sentimentality" for imagining the worst about corporations (see Sen 1999, 280). Indeed, not all social scientists writing about mining conflicts are skeptical about the prospects for reform; many of my colleagues are more willing to consider acceptable trade-offs, staking out the middle ground, or formulating win-win scenarios—language that is also used by industry representatives in contrast to the perspectives of the NGOs and communities with whom I have collaborated. To make constructive interventions into political debates about mining conflicts, scholars must remain clear-eyed about corporate power rather than starry-eyed about the prospects for change.

The demand for metals is unlikely to abate, even with more robust commitment to recycling and the substitution of alternative materials. Nor is it the case that indigenous peoples uniformly oppose mining on their lands and territories, although most seek to impose limits on its social and environmental impacts. The goal of political organizing on these issues is not to stop all new mining permanently but rather to compel the industry to improve its practices by raising international standards; to ensure that these standards are obligatory rather than just voluntary; and to establish fair, effective, and transparent mechanisms for complaint resolution, coupled with the swift application of strong sanctions to ensure compliance. These measures should be undertaken alongside steps to guarantee free, prior, and informed consent for the communities with the most at stake if these projects go forward, in terms of the risks to local livelihoods, environments, long-term health and well-being, and the ability to protect their values in the midst of development. This can only be accomplished through mechanisms that draw on the politics of time to enhance their political leverage.

Despite the widespread critique of the harms caused by mining, the industry continues to have a poor track record. On a number of occasions, I have been asked to present a positive example of a mining project that has fulfilled its commitments to local communities: protected the environment, safeguarded labor rights, ensured the equitable distribution of benefits, and adequately provided for mine closure and proper rehabilitation of the mine site. Indeed, it would enhance my scholarly credibility to be able to provide examples of projects meeting these criteria and point to them as exemplars for other mining projects to follow. Yet there are no mines that meet all of these criteria. A telling example of this dilemma occurred during discussion at a 2009 workshop on indigenous peoples, extractive industry, and human rights in Manila. Sponsored by the U.N. Permanent Forum on Indigenous Issues, it was the long-delayed follow-up to the 2001 meeting at the United Nations in Geneva. When a speaker from the Asian Development Bank was asked to identify a mining project that met all or most of the standards for best practice, he was unable to provide a single example from among the many mining projects in the Philippines or even all of Asia. The best he could do was make reference to a platinum mine in South Africa with a positive reputation, although he acknowledged that he had never visited the project and knew relatively little about it. The project to which he referred, Anglo American's Royal Bafokeng mine, is frequently touted by the mining industry as a model example of a Black Economic Empowerment program (Cook 2011). However, as John and Jean Comaroff (2009, 109) point out, Bafokeng land is so polluted that it can no longer be used for agriculture. The majority of the royalties earned by the mine are controlled by the king and self-appointed CEO of the Royal Bafokeng Nation instead of redistributed among the Bafokeng, who have been described as "a rich nation of poor people" (Comaroff and Comaroff 2009, 110). Anglo American's partnership with the Bafokeng enables the company to fulfill its Black Economic Empowerment quotas without having to adopt more radical changes to its other operations in South Africa (Dinah Rajak, pers. comm. 2012). In the ensuing discussion at the Manila workshop, I compared the search for a responsible mine to the pursuit of a mythical beast that people believe in because they have heard stories of its existence, even though no one claims to have seen it.[18]

Yet there has been progress on many fronts, giving cause for hope, even if optimism remains unrealistic. As a result of the efforts described here, there has been a significant shift in public awareness of the problems caused by mining, including widespread recognition that the mining industry rarely lives up to its commitments and promises. The sharing of information through international networks and other strategies to accelerate local learning curves have reached many of the communities most vulnerable to the impacts of mining. This can be seen most clearly in the referenda against mining in Latin America. New obligations to respect human rights and discussions about the rights of indigenous peoples to free, prior, and informed consent continue to percolate through international financial institutions and increasingly influence private lending through banks, despite simultaneous efforts by private equity and sovereign wealth funds to avoid these standards. Broader campaigns focused on transparency and accountability challenge the relationship of mining companies to public and private security forces. These calls for reform are not tied to specific mining projects or impacted communities but rather address the broader contexts in which mining conflicts occur. These initiatives have increased scrutiny of the mining industry, making it increasingly difficult for new mining projects to receive approval without first establishing stronger guarantees—a situation that illustrates the promise of the politics of time.

Conclusion

We must rid ourselves of the idea that dilemmas can be
resolved once and for all, so that we can start working in
earnest for a more livable society.
—Alberto Melucci

This book analyzes the relationships between corporations and their
critics in an era of neoliberal capitalism. Civil society plays a pivotal
role in questioning and challenging the deleterious consequences of
corporate conduct for human health and the environment. Corporations respond to their critics through social technologies that protect
their economic interests and minimize their reputational risks. They
ignore, refute, or appropriate the terms of the critique, manipulate
scientific research, and seek to co-opt or delegitimize their opponents.
Consequently, strategies that succeed in one campaign are circumvented
in the next, demanding constant innovation on the part of NGOs and
social movements.

The dialectical character of these relationships suggests the impossi-
bility of resolving the dilemmas of contemporary capitalism. It is illusory
to imagine that corporations will ever be entirely transparent or accountable, despite their virtuous claims to social responsibility and sustainability. However, this does not mean that resistance is futile. As Alberto
Melucci (1998, 429) argues, making these dilemmas apparent allows for
their renegotiation in new forms, opening up the possibilities for change.
By revealing the problems caused by contemporary corporations,
oppositional movements and critique represent one of the primary
defenses against the negative consequences of unrestrained capitalism.

The events discussed in this book illustrate the growth and development of nongovernmental politics that accompanied the spread of neo-

liberal economic policies. The mining conflicts analyzed here resulted in novel engagements between NGOs and corporations, yielding new organizational forms. Alliances based on the politics of space enabled critics of the industry to exert pressure on mining companies everywhere they operate. The mining industry responded to its heightened exposure by establishing new forms of collaboration among companies that previously regarded each other as fierce competitors. These industry initiatives led NGOs to establish international networks that could share information, promote reforms in the investment policies of multilateral organizations and financial institutions, and set the agenda for a global campaign against the mining industry. More recently, the rise of virtual NGOs operating primarily through new social media has expanded participation in these struggles.

The structural transformations of these nongovernmental organizations have had significant implications for their internal politics. There is a tension between horizontal political forms, which are effective in maintaining solidarity and democratic relationships but less successful in setting and achieving their goals, and vertical or centralized forms of organization, which facilitate decision making but may reduce participation and commitment. These dynamics are illustrated in the respective careers of the two NGO networks discussed here: the vertical organization of the Global Mining Campaign resulted in its truncated life span, whereas the horizontal politics of Mines and Communities has been responsible for its comparative longevity, but has also limited the kinds of engagements it has been able to undertake. The new virtual NGOs respond more quickly to events and avoid the political infighting associated with more traditional brick-and-mortar NGOs, but the low threshold for participation may inadvertently diminish the significance of the problems they seek to address.

It is a testament to the tenacity of nongovernmental organizations and the commitment of their members that they have been able to transform the political and economic environment in which the mining industry operates given the convergence of criticism of these organizations from the right, on the left, in the academy, and by the state. Despite their shortcomings, NGOs have played a central role in political struggles like the campaign against the Ok Tedi mine. The vitality and creativity of NGOs have allowed the political movements with which they collaborate to stay one step ahead of corporations and industries.

The book also compares two different kinds of political movement. The first example is the politics of space, which makes use of resources that are geographically distributed. It strives to create oppositional power through the development of extensive transnational alliances. The second is the politics of time, which pursues alternative strategies focused on the prevention of industrial activities that are almost certain to cause harm—activities that become very difficult to halt once set in motion given the huge capital investments they entail and the economic resources they provide to the state and other parties. The politics of space was characteristic of much of the environmental activism that emerged in the 1990s, which often addressed problems after the fact. In contrast, the politics of time leads to more hopeful forms of intervention given its potential to prevent harm from occurring.

Corporations also draw on the politics of time, especially in the promotion of doubt and uncertainty, in order to delay action against them, including regulation and potential delegitimization. This may not be surprising in the realm of so-called harm industries, like mining and tobacco, in which profit is predicated on negative environmental impacts and risks to human health (Benson and Kirsch 2010a), but it is also found in industries intended to enhance human health and well-being, including the pharmaceutical industry. The widespread corporate manipulation of scientific claims indicates that these practices are intrinsic to contemporary capitalism. The problems of corporate science are compounded by legal protections on confidentiality and trade secrets, as illustrated by Freeport's defense of its right to prevent disclosure of information about pollution downstream from the mine. Current efforts to force oil and gas companies to release proprietary information about the chemicals used in hydraulic fracturing provide another pertinent example of this dynamic.

Corporate responses to critique include the strategic use of audit culture, which conveys the message that problems are being addressed while avoiding any real changes to operating procedures. Audit culture also promotes the view that markets and corporations provide more efficient solutions to environmental problems than regulation. In addition, corporations partner with conservative political organizations that criticize NGOs for being unelected and not accountable to the public, and consequently to undermine democracy, even though these characterizations also apply to the corporation (B. Adam 1998, 15). They criticize social-choice and green investment funds for diverting attention away from the "profit motive" by forcing corporations to take social and environmental factors into account. The same alliances have sought to discredit public participation in science. These are all examples of the ways in which the relationships between corporations and their critics have come to influence larger social, political, and economic debates.

Indigenous politics has played an integral role in many of the campaigns against the mining industry discussed here, from the Ok Tedi case to many of the referenda in Latin America. Indigeneity has only recently become a source of symbolic capital. Like the definitional career of sustainability and sustainable development, international recognition of the legal rights of indigenous peoples emerged through a series of multilateral conferences and declarations. The example of the indigenous right to free, prior, and informed consent is a case in point. It was first established in binding international treaty law by ILO Convention No. 169 in 1989; subsequently debated at United Nations meetings on indigenous peoples, human rights, and extractive industry in 2001; and eventually incorporated into the 2007 U.N. Declaration on the Rights of Indigenous Peoples. Pressure on the World Bank resulted in the establishment of new safeguard policies for indigenous peoples in the 1990s, although it used the weaker standard of *consultation* rather than *consent*. More recently, however, the World Bank has recognized the indigenous right to free, prior, and informed consent under limited conditions. The mining industry is currently involved in a range of discussions about the implementation of free, prior, and informed consent, although these efforts simultaneously raise concerns about potential co-optation of these rights within new regimes of audit culture. Mining conflicts have featured prominently in many of these discussions and developments, providing compelling evidence in support of indigenous rights, even as these new rights have become fundamental resources in mining conflicts.

The campaigns against the mining industry discussed in this book overlap with the emergence of environmentalism as a global political movement. Environmental NGOs have played important roles in the politics of mining, including the ability of the Australian Conservation Foundation to raise BHP's public profile in relation to the Ok Tedi mine and Friends of the Earth to compel the World Bank to review its investments in the extractive industry. But the environmental movement is fractured in ways that have significant consequences for these mining conflicts. In the wake of the 1992 Rio "Earth Summit," conservation groups sought to collaborate with indigenous peoples (Conklin and Graham 1995; West 2005), but since the 2002 World Summit on Sustainable Development in Johannesburg, these groups are more likely to partner with mining companies and extractive industry (Chapin 2004), with the result that indigenous peoples increasingly regard conservationists as a threat to their interests rather than a potential ally. Another split is associated with the identification of environmentalism as a post-materialist value, which excludes the politics of marginalized populations disproportionately affected by pollution and environmental degradation. As the Ok Tedi case illustrates, the microeconomics of the resource curse poses a threat to both the subsistence practices and cultural survival of these groups. Yet another fracture in the environmental movement results from the mining industry's appropriation and redefinition of sustainable development in terms of "weak sustainability," which has the potential to result in a tragedy of the commons. But despite the contradictory elements of the environmental movement, the politics of sympathy in relation to the environmental degradation caused by mining continues to be an important source of recognition and public support for these social movements.

This book also examines the use of novel legal strategies that seek to hold corporations accountable in the countries in which they are incorporated for their international operations. The landmark settlement of the first Ok Tedi case, in 1996, established important precedents in terms of the judiciability of claims regarding subsistence rights by showing how they are analogous to more familiar claims based on economic damage to property, and it also recognized the associated liabilities for corporations. Unfortunately, the key component of the settlement—concerning the implementation of tailings containment—proved unenforceable, despite the plaintiffs' return to court in 2000. The decade-long legal process, which ran from 1994 to 2004, allowed the mining company to continue polluting the Fly River system, and had opportunity costs for the plaintiffs in terms of their failure to pursue other political strategies to achieve their goals. Nonetheless, negative publicity from the second legal case forced BHP Billiton to transfer its shares in the mine to an offshore trust, a decision that may eventually cost the company three billion dollars. The disposition of these funds remains a key focus of ongoing debates about the Ok Tedi mine, which continues to operate as an independent entity, without corporate investors, even as its environmental impacts intensify in their severity and longevity.

The other legal proceedings described here—against Freeport-McMoRan and its Grasberg mine in the militarized Indonesian territory of West Papua for its environmental impacts and collusion with the Indonesian military, which resulted in allegations of genocide, and against Rio Tinto for both the environmental impacts of its Panguna mine and its alleged collusion with the state during the decade of civil war in Bougainville—did not fare as well in the courts. The Freeport case, which made use of the U.S. Alien Tort Claims Act of 1789, failed in the U.S. District Court in New Orleans, although the case—in combination with the OPIC decision to withdraw its political risk insurance in 1995—exposed the company to contentious debate at U.N. meetings in Geneva, shareholder actions, and heightened NGO scrutiny. The long-running and fiercely contested case against Rio Tinto, which began in 2001, was dismissed after a U.S. Supreme Court ruling in 2013 restricted the application of the alien claims act, facilitating Rio Tinto's quest to resume mining in Bougainville. The demise of the U.S. Alien Tort Claims Act as a means of holding transnational corporations accountable for their international operations affected a series of cases pending in the U.S. courts, including the lawsuit against Royal Dutch Petroleum for its impact on the Niger Delta and the Ogoni people, the case in which the controversial Supreme Court ruling was issued.

Nonetheless, the Ok Tedi case helped to set an important precedent for transnational legal proceedings. Whether or not they result in successful judgments or settlements favorable to plaintiffs, international legal claims have proven to be a valuable resource in the struggle between communities and mining companies. A pivotal issue in many of these cases has been the status of international environmental norms, which are being progressively developed through the pressure that civil society puts on the World Bank to strengthen the conditionalities on its loans, which are generally regarded as the benchmark for other international financial institutions. These new standards have the potential to rise to the level of internationally recognized norms, crossing over from "soft law" to "hard law." As the 1997 Control Risks report *No Hiding Place* foretold (Bray 1997, 42), legal activism has become a standard component of NGO repertoires and shows no sign of abating. Litigation can play an important role in modifying corporate behavior given the significance of reputational costs to corporations in an era of shareholder capitalism. The recognition that corporations may be held accountable to higher standards than those prevailing in the countries in which they operate may also contribute to industry reform.

These legal cases provide evidence to support both the claims of the hegemony theorists, who view the law as a resource of the elite, and resistance theorists, who see the law as a strategy of counterglobalization (Santos and Rodríguez-Garavito 2005) and a valuable "weapon of the weak" (Scott 1987). But given that the recent proliferation of cases and the emergence of new international norms are counterbalanced by new restrictions on international legal proceedings and by the determination of companies like Rio Tinto not to settle claims against them, regardless of the negative publicity, it suggests that the dialectical relationship between corporations and their critics described throughout this book also applies to their legal contests.

The complex relationships between corporations and their critics also influence international financial institutions that promote capitalist expansion in the name of development. Pressure on these institutions has led to the imposition of stricter conditionalities on their investments. In the absence of formal standardization of these criteria, however, corporations remain able to shop for financial support from institutions willing to overlook their shortcomings. Sovereign wealth funds that are not subject to these restrictions and private equity funds that ignore the standards imposed by international financial institutions act like free riders by providing investors with significant economic advantages. However, there are significant exceptions to this trend; for example, concern about the environmental impact of the Freeport mine in West Papua led the Norwegian Government Pension Fund (2006) to divest from the project. Pressure from NGOs also encouraged the United Nations (2011) to establish a new framework that requires corporations and states to "protect, respect, and remedy" human rights and human rights violations, although these principles remain aspirational. Human rights groups, environmental NGOs, and indigenous movements have been remarkably successful in influencing these powerful and formerly intransigent organizations. But the incomplete realization of these transformations suggests that the dialectical relationship between corporations and their critics also operates at the level of capital and finance.

The relationship between corporations and their critics also influences debates about regulation. NGO campaigns have successfully promoted regulation in specific domains, including recent U.S. congressional requirements for financial disclosure of the use of metals procured from conflict zones in the "don't ask, don't tell" supply chains of the mobile telecommunications industry, which were aimed at mining operations in the Democratic Republic of the Congo. However, objections to the accompanying regulatory burden on manufacturers has led to efforts to roll back these requirements. There are also intermittent rumors that the mining industry may be willing to accept additional government regulation, which may be the only way solve the mining industry's collective action problem. Competition for access to minerals in conflict zones, which poses significant reputational risks to publicly traded corporations, may contribute to this sentiment.

But ultimately, the debate about regulation comes down to whether corporations are willing to accept higher production costs in return for the relief from criticism that this might bring versus their ability to increase their market share and profits by maintaining greater flexibility than their competitors (see Szablowski 2007, 99–100). The competitive relationship between mining companies with regard to operational flexibility is evident in BHP Billiton's decision not to build new mines using riverine tailings disposal, versus Rio Tinto's position that such decisions should be made on a case-by-case basis. It is unclear whether industry attempts at self-regulation, such as the International Council on Minerals and Mining's stated objective of serving as a "catalyst" in raising industry standards, can be successful given the problem of free riders that undermine voluntary agreements.

A related concern is how political ideologies and development models affect state policy regarding the mining industry. Despite the problems associated with the resource curse, Papua New Guinea remains committed to the development paradigm that promotes resource extraction as a vehicle for growth. The state's ideological commitment to dependency theory resulted in a fundamental conflict of interest between its contradictory roles as both regulator and shareholder—a problem that persists, as the state continues to invest in natural resource extraction projects, albeit through more complex financial arrangements. This runs counter to neoliberal policies that emphasize the privatization of national assets. However, the state's limited interest or capacity in monitoring or regulating corporations has consequences that resemble neoliberal policies of deregulation. Comparative questions can also be raised about how political ideologies influence policies toward extractive industry. In the Andean countries of Latin America, for example, the policies of left-of-center governments on these issues do not differ substantially from those of more conservative governments (Bebbington 2009), whereas in Papua New Guinea, politicians are not driven by commitment to either the left or the right, suggesting that political ideology has a relatively limited impact on resource extraction in these states. A colleague from Mines and Communities recently noted how startling it is to see the mining industry "claw back" against its catastrophic track record to convince states that mining is a productive form of development, especially given that mining conflicts continue to pose a threat to political stability in much of the world. The discourses of corporate social responsibility and sustainability have played a pivotal role in convincing the state that corporate tigers can change their stripes.

Three elements distinguish this work from previous ethnographic accounts of the corporation. First, rather than focus on organizational dynamics within the corporation, this book analyzes corporate efforts to manage their external operating environments, although the two approaches are complementary. The influence of external critics on corporate decision-making, however, suggests the need to study social movements and corporations within a single frame of analysis, as I have demonstrated here, rather than independently. A second difference is the political perspective of this work. Studying the mining industry requires a healthy dose of skepticism and perhaps even a measure of cynicism, especially in relation to the promotion of the virtuous discourses of sustainability and corporate social responsibility. In contrast to the anthropological tradition of suspending one's disbelief when conducting ethnographic research, I have declined to give the mining industry the benefit of the doubt: its track record demands a higher standard of proof. A final difference is that this ethnography was written by an active participant in political campaigns against the excesses of the mining industry, rather than by a neutral observer. Instead of jeopardizing access to key informants and events, engagement with these issues has provided me with an insider perspective on the interactions between corporations and their critics. It has offered new sites for ethnographic observation, new questions for research, and new perspectives on the corporation.

Finally, this work describes how social movements like the campaign against the Ok Tedi mine have the ability to make visible the dilemmas of contemporary capitalism and negotiate alternative outcomes. Despite being faced with steep learning curves, marginal economic status, and limited power, indigenous movements have raised the profile of an industry that had long been successful in avoiding the public gaze. The mining industry can no longer assume that the state is its only negotiating partner or that rural or indigenous communities lack the resources or capacity to challenge their operations, whether by forging international alliances with NGOs and other partners, through legal action in the countries in which the corporations are based, or by force—albeit at a terrible cost. The mining industry faces increasing pressure from NGOs mobilizing the discourses of environmentalism and indigenous rights. During the time I have been working on these issues, indigenous political movements and their NGO allies have been able to raise the status of these conflicts to the level of an existential threat to the mining industry, attract regular media coverage, demand attention at the highest levels of the state, and provoke debates at the World Bank and the United Nations. The mining industry has had to modify its policies and practices, although it has done so in ways that simultaneously push back against its critics. Mining conflicts have become contentious issues in electoral politics from Papua New Guinea to Peru. They have contributed to lengthy delays in the approval process for new mines and prevented some projects from going forward, consequences of the politics of time. Even though the campaign against the Ok Tedi mine was ultimately unable to save the river or the surrounding forests, its leaders, lawyers, and NGO allies did far more to stimulate debate and raise awareness about these issues than could possibly have been expected at the outset.

However, it is almost as difficult to identify a successful campaign against the mining industry as it is to find a mining project that operates according to the standards of best practice. One might point to the campaign at Tambogrande in Peru, the first public referendum on a mining project in Latin America, which invoked the politics of time in forcing the prospective investors to forfeit their concession. But like wolves at the door, other mining companies have already attempted to restart the project. The materiality of the resource—the minerals that lie dormant underground, without decaying, and that increase in value over the long run—is central to this dynamic, much as the anonymity of metals limits the possibilities for consumer politics. The Tambogrande example suggests that no campaign against mining is ever permanently victorious, as capital is nothing if not relentless in its pursuit of economic opportunity.

For every accomplishment in these struggles, there is an accompanying response. For the Yonggom and their neighbors, their astonishing international campaign and stunning legal victory seemed to achieve everything they had been fighting for, yet the company's steadfast refusal to stop discharging tailings into the river prevented the campaign from protecting the environment. BHP experienced a profound loss of face in its home court in Melbourne but was ultimately rewarded for dragging its feet on tailings containment. It only belatedly realized that the political cost of its failure to solve the problem was too great to continue operating the mine, a decision that cost the company billions of dollars.

The fundamental dilemmas of contemporary capitalism cannot be resolved; they are part of the dialectical relationship between corporations and their critics that inevitably leads to new forms of contestation on both sides. This dynamic defines both the possibilities and the limitations of political engagement during a neoliberal era of global capitalism in which corporations rival states in wealth and power. Understanding how this process operates may be a partial antidote to political resignation, although it comes at the cost of learning how to live with incremental progress.

Yet one must cherish the hope provided by Rex Dagi, Alex Maun, and the other activists from the Ok Tedi and Fly Rivers, who were able to take one of the world's largest corporations to the brink in fighting for their environment and their rights. Recounting their struggle does not bring back the river, but it provides motivation to remain politically engaged in shaping alternative futures.

Epilogue

After a largely uncontested and spectacularly profitable decade, Ok Tedi Mining Ltd. faced unexpected challenges in 2013 from the Papua New Guinea government, which sought to gain control over the company's economic assets, including the mine. On September 18, the parliament passed the Mining (Ok Tedi Tenth Supplemental Agreement) Act of 2013, which nationalized the Ok Tedi mine and attempted to repatriate the $1.4 billion trust fund in Singapore. The 2001 law granting BHP Billiton immunity from prosecution for environmental damage was also overturned. The state assumed ownership of the Ok Tedi mine on January 1, 2014, but its effort to expropriate the trust fund was blocked by the Singapore courts. The trust also owns 63.4 per cent of the mine, worth an estimated $1.1 billion, the status of which is currently under arbitration by the International Centre for Settlement of Investment Disputes in Washington, DC.

As this book was going to press in January 2014, I met with Rex Dagi, Alex Maun, and several other key figures in the long-running struggle against OTML and BHP. We discussed the different paths they have taken since their participation in the initial lawsuit against the mine and their reactions to recent events. While Dagi supported their return to the Supreme Court of Victoria in 2000, he opposed the out-of-court settlement reached in 2004 and subsequently left the province. Dagi and I met at his house in a squatter settlement in Port Moresby. We were joined by Dair Gabara, the lawyer from the South Fly who participated in both cases against OTML and BHP. We later met with Gabia Gagarimabu, who was the lead plaintiff in the 2000 legal case while serving as a member of parliament. All three of the former plaintiffs were eager to take advantage of the new opportunities to hold BHP Billiton accountable for destroying their river system.

In Kiunga, I met separately with Alex Maun and Moses Oti, neither of whom participated in the second lawsuit against BHP Billiton. Instead, they chose to work closely with Ok Tedi Mining Ltd. to manage the distribution of economic benefits to the people living downstream from the mine. Although the Tenth Supplemental Agreement commits the PNG government "to restructure [the Singapore-based trust] and its operations to ensure that [it] applies the funds for the exclusive benefit of Western Province," neither Maun nor Oti supports the government intervention. Instead, they argue that the affected communities should own the mine and control the trust without external interference. I asked Maun about his recent comments to the media, in which he called for the Ok Tedi mine to close. He pointed to environmental damage that continues to exceed predictions, with pollution spreading ever further from the river corridor, especially in the Middle Fly. Maun also expressed concern about the risk of acid mine drainage from the pyrite storage area at Bige on the lower Ok Tedi River, beside his home village of Ieran. On a personal note, Maun conveyed his disappointment that the people of Western Province failed to appreciate or even acknowledge the hard work and sacrifices made by the leaders of the campaign against the Ok Tedi mine.

The Papua New Guinea economy remains dependent on extractive industry, including the new $19 billion natural gas project that extends from the Southern Highlands to the Ok Tedi River. Other leases are under negotiation for nearby oil deposits. Although there is widespread support for these developments, people invoke the lessons they have learned from the Ok Tedi case, insisting that the new projects be held to stronger environmental standards. They also argue that the people most directly affected by these developments should receive a larger share of their economic benefits. They claim not to have received anything of real or lasting value from the Ok Tedi mine, leading Robin Moken to emphasize the need "to stop making excuses and make something for the people."

In the meantime, people living in rural areas are increasingly connected to urban areas by road and cell phone. The people in Dome Village on the lower Ok Tedi River, for example, regularly travel to the town of Kiunga by truck and increasingly depend on store-bought food purchased using compensation payments. There is also a small market in the village, a novel development given that in the past food was never bought and sold, only given away. This allows people without incomes to participate in the cash economy. Some of the people living on the west bank of the Ok Tedi River talk about moving away from the polluted watershed toward the border, where they own land, once the government builds a road connecting the area to town.

The recent legislation on BHP Billiton and the Ok Tedi mine has prompted a flurry of legal activity, despite lingering reservations about the ability of the law to solve these problems. As Paul Katut noted about the original lawsuit against BHP, "We were fighting with the law, but the law wasn't fighting for us." A case filed by several plaintiffs from the South Fly resulted in an injunction from the deputy chief justice of Papua New Guinea on January 14, 2014, that requires Ok Tedi Mining Ltd. to stop discharging tailings and waste rock into the river system, effectively closing down the mine. The injunction also freezes the expenditure of dividends from the mine in the South Fly and calls for an audit of past expenses. Finally, the injunction compels the mining company to set aside funds to conduct independent research on pollution in the South Fly and its effects on human health, the results from which are expected to refute the claim by Ok Tedi Mining Ltd. that the mine has no significant impacts below the junction with the Strickland River. The prime minister urged the court to reconsider its decision, which he plans to aggressively challenge, arguing that closing the mine would have "horrendous" economic consequences for the state. The media also revealed that the injunction could complicate behind-the-scenes discussions between the state and BHP Billiton aimed at settling their dispute over the trust fund in Singapore and its shares in the Ok Tedi mine.

The windfall profits earned by the Ok Tedi mine during the last decade—and the mining company's plan to continue operating until at least 2025—means that there are significant opportunities to make better use of the revenue from the project on behalf of the people living downstream. But even if these economic benefits are fully realized, they will inevitably be overshadowed by the project's catastrophic environmental impacts. The possibilities for improving the social and economic conditions along the Ok Tedi and Fly Rivers are not only compromised materially by the extent to which the river system has already deteriorated but are also constrained by the political and legal options available to the people living there. The challenging circumstances they face underscore the importance of the politics of time in preventing future environmental disasters.

Timeline of the Ok Tedi Mine and Related Events

	Ok Tedi Mine	Related Events
1876	Lawrence Hargrave finds gold while panning in lower Ok Tedi River.	
1921		Beginning of Wau gold rush (Australian territory of New Guinea).
1968	Ok Tedi ore body discovered in Star Mountains.	
1971		United States breaks from gold standard amidst oil crisis; price rises from $37/oz. to $850/oz. in 1980.
1972		Production begins at Panguna copper mine, Bougainville.
1975		Papua New Guinea independence from Australia.
1979		Partizans (People against Rio Tinto Zinc and its Subsidiaries) founded in London.
1980	Ok Tedi consortium formed after Kennecott walks away.	
		Gold prices peak at $850/oz.
1982	Construction of Ok Tedi mine begins.	

	Ok Tedi Mine	Related Events
1984	Landslip ends construction of tailings dam.	
	First gold pour at Ok Tedi mine	
	Loss of cyanide drums at the mouth of the Fly River	
	Cyanide spill in Ok Tedi River	
1986	Sixth Supplemental Agreement allows for continued riverine tailings disposal.	
1987	First copper concentrate produced	
1988	William Townsend publishes "Giving Away the River." David Hyndman publishes "Ok Tedi: New Guinea's Disaster Mine."	
		Mineral Policy Center in Washington, DC, founded.
	Dome village petition on pollution and the refugees	
1989		Rebellion in Bougainville leads to closure of Panguna mine.
	Stuart Kirsch publishes "Ok Tedi River a Sewer."	
		ILO Convention No. 169 recognizes indigenous right to free, prior, and informed consent.
1990	Protest march in Kiunga calls for $1 billion in compensation.	
1992	Alex Maun travels to Germany for conference on Starnberg report.	
	Rex Dagi speech on *Rainbow Warrior II* in Rio de Janeiro.	U.N. Conference on Environment and Development ("Earth Summit") in Rio de Janeiro.
	Dagi et al. attend meetings in Washington, DC, and New York.	
1993	ENECO founded in Kiunga	
	Australian Conservation Foundation report declares Ok Tedi River "almost biologically dead."	
	International Water Tribunal in the Netherlands finds BHP guilty, calls for early mine closure.	

Ok Tedi Mine	Related Events
Social impact study of Ok Tedi mine on Yonggom and Awin villages completed	
Debate on Ok Tedi mine at Waigani seminar on environment and development, Port Moresby	
1994 Lawsuit filed against BHP in Supreme Court of Victoria by Slater & Gordon, May 5	
1995 Eighth Supplemental Agreement bans participation in foreign legal proceedings	
	Mineral Policy Institute in Australia founded
	U.S. Overseas Private Investment Corporation (OPIC) cancels Freeport's political risk insurance.
Contempt of court judgment issued against BHP	
1996 Alex Maun visits Dene First Nation and testifies at public hearings in Yellowknife, Canada, regarding BHP's interest in diamond concession	
	U.S. Alien Tort Claims Act lawsuit filed against Freeport–McMoRan in New Orleans
	First international meeting on mining and indigenous peoples, in London, sponsored by World Council of Churches
First Ok Tedi case settled out of court, June 7	
1997 El Niño drought delays reporting on OTML waste management reports.	Slater & Gordon file suit against Gold Ridge mine in the Solomon Islands
1998	Case against Freeport in District Court of New Orleans dismissed
	Indian NGO mines, minerals & People established
	Corporate-sponsored Global Mining Initiative (GMI) established

	Ok Tedi Mine	Related Events
1999	OTML releases new studies describing impacts as "significantly greater than expected." BHP announces that Ok Tedi mine "is not compatible with our environmental values."	
		MiningWatch Canada founded
		Indonesian Mining Advocacy Network JATAM established
2000	World Bank review of Ok Tedi project calls for early mine closure.	
		Launch of Mines, Minerals and Sustainable Development (MMSD) program by mining industry
	Landowners lodge claim for breach of 1996 settlement against BHP and OTML, April 11.	
	CMCAs opt-out process instituted	
		U.S. Alien Tort Claims Act case filed against Rio Tinto re: the Panguna mine and Bougainville civil war
2001		Gold prices hit bottom at $255/oz.; start climb toward $1,787/oz. in 2012.
		Launch of short-lived Global Mining Campaign (GMC) in Washington, DC
		Mines and Communities international network of NGOs concerned with indigenous peoples and mining issues, foundational meeting in London
	BHP merges with Billiton to become BHP Billiton.	
		Launch of International Council on Mining and Metals (ICMM) in London
		Lawsuit against Gold Ridge Mine dismissed
		Bougainville peace agreement signed
		U.N. Office of the High Commissioner for Human Rights expert workshop on indigenous peoples, human rights, and resource extraction in Geneva

	Ok Tedi Mine	Related Events
	Ninth Supplemental Agreement allows BHP Billiton to exit Ok Tedi mine. PNG Sustainable Development Program Ltd. established with BHP Billiton's 52% stake in the mine in exchange for legal immunity	
2002	BHP Billiton officially withdraws from Ok Tedi Mining Ltd.	
		Toronto GMI meeting announces MMSD results.
		First major *consulta* in Tambogrande, Peru, against Manhattan Minerals
		World Summit on Sustainable Development (WSSD) in Johannesburg
2003		World Bank Extractive Industry Review workshop on indigenous peoples and resource extraction in Oxford
	Plaintiffs in second case against Ok Tedi mine instructed to settle, December 21	
2004	Out of court settlement approved, January 16	
2005		Esquel *consulta* against Meridian Gold, Argentina
		Sipacapa *consulta* against Goldcorp's Marlin mine, Guatemala
	Regional summit meeting in Kiunga fails to find a way forward.	
2006	OTML earns record $639 million profit after taxes.	
2007		U.N. Declaration on the Rights of Indigenous Peoples passes.
2009		Manila meeting on indigenous peoples and extractive industry
2012		Gold prices peak at $1,787/oz.

	Ok Tedi Mine	Related Events
2013	PNG Sustainable Development Program Ltd. worth US$1.4 billion (after $600 million in expenditures)	
		Preliminary talks with Rio Tinto regarding reopening of Panguna mine in Bougainville
	Community Mine Continuation Agreements renewed in advance of plans to extend operating life of Ok Tedi mine to 2025	
		Alien tort case against Rio Tinto regarding Panguna mine dismissed
		Gold prices bottom out at $1,192/oz. in June.
	PNG government nationalizes Ok Tedi mine, strips BHP Billiton of immunity from legal prosecution, and tries to take control of PNG Sustainable Development Program Ltd.	

Notes

1. In the United States, these views are generally referred to as market-based policies or neoconservatism.

2. Writing about the role of labor in open-cut mines in the Andes, David Szablowski (2007, 41–42) notes, "The new mining operations being developed since the boom of the 1990s essentially do not require local labour. This has contributed significantly to the militancy of contemporary mining and community conflicts. On one level, communities are denied an important source of the benefits and opportunities that are expected to arise from mining activity. On another, the absence of work has highlighted other sources of conflict that have often been overshadowed in mining development: conflicts over access to resources, the marginalization of local people, socio-economic impacts and environmental degradation."

3. The names of the largest oil companies in the world are familiar to most consumers through their advertising campaigns and gas stations, and increasingly, by their oil spills. In contrast, the major mining companies are less familiar except in mining centers.

4. The major exception has been the Kimberley Process regarding the sale of "blood diamonds" from conflict zones, as I discuss in chapter 5.

1. COLLIDING ECOLOGIES

1. Kennecott's assessment that Ok Tedi was a "high-risk, moderate-reward opportunity that would severely stretch the corporation's beleaguered financial capacity" led the company to withdraw from the project in 1975 (Pintz 1984, 46).

2. John Burton (1997, 29) describes how the mining industry exploits the trope *terra nugax,* which conflates distance from capital and markets with worthlessness.

3. From November to April, the ore is transported by barge to a transshipment point in the Gulf of Papua, and from May to October, to the harbor in Port Moresby, where it is off-loaded onto larger ships (Tingay 2007, 28)

4. *The Fourth Goal and Directive Principle of the Papua New Guinea Constitution* (Papua New Guinea 1975) states, "We declare our fourth goal to be for Papua New Guinea's natural resources and environment to be conserved and used for the collective benefit of us all, and to be replenished for the benefit of future generations."

5. Although Filer (1997b, 61) notes that the operating losses reported by Ok Tedi Mining Ltd. prior to the signing of the Seventh Supplemental Agreement were subsequently revised to indicate profits over the same period.

6. Literary critic Rob Nixon (2011) writes about the disproportionate impact on marginalized populations from the "slow violence" associated with oil spills, the use of toxic chemicals, and the environmental aftermath of war.

7. The mining industry has a long history of seeking to discredit compensation claims. A striking example comes from a mining museum in Waihi, New Zealand, which displays two human thumbs in formaldehyde, accompanied by a caption stating, "Some miners deliberately chopped off thumbs or fingers to obtain compensation." A claim like this could be made only because so many people lost their fingers, limbs, and lives while working in underground gold mines (Ryan 2005).

8. Many Americans had a similar response to the BP oil spill in the Gulf of Mexico after hearing stories about fishermen and others who lost their livelihood in the spill. A CNN headline read, "Gulf residents mourn oil disaster." Of the pollution along the coast, one person commented, "It breaks my heart." Others talked about feelings of sadness and loss. A politician became choked up and began to cry in the middle of his testimony. Signs posted by people living along the coast asked, "BP, how should I feed my family?" (Kirsch 2010).

9. Invasive species also pose new problems, including grasses introduced by the mining company to stabilize the tailings deposits along the river and several invasive fish species.

10. According to Alan Tingay (2007, 27), who assessed the threat of acid rock drainage (ARD) from the Ok Tedi mine in 2007, "The consequences of the failure of the ARD management strategy could vary in significance from small-scale increases in the amount of ARD flowing to the ecosystem to large scale pollution and the complete destruction of the Fly River ecosystem with catastrophic implications for communities that depend on that ecosystem."

11. Freeport CEO James R. Moffet once described the project as "thrusting a spear of economic development into the heartland of Irian Jaya" (Marr 1993, 71).

12. The distance traveled from Freeport's Grasberg mine to the Arafura Sea is only 120 kilometers, about one-ninth the distance from the Ok Tedi mine to the Gulf of Papua, although the drop in elevation is much greater.

13. These funds supported an estimated 550 armed forces personnel stationed in the vicinity of the mine (Robert F. Kennedy Memorial Center for Human Rights 2004).

14. Filer (1990, 79) argues that the unifying feature of Bougainville ethnic identity is "the massive hole in the middle of [the island]."

2. THE POLITICS OF SPACE

1. John Burton (2000, 99) refers to these discussions as the "turning-point for mine impact studies in Papua New Guinea."

2. Another possible tactic was violence against the mining company. Although some of the early protests included acts of vandalism, they were spontaneous rather than planned. The state, however, has not hesitated to use its mobile police forces, which have a history of human rights violations, in response to conflict. But the events leading to the civil war in Bougainville suggest that excessive use of force by the state can be a catalyst for the escalation of conflict rather than an effective deterrent.

3. Yonggom nicknames are reciprocal (Kirsch 2006, 65), and the three of us often address and refer to each other "*bot-korok.*"

4. ICRAF was cofounded by Brian Brunton, an Australian lawyer who became a national judge in Papua New Guinea and later worked with Slater & Gordon on their submissions to the PNG courts (Brunton 1997), and Powes Parkop, a Papua New Guinean lawyer and human rights activist who later became a member of Parliament and the governor of the National Capital District.

5. The recommendation for establishing the acceptable particulate level was produced by Applied Geology Associates, the New Zealand consulting firm responsible for the controversial report on the environmental impact of the Panguna mine that enraged Bougainville landowners (Connell 1991, 72)

6. Moses Oti also pointed to the suspension of the requirement to construct a tailings dam as a turning point in the campaign. He recalled that Ted Diro, then deputy prime minister, told him: "if the landowners want compensation, they have to provide evidence, scientific evidence, to the government." Oti said that Diro's admonition inspired them to solicit independent evaluations of the environmental impact of the mine (pers. comm. 1996).

7. The report from the Wau Ecology Institute (Sakulas and Tjamei 1991) benefitted from contributions by Jörg Hettler, a lecturer at the University of Papua New Guinea specializing in the environmental impact of resource extraction (see Hettler and Lehmann 1995).

8. A subsequent report from IUCN (International Union for Conservation of Nature 1995, 50–51) was more critical of pollution on the Fly River and BHP's presentation of scientific data, noting, "Currently OTML appear to project an image of continuing environmental impacts until mine closure after which the river systems will quickly revert to normal, pre-mining conditions. This is probably an unrealistic although convenient scenario. Even if the physical system reaches an equilibrium relatively rapidly, the ecological effects of elevated copper/metal levels, either actual or perceived, are likely to be an issue in the Fly for many years after the closure of the mine."

9. My first interactions with Roger Moody took the form of a debate about legal challenges to the mining industry that appeared in an activist journal

focused on the conflicts between Royal Dutch Petroleum and the Ogoni people in the Niger Delta of Nigeria (Moody 1996; Kirsch 1997e).

10. Moody was also an advisor to the second International Water Tribunal on mining issues.

11. The title comes from the comparison of political resistance by environmentalists and indigenous activists to the actions of the Lilliputians in Jonathan Swift's satirical novel: "Like Gulliver, the mining industry is a robust giant held down by a million silk strings" (Moody 1992, 9).

12. In 1987, Metallgeschaft created Metall Mining Company, a Canadian subsidiary responsible for Metallgeschaft's foreign mines, including OTML. Metallgeschaft retained a 50.1 percent interest in Metall Mining Co. (Metall also retained 35 percent interest in the Norddeutsche refinery in Germany, one of OTML's largest customers). In 1993, Metall purchased Degussa and DEG's shares of Ok Tedi Mining Ltd., which after a subsequent transfer of 2 percent equity to the Papua New Guinea state, increased Metall's stake in OTML to 18 percent (IWT 1994, Mining 60). In 1994, Metallgeschaft, after almost being forced to declare bankruptcy following huge losses on the derivative market, sold its stake in Metall Mining, although it repurchased its original interest in Norddeutsche Affinerie. In 1995, Metall Mining changed its name to Inmet Mining Corporation to dissociate itself from the troubled Metallgeschaft Corporation. Inmet was the final private investor in OTML until 2009, when it swapped its 18 percent equity interest in OTML for a 5 percent royalty on revenues from the mine, plus a cash payment equal to 18 percent of the company's working capital. In 2010, it sold its share of the mine's royalties back to the company for $335 million (Hill 2010).

13. The Australian Conservation Foundation, which had previously shown little inclination to campaign internationally, was provoked into taking up the issue by an unauthorized press release from several of its staff members about potential impacts from the Ok Tedi mine on the Torres Strait Islands in Australia. The media response to the press release was such that the organization felt compelled to act (Helen Rosenbaum, pers. comm. 2011).

14. In 1993, the Papua New Guinea kina was worth approximately US$1.01.

15. The oft-quoted phrase from the report is usually rendered as "biologically dead."

16. The Yonggom emphasize their ability to speak their own language in addition to the lingua franca of the state in contrast to their perception that Euro-Americans have forgotten their native tongues and are only able to speak the language of the state. They also point to their dependence on subsistence production in contrast to Euro-Americans, who buy their food in stores. A final distinction is that Papua New Guineans retain the customs and traditions that set them apart from their neighbors, whereas Euro-Americans appear homogenous to them by comparison.

17. Similar distinctions were invoked by Yonggom cargo cults during the 1950s, which, instead of seeking commodities or "cargo," demanded factories for the production of tools, cloth, and money (Schoorl 1993).

18. Colin Filer (1997c, 119) argues that mining conflicts in Melanesia represent "not just a failure to cooperate with the [mining industry], which many

people might applaud as a heroic act of resistance, but a lack of mutual cooperation in the pursuit, and even the definition, of that 'development' which
everyone agrees they want." He argues that Melanesians "make life unusually
difficult for multinational mining companies, not because they share philosoph-
ical assumptions or oppositional strategies which merit special sympathy or
the applause of Western environmentalists, but because of the characteristic
diversity and instability of political relationships between Melanesian persons,
institutions, and communities" (Filer 1997c, 94).

19. The Innu of Newfoundland combine traditional knowledge of elders and
hunters with scientific concepts that enable their "leaders to deal with the dominant society on its own terms and to challenge the ways in which science is
pressed into service by powerful interests" (Innes 2001, 14). "Terms like 'ecological integrity,' 'biological diversity,' and 'cumulative effects' are now frequently used by Innu spokespeople, . . . [who] have adapted and incorporated
those aspects of science that make sense to them, while contesting those aspects
that do not" (Innes 2001, 15).

3. DOWN BY LAW

1. Many of these complaints also address the use of force against local populations to secure access to their resources and labor.

2. During the 1990s, I was able to interview and share information with
attorneys in the cases against BHP, Freeport, Rio Tinto, and ChevronTexaco.

3. Most of the cases against mining companies discussed in this chapter were
class actions, which bring together a number of individuals based on common
interests, which may include exposure to harm. Class-action law is a means of
reducing the transaction costs of legal proceedings for plaintiffs and thereby
increasing their access to the courts, which is generally viewed as a democratic
good. Because American lawyers may be compensated by a percentage of
awards rather than by fees, they are able to use these funds to run class-action
cases with higher costs and uncertain prospects for success. The development of
modern class-action law in the United States from the 1970s to the 1980s is
associated with political movements that addressed civil rights, environmental
issues, and consumer rights (Yeazell 1987). Class actions against corporations
may also be intended to change the behavior of the class of defendants and thus
have a regulatory influence. However, the rulings in these cases are not prospective like ordinary government regulations, with which corporations can comply
to reduce their risk, but claim retroactive liability in their evaluation of the
harm done (Pring et al. 1999, 42). They are also somewhat controversial
because of the pressure they exert on the defendant to settle and because the
entire class of plaintiffs is legally bound by the outcome. For jurisdictions that
do not permit class actions, lawyers may bundle individual cases together and
run a series of test cases that, if successful, may be used to leverage a settlement
for the remainder of the claims, which was the strategy in the first Ok Tedi case.

4. Dair Gabara later resigned his government post and established a law
office in Port Moresby, where he represented Slater & Gordon in Papua New
Guinea.

5. It is generally sufficient to demonstrate that "legally significant acts" arose in the forum state in order to establish an adequate territorial nexus for a case (Akpan 2002, 68). The fundamental assumption is that a court should not decline to hear a case simply because alternatives exist. However, the doctrine of *forum non conveniens* permits the court to decline to hear a case for which fairness to the defendant dictates that the case would be more appropriately adjudicated in the country in which the alleged violation occurred. The responsibility for demonstrating that an alternative forum is more appropriate rests with the defendant, and claims of *forum non conveniens* are generally advanced on practical grounds, for example, that the evidence and the key witnesses are located in the host state in which the company operates rather than the home state of the corporation. Appropriate reasons to locate the forum in the home state of the corporation include questions about the independence of the judiciary in the host state, potential danger to the plaintiffs or witnesses, or other conditions that limit the viability of the forum. Although reference to more favorable laws or judicial processes, such as the availability of jury trials, are not permitted in arguments concerning forum, the identification of the most favorable forum for one's client is an important motivation for these claims.

6. Sovereign immunity is a well-established legal principle that recognizes the rights of states to manage their own affairs, including their natural resources. Consequently, acts by sovereign states are not subject to review by foreign courts. Thus, liability in cases against extractive industry may be skewed in the direction of holding transnational corporations accountable for actions that may be condoned, encouraged, or even required by the host state. In other words, corporations may be held accountable to standards above and beyond those required by the host state. The ability to enforce higher standards is a crucial resource for counteracting the "race to the bottom," by forcing corporations to adopt higher standards rather than shopping for less-demanding regulatory regimes.

7. Jurisdiction refers to the legal authority of the court over the defendants, subject matter, and property in question.

8. The term *yariman* also refers to other relationships. The central actor in divinations held to seek the cause of a persistent illness, or *anigat,* is known as the *anigat yariman.* Similarly, the sponsor of an *arat* pig feast is known as the *arat yariman.* The *yariman* relationship is based on the responsibilities of kinship, guardianship, and sponsorship. Given that *ambip kin* refers to both a particular block of land and the specific lineage or clan that holds the rights to that land, *ambip kin yariman* indicates the person or persons responsible for lineage or clan land.

9. The Native Title Act of Australia (1993), which provides a mechanism for settling Aboriginal land claims, was passed in response to the 1992 Australian High Court decision in *Mabo v. Queensland.*

10. Worth approximately US$86 million at the time.

11. The finding of contempt led the Australian aid agency Community Aid Abroad to observe, "The Big Australian has become a Big Bully" (Cannon 1998, 252).

12. In June 1995, one kina was worth approximately US$0.78.

13. Fifteen years later, when a lawsuit in Papua New Guinea sought to stop the Ramu nickel and cobalt mine from using submarine tailings disposal, the PNG Parliament hastily passed the Environment Bill Amendment 2010, a sweeping amendment that prohibits all challenges to permits issued by the Ministry of Environment except by developers. The act specifies that permits are "final and may not be challenged or reviewed in any court or tribunal." The amendment suggests that the Compensation (Prohibition of Foreign Legal Proceedings) Act 1995 was less about national sovereignty than the state's refusal to accept any challenges to resource extraction projects, regardless of the venue. The Environment Bill Amendment of 2010 was subsequently overturned, but not before it had the intended effect of scuttling the litigation against the Ramu mine's use of submarine tailings disposal.

14. During this process, Dair Gabara "cracked under a combination of threats and promises, cancelled his retainer arrangement with Slater & Gordon, and entered into private negotiations with the mining company to settle the villagers' claims out of court" (Gordon 1997, 254–55). However, Gabara later recanted and returned to work with the landowners and for Slater & Gordon.

15. The settlement also allowed Ellis to assume the chairmanship of BHP without the specter of Ok Tedi looming over him (Callick 1996).

16. Worth approximately US$86 million at the time.

17. Worth approximately US$31 million at the time.

18. The four preferred options at the time of the settlement were identified as: (1) a 110 km tailings pipeline from the mine to the lower Ok Tedi River, combined with dredging; (2) a 103 km tailings pipeline to the lower Ok Tedi River, combined with a conventional tailings pond; (3) dredging in the lower Ok Tedi River only; or (4) construction of a tailings dam in the mountains (Ok Tedi Settlement Agreement 1996; reproduced in Banks and Ballard 1997a, appendix 1, 216).

19. Worth approximately US$5.5 million at the time.

20. In Papua New Guinea, the expression "playing politics" means "to deceive or mislead someone."

21. Here Gabara is referring to the rumor that they "lost the case," because they did not receive the entire A$4 billion claim initially reported by the media.

22. "We're not backward [Tok Pisin *kanaka* literally means 'native,' but in the derogatory form *bus kanaka,* it means 'backward' or 'primitive']; we're determined [Yonggom *bot-korok* means 'stubborn' or, literally, 'stone-headed']. The Ok Tedi is our life. The Ok Tedi River is polluted [*Deri* is the Yonggom name for the river; the Yonggom *moraron* literally means 'spoiled' or 'rotten'], so it [the company] must pay. We worked together as one [the Yonggom *inamen mimo* means 'with one mind' or 'shared intentions']."

23. In Papua New Guinea Tok Pisin: "Tenkyu, Papa God. Yu bai givim dispela save long Rex Dagi long helpim mipela. Papa God yu yet yu putim gol na silva na kapa long graun. Em i no bilong mipela, em I bilong yu tasol. Mipela usim em. Fly Wara, em i no bilong mipela, em i bilong yu tasol."

24. The PNG kina was worth US$0.77 at the time of the June 1996 settlement. It subsequently declined as low as US$0.23 in November 2002 and recovered to US$0.475 by January 2013.

25. The literature on resource compensation in Papua New Guinea is extensive (see Bainton 2009; Crook 2004; Filer 1997a; Kirsch 2004, 2006; Strathern 1999, 2000).

26. Pitpit *(Saccharum edule)* is also known as "bush asparagus."

27. BHP's commitment to implement the preferred tailings option was subject to "unexpected or unforeseen circumstances which may render the tailings option economically or technically unfeasible" and "obtaining all necessary leases and other approvals required from the landowners and the state." In addition, BHP and OTML agreed that "if and as required by the State, the Companies will provide all necessary financial and other support for, and will bona fide participate in, the independent enquiry or review conducted by the State" (Ok Tedi Settlement Agreement 1996; reproduced in Banks and Ballard 1997a, appendix 1, 217).

28. Slater & Gordon had recently spent more than one million dollars in its unsuccessful case against Ross Mining over the Gold Ridge Mine in the Solomon Islands.

29. This principle had previously been articulated by Rex Dagi in a witness statement prepared before the initial lawsuit: "Decisions about the land are made by the clan and the clan leader then acts on the decisions. They have a clan meeting to make a decision" (Dagi n.d.). Dagi also made a similar claim about decision making within the village: "If there is a community project, the village councilor meets clan leaders and then they take it to their individual clans and then go back to the village councilor with the views of the clans and whether they will participate in the community project" (Dagi n.d.).

30. The *Post-Courier* (2001) reported, "The environmental disaster created by the Ok Tedi mine has been a financial and environmental nightmare for BHP."

31. I first learned of this proposal while at a bar in the mining township in Tabubil, where several mining executives asked me whether I would support running the mine as a nonprofit organization. My response was that I usually think of nonprofit organizations as doing good, not destroying the environment.

32. Slater & Gordon also felt that Australia's conservative political tilt at the time created bias against class-action lawsuits like the Ok Tedi case.

33. Efforts were made by the Mineral Policy Institute to find lawyers to continue the litigation, but its size and complexity, especially given that Slater & Gordon, one of the largest and most successful plaintiffs law firms in Australia, had walked away from it, discouraged any strong interest. There was also considerable "compassion fatigue" in Australia regarding the case, which was seen by many as a lost cause.

34. The CMCAs were renegotiated with the assistance of an American NGO that specializes in multi-stakeholder engagement. Despite being engaged for its expertise in environmental issues, the NGO treated the environmental problems downstream from the mine as secondary to the question of compensation. After prompting by the member of the multi-stakeholder engagement representing the interests of civil society, however, it sponsored the first independent environmental study of the mine's impacts (Tingay 2007).

35. OTML also sought to identify additional exploration and mining opportunities elsewhere in Papua New Guinea (Sheppard 2010).

36. The case was delayed several times by challenges to the Alien Tort Claims Act, including the question whether there is a requirement that the plaintiffs must first exhaust all possibilities for adjudication in the forum in which the alleged tort occurred and whether alien tort cases infringe on the authority of the executive branch to shape foreign policy, as argued in an amicus curiae brief from the U.S. Department of State under the pro-business administration of President George W. Bush.

37. In contrast, torts concerning human health are more amenable to adjudication, as indicated by several key victories in international tort claims in the British courts over workers' exposure to asbestos and radioactivity from uranium mining in South Africa (Meeran 1999).

38. The nineteenth-century legal fiction known as the "corporate veil" considers every company in a corporate group as a separate legal entity, which limits the liability of shareholders, including parent companies, which was historically seen as necessary to protect the capital raised for investment (Ward 2001, 469). Challenging this principle is referred to as piercing or lifting the corporate veil. There is "increasing recognition of the view that 'there are powerful economic, moral, and social factors' that may make parent companies liable" for their actions (Akpan 2002, 56).

4. CORPORATE SCIENCE

1. C.C. Little's commitment to eugenics led him to attribute most human traits to genetics, "including vulnerability to cancer" (Oreskes and Conway 2010, 17). Consequently, he argued that "genetic weakness" was responsible for lung cancer rather than smoking (17).

2. A popular history of the University of Michigan identifies Little only as a former director of the American Cancer Society and asserts that "his experimentation contributed invaluably to the study of the dread disease" (Peckham 1994, 190).

3. The Commissioner of the U.S. Food and Drug Administration forthrightly expressed his condemnation of these practices: "I don't want to live in peace with these guys. . . . If they cared at all for the public health, they wouldn't be in the business in the first place" (David Kessler, cited in Brandt 2007, 430–31).

4. Another example of this dynamic is provided by the food industry, as nutritionist Marion Nestle (2007, xiv) observes: "Food companies will make and market any product that sells, regardless of its nutritional value or its effect on health. In this regard, food companies hardly differ from cigarette companies. They lobby Congress to eliminate regulations that are perceived as unfavorable; they press federal regulatory agencies not to enforce such regulations; and when they don't like regulatory decisions, they file lawsuits. Like cigarette companies, food companies co-opt food and nutrition experts by supporting professional organizations and research, and they expand sales by marketing directly to children, members of minority groups, and people in developing countries—whether or not the products are likely to improve people's diets."

5. The cognitive psychologist Daniel Kahneman (2011) suggests that optimism is a pervasive heuristic bias. The "planning fallacy" is ordinarily counterbalanced by another heuristic bias that overvalues potential losses. But in the Ok Tedi case, the costs of production were externalized onto society and the environment, and consequently undervalued by the corporation.

6. Writing about the Ok Tedi mine, Simon C. Apte (2009, 369) argues that in the 1970s and early 1980s, "environmental science did not possess the predictive capability required to confidently assess mine impacts, as a result of which many of the assessments of the environmental impact were overoptimistic." However, OTML continued to deny that the mining project was having significant, long-lasting environmental impacts until 1999.

7. Elizabeth Povinelli (2002, 155) refers to this as the "liberal desire to escape, as individuals or as the authors and proponents of social projects, the unconditional of the future perfect proposition: . . . 'We will have been wrong.'"

8. Although George Frynas (1998) argues that, in contrast to conventional economic reasoning, in which it is assumed that the rule of law is a precondition for economic success, corporations may benefit from the lack of governance and regulation in weak or failed states. Frynas illustrates his argument with the example of Royal Dutch Petroleum in Nigeria, but the current mining free-for-all in the Democratic Republic of the Congo is another example of this phenomenon.

9. As Michael Goldman notes, "The difference between measuring downstream effects as 100 yards *or* 100 miles from a project site can translate into millions of dollars in compensation, land and water cleansing, or population resettlement. The incentive, hence, becomes to minimize project risk through the process of constructing environmental assessments." (2005, 119; emphasis in original).

10. The peer review group stopped functioning after the 2000 report, although their confidentiality agreement with the mining company prevents them from discussing their experiences (Patricia Townsend, pers. comm. 2002).

11. The sediment load of the Strickland River has been estimated at eight to ten times that of the Fly River (Pickup and Marshall 2009, 13).

12. Another example of this strategy is deployed by the nuclear industry, which attempts to allay concerns by pointing out that "uranium is a natural material" that can be found everywhere (Schramm 2010). The uranium-mining industry also argues that "radioactivity released by coal is greater than that released by nuclear power plants," at least in the normal course of affairs, i.e., excluding nuclear accidents (Schramm 2010).

13. Writing about the measurement of copper concentrations in the Ok Tedi River, Simon C. Apte (2009, 343) notes that "failure to take into account the variability that occurs at timescales of hours and days may result in erroneous or biased interpretation."

14. Arn Keeling (pers. comm. 2010) reports that mining company representatives in Canada used the same technique to reassure people that mining was safe.

15. Gold and copper prices are often countercyclical, that is, copper prices fall when there is a recession, because the demand for copper, much of which is used in construction, decreases, whereas gold prices tend to rise in relation to a

decline in the stock market, as people seek investment opportunities that are insulated from fluctuations in the stock market. However, in the recent recession, both gold and copper prices remained high, creating windfall profits at mines like Ok Tedi.

16. This included supporting the mine on behalf of elderly people in the community, so that they might receive some benefits from its operation. As one woman told me, "I want to taste some sugar before I die" (Kirsch 2006, 208).

17. I also argued that revealing the facts underlying OPIC's decision to terminate Freeport's political risk insurance would provide important information to other companies regarding the agency's standards. By congressional mandate, OPIC offers assistance only to operations that do not significantly degrade the environment.

18. Coumans (2011, S33) compares these anthropologists to journalists embedded in the military, who "gain access to experiences and information that would be [otherwise] difficult to obtain." However, the ability of anthropologists embedded in mining companies "to publicize those insights may be restricted, and their reporting may be biased by their operating environment" (Coumans 2011, S33).

19. Lawsuits against tobacco companies forced them to release internal documents revealing their practices (Brandt 2007; Proctor 2012). Numerous physicians have written about their experiences with the pharmaceutical industry (e.g., Angell 2005; Kassirer 2005). Comparable evidence is not available for the mining industry.

20. Charles Perrow's (1994, 219) argument that "production pressures, profit pressures, growth, prestige, department power struggles and so on will supplant safety concerns" may also apply to environmental impacts.

21. Perrow (1997, 66) argues that in the United States, "a fully wage-dependent workforce makes whistle-blowing risky, structural interests of employees limits the reform efforts of even an environmentally sensitive executive, decentralization limits accountability, consultants and public relations staff are available to reassure executives that trade-offs are in society's interests and that regulations mean waste, and organizations socialize all employees, making whistle blowing even rarer."

22. Jessica Smith Rolston (2010) makes a similar observation in her analysis of the corporate social responsibility policies of a gold mine in the Pacific Northwest. Given the strong environmental values of the people living in the region and negative public perceptions of mining, the company sought to convey to its employees that they worked for an environmentally responsible company.

5. INDUSTRY STRIKES BACK

1. However, Peter Sandman, one of the authors of the volume, subsequently adopted a much more aggressive approach to these issues, becoming a celebrity on the corporate risk management/public relations lecture circuit, characterizing journalism and activism as "outrage industries" (Sandman 2008).

2. Greenpeace's decision to accept a seat on Shell's board of directors after the Brent Spar controversy in 1995, when it opposed the company's plan to

scuttle an offshore oil storage platform at sea, provided the company with some welcome good news but presented a credibility gap for an organization whose reputation was based on contesting powerful corporations rather than collaborating with them (Kenneth MacDonald, pers. comm. 2010).

3. Another version of this strategy is the establishment of faux NGOs that purport to represent indigenous communities (Sawyer 2004) or consumer groups (Brandt 2007). These groups are sometimes referred to as "astroturf" NGOs in contrast to "grassroots" groups.

4. John Stauber and Sheldon Rampton (1995, 126) argue that the corporate "good cop, bad cop" strategy "skillfully creates and exploits divisions within the environmental movement. This strategy of 'divide and conquer' coopts and compromises mainstream environmental organizations, while simultaneously orchestrating extremist attacks against grassroots activists and others not willing to 'behave respectably' in exchange for industry cash."

5. Similarly, in Peru, the right-wing president Alan García accused environmentalists of being "dogs in the manger" for trying to stop others from using something that is of no value to them. Such accusations occur even though critics of the mining industry see themselves as working for the good of the nation by protecting the environment.

6. Development projects in nature reserves and parks may also be exempted from legislative requirements to negotiate with people who previously occupied and/or make use of the lands and territories in question (see Humphreys Bebbington 2012).

7. During the period between the 1997 Kyoto Protocol and the 2011 Fukushima crisis, when nuclear power received the reluctant endorsement of mainstream conservation organizations concerned about greenhouse gases and global climate change, the uranium-mining industry sought inclusion in green-choice funds, efforts that were subsequently delegitimized by the tsunami, which brought Japan's nuclear industry to the brink of disaster.

8. Early discussions about sustainability often emphasized the conservation of finite resources. This referred not only to biota but also to minerals and energy sources, arguments that were premised on the assumption of scarcity. However, there are reasons to question assumptions about resource scarcity in relation to minerals and fossil fuels. The total stock of gold to which humans have access increases every year rather than being consumed, as fossil fuels are. Similarly, it is unlikely that we will ever run out of copper, as not only is copper a relatively abundant element, but the total stock of copper available for human use also continues to increase. In both cases, the increasing environmental costs of extraction pose a greater threat than the risk of resource depletion. Recent discoveries of deep sea oil deposits and increased access to oil and natural gas using controversial hydraulic fracturing technology also suggest that the environmental risks of extraction and consumption outweigh concerns about resource scarcity or exhaustion.

9. Placer Dome, which at the time operated the Porgera mine in Papua New Guinea, which also discharges tailings into the Fly River, clearly had the lawsuit against the Ok Tedi mine in mind when formulating these policies (see Murray and Williams 1997).

10. The use of the language of conservation has an interesting history in the mining industry: minerals were seen as "wasting assets" that one had to use or lose, and restricting access to mineral resources in parks was viewed as "sterilizing" them (Keeling and Wynn 2011, 131).

11. As one anonymous industry correspondent observed about the industry's claim to practice *sustainable mining*, "Being discovered as an industry trying to fool people is the great risk being run by mining as it pretends to be something more than a business which digs, delivers, and moves on—each step being acceptable, essential in fact, to meeting the demands of industry and consumers—but definitely not sustainable" (Dryblower 2004).

12. The American satirist Stephen Colbert (2012, 128) asks how coal is converted to clean coal, diagramming the answer, "1) Start with coal. 2) Add the word 'clean' in front of it."

13. The MMSD report notes, "In some circumstances deep-sea mine disposal might be an option deserving serious consideration—when the mineral deposits are on islands that have little spare land, when available space is at risk of flooding or when the stability of land disposal facilities is uncertain because of high rainfall or seismicity" (Danielson 2002).

14. Instead, the industry successfully persuaded the World Summit on Sustainable Development (United Nations 2002, 37, 45) to include references to "sustainable mining practices" and "the contribution of the industrial sector, particularly mining, minerals and metals, to the sustainable development of Africa."

15. Writing about the Guadalupe oil spill described in the previous chapter, Tom Beamish (2002, 52–53) notes "how vulnerable we are to industrial excess with the weak system of industrial regulation (also referred to as 'self-audit') that is currently in place." One of the lessons learned from the BP oil spill in the Gulf of Mexico was that the federal regulatory body responsible for monitoring off-shore oil wells, despite conveying the appearance of providing appropriate oversight, was largely dependent on information supplied by the petroleum industry.

16. There are also a number of smaller programs that take the form of certification programs for "green gold" and "conflict-free" gemstones. One example is the No Dirty Gold campaign operated by the NGO Earthworks in Washington, DC (see chapter 2). The boutique size of these initiatives suggests the difficulties entailed in scaling them up to include a larger percentage of the market. In some cases, these programs are little more than marketing schemes intended to attract consumers and may have the perverse effect of alleviating general concerns about the mining industry.

17. In an allusion to the famous sign advertising rabbits for sale as "pets or meat" in Michael Moore's (2002) breakout film *Roger and Me,* which focuses on the economic hardships caused by automobile plant closures in Michigan, the film's primary Romanian character, Gheorghe Lucian, is introduced for the first time standing beside his rabbit hutch. However, Lucian looks genuinely shocked when McAleer asks him whether he intends to eat his pet rabbit.

18. The film also deploys a familiar trope symbolizing the postsocialist economic collapse by showing footage of people at an abandoned factory pulling steel reinforcement rods from concrete to sell as scrap metal.

19. In 2013, the Pascua Lama project was cited for major environmental violations, leading the Chilean government to suspend construction.

20. Expanding their antienvironmentalist oeuvre, McAleer and McElhinney's next project was a film attacking "global warming hysteria."

21. Andrew J. Hoffman (1997, 180) argues that there are two constructive roles for environmental activists: as consultants who work within existing power structures to bring about change, although they risk being co-opted, and as "militants" who help set the agenda by remaining outside of institutional fields.

22. Here I follow Marc Edelman's (2001, 301–3) call for anthropologists to study conservative political organizations.

23. For example, at a presentation of the film *Mine Your Own Business*, the CEO of Gabriel Resources, which seeks to develop a gold mine in Roşia Montană, complained, "The opposition has sued us at least 50 times, sued politicians and bureaucrats personally," intimidating the Romanian government. The company has had "to respond to 5,610 questions from NGOs and 93 contestations, some 100 pages long. The completed response is 12,600 pages in English and 12,900 pages in Romanian" (Heritage Foundation 2007).

24. Nahan (2003) was speaking on behalf of the Institute for Public Affairs, the Australian counterpart to the American Enterprise Institute.

25. See Oreskes and Conway (2010, 216–39) for discussion and critique of the "revisionist attack" on Rachel Carson in relation to the ban on DDT.

26. The ad was published to accompany a congratulatory essay on "Closing BHP's Island Copper Mine" in the *Mining and Engineering Journal* (J. J. Marcus 1997).

6. NEW POLITICS OF TIME

1. According to Alan Tingay (2007, 28), who assessed the threat of acid rock drainage (ARD) from the Ok Tedi mine in 2007, "In my opinion the ARD mitigation strategy should be regarded as a large-scale engineering experiment that the decision-makers believe has a low risk of failure and a high chance of success, but for which the actual outcome is unknown and may be catastrophic for the environment."

2. According to this point of view, "A politics of time is concerned with the appropriation of the time of others, the institutionalization of a dominant time, and the legitimization of power by means of the control of time. And above all, a politics of time is based on the struggle for control and forms of resistance or acquiescence" (Rutz 1992, 7). Katherine Verdery (1992, 37) defines the politics of time as a political contest between "social actors who seek to create or impose new temporal disciplines . . . and the persons subjected to these transformative projects."

3. In the interest of full disclosure, I am a founding member and active participant in the Mines and Communities network.

4. The division of labor between scholars and activists has sometimes been taken to imply that activists lack the knowledge or perspective of their academic counterparts (Appadurai 2002, 16–7), although in practice there is considerable overlap between the two groups.

5. One of the founding members of the Mines and Communities network points with frustration to its failure to prevent the inclusion of references to mining as a form of sustainable development in the resolutions of the 2002 World Summit on Sustainable Development in Johannesburg (United Nations 2002, 37, 45; see chapter 5, n. 14).

6. The website for the campaign against the Ramu mine is www.ramumine. wordpress.com. The online campaign against deep-sea mining is located at www.deepseaminingoutofourdepth.org. The Greenpeace report is available at www.greenpeace.org/international/en/publications/Campaign-reports/Oceans-Reports/deep-seabed-mining. The Woods Hole Oceanographic Institution and the National Geographic Society have also recently addressed these issues. The artists' collective can be found online at http://akrockefeller.com.

7. The findings of the multi-stakeholder World Commission on Dams were considered too critical by the World Bank, and consequently, the choice of a single eminent person for the Extractive Industries Review was intended to produce a more moderate result.

8. The lower standard of *consultation* has also been deployed by states as a means of blocking demands for free, prior, and informed consent (see Reuters 2011)

9. U.N. interest in transnational corporations dates back to the 1970s, sparked by the links between ITT (International Telegraph and Telephone Corporation) and the CIA-backed coup in Chile that led to the death of leftist president Salvador Allende. The United Nations Centre for Transnational Corporations was established in 1974 and operated until 1993.

10. Even when an NGO was supposed to take them to visit a poorly rehabilitated bauxite mine in East Suriname, they were brought to the plant nursery for the project instead of the former mine, which was further away.

11. The other members of the team were an environmental lawyer, a hydrologist, a pair of ecologists, a specialist on indigenous rights and development, and an expert on social and environmental impact assessment (Goodland 2009).

12. For a similar independent review of the environmental and social impact assessment of the proposed Rio Blanco mine in Piura, Peru, see Bebbington et al. (2007).

13. However, Dipesh Chakrabarty (2000, 44–45) argues against the identification of the modern state with freedom, as the state achieves its goals through projects of reform, progress, and development that may be coercive or violent.

14. A shortcoming of many NGOs working on these issues is that they are unable to offer communities alternative forms of development at a more appropriate scale, which may lead the communities to conclude that the mining industry is their only partner for development.

15. Oxfam provided financial support for an independent review of the project's environmental impact assessment and the referendum (McGee 2009, 606).

16. There is evidence that this is becoming an international practice, including recent examples from the United States. For instance, in 2008, a statewide referendum was held in Alaska to determine whether the controversial Pebble copper and gold mine, which threatens the Bristol Bay salmon fishery, should go forward (New York Times 2008). The proposal lacked sufficient electoral

support to block the mine, although the project remains controversial. After the U.S. Environmental Protection Agency released a negative review, Anglo American withdrew from the project in September 2013, walking away from its $541 million investment (Eilperin 2013). Rio Tinto followed suit in April 2014, donating its shares in the mine to two Alaskan foundations and leaving the project without financial backing or experienced partners.

17. By requiring a positive demonstration that an action is safe, the precautionary principle reverses the ordinary practice of permitting an action unless and until it is shown to be harmful, and consequently is an example of the politics of time. In contrast, the practice of "disaster capitalism" (Klein 2008), which treats catastrophe as an opportunity to pursue transformative political and economic projects, is the opposite of the politics of time as used here.

18. A similar point was made in an anonymous comment posted online in reference to a symposium about the proposed Pebble gold mine in Alaska that included several industry representatives (Keystone Center 2010). The comment noted how, in response to multiple questions from the audience, none of the speakers were able to identify a single mining project they were willing to endorse.

References

Abu-Lughod, Lila. 1990. "The Romance of Resistance: Tracing Transformations of Power through Bedouin Women." *American Ethnologist* 17 (1): 41–55.

Adam, Barbara. 1998. *Timescapes of Modernity: The Environment and Invisible Hazards.* New York: Routledge.

Adam, W. M. 2001. *Green Development: Environment and Sustainability in the Third World.* New York: Routledge.

Africa Fighting Malaria. 2008. Homepage. www.fightingmalaria.org.

Aguilar, Ephraim. 2007. "Fish Kill Hits 5 Villages in Rapu-Rapu—Environmental Group." *Inquirer* (Philippines). October 29. www.inquirer.net/specialreports /theenvironmentreport/view.php?db=1&article=20071029-97433.

Akpan, George A. 2002. "Litigating Problems That Arise from Natural Resources Exploitation in Foreign Courts: Impediments to Justice." *Journal of Energy and Natural Resources Law* 20: 55–78.

Allen, N. T., and T. P. Mugavin. 1991. "Starnberg Commentary." Second Confidential Draft. Melbourne: BHP Minerals Asia Pacific Division in Consultation with Ok Tedi Mining.

American Enterprise Institute. 2003. "Nongovernmental Organizations: The Growing Power of an Unelected Few." www.aei.org/article/foreign-and-defense-policy/international-organizations/ngos--the-growing-power-of-an-unelected-few.

Amnesty International. 2010. "Undermining Right: Forced Evictions and Police Brutality around the Porgera Gold Mine, Papua New Guinea." London: Amnesty International.

Anaya, S. James. 2004. *Indigenous Peoples in International Law.* Second Edition. Oxford: Oxford University Press.

Angell, Marcia. 2005. *The Truth about the Drug Companies: How They Deceive Us and What to Do about It.* New York: Random House.

Anglo American. 2009. Homepage. www.angloamerican.com.

Appadurai, Arjun. 2000. "Grassroots Globalization and the Research Imagination." *Public Culture* 12 (1): 1–19.

———. 2002. "Deep Democracy: Urban Governmentality and the Horizon of Politics." *Public Culture* 14 (1): 21–47.

Applied Geology Associates Pty. 1989. "Environmental, Socio-Economic, Public Health Review of Bougainville Copper Mine, Panguna." Review Completed for the National Executive Council of Papua New Guinea. Wellington: AGA.

Apte, Simon C. 2009. "Biogeochemistry of Copper in the Fly River." In Bolton 2009, 321–73.

Arellano-Yanguas, Javier. 2012. "Mining and Conflict in Peru: Sowing the Minerals, Reaping a Hail of Stones." In Bebbington 2012a, 89–111.

Auty, Richard M. 1993. *Sustaining Development in Mineral Economies: The Resource Curse Thesis.* London: Routledge.

Ayres, Mary C. 1983. "This Side, That Side: Locality and Exogamous Group Definition in the Morehead Area, Southwestern Papua." PhD diss., University of Chicago.

Bainton, Nicholas A. 2009. "Keeping the Network Out of View: Mining, Distinctions and Exclusion in Melanesia." *Oceania* 79 (1): 18–33.

Baker, Russell. 1996. "Clean Up or Shut Up." *Bulletin* (Sydney), June 11, 50.

Ballard, Chris, and Glenn Banks. 2003. "Resource Wars: The Anthropology of Mining." *Annual Review of Anthropology* 32: 287–313.

Banks, Glenn. 1998. "Compensation for Communities Affected by Mining and Oil Developments in Melanesia." *Malaysian Journal of Tropical Geography* 29 (1): 53–67.

———. 2002. "Mining and the Environment in Melanesia: Contemporary Debates Reviewed." *The Contemporary Pacific* 14 (1): 39–67.

Banks, Glenn, and Chris Ballard, eds. 1997a. *The Ok Tedi Settlement: Issues, Outcomes and Implications.* Pacific Policy Paper 27. Canberra: National Centre for Development Studies and Resource Management in Asia-Pacific, The Australian National University.

———. 1997b. "Introduction: Settling Ok Tedi." In Banks and Ballard 1997a, 1–11.

Barker, Geoffrey, and Stewart Oldfield. 1999. "BHP Admits Mine Is a Mess, but Downer Says Dig In." *Australian Financial Review,* August 12, 1.

Barsh, Russell Lawrence. 1994. "Indigenous Peoples in the 1990s: From Object to Subject of International Law." *Harvard Human Rights Journal* 7: 33–86.

Barth, Fredrik. 1983. "Cultural Impact Study of the Ok Tedi Project." *Bikmaus* 4 (1): 56–65.

Basu, Niladri, and Howard Hu. 2010. "Toxic Metals and Indigenous Peoples Near the Marlin Mine in Western Guatemala: Potential Exposures and Impacts on Health." Cambridge, MA: Physicians for Human Rights. https://s3.amazonaws.com/PHR_Reports/guatemala-toxic-metals.pdf

Bate, Roger, and Richard Tren. 2003. "Do NGOs Improve Wealth and Health in Africa?" Washington, DC: American Enterprise Institute. www.aei.org/files/2003/06/11/20040402_20030611_Bate.pdf.

Batha, Emma. 2000. "Death of a River." *BBC,* February 15. http://news.bbc.co.uk/2/hi/europe/642880.stm.

Baviskar, Amita. 2004. *In the Belly of the River: Tribal Conflicts over Development in the Narmada Valley.* Second Edition. New Delhi: Oxford University Press.

BBOP (Business and Biodiversity Offsets Programme). 2009. "Compensatory Conservation Case Studies." Washington, DC: BBOP. http://content.undp. org/go/cms-service/stream/asset/?asset_id=2469112.

Beamish, Thomas D. 2002. *Silent Spill: The Organization of an Industrial Crisis.* Cambridge, MA: MIT Press.

Bebbington, Anthony. 2009. "The New Extraction: Rewriting the Political Ecology of the Andes." *NACLA Report on the Americas* 42 (5): 12–20.

———, ed. 2012a. *Social Conflict, Economic Development and the Extractive Industry: Evidence from South America.* New York: Routledge.

———. 2012b. "Social Conflict and Emergent Institutions: Hypotheses from Piura, Peru." In Bebbington 2012a, 67–88.

Bebbington, Anthony, and Jeffrey Bury. 2009. "Institutional Challenges for Mining and Sustainability in Peru." *Proceedings of the National Academy of Sciences* 106 (41): 17, 296–301.

Bebbington, Anthony, Michael Connarty, Wendy Coxshall, Hugh O'Shaughnessy, and Mark Williams. 2007. "Mining and Development in Peru: With Special Reference to the Rio Blanco Project, Piura." London: Peru Support Group. www.perusupportgroup.org.uk.

Beck, Ulrich. 1992. *Risk Society: Towards a New Modernity.* Translated by Mark Ritter. London: Sage.

Benson, Peter. 2011. *Tobacco Capitalism: Growers, Migrant Workers, and the Changing Face of a Global Industry.* Princeton: Princeton University Press.

Benson, Peter, and Stuart Kirsch. 2010a. "Capitalism and the Politics of Resignation." *Current Anthropology* 51 (4): 459–86.

———. 2010b. "Corporate Oxymorons." *Dialectical Anthropology* 34 (1): 45–48.

BHP (Broken Hill Proprietary Ltd). 1995a. "Ok Tedi. Are You Getting the Full Picture?" Melbourne: BHP.

———. 1995b. "BHP and Ok Tedi: The Facts." Melbourne: BHP.

———. 1995c. Advertisements in *Australian Financial Review,* September 26 and October 9.

BHP Billiton. 2009. "Our Approach to Sustainability." www.bhpbilliton.com/ bb/sustainableDevelopment/ourApproachToSustainability.jsp. Accessed September 15, 2006.

———. 2010. "Our Sustainability Framework." September. www.bhpbilliton. com/home/aboutus/Documents/ourSustainabilityFramework2010.pdf.

Biersack, Aletta. 2006. "Red River, Green River: The Politics of Place along the Porgera River." In *Reimaging Political Ecology,* edited by Aletta Biersack, 233–80. Durham, NC: Duke University Press.

Blumenstyk, Goldie. 2007. "Mining Company Involved in Environmental Disaster Now Advises Sustainability Institute at U. of Michigan." *Chronicle of Higher Education* 54 (15): A22.

Bolton, Barrie R., ed. 2009. *The Fly River, Papua New Guinea: Environmental Studies in an Impacted Tropical River System.* Developments in Earth & Environmental Sciences 9. Amsterdam: Elsevier.

Bourdieu, Pierre. 1977. *Outline of a Theory of Practice*. Cambridge: Cambridge University Press.

Boyd, Stephanie. 2002. "Tambogrande Referendum Has Domino Effect in Peru." Americas Program, International Relations Center (IRC). July 16. http://www.cipamericas.org/archives/1162.

Brandt, Allan M. 2007. *The Cigarette Century: The Rise, Fall, and Deadly Persistence of the Product that Defined America*. New York: Basic Books.

Bray, John, ed. 1997. *No Hiding Place*. London: Control Risks Group.

Bridge, Maurice, and Angus Wong. 2011. "Consenting Adults: Changes to the Principle of Free, Prior and Informed Consent Are Changing the Way in which Firms Engage Communities." *Mining, People and the Environment* (July): 12–15.

Broderick, Judge Vincent L. 1994. Memorandum. Maria Aguinda et al., Individually and on Behalf of All Others Similarly Situated, Plaintiffs, against Texaco, Inc., Defendant. United States District Court, Southern District of New York. 93 Civ 7527. April 11. White Plains.

Brodeur, Paul. 1985. *Outrageous Misconduct: The Asbestos Industry on Trial*. New York: Pantheon.

Brosius, J. Peter. 1999. "Green Dots, Pink Hearts: Displacing Politics from the Malaysian Rain Forest." *American Anthropologist* 101 (1): 36–57.

Brown, Michael. 1993. "Facing the State, Facing the World: Amazonia's Native Leaders and the New Politics of Identity." *L'Homme* 33 (2–4): 307–26.

Brundtland, Gro Harlem, ed. 1987. "Our Common Future." The World Commission on Environment and Development. http://conspect.nl/pdf/Our_Common_Future-Brundtland_Report_1987.pdf.

Brunton, Brian. 1997. "The Perspective of a Papua New Guinea NGO." In Banks and Ballard 1997a, 167–82.

Bryce, Robert. 1995a. "Written in Stone: UT's Jim Bob Moffett and Freeport-McMoRan Ride a New Wave of Allegations." *Austin Chronicle*, September 23. www.austinchronicle.com/news/2005-09-23/292538.

———. 1995b. "U.S. Cancels Indonesian Mine's Insurance." *New York Times*, November 2. www.nytimes.com/1995/11/02/business/international-business-us-cancels-indonesian-mine-s-insurance.html.

———. 1996. "Spinning Gold." *Mother Jones* (September/October): 66–69.

———. 2003. "Freeport's Mercenary Murderers?" *Austin Chronicle*, March 28. www.austinchronicle.com/news/2003-03-28/151851.

Burton, John. 1997. "Terra Nugax and the Discovery Paradigm: How Ok Tedi Was Shaped by the Way It Was Found and How the Rise of Political Process in the North Fly Took the Company by Surprise." In Banks and Ballard 1997a, 27–55.

———. 1998. "Mining and Maladministration in Papua New Guinea." In *Governance and Reform in the South Pacific*, edited by Peter Larmour, 154–182. Pacific Policy Paper 23. Canberra: National Centre for Development Studies, Australian National University.

———. 2000. "Knowing about Culture: The Handling of Social Issues at Resource Projects in Papua New Guinea." In *Culture and Sustainable Development in the Pacific*, edited by Anthony Hooper, 98–110. Canberra: Asia Pacific Press.

Busse, Mark. 1991. "Environment and Human Ecology in the Lake Murray-Middle Fly Area." In Lawrence and Cansfield-Smith 1991, 441–49.

Buttel, Frederick H. 2000. "Ecological Modernization as Social Theory." *Geoforum* 31 (1): 57–65.

Byrne, Justice David. 1995. Judgment. Rex Dagi and Others, Plaintiffs, and The Broken Hill Proprietary Company Limited and Ok Tedi Mining Limited, Defendants. Supreme Court of Victoria. No. 5782 of 1994. November 10. Melbourne.

Calhoun, Craig. 1993. "'New Social Movements' of the Early Nineteenth Century." *Social Science History* 17 (3): 385–427.

Callick, Rowan. 1994. "Australia: BHP Hit by $4bn Claim—PNG Villagers Allege Pollution." *Australian Financial Review*, May 4.

———. 1996. "Ok Tedi Win for Villagers and a Lesson for all Miners." *Australian Financial Review*, June 12.

Cannon, Michael. 1998. *That Disreputable Firm . . . the Inside Story of Slater & Gordon*. Melbourne: University of Melbourne Press.

Carlat, Daniel. 2007. "Dr. Drug Rep: Physicians and the Pharmaceutical Industry." *New York Times Magazine*, November 25.

Caruso, Emily, Marcus Colchester, Fergus MacKay, Nick Hildyard, and Geoff Nettleton. 2003. "Synthesis Report: Indigenous Peoples, Extractive Industries and the World Bank." In Colchester et al. 2003, 17–172.

Cavadini, Fabio, dir. 2010. *Color Change*. Frontyard Films, DVD.

Chadwick, John. 2002. "Non-Governmental Organizations (NGOs)." *Mining Environmental Management* (September): 20–23.

Chakrabarty, Dipesh. 2000. *Provincializing Europe*. Princeton: Princeton University Press.

Chapin, Mac. 2004. "A Challenge to Conservationists." *World Watch*, November/December: 17–31.

Chapman, Peter, Margaret Burchett, Peter Campbell, William Dietrich, and Barry Hart. 2000. "Ok Tedi Mining Ltd. Environment Peer Review Group: Comments on Key Issues and Review Comments on the Final Human and Ecological Risk Assessment Documents." Tabubil, PNG: Ok Tedi Mining Ltd.

Chauvel, Richard. 2005. *Constructing Papuan Nationalism: History, Ethnicity, and Adaption*. Policy Studies 14. Washington, DC: East-West Center.

Clifford, James, and George Marcus, eds. 1986. *Writing Culture: The Poetics and Politics of Ethnography*. Berkeley: University of California Press.

Colbert, Stephen. 2012. *American Again: Re-becoming the Greatest We Never Weren't*. New York: Grand Central.

Colchester, Marcus, Ann Loreto Tamayo, Raymundo Rovillos, and Emily Caruso, eds. 2003. *Extracting Promises: Indigenous Peoples, Extractive Industries and the World Bank*. Baguio City, Philippines: Tebtebba Foundation.

Comaroff, John L., and Jean Comaroff. 2006. "Law and Disorder in the Postcolony: An Introduction." In *Law and Disorder in the Postcolony*, edited by Jean Comaroff and John L. Comaroff, 1–56. Chicago: University of Chicago Press.

———. 2009. *Ethnicity, Inc.* Chicago: University of Chicago Press.

Conklin, Beth. 1997. "Body Paint, Feathers, and VCRs: Aesthetics in Authenticity in Amazonian Activism." *American Ethnologist* 24 (4): 711–737.

Conklin, Beth, and Laura Graham. 1995. "The Shifting Middle Ground: Amazonian Indians and Ecopolitics." *American Anthropologist* 97 (4): 1–17.

Connell, John. 1991. "Compensation and Conflict: The Bougainville Copper Mine, Papua New Guinea." In *Mining and Indigenous Peoples in Australasia,* edited by John Connell and Richard Howitt, 55–76. Sydney: Sydney University Press.

———. 1997. *Papua New Guinea: The Struggle for Development.* New York: Routledge.

Connolly, Bob, and Robin Anderson. 1988. *First Contact: New Guinea's Highlanders Encounter the Outside World.* New York: Penguin Books.

Cook, Susan E. 2011. "The Business of Being Bafokeng: The Corporatization of a Tribal Authority in South Africa." *Current Anthropology* 52 (3): S151–S159.

Cooley, Alexander, and James Ron. 2002. "NGO Scramble: Organizational Insecurity and the Political Economy of Transnational Action." *International Security* 27 (1): 5–39.

Coumans, Catherine. 1995. "Ideology, Social Movement Organization, Patronage and Resistance in the Struggle of Marinduqueños against Marcopper." *Pilipinas* 24 (1): 37–74.

———. 2011. "Occupying Spaces Created by Conflict. Anthropologists, Development NGOs, Responsible. Investment, and Mining." *Current Anthropology* 52 (S3): S29–S43.

Cronon, William. 1996. "The Trouble with Wilderness; or, Getting Back to the Wrong Nature." In *Uncommon Ground: Rethinking the Human Place in Nature,* edited by William Cronon, 69–90. New York: W.W. Norton.

Crook, Tony. 2004. "Transactions in Perpetual Motion." In *Transactions and Creations: Property Debates and the Stimulus of Melanesia,* edited by Eric Hirsch and Marilyn Strathern, 110–31. Oxford: Berghahn.

———. 2007. *Anthropological Knowledge, Secrecy and Bolivip, Papua New Guinea: Exchanging Skin.* Oxford: Oxford University Press.

Csagoly, Paul, ed. 2000. "The Cyanide Spill at Baia Mare, Romania: Before, During and After." Baire Mare Task Force Szentendre, Hungary. The Regional Environmental Center for Central and Eastern Europe (REC). www.rec.org/REC/Publications/CyanideSpill/ENGCyanide.pdf.

CSIRO (Commonwealth Scientific and Industrial Research Organization) Australia. 1996. "Review of Riverine Impacts, Porgera Joint Venture." Dickson, Australia: CSIRO Environmental Projects Office.

Dagi, Rex. n.d. Witness proof. Undated document in the possession of the author.

Dakop, David, Karup Dumun, and Jacob Aron. 2004. Notice from Komokpin, Papua New Guinea, to the Prothonotary of the Supreme Court of Victoria. Case No. 5003 of 2000. January 7. Melbourne.

Daly, Herman E. 1996. *Beyond Growth: The Economics of Sustainable Development.* Boston: Beacon Press.

Danielson, Luke, ed. 2002. *Breaking New Ground: Mining, Minerals and Sustainable Development.* International Institute for Environment and Development. London: Earthscan. www.iied.org/mmsd/finalreport/index.html.

———. 2006. *Architecture for Change: An Account of the Mining Minerals and Sustainable Development Project.* Berlin: Global Public Policy Institute. http://pubs.iied.org/pdfs/G00976.pdf.

Das, Samarendra, and Felix Padel. 2010. *Out of This Earth: East India Adivasis and the Aluminum Cartel.* New Delhi: Orient BlackSwan.

Das, Veena. 1989. "Subaltern as Perspective." In *Subaltern Studies: Writings on South Asian History and Society,* vol. 6, edited by Ranajit Guha, 310–24. New Delhi: Oxford University Press.

Davis, Devra. 2002. *When Smoke Ran Like Water: Tales of Environmental Deception and the Battle against Pollution.* New York: Basic Books.

Davis, John P. 1961. *Corporations: A Study of the Origin and Development of Great Business Combinations and of Their Relation to the Authority of the State.* New York: Capricorn Books.

Deegan, Denise. 2001. *Managing Activism: A Guide to Dealing with Activists and Pressure Groups.* Institute of Public Relations, PR in Practice Series. London: Kogan Page.

de la Cadena, Marisol, and Orin Starn. 2007. Introduction to *Indigenous Experience Today,* edited by Marisol de la Cadena and Orin Starn, 1–30. Oxford: Berg.

Depew, Robert C. 1987. "The Aekyom: Kinship, Marriage and Descent on the Upper Fly River." PhD diss., University of Edinburgh.

Diamond, Jared. 2005. *Collapse: How Societies Choose to Fail or Succeed.* New York: Penguin Books.

Divecha, Simon. 2001. "Private Power." ZNET. December 18. www.znet.org.

Dove, Michael. 1993. "A Revisionist View of Tropical Deforestation and Development." *Environmental Conservation* 20 (1): 17–56.

———. 1996. "Center, Periphery, and Biodiversity: A Paradox of Governance and a Development Challenge." In *Valuing Local Knowledge: Indigenous People and Intellectual Property Rights,* edited by Stephen B. Brush and Dorren Stabinsky, 41–67. Washington, DC: Island Press.

Downing, Ted. 2001. "Why Comment on the World Bank's Proposed Indigenous Peoples Policy?" *Anthropology News* 42 (9): 23–24.

Doyle, Cathal, and Jill Cariño. 2013. "Making Free, Prior & Informed Consent a Reality: Indigenous Peoples and the Extractive Sector." www.piplinks.org/system/files/Consortium+FPIC+report+-+May+2103+-+web+version.pdf.

Dryblower [pseud.]. 2004. "Sustainable Mining? Who Are We Trying to Fool?" *Mining News,* January 20. www.miningnews.net/StoryView.asp?StoryID=21678.

Dumit, Joseph. 2005. "The Depsychiatrisation of Mental Illness." *Journal of Public Mental Health* 4 (3): 8–13.

Duval, Judge Stanwood R. 1997. Minute Entry. Tom Beanal, On Behalf of Himself and All Others Similarly Situated, Versus Freeport-McMoRan, Inc., and Freeport-McMoRan Copper and Gold, Inc. United States District Court, Eastern District of Louisiana. Civil Action No. 96–1474. April 9. New Orleans.

Eagle, E. M. 1994. "Copper Mining and the Environment in Papua New Guinea—The Ok Tedi Case Study." In Schoell 1994a, 59–80.

Eckert, Julia. 2012. "Rumours of Rights." In Eckert et al. 2012b, 147–70.

Eckert, Julia, Brian Donahoe, Zerrin Özlem Biner, and Christian Strümpell. 2012a. "Introduction: Law's Travels and Transformations." In Eckert et al. 2012b, 1–22.

———, eds. 2012b. *Law Against the State: Ethnographic Forays into Law's Transformations*. Cambridge: Cambridge University Press.

Economist. 1999. "Mea Copper, Mea Culpa. Australia's Broken Hill Proprietary May Pull Out of New Guinea." August 21, 58.

Edelman, Marc. 2001. "Social Movements: Changing Paradigms and Forms of Politics." *Annual Review of Anthropology* 30: 285–317.

Eilperin, Juliet. 2013. "Major Backer of Pebble Mine Project Pulls Financial Support." *Washington Post*. September 16. www.washingtonpost.com/blogs/post-politics/wp/2013/09/16/major-backer-of-pebble-mine-project-pulls-financial-support.

Emel, Jody. 2002. "An Inquiry into the Green Disciplining of Capital." *Environment and Planning* A 34 (5): 827–43.

Entine, Jon. 2003. "Capitalism's Trojan Horse: Social Investment and Anti-Free Market NGOs." www.aei.org/files/2003/06/11/200404022_200306 11_entine.pdf.

Escobar, Arturo. 2001a. "Culture Sits in Places: Reflections on Globalism and Subaltern Strategies of Localization." *Political Geography* 20 (2): 139–74.

———. 2001b. Comment on Stuart Kirsch, "Lost Worlds: Environmental Disaster, 'Culture Loss,' and the Law." *Current Anthropology* 42 (2): 183–84.

———. 2008. *Territories of Difference: Place, Movements, Life, Redes*. Durham, NC: Duke University Press.

Evans, D. 2010. "Tensions at the Gold Ridge Mine, Guadalcanal, Solomon Islands." *Pacific Economic Bulletin* 25 (3): 121–34.

Evans, Geoff. 2002. "Dealing with the Hardest Issues." *Mining Monitor* 7 (1): 11.

Ferguson, James. 1999. *Expectations of Modernity: Myths and Meanings of Urban Life on the Zambian Copperbelt*. Berkeley: University of California Press.

———. 2006. *Global Shadows: African the Neoliberal World Order*. Durham, NC: Duke University Press.

Filer, Colin. 1990. "The Bougainville Rebellion, the Mining Industry and the Process of Social Disintegration in Papua New Guinea." In *The Bougainville Crisis*, edited by R. J. May and M. Spriggs, 73–112. Bathurst: Crawford House Press.

———. 1997a. "Resource Rents: Distribution and Sustainability." In *Papua New Guinea: A 20/20 Vision*, edited by Ila Temu, 222–60. Boroko, Papua New Guinea, and Canberra: PNG National Research Institute and the National Centre for Development Studies, Australian National University.

———. 1997b. "West Side Story: The State's and Other Stakes in the Ok Tedi Mine." In Banks and Ballard 1997a, 56–93.

———. 1997c. "The Melanesian Way of Menacing the Mining Industry." In *Environment and Development in the Pacific Islands*, edited by Ben Burt and Christian Clerk, 91–122. Pacific Policy Paper 25. Canberra and Port

Moresby: Australian National University and University of Papua New Guinea Press.

———. 1999a. Introduction to *Dilemmas of Development: The Social and Economic Impact of the Porgera Gold Mine, 1989–1994*, edited by Colin Filer, 1–18. Pacific Policy Paper 34. Canberra: Asia Pacific Press.

———. 1999b. "The Dialectics of Negation and Negotiation in the Anthropology of Mineral Resource Development in Papua New Guinea." In *The Anthropology of Power: Empowerment and Disempowerment in Changing Structures,* edited by Angela Cheater, 88–102. ASA Monographs 36. New York: Routledge.

Filer, Colin, Glenn Banks, and John Burton. 2008. "The Fragmentation of Responsibilities in the Melanesian Mining Sector." In *Earth Matters: Indigenous Peoples, Extractive Industries and Corporate Social Responsibility,* edited by Ciaran O'Faircheallaigh and Saleem Ali, 163–79. Sheffield, UK: Greenleaf.

Filer, Colin, and Martha Macintyre. 2006. "Grass Roots and Deep Holes: Community Responses to Mining in Melanesia." *The Contemporary Pacific* 18 (2): 215–31.

Finau, Bishop Patelisio. 1994. "Becoming Involved—for the Sake of the People." In Schoell 1994a, 109–13.

Finn, Janet. 1998. *Tracing the Veins: Of Copper, Culture, and Community from Butte to Chuquicamata.* Berkeley: University of California Press.

Fisher, William F. 1997. "Doing Good? The Politics and Antipolitics of NGO Practices." *Annual Review of Anthropology* 26: 439–64.

Fishman, Chuck, Noel Brown, and Tom Cooke. 1983. *Ok Tedi 24:00.* Tabubil, PNG: Ok Tedi Mining Ltd.

Fortun, Kim. 2001. *Advocacy after Bhopal: Environmentalism, Disaster, New Global Orders.* Chicago: University of Chicago Press.

Fortun, Kim, and Mike Fortun. 2005. "Scientific Imaginaries and Ethical Plateaus in Contemporary U.S. Toxicology." *American Anthropologist* 107 (1): 43–54.

Foster, Robert J. 2008. *Coca-Globalization: Following Soft Drinks from New York to New Guinea.* New York: MacMillan.

Fox, Julia D. 1997. "Leasing the Ivory Tower at a Social Justice University." *Organization & Environment* 10 (3): 259–77.

Frynas, Jedrzej George. 1998. "Political Instability and Business: Focus on Shell in Nigeria." *Third World Quarterly* 19 (3): 457–78.

Fultz, Katherine. 2011. "Local Referendums on Mining Projects in Latin America." Unpublished report in the possession of the author.

Gabriel Resources, 2008. Homepage. www.gabrielresources.com/home.htm.

Gao, Zhiguo, George Akpan, and Jim Vanjik. 2002. "Public Participation in Mining and Petroleum in Asia and the Pacific: The Ok Tedi Case and Its Implications." In *Human Rights in National Resource Development: Public Participation in the Sustainable Development of Mining and Energy Resources,* edited by Donald N. Zillman, Alastair R. Lucas, and George (Rock) Pring, 679–94. Oxford: Oxford University Press.

Garnaut, John. 2004. "PNG Has New Best Friends." *Sydney Morning Herald.* February 9.

Gedicks, Al. 1993. *The New Resource Waters: Native and Environmental Struggles against Multinational Corporations.* Boston, MA: South End Press.

———. 2001. *Resource Rebels: Native Challenges to Mining and Oil Corporations.* Cambridge, MA: South End Press.

Gedicks, Al, and Zoltán Grossman. 2005. "Defending a Common Home: Native/Non-Native Alliances against Mining Corporations in Wisconsin." In *In the Way of Development: Indigenous Peoples, Life Projects and Globalization,* edited by Mario Blaser, Harvey A. Feit, and Glenn McRae, 187–203. London: Zed.

Gerritsen, Rolf, and Martha Macintyre. 1991. "Dilemmas of Distribution: The Misima Gold Mine, Papua New Guinea." In *Mining and Indigenous Peoples in Australasia,* edited by John Connell and Richard Howitt, 35–54. Sydney: Sydney University Press.

Gewertz, Deborah B., and Frederick K. Errington. 1991. *Twisted Histories, Altered Contexts: Representing the Chambri in the World System.* New York: Cambridge University Press.

Gilbertson, Brian. 2002. Speech to the World Business Council for Sustainable Development / International Institute for Economy Development, Mining, Minerals & Sustainable Development Meeting. World Summit on Sustainable Development, Johannesburg. August 30. www.bhpbilliton.com/home/investors/reports/Documents/worldsummit.pdf.

Gladman, Darren, David Mowbray, and John Duguman, eds. 1996. *From Rio to Rai: Environment and Development in Papua New Guinea up to 2000 and Beyond.* Papers from the Twentieth Waigani Seminar, 1993. Vols. 1–6. Port Moresby: University of Papua New Guinea Press.

Gladwell, Malcolm. 2010. "Small Change: Why the Revolution Will Not Be Tweeted." *New Yorker,* October 4. www.newyorker.com/reporting/2010/10/04/101004fa_fact_gladwell.

Global Witness. 2005. *Paying for Protection: The Freeport Mine and the Indonesian Security Forces.* Washington, DC: Global Witness. www.globalwitness.org.

Goode, John. 1977. *Rape of the Fly: Exploration in New Guinea.* Melbourne: Nelson.

Goodland, Robert. 2000. "Social and Environmental Assessment to Promote Sustainability: An Informal View from the World Bank." Environment Department Papers 74. Environmental Management Series. Washington, DC: World Bank. www-wds.worldbank.org/external/default/WDSContentServer/WDSP/IB/2000/10/21/000094946_00101305481390/Rendered/PDF/multi_page.pdf

———, ed. 2009. "Suriname's Bakhuis Bauxite Mine: An Independent Review of SRK's Impact Assessment." Paramaribo, Suriname: Bureau VIDS.

Goldman, Michael. 2005. *Imperial Nature: The World Bank and Struggles for Social Justice in the Age of Globalization.* New Haven, CT: Yale University Press.

Gordon, John. 1997. "The Ok Tedi Lawsuit in Retrospect." In Banks and Ballard 1997a, 141–66.

Graeber, David. 2013. *The Democracy Project: A History, A Crisis, A Movement.* New York: Spiegel & Grau.

Graham, Laura. 2002. "How Should an Indian Speak? Amazonian Indians and the Symbolic Politics of Language in the Global Public Sphere." In *Indigenous Movements, Self-representation and the State in Latin America,* edited by Kay B. Warren and Jean E. Jackson, 181–228. Austin: University of Texas Press.

Grech, Andrew. 2004. Affidavit. Gabia Gagarimabu, For Himself and As Representing Certain Parties to the Agreement Made with BHP and OMTL on the 7th Day of June, 1996, and BHP Billiton Limited and Ok Tedi Mining Limited. Supreme Court of Victoria No. 5003 of 2000. January 15. Melbourne.

Greenberg, Daniel S. 2007. *Science for Sale: The Perils, Rewards, and Delusions of Campus Capitalism.* Chicago: University of Chicago Press.

Griffin, James. 1990. "Logic is a Whiteman's Trick." In *Australian-Papua New Guinea Relations: Problems and Prospects,* edited by D. Anderson, 70–80. Sydney: Pacific Security Research Bureau.

Grimaldi, James V. 2007. "Smithsonian Project Loses Oil Sponsor." *Washington Post,* November 17. www.washingtonpost.com/wp-dyn/content/article/2007/11/16/AR2007111601495.html.

Grossman, Zoltán. 2005. "Unlikely Alliances: Treaty Conflicts and Environmental Cooperation between Native American and Rural White Communities." *American Indian Culture and Research Journal* 29 (4): 21–43.

Halvaksz, Jamon Alex II. 2010. Review of *Reverse Anthropology* by Stuart Kirsch and *Conservation Is Our Government Now* by Paige West. Book Review Forum. *Pacific Studies* 33 (1): 59–67.

Hance, B.J., Caron Chess, and Peter M. Sandman. 1990. *Industry Risk Communication Manual: Improving Dialogue with Communities.* Boca Raton, FL: Lewis Publishers.

Hardt, Michael, and Antonio Negri. 2000. *Empire.* Cambridge, MA: Harvard University Press.

Harris, Chris. 1997. "An Australian NGO Perspective: On the Implications of Ok Tedi." In Banks and Ballard 1997a, 189–95.

Harvey, David. 2000. *Spaces of Hope.* Berkeley: University of California Press.

———. 2003. *The New Imperialism.* Oxford: Oxford University Press.

———. 2005. *A Brief History of Neoliberalism.* Oxford: Oxford University Press.

Healy, David. 2006. "The New Medical Oikumene." In Petryna, Lakoff, and Kleinman 2006, 61–84.

Hecht, Gabrielle. 1998. *The Radiance of France: Nuclear Power and National Identity after World War II.* Cambridge, MA: MIT Press.

———. 2012. *Being Nuclear: Africans and the Global Uranium Trade.* Cambridge, MA: MIT Press.

Helfgott, Federico. 2013. "Transformations in Labor, Land and Community: Mining and Society in Pasco, Peru, 20th Century to the Present." PhD diss., University of Michigan.

Heller, Michael. 1998. "The Tragedy of the Anticommons: Property in the Transition from Marx to Markets." *Harvard Law Review* 111 (3): 621–88.

Heritage Foundation. 2007. Presentation of the film *Mine Your Own Business,* May 30. Digital sound recording, www.heritage.org/Press/Events/evo53007a.cfm.

Hettler, Jörg, and Bernd Lehmann. 1995. "Environmental Impact of Large Scale Mining in Papua New Guinea: Mining Residue Disposal by the Ok Tedi Copper-Gold Mine." Final Report on a Study Funded by the United Nations Environment Programme (UNEP/SPREP). Berlin: Berlin Fachbereich Geowiss.

Hextall, Bruce. 1996. "Removing the Fly in BHP'S Ointment." *Sydney Morning Herald*. June 12.

Higgins, Roger J. 2002. "Ok Tedi: Creating Community Partnerships for Sustainable Development." Paper presented at the annual general meeting of the Canadian Institute of Mining, Metallurgy, and Petroleum, Vancouver.

Hill, Liezel. 2010. "Inmet Will Sell Ok Tedi Royalty for $335 Million." *Mining Weekly*, December 2. www.miningweekly.com/article/inmet-will-sell-ok-tedi-royalty-for-335m-2010-12-02.

Hirt, Paul W. 1994. *A Conspiracy of Optimism: Management of the National Forests since World War Two*. Lincoln: University of Nebraska Press.

Ho, Karen. 2009. *Liquidated: An Ethnography of Wall Street*. Durham, NC: Duke University Press.

Hoffman, Andrew J. 1997. *From Heresy to Dogma: An Institutional History of Corporate Environmentalism*. San Francisco: The New Lexington Press.

Howard, Michael. 1993. "Competing Views of the Environment and Development in Irian Jaya." Paper presented at the annual meeting of the American Anthropological Association, Washington, DC.

Human Rights Watch. 2010. "Gold's Costly Dividend: Human Rights Impacts of Papua New Guinea's Porgera Gold Mine." New York: Human Rights Watch.

Humphreys Bebbington, Denise. 2012. "State-Indigenous Tensions over Hydrocarbon Expansion in the Bolivian Chaco." In Bebbington 2012a, 29–47.

Hyndman, David. 1988. "Ok Tedi: New Guinea's Disaster Mine." *The Ecologist* 18 (1): 24–29.

———. 1991. "Zipping Down the Fly on the Ok Tedi Project." In *Mining and Indigenous Peoples in Australasia,* edited by John Connell and Richard Howitt, 76–90. Sydney: Sydney University Press.

———. 1994. *Ancestral Rain Forests and the Mountain of Gold: Indigenous Peoples and Mining in New Guinea*. Boulder, CO: Westview.

ICMM (International Council on Mining and Metals). 2008. Homepage. www.icmm.com.

———. 2013. Homepage. www.icmm.com.

ICRAF (Individual and Community Rights Advocacy Forum). 1995. "Ten Good Reasons Why They Should Vote against the Mining Bill." Advertisement. *The National* (Papua New Guinea).

———. 2000. "Trip One to Ok Tedi as Independent Observer," March 26–31. Unpublished report in the possession of the author.

IIED (International Institute for Environment and Development). 2001. "Challenges and Opportunities Facing the Minerals Sector." February 11. Unpublished report in the possession of the author.

Inglehart, Ronald. 1977. *The Silent Revolution*. Princeton, NJ: Princeton University Press.

———. 1990. *Culture Shift in Advanced Industrial Society*. Princeton, NJ: Princeton University Press.

Innes, Larry. 2001. "Staking Claims: Innu Rights and Mining Claims at Voisey's Bay." *Cultural Survival Quarterly* 25 (1): 12–16.

IUCN (International Union for Conservation of Nature). 1980. *World Conservation Strategy: Living Resource Conservation for Sustainable Development.* Gland, Switzerland: IUCN, UNEP, and WWF.

———. 1992. "The Ok Tedi Copper Mine in Papua New Guinea: Review of the Starnberg Report." Gland, Switzerland: IUCN.

———. 1995. "The Fly River Catchment, Papua New Guinea: A Regional Environmental Assessment." Published in collaboration with the Department of Environment and Conservation, Boroko, Papua New Guinea. Cambridge: IUCN.

IWT (International Water Tribunal). 1994. *Second International Water Tribunal, 1992–1994. The Case Books.* 7 vols. Utrecht, Netherlands.

Jackson, Richard, 1979. "The Awin: Free Resettlement on the Upper Fly River (Western Province)." In *Going through Changes: Villagers, Settlers and Development in Papua New Guinea,* edited by C. A. Valentine and B. L. Valentine, 1–14. Boroko: Institute of Papua New Guinea Studies.

———. 1982. *Ok Tedi: The Pot of Gold.* Port Moresby: Word Publishing.

———. 1993. *Cracked Pot of Copper Bottomed Investment? The Development of the Ok Tedi Project 1982–1991, A Personal View.* Brisbane, Queensland: Melanesian Studies Centre, James Cook University.

———. 1998. "David and Goliath on the Fly." Review of Glenn Banks and Chris Ballard, *The Ok Tedi Settlement. Journal of Pacific History* 33 (3): 307–11.

Jackson, Richard, C. A. Emerson, and Robert L. Welsch. 1980. "The Impact of the Ok Tedi Project." A Report Prepared for the Department of Minerals and Energy. July.

Jameson, Fredric. 1994. *The Seeds of Time.* New York: Columbia University Press.

Jamieson, Lisa. 1996. "BHP Faces $500M Bill to Mine Ok Tedi." *The Daily Telegraph* (Sydney). June 12.

Joseph, Sarah. 2004. *Corporations and Transnational Human Rights Litigation.* Oxford: Hart.

Juris, Jeffrey S. 2008. *Networking Futures: The Movements against Corporate Globalization.* Durham, NC: Duke University Press.

Kahneman, Daniel. 2011. *Thinking Fast and Slow.* New York: Farrar, Straus and Giroux.

Kalinoe, Lawrence. 2003. "Independent Review Report on the Ok Tedi Community Mine Continuation Agreements and Related Matters." Prepared for Oxfam Community Aid Abroad, Australia.

Kassirer, Jerome P. 2005. *On the Take: How Medicine's Complicity with Big Business Can Endanger Your Health.* Oxford: Oxford University Press.

Katat, Paul, et al. 2004. Notice from Ulawas, Moian, Membok, Erekta, and Karemgo, Papua New Guinea, to the Prothonotary of the Supreme Court of Victoria. Case No. 5003 of 2000. January 12. Melbourne.

Kaye, Tony. 1996. "Australia: Costly Lesson on Being the Good Guy Next Door—BHP." *The Age* (Melbourne), June 12.

Keck, Margaret E., and Kathryn Sikkink. 1998. *Activists beyond Borders: Advocacy Networks in International Politics.* Ithaca: Cornell University Press.

Keeling, Arn. 2004. "The Effluent Society: Water Pollution and Environmental Politics in British Columbia, 1889–1980." PhD diss., University of British Columbia.

Keeling, Arn, and Graeme Wynn. 2011. "'The Park . . . Is a Mess': Development and Degradation in British Columbia's First Provincial Park." *BC Studies* 170: 119–50.

Keenan, Karyn, José de Echave, and Ken Traynor. 2007. "Mining Rights and Community Rights: Poverty Amidst Wealth." In *Reclaiming Nature: Environmental Justice and Ecological Restoration,* edited by Sunita Narain, James K. Boyce, and Elizabeth A. Stanton, 181–201. London: Anthem Press.

Keystone Center. 2010. "Responsible Large-Scale Mining: Global Perspectives. Panel of Independent Experts on the Potential Development of Pebble Mine." Sponsored by the Keystone Center, Colorado. December 3. Video and comments. https://www.keystone.org/9-uncategorised/302-pebble-webcast.html

Kirsch, Stuart. 1989a. "Ok Tedi River a Sewer." *The Times of Papua New Guinea,* June 1–7.

———. 1989b. "The Yonggom, the Refugee Camps along the Border, and the Impact of the Ok Tedi Mine." *Research in Melanesia* 13: 30–61.

———. 1995. "Social Impact of the Ok Tedi Mine on the Yonggom Villages of the North Fly, 1992." *Research in Melanesia* 19: 23–102. Originally produced as "Ok-Fly Social Monitoring Programme, Report 5." Port Moresby: Unisearch PNG Pty. Ltd., 1993.

———. 1996. "Anthropologists and Global Alliances." *Anthropology Today* 12 (4): 14–16.

———. 1997a. "Is Ok Tedi a Precedent? Implications of the Settlement." In Banks and Ballard 1997a, 118–40.

———. 1997b. Affidavit. Robert Bryce. The Austin Chronicle Corporation, Inc. and Pratap Chatterjee, Plaintiffs, v. The Overseas Private Investment Corporation, Defendant, and Freeport-McMoRan Copper and Gold, Inc., Defendant Intervenor. United States District Court, Western District of Texas. Cause No. 96 CA 595 JN. April 11. Austin.

———. 1997c. "Indigenous Response to Environmental Impact along the Ok Tedi." In Toft 1997, 143–55.

———. 1997d. "Regional Dynamics and Conservation in Papua New Guinea: The Lakekamu River Basin Project." *The Contemporary Pacific* 9 (1): 97–121.

———. 1997e. "*Kotim Ol* (Take Them to Court)." *Delta: News and Background on Ogoni, Shell and Nigeria* 3: 32–35.

———. 2001a. "Lost Worlds: Environmental Disaster, 'Culture Loss' and the Law." *Current Anthropology* 42 (2): 67–98.

———. 2001b. "Property Effects: Social Networks and Compensation Claims in Melanesia." *Social Anthropology* 9 (2): 147–63.

———. 2002. "Anthropology and Advocacy: A Case Study of the Campaign against the Ok Tedi Mine." *Critique of Anthropology* 22 (2): 175–200.

———. 2003. "Mining and Environmental Human Rights in Papua New Guinea." In *Transnational Corporations and Human Rights,* edited by George Jedrzej Frynas and Scott Pegg, 115–36. London: Palgrave.

———. 2004. "Property Limits: Debates on the Body, Nature, and Culture." In *Transactions and Creations: Property Debates and the Stimulus of Melanesia,* edited by Erich Hirsch and Marilyn Strathern, 21–39. Oxford: Berghahn.

———. 2006. *Reverse Anthropology: Indigenous Analysis of Social and Environmental Relations in New Guinea.* Stanford, CA: Stanford University Press.

———. 2007. "Indigenous Movements and the Risks of Counterglobalization: Tracking the Campaign against Papua New Guinea's Ok Tedi Mine." *American Ethnologist* 34 (2): 303–21.

———. 2008. "Social Relations and the Green Critique of Capitalism in Melanesia." *American Anthropologist* 110 (3): 288–98.

———. 2009. "Comments on the Bakhuis Draft Environmental and Social Impact Report." In Goodland 2009, 26–59.

———. 2010. "Sustainability and the BP Oil Spill." *Dialectical Anthropology* 34 (3): 295–300.

———. 2012a. "Afterward: Extractive Conflicts Compared." In Bebbington 2012a, 201–13.

———. 2012b. "Juridification of Indigenous Politics." In Eckert et al. 2012b, 23–43.

Klein, Naomi. 2008. *The Shock Doctrine: The Rise of Disaster Capitalism.* New York: Random House.

Koebele, Michael. 2010. *Corporate Responsibility under the Alien Tort Statute: Enforcement of International Law through U.S. Torts Law.* Leiden: Martinus Nijhoff.

Koma, Matilda. 2003. "Papua New Guinea: A Guarantee for Poverty." In Colchester et al. 2003, 179–99.

Kreye, Otto, and Lutz F.P. Castell. 1991. "Development and the Environment in PNG. A Study by the Starnberg Institute." *Catalyst: Social Pastoral Magazine for Melanesia* 21 (3): 1–119.

Krimsky, Sheldon. 2003. *Science in the Private Interest: Has the Lure of Profits Corrupted Biomedical Research?* New York: Rowman & Littlefield.

Krockenberger, Michael. 1996. Media release. Australian Conservation Foundation. June 11.

Kuipers, J. R., A. S. Maest, K. A. MacHardy, and G. Lawson. 2006. "Comparison of Predicted and Actual Water Quality at Hardrock Mines: The Reliability of Predictions in Environmental Impact Statements." Washington, DC: Earthworks. www.earthworksaction.org/files/publications/ComparisonsReportFinal.pdf

Lawrence, David, 1991. "The Subsistence Economy of the Kiwai-Speaking People of the Southwest Coast of Papua New Guinea." In Lawrence and Cansfield-Smith 1991, 367–77.

Lawrence, David, and Tim Cansfield-Smith, eds. 1991. *Sustainable Development of Traditional Inhabitants of the Torres Strait Region.* Canberra: Great Barrier Reef Marine Park Authority.

Leith, Denise. 2003. *The Politics of Power: Freeport in Suharto's Indonesia.* Honolulu: University of Hawai'i Press.

Lepani, Charles W. 1994. "The Challenges of Economic and Social Development in the Pacific Islands Region." In Schoell 1994a, 41–58.

Li, Fabiana. 2009. "Documenting Accountability: Environmental Impact Assessment in a Peruvian Mining Project." *Political and Legal Anthropology Review* 32 (2): 218–36.

Li, Tania Murray. 2000. "Articulating Indigenous Identity in Indonesia: Resource Politics and the Tribal Slot." *Comparative Studies in Society and History* 42 (1): 149–79.

Lobe, Jim. 2003. "U.S. Conservatives Take Aim at NGOs." *Oneworld.net*. www.commondreams.org/headlines03/0612–09.htm.

Lyons, Kristen, and Carol Richards. 2013. "Mining Universities." *Arena: The Website of Left Political, Social and Cultural Commentary*. July. www.arena.org.au/2013/07/mining-universities-by-kristen-lyons-and-carol-richards.

Macdonald, Gaynor, 2002. "Ethnography, Advocacy and Feminism: A Volatile Mix. A View from a Reading of Diane Bell's *Ngarrindjeri Wurruwarrin*." *The Australian Journal of Anthropology* 13 (1): 88–110.

MacKay, Fergus. 2004. "Indigenous People's Right to Free, Prior and Informed Consent and the World Bank's Extractive Industries Review." *Sustainable Development Law & Policy* 4 (2): 43–65.

Maclean, Neil. 1994. "Freedom or Autonomy: A Modern Melanesian Dilemma." *Man* 29 (3): 667–688.

Malinowski, Bronislaw. 1935. *Coral Gardens and Their Magic*. London: Allen and Unwin.

Manheim, Jarol B. 2003. "Biz-War: Foundation-NGO Network Warfare on Corporations in the United States." www.aei.org/files/2003/06/11/20040402_20030611_Manheim.pdf.

———. 2004. *Biz-War and the Out-of-Power Elite: The Progressive-Left Attack on the Corporation*. Mahwah, NJ: Lawrence Erlbaum Associates.

Manson, Andrew, and Bernard Mbenga. 2003. "'The Richest Tribe in Africa': Platinum-Mining and the Bafokeng in South Africa's North West Province, 1965–1999." *Journal of Southern African Studies* 29 (1): 25–47.

Marchand, Roland. 1998. *Creating the Corporate Soul: The Rise of Public Relations and Corporate Imagery in American Big Business*. Berkeley: University of California Press.

Marcus, George E. 1995. "Ethnography in/of the World System: The Emergence of Multi-Sited Ethnography." *Annual Review of Anthropology* 24: 95–117.

Marcus, Jerrold J. 1997. "Closing BHP's Island Copper Mine: A Study in Dignity, Honor, and Pride." *Engineering and Mining Journal* 198 (2): 28–34.

Markowitz, Gerald, and David Rosner. 2002. *Deceit and Denial: The Deadly Politics of Industrial Pollution*. Berkeley: University of California Press.

Marr, Carolyn. 1993. *Digging Deep: The Hidden Costs of Mining in Indonesia*. London: Down to Earth.

Martinez-Alier, Joan. 2003. *The Environmentalism of the Poor: A Study of Ecological Conflicts and Valuation*. Northampton, MA: Edward Elgar Publishing.

Maun, Alex. 1997. "The Impact of the Ok Tedi Mine on the Yonggom People." In Banks and Ballard 1997a, 113–17.

Maunsell and Partners. 1982. *Ok Tedi Environmental Study.* 7 vols. Melbourne: Maunsell and Partners Pty. Ltd. for Ok Tedi Mining Ltd.

May, R. J., ed. 1986. *Between Two Nations: The Indonesia-Papua New Guinea Border and West Papua Nationalism.* Bathurst, Australia: Robert Brown.

McAleer, Phelim, and Ann McElhinney, dirs. 2006. *Mine Your Own Business: The Dark Side of Environmentalism.* Bucharest: New Bera Media, DVD.

McEachern, Doug. 1995. "Mining Meaning from the Rhetoric of Nature—Australian Mining Companies and Their Attitudes to the Environment at Home and Abroad." *Policy Organisation & Society,* Winter: 48–69.

McGee, Brant. 2009. "The Community Referendum: Participatory Democracy and the Right to Free, Prior and Informed Consent to Development." *Berkeley Journal of International Law* 27 (2): 570–635.

McLaren, John, A. R. Buck, and Nancy E. Wright, eds. 2005. *Despotic Dominion: Property Rights in British Settler Societies.* Vancouver: University of British Columbia Press.

McWilliams, James E. 2008. *American Pests: The Losing War on Insects from Colonial Times to DDT.* New York: Columbia University Press.

Meeran, Richard. 1999. "The Unveiling of Transnational Corporations: A Direct Approach." In *Human Rights Standards and the Responsibility of Transnational Corporations,* edited by Michael K. Addo, 161–70. London: Kluwer Law International.

Merry, Sally Engle. 2006. *Human Rights and Gender Violence: Translating International Law into Local Justice.* Chicago: University of Chicago Press.

Melucci, Alberto. 1980. "The New Social Movements: A Theoretical Approach." *Social Science Information* 19 (2): 199–226.

———. 1998. "Third World or Planetary Conflicts?" In *Cultures of Politics, Politics of Cultures: Re-Visioning Latin American Social Movements,* edited by Sonia E. Alvarez, Evelina Dagnino, and Arturo Escobar, 422–29. Boulder, CO: Westview Press.

Michaels, David. 2008. *Doubt Is Their Product: How Industry's Assault on Science Threatens Your Health.* Oxford: Oxford University Press.

Mines and Communities. 2001. London Declaration. www.minesandcommunities.org/article.php?a=8470.

Mining Journal. 2001. "Industry in Transition." April 13, 267–68.

Mining, People and the Environment. 2010. "Enemies or Allies." July 6. www.mpe-magazine.com/reports/enemies-or-allies.

Miyazaki, Hirokazu. 2006. "Economy of Dreams: Hope in Global Capitalism and Its Critiques." *Cultural Anthropology* 21 (2): 147–72.

Moken, Robin. 2004. Notice from Kawok, Papua New Guinea, to the Prothonotary of the Supreme Court of Victoria. Case No. 5003 of 2000. January 8. Melbourne.

Mongoven, Bart. 2007. "A Potential Tool for Protecting Human Rights in the Third World." Stratfor Public Policy Intelligence Report, August 16. www.stratfor.com.

Moody, Roger. 1992. *The Gulliver File: Mines, People, and Land: A Global Battleground.* London: Minewatch.

———. 1996. "Mining the World: The Global Reach of Rio Tinto Zinc." *The Ecologist* 26 (2): 46–52.

———. 2005. *The Risks We Run: Mining, Communities, and Political Risk Insurance.* London: International Books.

———. 2007. *Rocks and Hard Places: The Globalization of Mining.* New York: Zed Books.

———. 2012. "Financial Innovations and the Extractive Industries." *Pitfalls and Pipelines: Indigenous Peoples and Extractive Industries,* edited by Andrew Whitmore, 39–67. Baguio City, Philippines: Tebtebba Foundation, International Work Group on Indigenous Affairs (IWGIA), and Indigenous Peoples Links.

Moore, Henrietta. 2004. "Global Anxieties. Concept Metaphors and Pre-Theoretical Commitments in Anthropology." *Anthropological Theory* 4 (1): 71–88.

Moore, Michael, dir. 2002. *Roger & Me.* Burbank, CA: Warner Home Video, DVD.

Moore, W. Henson. 1996. "The Social License to Operate." *Paper Industry Manufacturing Association* 78 (10): 22–23.

Mowbray, David. 1995. Foreword to *Environmental Impact of Large-Scale Mining in Papua New Guinea: Mining Residue Disposal by the Ok Tedi Copper-Gold Mine,* by Jörg Hettler and Bernd Lehmann, 2–4. United Nations Environmental Program. Berlin: FU.

Mudder, Terry. 2002. The NGOs. *Mining Environmental Management* (September). www.infomine.com/library/publications/docs/Mudder_NGOs.pdf.

Mundo, Bineet. 2003. "India: Breaking the Trust." In Colchester et al. 2003, 297–334.

Munro, Kelsey. 2004. "Ok Tedi: Litigation Drowned in Tailings." *Justinian,* May 24. www.justinian.com.au.

Murray, Gavin, and Ian Williams. 1997. "Implications for the Australian Minerals Industry: A Corporate Perspective." In Banks and Ballard 1997a, 196–204.

Nader, Laura. 1972. "Up the Anthropologist: Perspectives Gained from Studying Up." In *Reinventing Anthropology,* edited by Dell Hymes, 284–311. New York: Pantheon.

Nader, Ralph. 1996. "BHP Still Stained by Ok Tedi Runoff." *Australian Financial Review,* September 24: 19.

Nahan, Mike. 2003. "Foreign Aid NGOs: The New Merchants of Poverty." www.aei.org/files/2003/06/11/20040402_20030611_Nahan.pdf.

Nash, Jill. 1993. "Mining, Ecocide, and Rebellion: The Bougainville Case." Paper presented at the annual meeting of the American Anthropological Association, Washington, DC.

Nash, June. 1973. *We Eat the Mines and the Mines Eat Us: Dependency and Exploitation in Bolivian Tin Mines.* New York: Columbia University Press.

Negri, Antonio. 1999. "The Specter's Smile" In *Ghostly Demarcations: A Symposium on Jacques Derrida's Specters of Marx,* edited by Michael Sprinkler, 5–16. New York: Verso.

Nestle, Marion. 2007. *Food Politics: How the Food Industry Influences Nutrition and Health.* Second edition. Berkeley: University of California Press.

New York Times. 2008. "Alaska Voters Reject Water Regulation at Mines." August 27. www.nytimes.com/2008/08/27/world/americas/27iht-mining .3.15685151.html.

Niezen, Ronald. 2003. *The Origins of Indigenism: Human Rights and the Politics of Identity.* Berkeley: University of California Press.

Nixon, Rob. 2011. *Slow Violence and the Environmentalism of the Poor.* Cambridge: Harvard University Press.

Norwegian Government Pension Fund—Global, Council on Ethics. 2006. Unpublished recommendation to the Ministry of Finance, Norway. February 15. Unofficial English Translation. www.regjeringen.no/upload/FIN/ etikk/Recommendation%20RT.pdf.

Nouah, Jeanne, Joachim Gwodog, Félix Devalois Ndiomgbwa, Armand Noahmvogo, Constant Félix Amougou Mbatsogo, Belmond Tchoumba, and Adrien Didier Amougoua. 2003. "Chad-Cameroon: Pushed by the Pipeline." In Colchester et al. 2003, 266–280.

Nowlin, Judge James R. 1999. Judgment. The Austin Chronicle Corporation, Inc. and Pratap Chatterjee, Plaintiffs, v. The Overseas Private Investment Corporation, Defendant, and Freeport-McMoRan Copper and Gold, Inc., Defendant Intervenor. United States District Court, Western District of Texas. Cause No. 96 CA 595 JN. July 28. Austin.

Nowotny, Helga, Peter Scott, and Michael Gibbons. 2001. *Re-Thinking Science: Knowledge and the Public in an Age of Uncertainty.* Cambridge: Polity.

OBS (The Observatory for the Protection of Human Rights Defenders). 2013. "Violations of the Right of NGOs to Funding: From Harassment to Criminalisation." Annual Report. www.omct.org/files/2013/02/22162/obs_annual _report_2013_uk_web.pdf.

Office of the Inspector General. 2004. "Nationwide Identification of Hardrock Mining Sites." Evaluation Report 2004-P-00005. March 31. Washington, DC: United States Environmental Protection Agency. www.epa.gov/oig/reports/2004 /20040331-2004-p-00005.pdf.

Offor Sharp. 2006. Offor Sharp (Stakeholder Engagement and Public Dispute Resolution) Homepage. www.offorsharp.com.au. Accessed September 15, 2006.

Ohtsuka, R. 1983. *Oriomo Papuans: Ecology of Sago-Eaters in Lowland Papua.* Tokyo: University of Tokyo Press.

Ok Tedi Settlement Agreement. 1996. Agreement between Rex Dagi et al., Slater & Gordon et al., Broken Hill Proprietary Limited, and Ok Tedi Mining Limited. June 7. Melbourne. Reproduced in Banks and Ballard 1997a, appendix 1, 211–20.

Oliver, Douglas. 1991. *Black Islanders: A Personal Perspective of Bougainville, 1937–1991.* Honolulu: University of Hawai'i Press.

Ong, Aihwa. 2006. *Neoliberalism as Exception: Mutations in Citizenship and Sovereignty.* Durham, NC: Duke University Press.

Oreskes, Naomi, and Erik M. Conway. 2010. *Merchants of Doubt: How a Handful of Scientists Obscured the Truth on Issues from Tobacco Smoke to Global Warming.* New York: Bloomsbury Press.

Orihuela, Jose Carlos, and Rosemary Thorp. 2012. "The Political Economy of Managing Extractives in Bolivia, Ecuador and Peru." In Bebbington 2012a, 29–47.

Orwell, George. 2003 [1949]. *Nineteen Eighty-Four.* New York: Plume.

OTML (Ok Tedi Mining Ltd.). 1993a. "The Australian Conservation Foundation Draft Report on the Impacts of the Ok Tedi Mine in Papua New Guinea by Dr. Helen Rosenbaum and Michael Krockenberger." October. Comments compiled by OTML Environment Department. Tabubil, PNG: Ok Tedi Mining Ltd.

———. 1993b. "ACF Distorting the Facts." News release, November 10. Tabubil, PNG: Ok Tedi Mining Ltd.

———. 1995. Advertisement, *The National* (Papua New Guinea), November 30.

———. 1999. Mine Waste Management Status Report. Media release. June 4. Tabubil, PNG: Ok Tedi Mining Ltd.

———. 2005. CMCA Environmental Predictions Update. Tabubil, PNG: Ok Tedi Mining Ltd.

———. 2013. Annual Environmental Report (ENV130920). September. Tabubil, PNG: Ok Tedi Mining Ltd.

Papua New Guinea, Independent State of. 1975. The Constitution of the Independent State of Papua New Guinea. Port Moresby: Department of the Prime Minister.

———. 1976. Mining (Ok Tedi Agreement) Act 1976.

———. 1986. Mining (Ok Tedi Sixth Supplemental Agreement) Act 1986.

———. 1995a. Draft Hansard (Papua New Guinea Parliament). Ninth Day. Tuesday December 5, 1995.

———. 1995b. Draft Hansard (Papua New Guinea Parliament). Tenth Day. Tuesday December 6, 1995.

———. 1995c. Mining (Ok Tedi Restated Eighth Supplemental Agreement) Act 1995.

———. 1995d. Compensation (Prohibition of Foreign Legal Proceedings) Act 1995.

———. 2001. Mining (Ok Tedi Mine Continuation (Ninth Supplement) Agreement) Act 2001.

Parametrix. 2002. Aquatic Ecological Risk Assessment Prepared for PT Freeport Indonesia. Vol. 1.

Parametrix and URS Greiner Woodward Clyde. 1999. "Draft Executive Summary: Assessment of Human Health and Ecological Risks for Proposed Mine Waste Mitigation Options at the Ok Tedi Mine, Papua New Guinea. Detailed Level Risk Assessment." Prepared for Ok Tedi Mining Ltd. August 6.

Peckham, Howard H. 1994. *The Making of The University of Michigan, 1817–1992.* Edited and updated by Margaret L. Steneck and Nicholas H. Steneck. Ann Arbor: Bentley Historical Library, University of Michigan.

Perrow, Charles. 1994. "The Limits of Safety: The Enhancement of a Theory of Accidents." *Journal of Contingencies and Crisis Management* 29 (4): 212–20.

———. 1997. "Organizing for Environmental Destruction." *Organization & Environment* 10 (1): 66–72.

Petryna, Adriana, Andrew Lakoff, and Arthur Kleinman, eds. 2006. *Global Pharmaceuticals: Ethics, Markets, Practices*. Durham, NC: Duke University Press.

Pheasant, Bill. 1994. "Clan Member Sues BHP for $4BN damages." *Australian Financial Review*. May 6, 15.

Pickup, Geoff, and Yantao Cui. 2009. "Modeling the Impact of Tailings and Waste Rock Disposal in the Fly River System." In Bolton 2009, 257–89.

Pickup, Geoff, and Andrew R. Marshall. 2009. "Geomorphology, Hydrology, and Climate of the Fly River System." In Bolton 2009, 3–49.

Pintz, William S. 1984. *Ok Tedi: Evolution of a Third World Mining Project*. London: Mining Journal Books.

Placer Dome Asia Pacific. 2000. "Porgera Mine Sustainability Report 2000: Towards a Sustainable Future." www.placerdome.com.

PNG Industry News. 2008. "Developments Mark PNG Mining." March 4. www.pngindustrynews.net.

PNGSDP (Papua New Guinea Sustainable Development Program Ltd.) 2012. "A Report on PNG Sustainable Development Program Ltd and Ok Tedi Mining Ltd." Media Statement. www.pngsdp.com/index.php/press-releases/113.

Pocock, J. G. A. 1992. "Tangata Whenua and Enlightenment Anthropology." *New Zealand Journal of History* 26 (1): 28–56.

Post-Courier (Papua New Guinea). 2000. "OTML Client to Pressure BHP." November 10.

———. 2001. "BHP Quits Mine." September 27.

———. 2002. "Closing All Mines Good for Us: Expert." September 20–22, weekend edition.

———. 2007. "Mining Gains Pose Woes." November 28.

Povinelli, Elizabeth. 2002. *The Cunning of Recognition: Indigenous Alterities and the Making of Australian Multiculturalism*. Durham, NC: Duke University.

Powdermaker, Hortense. 1962. *Copper Town: Changing Africa, the Human Situation of the Rhodesian Copperbelt*. New York: Harper Colophon.

Power, Michael. 1994. *The Audit Explosion*. London: Demos.

———. 1997. *The Audit Society: Rituals of Verification*. Oxford: Oxford University Press.

Prince, William, and David Nelson. 1996. *Colorado Journal of International Environmental Law and Policy* 7: 247–317.

Pring, George, James Otto, and Koh Naito. 1999. "Trends in International Environmental Law Affecting the Minerals Industry." 2 parts. *Journal of Energy and Natural Resources Law* 17: 39–55 and 151–77.

Proctor, Robert N. 2012. *Golden Holocaust: Origins of the Cigarette Catastrophe and the Case for Abolition*. Berkeley: University of California Press.

Rabinow, Paul. 2002. "Midst Anthropology's Problems." The David M. Schneider Distinguished Lecture. *Cultural Anthropology* 17 (2): 135–49.

Rajak, Dinah. 2011a. *In Good Company: An Anatomy of Corporate Social Responsibility*. Stanford, CA: Stanford University Press.

———. 2011b. "Theatres of Virtue: Collaboration, Consensus, and the Social Life of Corporate Social Responsibility." *Focaal* 60: 9–20.

Ramos, Alcida. 1998. *Indigenism: Ethnic Politics in Brazil*. Madison: University of Wisconsin Press.

———. 1999. "Anthropologist as Political Actor." *Journal of Latin American Anthropology* 4 (2): 172–89.

Reed, Darryl. 2002. "Resource Extraction Industries in Developing Countries." *Journal of Business Ethics* 39: 199–226.

Regan, Anthony J. 2010. *Light Intervention: Lessons from Bougainville*. Washington, DC: United States Institute of Peace Press.

Reuters. 2011. "Peru Congress Passes Consultation Law Unanimously." August 24.http://af.reuters.com/article/commoditiesNews/idAFN1E77M1fl20110824.

———. 2013. "Peru Deputy Minister Resigns as Humala Rolls Back Indigenous Law." May 4. www.reuters.com/article/2013/05/04/us-peru-mining-indigenous-idUSBRE9430AB20130504.

Revenga, Álvaro. 2005. *Sipakapa No se vende / Sipakapa Is Not for Sale*. Guatemala: Caracol Productions, 55 minutes.

Riles, Annelise. 2000. *The Network Inside Out*. Ann Arbor: University of Michigan Press.

Rio Tinto. 2008. "Rio Tinto and Biodiversity: Biodiversity Offset Design. Achieving Results on the Ground." London: Rio Tinto. www.riotinto.com/documents/ReportsPublications/RTBiodiversitystrategyfinal.pdf.

———. 2009. Corporate website. www.riotinto.com.

Ripley, Earle A., and Robert E. Redman, with James Maxwell. 1978. *Environmental Impact of Mining in Canada*. National Impact of Mining 7. Centre for Resource Studies. Kingston, Canada: Queen's University.

Robert F. Kennedy Memorial Center for Human Rights—Indonesia Support Group. 2004. The West Papua Report no. 6. Robert F. Kennedy Memorial Center for Human Rights, June/July.

Rogers, Douglas. 2012. "The Materiality of the Corporation: Oil, Gas, and Corporate Social Technologies in the Remaking of a Russian Region." *American Ethnologist* 39 (2): 284–96.

Rolston, Jessica Smith. 2010. "Corporate Social Responsibility in the Mining Industry: A Comparison." Paper presented at the annual meeting of the American Anthropological Association, New Orleans.

Rose, Carol M. 1994. *Property and Persuasion: Essays on the History, Theory, and Rhetoric of Ownership*. Boulder, CO: Westview Press.

Rose, Deborah Bird. 1999. "Hard Times: An Australian Study." In *Quicksands: Foundational Histories in Australia and Aotearoa New Zealand*, edited by Klaus Neumann, Nicholas Thomas, and Hilary Ericksen, 2–19. Sydney: University of New South Wales Press.

Rosenbaum, Helen, and Catherine Coumans. 2011. "Out of Our Depth: Mining the Ocean Floor in Papua New Guinea." November. Deep Sea Mining Campaign, an affiliate of Friends of the Earth Australia. www.deepseaminingoutofourdepth.org/report.

Rosenbaum, Helen, and Michael Krockenberger. 1993. "Report on the Impacts of the Ok Tedi Mine in Papua New Guinea." Melbourne: Australian Conservation Foundation.

Ross, Michael. 1999. "The Political Economy of the Resource Curse." *World Politics* 51 (2): 297–322.

Rutz, Henry J., ed. 1992. *The Politics of Time*. American Ethnological Society monograph series 4. Washington, DC: American Anthropological Association.

Ryan, Tom. 2005. "The Miners' Thumbs: Re-Membering the Past in the Waihi Museum." *Journal of New Zealand Literature* 23 (1): 71–97.

Sachs, Jeffrey D., and Andrew M. Warner. 1995. "Natural Resource Abundance and Economic Growth." Development Discussion Paper 517a. Cambridge, MA: Harvard Institute for International Development.

Sahlins, Marshall. 1999. "What Is Anthropological Enlightenment? Some Lessons of the Twentieth Century." *Annual Review of Anthropology* 28:i–xxiii.

Sakulas, Harry, and Lawrence Tjamei. 1991. "Ecological Damage Caused by the Discharges from the Ok Tedi Copper and Gold Mine, Papua New Guinea." Case Document on the Ok Tedi Mine for the International Water Tribunal. Wau, Papua New Guinea: Wau Ecology Institute.

Salim, Emil. 2003. "Striking a Better Balance: The World Bank Group and the Extractive Industries Review." The Final Report of the Extractive Industries Review 1. www.eireview.org.

———. 2004. "Business as Usual with Marginal Change: Final Comment on the World Bank Group Management Response to the Extractive Industry Review by the Extractive Industry Review Eminent Person." Washington, DC: Extractive Industries Review.

Sandman, Peter. 2008. The Peter Sandman Risk Communication Website. www.psandman.com/index.htm.

Santos, Boaventura de Sousa, and César A. Rodríguez-Garavito. 2005. "Law, Politics, and the Subaltern in Counter-Hegemonic Globalization." In *Law and Globalization from Below*, edited by Boaventura de Sousa Santos and César A. Rodríguez-Garavito, 1–26. Cambridge: Cambridge University Press.

Sassen, Saskia. 1998. *Globalization and Its Discontents*. New York: The New Press.

Sawyer, Suzana. 2004. *Crude Chronicles: Indians, Multinational Oil, and Neoliberalism in Ecuador*. Durham, NC: Duke University Press.

Sawyer, Suzana, and Edmund Terence Gomez, eds. 2012. *The Politics of Resource Extraction: Indigenous Peoples, Multinational Corporations, and the State*. New York: Palgrave Macmillan.

Schoell, Hans Martin, ed. 1994a. "Development and Environment in Papua New Guinea: An Overview." *Point* 18. Goroka, Papua New Guinea: The Melanesian Institute.

———. 1994b. Introduction to Schoell 1994a, 9–16.

Schoorl, J. W. 1993. *Culture and Change among the Muyu*. Translated by G. J. van Exel. KITLV Translation Series 23. Leiden: KITLV Press. Originally published as *Kultuur en Kultuurveranderingen in het Moejoe-Gebied* (Leiden: Proefschrift, 1957).

Schramm, Manuel. 2010. "Uranium Mining and the Environment in East and West Germany. A Comparison." Paper presented at the conference "History Underground," Rachel Carson Center for Environment and Society, University of Munich, Germany.

Scott, James C. 1987. *Weapons of the Weak: Everyday Forms of Peasant Resistance*. New Haven, CT: Yale University Press.

———. 1999. *Seeing Like a State: How Certain Schemes to Improve the Human Condition Have Failed*. New Haven, CT: Yale University Press.

Seagle, Caroline, 2012. "Inverting the Impacts: Mining, Conservation, and Sustainability Claims Near the Rio Tinto/QQM Ilmenite Mine in Southeast Madagascar." *Journal of Peasant Studies* 39 (2): 447–77.

Sen, Amartya. 1999. *Development as Freedom*. Oxford: Oxford University Press.

Shamir, Ronen. 2010. "Capitalism, Governance, and Authority: The Case of Corporate Social Responsibility." *Annual Review of Law and Social Science* 6: 531–53.

Sheppard, Ian. 2010. "Ok Tedi Mining. Building Our Future: More than One Mine." Paper presented at the PNG Mining and Petroleum Conference, Sydney, Australia.

Shore, Cris, and Susan Wright. 2002. "Coercive Accountability: The Rise of Audit Culture in Higher Education." In Strathern 2002a, 57–89.

Simmel, Georg. 1978. *The Philosophy of Money*. Translated by T. Bottomore and D. Frisby. London: Routledge and Kegan Paul.

Singer, Merrill, and Hans Baer. 2008. *Killer Commodities: Public Health and the Corporate Production of Harm*. Lanham, MD: AltaMira Press.

Smith, Craig S. 2007. "Fighting Over Gold in the Land of Dracula." *New York Times,* January 3.

Smith, Jessica, and Federico Helfgott. 2010. "Flexibility or Exploitation? Corporate Social Responsibility and the Perils of Universalization." *Anthropology Today* 26 (3): 20–23.

Speed, Shannon. 2008. *Rights in Rebellion: Indigenous Struggle and Human Rights in Chiapas*. Stanford, CA: Stanford University Press.

SRK Consulting. 2008. "Environmental and Social Impact Assessment of Mining Aspects of the Proposed Bakhuis Bauxite Project Draft Environmental and Social Impact Report." Volume 1. January. Prepared for NV BHP Billiton Maatschappij Suriname and Suriname Aluminium Company LLC.

Stauber, John, and Sheldon Rampton. 1995. *Toxic Sludge Is Good for You: Lies, Damn Lies and the Public Relations Industry*. Monroe, ME: Common Courage Press.

Storey, A.W., Markson Yarrao, Charles Tenakanai, Boga Figa, and Jessica Lynas. 2009. "Fish Assemblages in the Fly River System and Effects of the Ok Tedi Copper Mine." In Bolton 2009, 427–59.

Strathern, Marilyn. 1996. "Cutting the Network." *Journal of the Royal Anthropological Institute* 2 (3): 517–35.

———. 1998. Comment on "Can Culture Be Copyrighted?" by Michael F. Brown. *Current Anthropology* 39 (2): 216–17.

———. 1999. "What Is Intellectual Property After?" In *Property, Substance and Effect: Anthropological Essays on Persons and Things*, edited by Marilyn Strathern, 179–203. London: Athlone.

———. 2000. "Environments Within: An Ethnographic Commentary on Scale." In *Culture, Landscape, and the Environment: The Linacre Lectures,*

1997, edited by Howard Morphy and Kate Flint, 44–71. New York: Oxford University Press.

———, ed. 2002a. *Audit Cultures: Anthropological Studies in Accountability, Ethics and the Academy.* New York: Routledge.

———. 2002b. "Introduction: New Accountabilities." In Strathern 2002a, 1–18. New York: Routledge.

———. 2002c. "Afterward: Accountability . . . and Ethnography." In Strathern 2002a, 279–304. New York: Routledge.

———. 2003. "Re-Describing Society." *Minerva* 41 (3): 263–76.

Studnicki-Gilbert, Daviken. 2010. "Exhausting the Sierra Madre: Mining Ecologies in Mexico over the Longue Durée." Paper presented at the conference "History Underground," Rachel Carson Center for Environment and Society, University of Munich, Germany.

Supreme Court of Victoria. 1995. Court Transcript. Rex Dagi and Others, Plaintiffs, and The Broken Hill Proprietary Company Limited and Ok Tedi Mining Limited, Defendants. Supreme Court of Victoria. No. 5782 of 1994. October 24. Melbourne.

———. 2004. Court Transcript. Gabia Gagarimabu, For Himself and As Representing Certain Parties to the Agreement Made with BHP and OMTL on the 7th Day of June, 1996, and BHP Billiton Limited and Ok Tedi Mining Limited. No. 5003 of 2000. January 15. Melbourne.

Swadling, Pamela. 1996. *Plumes from Paradise: Trade Cycles in Outer Southeast Asia and Their Impact on New Guinea and Nearby Islands until 1920.* Boroko: Papua New Guinea National Museum, in association with Robert Brown and Associates.

Swartzendruber, J.F. 1993. "Papua New Guinea Conservation Needs Assessment: Synopsis Report." Washington, DC: Biodiversity Support Program and Boroko: Government of Papua New Guinea, Department of Conservation and Environment.

Sydney Morning Herald. 1995. "Not Just Big, This Australian." Editorial. September 26.

Szablowski, David. 2007. *Transnational Law and Local Struggles: Mining, Communities and the World Bank.* Portland, OR: Hart.

———. 2010. "Operationalizing Free, Prior, and Informed Consent in the Extractive Industry? Examining the Challenges of a Negotiated Model of Justice." *Canadian Journal of Development Studies* 30 (1–2): 111–30.

Tait, Nikki. 2006. "Ok Tedi Copper Mine Damage Claim Settled." *Financial Times.* June 12.

Tamang, Parshuram. 2005. "An Overview of the Principle of Free, Prior and Informed Consent and Indigenous Peoples in International and Domestic Law and Practices." U.N. Workshop on Free, Prior and Informed Consent. New York, January 17–19. U.N. Department of Economic and Social Affairs. www.un.org/esa/socdev/unpfii/documents/workshop_FPIC_tamang.doc.

Taussig, Michael T. 1980. *The Devil and Commodity Fetishism in South America.* Chapel Hill: The University of North Carolina Press.

Thomas, Andrew. 2004. "World Bank Board Backs Management over EIR." *The Mining Journal,* August 6, 5.

Thomas, Nicholas. 1992. "The Inversion of Tradition." *American Ethnologist* 19 (2): 213–32.

Thompson, Herb, and Scott MacWilliam. 1992. *The Political Economy of Papua New Guinea: Critical Essays.* Manila, Philippines: Journal of Contemporary Asia Publishers.

Thomson, Ian, and Robert G. Boutilier. 2011. "Social License to Operate." *SME Mining Engineering Handbook,* edited by P. Darling, chapter 17.2, 1779–96. Littleton, CO: Society for Mining, Metallurgy, and Exploration.

Timperly, Mike. 1994. "Ok Tedi, the Environment and You. The Effects of the Ok Tedi Mine on the People, Plants and Animals Living along the Ok Tedi, the Fly River and the Coastal Area of Western Province." Department of Mining and Petroleum. Sponsored by Ok Ted Mining.

Tingay, Alan. 2007. "The Ok Tedi Mine, Papua New Guinea: A Summary of Environmental and Health Issues." November. Unpublished report sponsored by Ok Tedi Mining Ltd.

Toft, Susan, ed. 1997. *Compensation for Resource Development in Papua New Guinea.* Law Reform Commission of Papua New Guinea Monograph 6 and Pacific Policy Paper 24. Canberra: Australian National University Press.

Touraine, Alain. 1985. "An Introduction to the Study of Social Movements." *Social Research* 52: 747–87.

Townsend, Patricia K., and William H. Townsend. 1996. "Giving Away the River, Continued: The Environmental Impact of the Ok Tedi Mine, Papua New Guinea." Paper presented at the biannual meeting of the European Society of Oceanists, Copenhagen.

———. 2004. "Assessing an Assessment: The Ok Tedi Mine." Paper presented at the conference "Bridging Scales and Epistemologies," Alexandria. www.maweb.org/en/Bridging.Proceedings.aspx.

Townsend, William. 1988. "Giving Away the River: Environmental Issues in the Construction of the Ok Tedi Mine, 1981–84." In *Potential Impacts of Mining on the Fly River,* edited by J.C. Pernetta, 107–19. UNEP Regional Seas Reports and Studies No. 99 and SPREP Topic Review No. 33. Nairobi: United Nations Environment Programme.

Trouillot, Michel-Rolph. 1991. "Anthropology and the Savage Slot: The Poetics and Politics of Otherness." In *Recapturing Anthropology,* edited by Richard Fox, 17–44. Santa Fe: SAR Press.

Trueman, Justine. 1996. "BHP Jumped 16c to $18.74 after News that the Company Had Settled Compensation Claims by PNG Landowners." *Sydney Morning Herald.* June 12.

Tsing, Anna Lowenhaupt. 1993. *In the Realm of the Diamond Queen: Marginality in an Out-of-the-way Place.* Princeton, NJ: Princeton University Press.

———. 2004. *Friction: An Ethnography of Global Connection.* Princeton, NJ: Princeton University Press.

Tucker, Kenneth H. 1991. "How New Are the New Social Movements." *Theory, Culture and Society* 8: 75–98.

Turner, Terence. 1991. "Representing, Resisting, Rethinking: Historical Transformations of Kayapó Culture and Anthropological Consciousness." In *Colonial Situations: Essays on the Contextualization of Ethnographic Knowledge*, edited by George W. Stocking Jr., 285–313. Madison: University of Wisconsin.

Tzeutschler, Gregory G. A. 1999. "Corporate Violator: The Alien Tort Liability of Transnational Corporations for Human Rights Abuses Abroad." *Columbia Human Rights Law Review* 30: 359–419.

Uiari, Kipling. 1995. "Sustainable Development: Challenges and Opportunities in the Evolution of Resource Projects as Agents for Development in PNG." Paper presented at the Mining and Petroleum Investment in Papua New Guinea conference, Sydney, Australia, March 20–21.

United Nations. 2002. Report of the World Summit on Sustainable Development. Johannesburg, South Africa, 26 August–4 September. www.un.org/jsummit/html/documents/summit_docs/131302_wssd_report_reissued.pdf

———. 2011. "Guiding Principles on Business and Human Rights: Implementing the United Nations 'Protect, Respect and Remedy' Framework." Report of the Special Representative of the Secretary-General on the issue of human rights and transnational corporations and other business enterprises, John Ruggie. March 21. www.business-humanrights.org/media/documents/ruggie/ruggie-guiding-principles-21-mar-2011.pdf

United Nations Economic and Social Council. 2003. "Norms on the Responsibilities of Transnational Corporations and other Business Enterprises with Regard to Human Rights." E/CN.4/Sub.2/2003/12/Rev.2. www1.umn.edu/humanrts/links/norms-Aug2003.html.

United Nations Environment Programme. 1972. Report of the United Nations Conference on the Human Environment, Stockholm. www.unep.org/Documents.Multilingual/Default.asp?DocumentID = 97.

Vaughan, Diane. 1999. *The Challenger Launch Decision: Risky Technology, Culture, and Deviance at NASA*. Chicago: University of Chicago Press.

Verdery, Katherine. 1992. "The 'Estatization' of Time in Ceausescu's Romania." In Rutz 1992, 37–61.

Verschuuren, Jonathan. 2010. "Overcoming the Limitations of Environmental Law in a Globalised World." Tilburg University Legal Studies Working Paper Series, no. 020/2010. http://papers.ssrn.com/sol3/papers.cfm?abstract_id=1582857

Vesalon, Lucian, and Remus Creţan. 2013. "'Cyanide Kills!' Environmental Movements and the Construction of Environmental Risk at Roşia Montană, Romania." *Area* 45(4): 443–51.

Vukosavic, Irina. 2012. "Anti-Munk Author Speaks on Campus. Alain Denault's Visit Comes as Longstanding Development Seminar Series Distances Itself from the Munk School." *The Varsity*. September 24. http://thevarsity.ca/2012/09/24/anti-munk-author-speaks-on-campus.

WALHI (Indonesia Forum for the Environment). 2006. "The Environmental Impacts of Freeport-Rio Tinto's Copper and Gold Mining Operation in Papua." Jakarta, Indonesia: WALHI. http://freewestpapua.org/documents

/the-envronmental-imacts-of-freeport-rio-tintos-copper-and-gold-mining-operation-in-indonesia-june-2006/

Wall Street Journal. 1993. "Amoco Sells Stake in Ok Tedi." October 28.

Ward, Barbara, and René J. Dubos. 1972. *Only One Earth: The Care and Maintenance of a Small Planet.* New York: W.W. Norton.

Ward, Halina. 2001. "Securing Transnational Corporate Accountability through National Courts: Implications and Policy Options." *Hastings International and Comparative Law Review* 24: 451–74.

Warren, Christian. 2001. *Brush with Death: A Social History of Lead Poisoning.* Baltimore: Johns Hopkins University Press.

Welker, Marina. 2009. "Corporate Security Begins in the Community: Mining, the Corporate Social Responsibility Industry, and Environmental Advocacy in Indonesia." *Cultural Anthropology* 24 (1): 142–79.

Welsch, R. L. 1994. "Pig Feasts and Expanding Networks of Cultural Influence in the Upper Fly- Digul Plain." In *Migration and Transformations: Regional Perspectives on New Guinea,* edited by A. J. Strathern and G. Stürzenhofecker, 85–119. Pittsburgh: University of Pittsburgh Press.

West, Paige. 2005. *Conservation Is Our Government Now: The Politics of Ecology in New Guinea.* Durham, NC: Duke University Press.

Williams, Lawrence. 2007. "Environmental Fascism: Mining Facing Misinformation and Downright Lies from Anti-Mining NGOs." March 7. http://www.mineweb.co.za/mineweb/content/en/mineweb-sustainable-mining?oid=15739&sn=detail

Wilson, Edward O. 1992. *The Diversity of Life.* Cambridge, MA: Harvard University Press.

Windybank, Susan, and Mike Manning. 2003. "Papua New Guinea on the Brink." *Issue Analysis* 30: 1–16.

World Bank. 2000. "Ok Tedi Mining Ltd. Mine Waste Management Project Risk Assessment and Supporting Documents." Unpublished technical note. www.abc.net.au/4corners/content/2000/worldbankreview.doc.

World Commission on Dams. 2000. "Dams and Development: A New Framework for Decision-Making." A Report of the World Commission on Dams. Sterling, VA: Earthscan.

Worster, Donald. 1992. *Under Western Skies: Nature and History in the American West.* Oxford: Oxford University Press.

Yeazell, Stephen C. 1987. *From Medieval Group Litigation to the Modern Class Action.* New Haven, CT: Yale University Press.

York, Richard, and Eugene A. Rosa. 2003. "Key Challenges to Ecological Modernization Theory." *Organization and Environment* 16 (3): 273–88.

Young, John, and Alan Septoff, eds. 2002. *Digging for Change: Towards a Responsible Minerals Future. An NGO and Community Perspective.* Washington, DC: Mineral Policy Center.

Zorn, Stephen A. 1977. "New Developments in Third World Mining Agreements." *Natural Resources Forum* 1 (3): 239–50.

Index